T0331726

Routledge Revivals

Mathematical Programming Methods for Geographers and Planners

Originally published in 1983, this was the first text to offer an in-depth treatment of mathematical programming methods explained from first principles. It considers all the major programming techniques and fully explains key terms, illustrates theories with detailed examples and show how the various skills are applied in practice. It will be invaluable in both the academic world and to policy formulators and planners, who make extensive use of the methods described.

Mathematical Programming Methods for Geographers and Planners

James Killen

Routledge
Taylor & Francis Group

First published in 1983
by Croom Helm Ltd

This edition first published in 2021 by Routledge
2 Park Square, Milton Park, Abingdon, Oxon, OX14 4RN
and by Routledge
605 Third Avenue, New York, NY 10158

Routledge is an imprint of the Taylor & Francis Group, an informa business

© 1983 J. E. Killen

Publisher's Note
The publisher has gone to great lengths to ensure the quality of this reprint but points out that some imperfections in the original copies may be apparent.

Disclaimer
The publisher has made every effort to trace copyright holders and welcomes correspondence from those they have been unable to contact.
A Library of Congress record exists at LCCN:82043829

ISBN 13: 978-1-032-01542-2 (hbk)
ISBN 13: 978-1-003-17903-0 (ebk)

DOI: 10.4324/9781003179030

Mathematical Programming Methods for Geographers and Planners

James Killen

CROOM HELM
London & Canberra

© 1983 J.E.Killen
Croom Helm Ltd, Provident House, Burrell Row,
Beckenham, Kent BR3 1AT

British Library Cataloguing in Publication Data

Killen, James
    Mathematical programming methods for geographers
    and planners.
    1. Progamming (Mathematics)
    2. Geography, Mathematical
    I. Title
    519.7'02491   GA21.5M33

ISBN 0-7099-1512-8

All rights reserved. For information write:
St. Martin's Press, Inc., 175 Fifth Avenue, New York, N.Y. 10010
Printed in Great Britain
First published in the United States of America in 1983

Library of Congress Cataloging in Publication Data

Killen, James E.
    Mathematical programming method for geographers
and planners.

    Includes bibliographical references and indexes.
    1. Land use—Planning—Mathematical models.
2. Transportation planning—Mathematical models.
3. Industries, Location of—Planning—Mathematical
models. 4. Programming (Mathematics) 5. Mathematical
optimization. I. Title.
HD108.4.K54   1983   658.4'033   82-42839

ISBN 0-312-50133-1

Printed and bound in Great Britain

CONTENTS

LIST OF FIGURES

Figure		Page

LIST OF TABLES

To My Mother, *Elsa M. Killen*, and in memory of My Father, *James T. Killen*.

PREFACE

I first became interested in mathematical programming methods and their geographical and planning applications when I was a postgraduate student in the Department of Geography at Northwestern University. On returning to Ireland, first as a research scholarship holder in Coras Iompair Eireann (Ireland's Transport Company) and later as a staff member in the Department of Geography at Trinity College, I was encouraged to develop this interest. It has now led to this book.

This work has taken over two years to write and during that time, I have been aided by many individuals. I wish to thank Alan Wilson, Professor of Urban and Regional Geography at the University of Leeds for many helpful comments on the entire text. A number of other individuals read various parts of it and, in particular, I wish to thank Paul Baird, John Cahill, Helen Deane and Mary Kennelly who took my course option in mathematical programming during the academic year 1981/2 and provided many useful reactions.

The preparation of almost 400 pages of camera-ready type-script comprises a major task. In my case, this task would not have been achieved without the willing, helpful and efficient assistance of three individuals: Martha Lyons who drew the diagrams, Terence Dunne who undertook the photographic work and Eileen Russell who typed both the draft text and the final copy. I wish to acknowledge the immense debt I owe to all of these and especially to Eileen Russell who typed virtually everything the reader shall see while, simultaneously, running a busy office and dealing with the requirements of other staff members. For Croom Helm Limited, Peter Sowden's efficiency and helpfulness enabled production to proceed smoothly while at home, such diverse individuals and items as Gerry, Liz, Lynn, Stephanie, Rufus and Boris, Sunday hospitality, Maura O'Shea's bridge class and what it led to and good music helped to keep the writer (more or less) sane.

During the latter stages of producing this work, it be-

came clear that a sum of money would be required to meet
certain costs associated with reproducing certain of the
figures and tables. I wish to acknowledge my indebtedness
to the University of Dublin U.S.A. Fund which most generously
provided a grant to cover this expense and to thank Professor Aidan Clarke, Mr. George Clarke and Professor Charles
Holland all of Trinity College for their valuable assistance
in this matter.

Finally, I wish to thank Professor Joseph P. Haughton,
my academic colleagues and all of the students with whom
I have been privileged to deal for making my university
teaching career such a positive and enjoyable experience.

1

INTRODUCTION

1.1 MATHEMATICAL PROGRAMMING

This is a book about mathematical programming methods and
their use in investigating phenomena of interest to geographers and planners. The term *programming*** as used here refers
to the task of finding the best or *optimal solution* to a
problem. *Mathematical programming* involves finding the
optimal solution to problems which can be expressed using
mathematical notation and which can be solved using
mathematical methods. Such problems are often referred to as
optimisation problems.

The number of geographical and planning topics which can
be viewed in terms of optimisation is immense. In order to
appreciate the overall structure of such problems, we mention
three here which will be treated in further detail later ;
the reader should pause to think of some others.

A development company has purchased a tract of land and
is currently devising a landuse development plan for it.
Various landuse possibilities are available e.g. high density
housing, medium density housing, low density housing,
industry, open space, educational facilities etc. and, as a
first step, the company wishes to determine the amount of
land to be given over to each landuse. The company wishes
to maximise the monetary return it will receive for the
complete development and, as a first step in this direction,
has worked out for each landuse possibility the return it
would receive per acre of land devoted to that use. If
maximisation of monetary return was the sole concern of the
company, the optimal landuse plan would obviously comprise
devoting the complete tract of land to that landuse offering

---

*Important terms which are defined where they first appear in
the text are given in italics.

the greatest return per acre. In practice, it is unlikely that this would be acceptable to the government agency responsible for planning control which, undoubtedly, would lay down certain criteria to be met by any development e.g. concerning the amount of open space and educational places to be provided per acre of residential development. Given these criteria, the problem facing the corporation involves determining the amount of land to be allotted to each landuse type in order to :

Maximise : Return

Subject to the condition that (s.t.) :

All planning criteria are met.

This is an example of an optimisation problem. It will be shown in Chapter Four that it can be expressed in mathematical terms and that it can be solved using a well defined mathematical method or *algorithm* to yield the optimal solution.

For a second example, consider the case of an industrial concern with a number of factories each capable of producing a given amount of some product. The product is demanded at a set of destinations (towns) and the demand level at each town is known. The cost of transporting a unit of product from a given factory to a given town is known. The per unit transport costs vary for each factory-town pair i.e. for each possible delivery route. In this situation, an optimisation problem of considerable interest involves finding the flow that should be assigned to each route in order to :

Minimise : Total Transport Costs

    s.t.   No factory is required to send out more product than it can produce
                  Each town receives its demand requirement.

This optimisation problem is discussed in Chapter Three.

For a third example, consider the case of a health authority which is faced with the task of providing a region with some central service e.g. hospitals. Specifically, suppose that the region contains m towns and that hospitals are to be constructed in some of these. If finance is scarce, the authority will presumably wish to provide as few hospitals as possible. Yet, some minimum level of service must be provided e.g. each town must lie within some distance, d, of a hospital. Thus an optimisation problem of interest concerns finding the subset of towns in which hospitals should be located in order to :

Minimise : Number of hospitals required

s.t.   Each town is within some distance, d, of a
            hospital.

This and related optimisation problems are discussed in
Chapter Seven.
      The preceding examples demonstrate some important
general properties of optimisation problems. First, each
problem comprises an aim or *objective* which is expressed as
making some entity e.g. return or costs as large (maximisation) or as small (minimisation) as possible. Second,
conditions or *constraints* which must be fulfilled by the
optimal solution are specified. Optimisation problems which
involve both an objective and constraints are said to involve
constrained optimisation. Very occasionally, a problem lacks
constraints i.e. involves *unconstrained optimisation*.
Occasionally too, a constrained optimisation problem is
solved by converting it to an unconstrained problem. Examples
of both of these situations occur in Chapter Eight.
      A further feature of optimisation problems which the
examples highlight is that they involve two types of variables:
decision variables and *fixed variables*. The former are
those variables for which optimal values are to be determined
by the solution process ; the latter are those variables
whose values are given at the outset. Thus, in the case of
the second example, the decision variables are the flows on
each factory - town route while the fixed variables are the
production capacities of the factories, the demand requirements of the towns and the per unit transport costs associated
with the routes.
      When representing an optimisation problem mathematically,
the usual practice, which is followed throughout this text,
is to denote decision variables by upper case notation and
fixed variables by lower case notation. Thus, following the
format used to summarise each of the examples, an optimisation problem can be viewed as finding the values of for a set
of decision variables X_1, X_2, ..., X_n in order to :

Optimise : $f(X_1, X_2, ..., X_n)$ ---- (1.1)

s.t. $g_i(X_1, X_2, ..., X_n) \leq$ or $=$ or $\geq b_i$

                for i $= 1, ..., m$ ---- (1.2)

where $f(X_1, X_2, ..., X_n)$ is some mathematical expression
involving n decision variables, $g_i(X_1, X_2, ..., X_n)$, i=1,...,m
represent the left hand sides of m constraints and b_i,
i = 1,....,m are given fixed variable values which occur on the

right hand sides of the m constraints. The task of optimising involves either maximisation or minimisation. The constraints involve equalities and/or inequalities. In general, the form of the constraints tends to be opposite in sense to the direction of the optimisation i.e. in a maximisation problem some or all of the constraints are generally of the 'less than or equals' type while in a minimisation problem some or all of the constraints are generally of the 'greater than or equals' type. Finally, in the context of Geography and Planning, the decision variables under consideration e.g. flow levels on routes, amounts of land to be assigned to various landuses are usually such that they cannot take negative values. Thus the condition :

$$X_j \geq 0 \text{ for } j = 1, \ldots, n \qquad \qquad ----(1.3)$$

is usually appended to (1.1), (1.2).

1.2 THE ROLE AND IMPORTANCE OF MATHEMATICAL PROGRAMMING

In recent years, increasing emphasis has been placed on optimisation problems and on mathematical programming by both geographers and planners. This reflects a number of important trends which have been occurring both within and without these disciplines. One such trend has been a greater emphasis on what can loosely be called a 'scientific approach'. This has led to the increased collection and use of numerical data and to a quest for mathematical methods appropriate to dealing with this data. In the case of Geography, another important recent trend has been an increasing interest in such matters as policy formulation, the implications of following different policies and on decision making. To some extent, this reflects a greater realisation that the environment as it currently exists represents the end product of numerous decisions taken with various objectives in mind and constrained in various ways. Thus, increased insights into many environmental phenomena can presumably be obtained if these objectives and constraints and their logical end-products are defined and analysed explicitly. As many of the examples in this book show, mathematical programming provides the means by which this can be attempted.

Unlike the geographer, the role of the planner has always been such as to place him firmly within the orbit of policy formulation and decision making. In an actual planning exercise e.g. the devising of a landuse development plan for an urban area, the underlying objective and constraints are seldom defined precisely. Nevertheless, there is usually much to be gained by conceptualising a problem mathematically (and, perhaps, in a number of different ways) and of determining and evaluating the solution(s) which emerge. Methodologically, as will be shown, these tasks fall squarely within the area of mathematical programming.

A number of developments and trends outside the immediate spheres of Geography and Planning have encouraged the use of mathematical programming methods within these subjects. One of these has been the increasing interest in mathematical programming *per se* notably by workers in the related fields of Operational Research and Management Science. Operational Research (or Operations Research as it is known in North America) had its origins during World War II when the military management called upon a team of scientists to study various problems concerning how the best use could be made of available resources. After World War II, studies of this type continued and widened in scope, notably to consider various problems commonly faced by large industrial corporations e.g. concerning inventory control, production and delivery patterns, factory design etc. The major outcome of this research thrust has been the development of a large number of methods which can be employed to solve many types of optimisation problem. The major part of this book is devoted to describing these methods and the uses to which they can be put by geographers and planners.

Another development which has encouraged the use of mathematical programming in Geography and Planning has been that of the modern computer with its ability to handle large problems efficiently. The development of successful mathematical programming methods has depended very much on the availability of computers with an ability to handle the required computations. This availability has been particularly crucial to workers in such areas as Geography and Planning where, very frequently, the problems of interest involve large amounts of data.

A final development which has stimulated interest in mathematical programming has stemmed from a greater awareness on a world scale that resources of all types - financial, ecological, mineral etc. - are finite and, in many instances, scarce. This has led to an increased emphasis being placed on the importance of determining how these resources can be used most efficiently - a task which falls squarely within the sphere of interest of the geographer and planner and in a methodological sense, within the subject area of mathematical programming.

1.3 OBJECTIVES AND PLAN OF BOOK

This book has two major objectives. The first is to familiarise the reader with the most commonly used mathematical programming techniques. The treatment does not claim to be exhaustive. However, an individual who has mastered

the material here should have little difficulty in consulting
more advanced works for information on specific topics not
covered. The second major objective is to acquaint the
reader with a large number of mathematical programming
examples from the fields of Geography and Planning. The
importance of the examples cannot be over-emphasised for they
demonstrate both the range of problems to which mathematical
programming can be applied and the way in which specific
problems can be conceptualised and formulated in mathematical
terms. One of the great challenges of using mathematical
methods to investigate real-world problems is that of
reconciling the need for mathematical tractability on the one
hand with that of achieving a sufficiently accurate representation of a complicated real-world situation on the other. It
is hoped that the various examples given here will highlight
this challenge and demonstrate some of the skills that may be
used in meeting it.

The most straightforward types of mathematical programming problem are those which deal with problems relating to
some type of network. These are treated in Chapters Two and
Three which lead logically to a consideration of the most
widely used programming method of all : linear programming.
This forms the subject of Chapter Four. An important question
which arises in the context of many mathematical programming
applications concerns how the optimal solution would change
for given changes in the fixed variables e.g. in the case of
the second example of Section 1.1 how the optimal delivery
pattern would change for given specified alterations in the
per unit transport costs associated with certain factory-town
routes. Answering questions of this type falls within the
scope of what is known as *sensitivity analysis*. Chapter Five
discusses sensitivity analysis as applied to linear programming problems. Chapters Six, Seven and Eight deal with the
methods of integer programming, zero-one programming and
nonlinear programming respectively paying special attention
to examples and techniques which are likely to be of use to
geographers and planners. Particular emphasis is placed on
zero-one programming models (Chapter Seven) which can be used
to investigate situations where a series of 'Yes' or 'No'
decisions are to be made in some optimal manner. The topic
of dynamic programming forms the subject matter of Chapter
Nine. Dynamic programming comprises a solution approach in
which a complex problem is subdivided into a number of
related sub-problems each of which is solved in turn with the
information so gained being used to bring one further towards
the optimal solution. The technique of dynamic programming
would appear to offer particular promise to geographers and
planners who so often find themselves analysing complex real-
world situations which cannot be dealt with mathematically as
a single entity. The final chapter of the book deals with
goal programming which treats problems in which the objective

is to come as close as possible to achieving a number of
specified goals simultaneously.

Of all the chapters in the book, Chapter Four is the
most important and should be read before any of those which
follow. The material in this chapter will be appreciated
better if those preceding it are studied first. Each of the
chapters which follow Chapter Four can be taken independently
with the exception of Chapter Seven for which Section 6.3 is
a pre-requisite. The reader seeking a thorough grounding in
and appreciation of mathematical programming is advised to
take the chapters in order for, by doing this, he will come
to understand the important relationships which exist between
the various model types and methods discussed.

One point which will strike the reader as he peruses
this text is that many real-world mathematical programming
problems are of such a size e.g. in terms of the number of
decision variables and constraints as to require solution by
computer. He will notice also that we do not discuss
explicitly the availability or otherwise of relevant computer
programmes. Rather, we simply remark here that most general
purpose computer facilities e.g. in universities will have
available package programmes relating to the major solution
methods discussed in the text and that the reader, having
studied it, should encounter few difficulties in using these.

Much of the material in this book is of a mathematical
nature. Yet, the text assumes no more than an elementary
mathematical knowledge namely a familiarity with such basic
topics as: algebraic manipulations on inequalities and
equations, the representation of lines and planes by equations
and *vice versa* and the use of summation notation (Σ). The
Appendix summarises concepts from Matrix Algebra and Calculus
which are required to support certain chapters.

2

NETWORK MODELS

2.1 INTRODUCTION

We begin our study of mathematical programming with a review of a number of models each of which relates to a network. Network models provide a convenient starting point for two main reasons : first, the underlying mathematics are fairly straightforward and, indeed, provide a useful base for the more complicated material to follow ; second, the range of actual and potential applications can be seen and appreciated fairly readily.

Network models may be subdivided into four categories :

1. Network design models
2. Shortest route models
3. Network flow models
4. The transportation and related models

The first three model types are discussed in this chapter.

2.2 NETWORK DESIGN MODELS

A network comprises a set of *nodes* or vertices some of which are joined by *links*, arcs or edges. A network design problem is one which commences with a given number of nodes and their locations and which seeks to link these in order to fulfill a given objective.

2.2.1 Two Simple Network Design Models

In order to illustrate the first two models, consider the problem of constructing a high speed road network in the State of Texas, U.S.A. It is required that the six largest cities in the state (Figure 2.1) be placed on the network. The

DOI: 10.4324/9781003179030-2

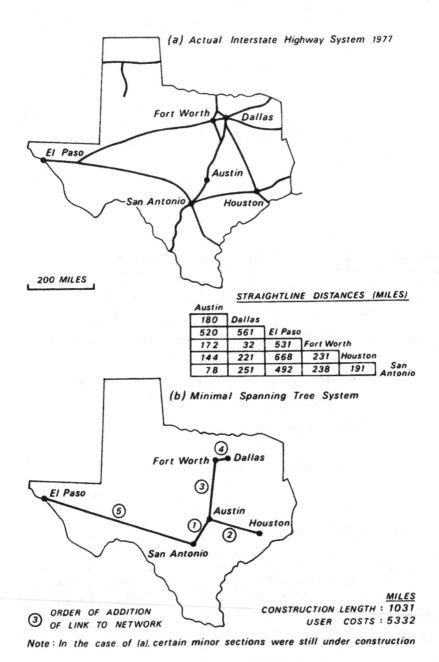

(a) Actual Interstate Highway System 1977

Fort Worth

Dallas

El Paso

Austin

San Antonio

Houston

200 MILES

STRAIGHTLINE DISTANCES (MILES)

Austin					
180	Dallas				
520	561	El Paso			
172	32	531	Fort Worth		
144	221	668	231	Houston	
78	251	492	238	191	San Antonio

(b) Minimal Spanning Tree System

Fort Worth ④ Dallas

③

El Paso

⑤ Austin

① Houston

②

San Antonio

MILES
CONSTRUCTION LENGTH : 1031
USER COSTS : 5332

③ ORDER OF ADDITION
OF LINK TO NETWORK

Note: In the case of (a). certain minor sections were still under construction

Figure 2.1 Texas Interstate Highway System

location of each of the cities and thus the straightline distance between each pair is known . It   is assumed that the cost of constructing a high speed road between any two cities is proportional to the straightline distance between them. It is assumed further that the cost to those who will use the network once it is completed i.e. in terms of fuel consumption, journey times etc. is proportional to the sum of the distances between every pair of nodes.

Bearing the latter in mind, one possible objective in constructing the road network might be to minimise total user costs i.e. to make all possible journeys as short (cheap) as possible. This would obviously be achieved by linking all nodes to give what is called the *maximally connected network*. An alternative objective might be to minimise construction costs i.e. to construct as short a network as possible subject to the constraint that all nodes are connected. Such a network is known as the *minimal spanning tree* and may be found as follows (Figure 2.1(b)). Start with any node (say Austin) and link it to the next nearest node (San Antonio). Consider the two nodes now on the network i.e. Austin and San Antonio and all possible links which could be constructed between these and the remaining unconnected nodes; construct the link which involves adding the minimum additional distance. In terms of Fig. 2.1, the task of deciding which link should be added to the network next may be viewed as inspecting the mileage values   relating   to nodes already linked (Austin, San Antonio), ignoring mileages between pairs of towns already on the network and of choosing the minimum mileage value - in this case from Austin to Houston (144 miles). Continuing in this manner, all possible links between Austin/San Antonio/ Houston and the remaining unconnected nodes are now inspected and that between Austin and Fort Worth is added. Two further applications of the process yield the full network. That this is truly the optimal solution can be checked by noting that no matter with which node one begins, the solution will be the same. If, for example, the solution was initiated at El Paso, the   last node to be joined previously, the first link added would be that to San Antonio; thereafter the links would be added in the same order as before.

2.2.2 The Optimal Network Problem

A characteristic of both the maximally connected and minimal spanning tree problems is that each may be expressed easily and solved rapidly to yield what is known to be the optimal solution. In terms of applications however, their use is limited for it is unlikely that a planner would pursue either of the two objectives underlying these models on the ground. With the minimal spanning tree solution, construction costs are minimised but user costs are exceptionally (and probably exorbitantly) high. As additional links are added over and above the minimal spanning tree, construction costs rise while user costs fall (Figure 2.2). The latter are minimised in the

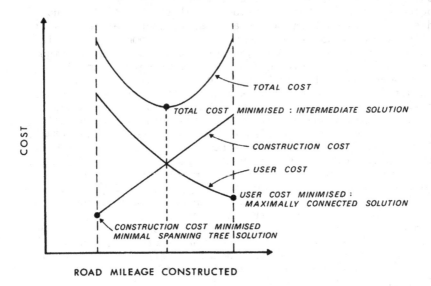

ROAD MILEAGE CONSTRUCTED

Figure 2.2 Road Cost Interrelationships

Source: O'SULLIVAN, P., HOLTZCLAW, G.D. and BARBER, G., (1979) *Transport Network Planning*, Croom Helm, London, 115.

Redrawn by permission

case of a maximally connected network but, by this stage, construction costs are exceptionally (and probably exorbitantly) high. Combining construction and user costs to give total costs demonstrates that these fall to a minimum at some point between the minimal spanning tree and maximally connected solutions. Bearing this in mind, Scott (1969a, 1971a) suggests that one reasonably realistic scenario is that in which finance is available to construct up to a certain maximum length of network and it is required that this be done in such a way as to minimise total user costs. Formally, this problem, which is usually referred to as *the optimal network problem* is :

$$
\begin{aligned}
&\text{Minimise : Total User Costs} \\
&\quad \text{s.t.} \quad L < \ell_{MAX}
\end{aligned}
\qquad \text{---- (2.1)}
$$

where L = Length of network actually constructed

ℓ_{MAX} = Maximum length of network permitted.

At first sight, the optimal network problem would appear to be only slightly more complex than the two problems of the previous section. Given that they could be solved relatively easily, one might guess that the same would be true here. Yet, as is often the case in mathematical programming, an apparently slight increase in realism leads to a considerable increase in mathematical complexity. The main cause of this complexity in the case of the optimal network problem is the large number of possible solutions which exist for any given problem. In general, n nodes can be linked in $_2n(n-1)/2$ ways. Thus in the case of the Texas highway example, there are $2^{15} = 32678$ possible ways in which the six cities could be connected i.e 32678 possible solutions, all of which should be presumably be inspected in turn if the true optimum is to be deduced. Because this task of total inspection will generally be of unrealistic magnitude (for a further discussion, see Section 7.2), we are forced in most cases to adopt what is known as a *heuristic solution method* by which is meant one which involves following a set of rules which should ultimately yield a near optimal solution and may indeed yield that solution but which is not guaranteed in advance so to do.

Scott suggests two heuristic strategies for dealing with the optimal network problem. The first involves starting with the minimal spanning tree solution (Section 2.2.1) and of approaching the (hopefully optimal) solution by successively interchanging/adding links which reduce user costs by the greatest amounts whilst not exceeding ℓ_{MAX} in (2.1). Specifically, with n nodes, the minimal spanning tree comprises (n-1) links. The solution process begins by removing one of these and by replacing it with all other possible links which still retain all nodes on the network. The user cost associated with each of these revised networks (which is interpreted once more as the sum of the distances of the journeys between all node pairs and which is set to infinity if the length of the network concerned exceeds the maximum permitted) is noted. If the minimum of these values is less than that associated with the minimal spanning tree solution, the associated network is retained as the best achieved so far. Then the possibility of interchanging links on it to yield a (n-1) link network with yet lower associated user costs, is investigated as above. This process continues until, ultimately, one arrives at an (n-1) link network in which there are no possibilities for a further interchanging of two links to reduce user cost. Once this network has been obtained, that new link which reduces user costs by the greatest amount without exceeding the maximum length limit is added. This n link network is then subjected to the inter-

change procedures outlined above. The process of inter-
changing/adding links continues until no further solution
which offers a reduction in user costs while keeping within
the length limit can be detected.

Scott's second heuristic strategy is similar in terms of
underlying logic to that described in the previous paragraph.
In this instance, the method begins with a maximally connected
network (i.e. that associated with minimum user costs but
whose length exceeds the maximum permitted). It then
successively removes/interchanges links in order to reduce
construction length to, ultimately, a permitted level whilst
raising user costs by as small amounts as possible.

Scott refers to the foregoing heuristic solution strategies as the *forwards* and *backwards* methods respectively. An
important contrast between them is that they approach the
final solution from different directions. The forwards method
begins with a possible or *feasible* solution but one which is
almost certainly sub-optimal; the underlying logic is to
approach optimality whilst always retaining feasibility i.e.
networks of permissible total length. The backwards method
begins with the 'ultimate' solution in terms of optimality
but one which is infeasible; the underlying logic is to
approach feasibility whilst departing from the 'ultimate' in
optimality as expressed by total user costs by as small an
amount as possible. Their value within the context of heuristic solution methods in general arises from the fact that while
neither is guaranteed to yield the true optimum, if a
particular problem is solved heuristically first *via* a forwards
method and then *via* a backwards method and if the same final
solution emerges, one can feel more confident that this is
indeed the true optimum.

Scott reports on results obtained using the forwards
and backwards algorithms for solving 26 optimal network
problems varying in size from seven to ten nodes. The
optimal solution to each problem was known in advance and
thus the performance of the algorithms could be checked. 21
of the 26 forwards runs and 24 of the 26 backwards runs
yielded the true optimum. The non-optimal solutions closely
approached the true optima. Thus, the foregoing heuristic
approaches do appear to yield good solutions. The reader is
referred to MacKinnon and Hodgson (1970) for a further
discussion and application of these techniques.

2.2.3 Steiner Minimal Spanning Trees

In this section, we consider further the problem of linking a
set of nodes at minimum total construction cost i.e. by a
network of minimum total distance. Recall the minimal
spanning tree solution (Section 2.2.1) which is illustrated
for a three node problem in Figure 2.3(a). An assumption
underlying this solution (and, indeed underlying the optimal

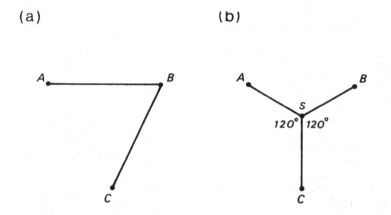

(a)   (b)

		MILES
CONSTRUCTION LENGTH		365
USER COST	A → B	180
	B → C	185
	A → C	365
TOTAL		730

		MILES
CONSTRUCTION LENGTH		325
USER COST	A → B	205
	B → C	215
	A → C	230
TOTAL		650

Figure 2.3 Comparison of Minimal Spanning Tree and Steiner Minimal Spanning Tree Networks for a Three Node Problem

network problem discussed in the previous section) is that any link incorporated into the network under design must join two of the initial nodes making up the problem. Consider now the alternative minimal spanning tree solution shown in Figure 2.3(b). Each of the three original nodes, A,B,C has been linked to a newly created additional node, S which is called a *Steiner point*. The revised solution is superior to that in Figure 2.3(a) for it involves a shorter network with lower associated user costs.

Many real-world networks exhibit the equivalent of Steiner points. Note in the case of the Texas interstate highway system (Figure 2.1(a)) that the routes from Fort Worth and San Antonio to El Paso converge at a junction east of the latter while the routes southwards from Fort Worth and Dallas converge to form a single route to Austin.

    While the facility to create additional nodes can
obviously yield superior solutions to network design problems,
the underlying solution processes increase once more in complexity. The geometry and mathematics underlying the
definition of Steiner points for networks have been examined
by Gilbert and Pollack (1968) and by Werner (1968, 1969). In
the case of three nodes, it can be shown that if one of the
angles in the triangle created by linking the nodes exceeds
120°, the minimal spanning tree is given by the two links
subtended by this angle. On the other hand, if no angle in
the triangle subtended by the three nodes exceeds 120°, the
minimal spanning tree may be found by locating a Steiner point
within the triangle such that the angles between three links
constructed to the three original nodes each equal 120°
(Figure 2.3(b)). Gilbert and Pollack present a straightforward geometric construction method for locating the Steiner
point.
    The same principles for Steiner point location apply to
networks with larger numbers of nodes. Turning again to the
minimal spanning tree solution for the Texas highway example
(Figure 2.1(b)), it might be felt that an undesirable property
of this solution is that El Paso is very inaccessible to the
rest of the network and, in particular, to the important area
of Dallas/Fort Worth. One way of alleviating this problem
would be to link El Paso/Fort Worth/Austin to a common
Steiner point (S in Figure 2.4); in fact, this solution
raises construction length slightly whilst offering a modest
reduction in user costs.
    A difficulty which arises when designing a network to
serve a number of nodes is that there are many possibilities
for the insertion of Steiner points. For the Texas example,
just one other possibility would be to insert an additional
Steiner point in Figure 2.4 to obviate the necessity for
traffic to Dallas to be routed via Fort Worth. In general,
if n is the number of original nodes and m is the number of
Steiner points introduced into the network (m $\leq$ n-2), the
maximum number of different possible Steiner topologies i.e.
arrangement patterns of Steiner points relative to the original nodes is given by :

$$\sum_{m=1}^{(n-2)} \left(\frac{2^{-m} \left(\begin{array}{c} n \\ n+2 \end{array} \right) (n+m-2)!}{m!} \right) \quad \text{---- (2.2)}$$

which, in the case of the Texas example with n=6 yields 3285
possible solutions. Because of this proliferation of possible
solutions i.e. possible ways of inserting Steiner points among
the original nodes, the only practical advice which can be
given is to inspect any Steiner network which would appear to
offer a desirable solution.

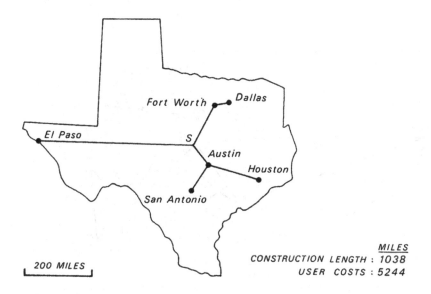

Figure 2.4 One Possible Topology for the Insertion of One
Steiner Point in the Texas Interstate Highway System

2.3. SHORTEST ROUTE MODELS

In these problems, a network is given. Each link has a value
associated with it which might represent the travel cost or
time or distance associated with that link. The route between
a given pair of nodes which minimises the sum of the values
associated with the links traversed i.e. which minimises the
total travel cost or time or distance is required.

2.3.1 Shortest Route Algorithm

In order to demonstrate the methods which follow, consider
the case of an airline company which flies the routes shown
in Figure 2.5. The value associated with each link is the
fare charged for traversing that link. The cheapest route
i.e. the 'shortest' route from New York City to San Francisco

17

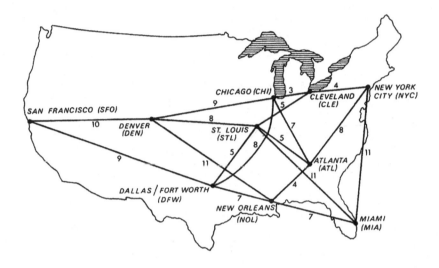

Figure 2.5 Shortest Route Problem: Airline Routes and Fares

is required.

The method used here to solve this problem is sometimes referred to as Moore's algorithm, Dantzig's algorithm or Dijkstra's algorithm. The overall strategy is to begin at the origin node, or *source* (New York City) and to build a tree-like network link by link outwards from it such that each node brought into the network is linked back to the source node *via* the least cost route. At each stage of the link addition process, all possible candidates for addition are inspected; the link chosen for addition is that to a currently unserved node and for which the minimum total travel cost back to the source is smallest. The network building process continues until the destination node or *sink* (San Francisco) is incorporated into the network.

Applying this method to the airline problem, the solution process commences at New York City. Three links are potential candidates for initiating the least cost network : NYC→CLE, NYC→ATL and NYC→MIA. The associated travel costs are 4, 8 and 11 respectively. The link NYC→CLE has the lowest associated cost and is thus incorporated into the network. For the second stage of the solution process, there are four potential additions to the least cost network : NYC→ATL; NYC→MIA: CLE→CHI and CLE→STL. The associated costs from New York City to

the respective end nodes are 8, 11, 7, 9 respectively. Thus
the link CLE→CHI is incorporated (Figure 2.6(i)). For the

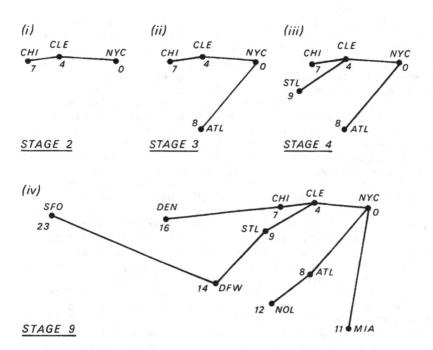

(i)

CLE
CHI   NYC
7   4   0

STAGE 2

(ii)

CLE
CHI   NYC
7   4   0

8 ATL

STAGE 3

(iii)

CLE
CHI   NYC
7   4   0
STL
9

8 ATL

STAGE 4

(iv)

SFO   DEN   CHI   CLE   NYC
23   16   7   4   0
                            STL
                             9

                                      8 ATL

        14 DFW

              12 NOL

STAGE 9   11 MIA

Figure 2.6 Shortest Route Problem: Least Cost Route Networks
    for Chosen Solution Stages

third stage of the solution process, the potential additions
to the network (cost from New York City in brackets) are :
NYC→ATL (8); NYC→MIA (11); CLE→STL (9); CHI→DEN (16); CHI→DFW
(15). Thus NYC→ATL is added. Continuing in this manner, the
reader should check that San Francisco is finally incorporated
into the least cost network at stage nine of the solution
process. Inspection of the network shows the least cost route
to be :

         NYC → CLE → STL → DFW → SFO

The associated cost is 23.

2.3.2 Some Applications

In the preceding example, attention focussed on determining
the shortest (least cost) route between two specified points.

19

It will be noted however that by chance, because San Francisco was the last node to be incorporated in the least cost route network, the shortest distance between the source node and *all* other nodes was found (Figure 2.6(iv)). Quite often, this is the purpose for which the algorithm is used.

One situation in which a determination of the shortest route between a node and all other nodes on a network is of interest arises within the context of urban transportation planning. The urban transportation planning process (for a summary see, for example, Bruton (1975) and Stopher and Meyburg (1975) commences by subdividing the area for which the transport plan is to be produced into small subareas or zones. Using various statistical methods, predictions are produced for the plan year of how many trips will be occurring between each pair of zones by each major transport node. Consider the case of trips by road. For any given set of roads proposals e.g. concerning motorway construction, improvement of existing roads etc, the planner will want to attempt an evaluation of how well this hypothesised road network will cater for the predicted demand. This is usually investigated using the shortest route algorithm. First, the proposed road network is drawn as a series of links and nodes. With each link is associated a travel time value which reflects the length of the link and the quality of the road it represents. The location of each of the zones between which a prediction for travel has been made is incorporated on the network as a node located at its centre. Now, given a prediction for the travel volume between each pair of zones and if the assumption is made that the trips between two zones will always take the shortest route in terms of travel time, the routes taken by all trips and thus the number of journeys to be expected on any part of the proposed network can be determined *via* repeated applications of the shortest route algorithm.

Figure 2.7 depicts the output from part of such an exercise carried out during the devising of a transport plan for Dublin, Ireland. It shows the least time routes on a proposed road network from a zone in the north-east of the city to various other zones. Given predictions for the number of trips between the origin zone and these other zones and assuming that trips take the least time route, the resulting flows on each link of the network caused by travel from the source zone in question to the destination zones in question can be determined. Further, repeating this exercise for each origin zone in turn enables the total flow to be predicted for each link from which the overall ability of the proposed road network to deal with the predicted travel demands can be evaluated.

A rather different application of the shortest route model is that discussed by Smith *et al.* (1972) who consider railroad and airline communications in north-east United

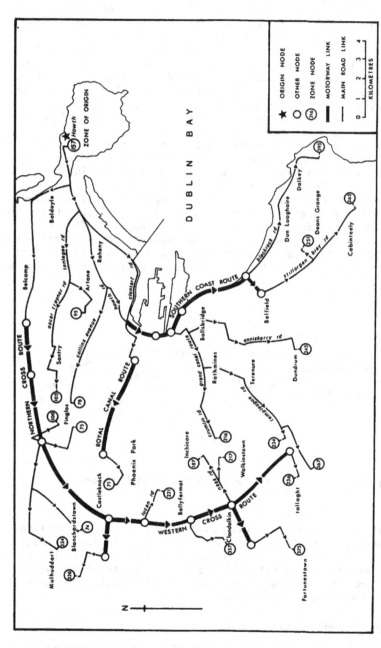

Figure 2.7 Shortest Route Network for a Given Origin Node and a Proposed Transport Network
From: AN FORAS FORBARTHA, (1972), *Dublin Transportation Study Technical Reports*, An Foras Forbartha,
Dublin, 8.13. Redrawn by permission of An Foras Forbartha.

21

States. In this study, the value assigned to each network
link comprises an index compounded of five summary attributes
of a journey on that link : travel time, travel cost, safety/
security, convenience and comfort. The index is calculated
in such a way as to be high for a link with generally undesirable characteristics. Thus finding the shortest path
between an origin and destination is equivalent to defining
the most desirable routing. Smith *et al.* claim that their
model could have particular value in evaluating usage shifts
as a result of specified changes in travel conditions on
certain links e.g. a speeding up of train service. Hypothesised routings for various journeys are given.

A final point worth making within the context of shortest
route problem applications is that the network under consideration need not necessarily represent a network which exists
in reality. Consider the case of a firm which has just
purchased a new truck. Assume for simplicity that a replacement will definitely be purchased in five years time but also,
that the firm may opt to purchase a replacement after one,
two, three and/or four years. The decision making strategies
open to the firm may be represented by a network of the form
(Figure 2.8) where each node represents a decision to purchase

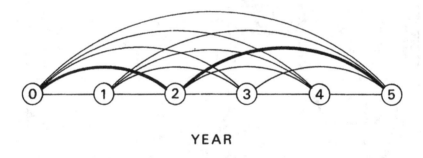

YEAR

Figure 2.8 A Network of Possible Decision Strategies

a replacement vehicle. Thus the strategy in darker outline
represents that of keeping the initial vehicle for two years
and then of keeping its replacement until the end of the five
year period. In reality, if a cost can be associated with
each link in the network, the least cost decision strategy is
that given by the shortest route.

2.3.3. Second Shortest Route

A question which sometimes arises within the context of

shortest route problems is that of determining the second
shortest route between (a) given pairs of node(s). One
situation in which such a determination is of relevance is
in the assigning of trips to a proposed transport network as
discussed in the previous section. An assumption made in that
discussion was that all trips between two zones (nodes) take
the shortest route between them; yet, in reality, some trips
will probably take the second shortest route especially if
the 'distance' difference between this route and the shortest
is small. This leads to the suggestion that when assigning
the trips predicted to take place between two zones to the
links of a proposed transport network, they should be split
between the shortest and second shortest routes bearing in
mind the relative total 'distances' involved. This presupposes that the second shortest route can be found.

In practice, the second shortest route can be readily
found by taking each link which comprises the shortest route
in turn, setting the 'distance' value associated with it to
infinity and re-solving the problem to yield a revised
minimum total 'distance' value and route. The second shortest
route is then the revised route for which the associated
total 'distance' value is lowest. Taking the case of the
airline routes between New York City and San Francisco,
recall that the shortest (least cost) route is :

$$NYC \rightarrow CLE \rightarrow STL \rightarrow DFW \rightarrow SFO.$$

Setting the cost associated with the NYC→CLE link to infinity
and re-solving yields the revised solution :

$$NYC \rightarrow ATL \rightarrow STL \rightarrow DFW \rightarrow SFO$$

which has an associated cost of 27. Now, setting the cost of
the CLE→STL link to infinity yields the revised solution :

$$NYC \rightarrow CLE \rightarrow CHI \rightarrow DEN \rightarrow SFO$$

which has an associated cost of 26. Setting the STL→DFW and
DFW→SFO links to infinity in turn also yields this solution.
Because it has the lowest associated cost of all of the
revised solutions, it comprises the second shortest route.

It should be noted that the preceding method defines as
the second shortest route that which contains at least one
link which is not in the shortest route and for which the
total distance value is lowest. An alternative definition of
the second shortest route is that it is route of minimum
total distance which has *no* link in common with the shortest
route. The route defined in this way can be found by setting
the values associated with all the links comprising the
shortest route simultaneously to infinity and re-solving.
In the case of the airline example, the resultant second

shortest route is :

$$NYC \rightarrow ATL \rightarrow STL \rightarrow DEN \rightarrow SFO$$

with an associated cost of 31.

2.4 NETWORK FLOW MODELS

2.4.1 Maximum Flow Problem

In this problem, a network is given. For each link, an upper capacity limit is stated for the flow of some commodity which that link can accommodate. It is required that the maximum flow possible of the commodity between a given source node and sink node be found together with the actual flow routings. Suppose in the case of the previously discussed airline problem that the maximum capacity of each route measured in hundreds of passengers that can be accommodated per day is as given in Figure 2.9. If New York City is taken as the source

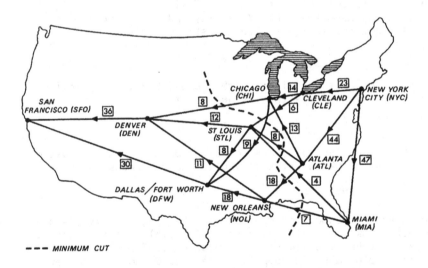

Figure 2.9 Maximum Flow Problem: Capacity Constraints

node and San Francisco as the sink node, the maximum flow problem involves determining the maximum number of passengers that can be transported from New York City to San Francisco in a day and the required routings. (It will be assumed for convenience that passengers can only be transported in the direction indicated by the arrow.)

The strategy used for solving the maximum flow problem involves finding what are known as *flow incrementable routes* from source to sink i.e. routes which facilitate an additional flow being introduced from source to sink. As each flow incrementable route is identified, the maximum possible flow is directed along it. The solution process ceases when no more flow incrementable routes are available. In the case of the airline problem, the route :

$$NYC \rightarrow CLE \rightarrow CHI \rightarrow DEN \rightarrow SFO$$

is a flow incrementable route. The maximum flow that can be directed along it equals the minimum of the capacities of the individual links comprising it i.e.

$$Min \{23, 14, 8, 36\} \quad = \quad 8.$$

Before proceeding to solve the maximum flow problem, we indicate *via* a simple example (Figure 2.10) a complication

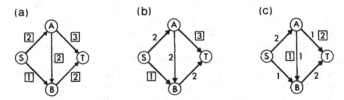

(a)   (b)   (c)

$\boxed{2}$ Remaining link capacity (if any)

Figure 2.10 Hypothetical Maximum Flow Problem

which can arise within the context of defining flow incrementable routes and hence the precise way in which these must
be defined in network terms. The maximum flow possible from
the source (S) to the sink (T) in the network in Figure 2.10(a)
is three units. One way in which this can be achieved is
as shown in Figure 2.10(c); an alternative would be to add a
unit flow to A → T and to remove it from A → B and B → T.

Consider now the task of deducing the maximum possible
flow *via* the successive indentification of flow incrementable
routes. Three initial possibilities present themselves
(Figure 2.10(a)):

$$S \rightarrow A \rightarrow B \rightarrow T$$

$$S \rightarrow A \rightarrow T$$

$$S \rightarrow B \rightarrow T$$

Suppose that the first of these is chosen. Assigning the
maximum possible flow to each link comprising the route (two
units) simultaneously exhausts the three link capacities.
Inspection of the resultant network (Figure 2.10(b)) yields
no obvious flow incrementable route. Yet, as demonstrated
already, a maximum of three units can flow through the network.

In order to surmount the type of difficulty highlighted
by this example, define any link to which flow can be added
as being *incrementable* and any link from which flow can be
removed as being *reducible*. (A link carrying a flow which is
below its maximum capacity is thus simultaneously incrementable and reducible). Define a flow incrementable route from
S to T as one which moves in the direction of flow along
incrementable links and against the direction of flow on
reducible links. When such a route is found, note the current
available capacity on each of the incrementable links and the
current flow on each of the reducible links. Find the minimum
of these values. In order to achieve the revised flow pattern,
add a flow equal to this minimum value to the incrementable
links and subtract it from the reducible links.

Reconsider Figure 2.10(b) in the light of the revised
definition of a flow incrementable route. The links
S → B ← A → T now form such a route because S → B and A → T
are incrementable while B ← A is reducible. The minimum of
the current capacities on the two incrementable routes
together with the flow on the reducible route is :

$$\text{Min} \quad \{ 1, 2, 3 \} = 1$$

Thus, an improved solution to that depicted in Figure 2.10(b)
can be obtained by adding a unit of flow to S → B and A → T
and by subtracting it from A → B which transforms the solution
in 2.10(b) to that in 2.10(c). Inspection of the flow pattern
in Figure 2.10(c) yields no further flow incrementable routes.

Thus this represents the optimal solution.

Returning now to the airline problem, nine routes can be found from New York City to San Francisco comprising incrementable links only. The solution after assigning the maximum possible flow to these in the order shown in Table 2.1 is shown in Figure 2.11. No further flow incrementable route is

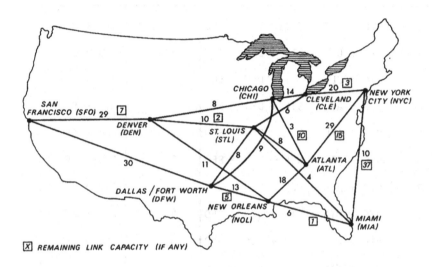

Figure 2.11 Maximum Flow Problem: Solution After Nine Stages

immediately apparent. Yet, in terms of the foregoing definition one exists :

$$NYC \rightarrow MIA \rightarrow NOL \rightarrow DFW \leftarrow STL \rightarrow DEN \rightarrow SFO$$

The maximum additional flow is given by :

$$Min \{37, 1, 5, 8, 2, 7\} = 1$$

Thus, one unit of flow is added to each of the incrementable links and subtracted from the reducible link, DFW ← STL. Inspection of the revised solution yields no further flow incrementing possibilities. Thus the maximum possible flow through the network is 60 units.

The foregoing solution to the maximum flow problem demonstrates what is often referred to as the *maximum flow* -

TABLE 2.1

MAXIMUM FLOW PROBLEM : ASSIGNMENT OF FLOWS TO ROUTES

Stage	Route	Flow Assigned	Link Achieving Maximum Capacity
1	NYC → CLE → CHI → DEN → SFO	8	CHI → DEN
2	NYC → CLE → STL → DEN → SFO	6	CLE → STL
3	NYC → CLE → CHI → DFW → SFO	6	CLE → CHI
4	NYC → ATL → STL → DFW → SFO	8	ATL → STL
5	NYC → ATL → CHI → DFW → SFO	3	CHI → DFW
6	NYC → ATL → NOL → DFW → SFO	13	DFW → SFO
7	NYC → ATL → NOL → DEN → SFO	5	ATL → NOL
8	NYC → MIA → STL → DEN → SFO	4	MIA → STL
9	NYC → MIA → NOL → DEN → SFO	6	NOL → DEN
10	NYC → MIA → NOL → DFW ← STL → DEN → SFO	1	MIA → NOL [1]
MAXIMAL FLOW		60	

[1] Unit capacity created STL → DFW

Minimum Cut	Capacity
CHI → DEN	8
CLE → STL	6
CHI → DFW	9
ATL → STL	8
MIA → STL	4
ATL → NOL	18
MIA → NOL	7
TOTAL	60

minimum cut principle which states that the maximum flow possible through a network equals the sum of the capacities of the links comprising the minimum cut. A network *cut* comprises a set of links which, if removed, divides the network into two separate entities, one containing the source node and the other the sink node. Thus, in the case of the airline example, the links :

CHI → DEN; STL → DEN; NOL → DEN; DFW → SFO

comprise a cut whose capacity is 61. By inspection the links:

CHI → DEN; CLE → STL; CHI → DFW; ATL → STL;

MIA → STL; ATL → NOL; MIA → NOL

comprise the minimum cut (Figure 2.9). The total capacity is 60 units which equals the maximum flow.

2.4.2 Least Cost Flow Problem With Capacity Constraints

The least cost flow problem with capacity constraints combines the ideas underlying the shortest route problem (Section 2.3.1) with those underlying the maximum flow problem to pose the question : *via* which links should k units of some product be routed through a network from source to sink such that total transport costs are minimised while no link capacities are transgressed. The link capacities express the upper and/ or lower bounds to the flow permitted on each link. Sometimes, it is required that the maximum possible volume of product (rather than k units) be shipped through the network from source to sink as cheaply as possible. We refer to this problem as the *least cost maximum flow problem.*

Given that the least cost flow problem with capacity constraints combines aspects of both the shortest route and maximum flow problems, one possible solution strategy would obviously be to combine the methods described in Section 2.3.1 and 2.4.1. Minieka (1978) describes such a strategy applicable in the case where the capacity constraints are all in the form of upper limits. First, the shortest (least cost) route i.e. shortest flow incrementable route from source to sink is found and the maximum amount of product is shipped along it. Then, assuming there is still more product to be shipped, the second shortest flow incrementable route is found and the maximum amount of product is directed along it. This process continues until the required amount of product has been shipped or, if the maximum amount of product possible is to be shipped, until no further flow incrementable route is available.

In terms of the methods discussed in Sections 2.3.1 and 2.4.1, the only additional complication which arises in this

revised formulation stems from the fact that at each stage of
the solution process we seek the next shortest flow incrementable route which, as discussed, may be a route which involves
'backtracking' along i.e. removing flow from certain links.
Minieka demonstrates how the shortest route methods given
previously (which always identify a series of 'forwards' links
from source to sink) can be adapted to identify flow incrementable routes.

An alternative method for solving the least cost flow
problem with capacity constraints is the so-called *out-of-
kilter algorithm* introduced by Fulkerson (1961) and summarised
by Minieka (1978) and by Taaffe and Gauthier (1973).   One
advantage of this algorithm is that it can deal with a problem
where certain links must have at least a stated minimum flow
in the final solution.   In summary, the algorithm commences
with an attempted solution which may or may not be feasible in
terms of the capacity constraints and which may or may not be
particularly efficient in terms of the costs associated with
individual links used.   Then, a set of rules are invoked to
successively improve the solution until, ultimately, optimality is reached.   The reader should consult the previously
cited works for details.

Two notable studies which involve solving a least cost
flow problem with capacity constraints are those of King *et al.*
(1971) and Gauthier (1968).   The former determines the least
cost pattern of flows for bituminous coal in the Mid-West/
Great Lakes area of the United States taking account of transport costs and of the capacities on the various available
routes.   The latter study is set within the context of the
State of São Paulo, Brazil highway network and seeks to
investigate such matters as the potential for interaction
between pairs of regional centres given the present road
network and the possible impact on both transport costs and
potential interaction levels of suggested transport network
improvements.

Gauthier's study commences by representing the São Paulo
road system as a network of nodes and links.   For each link,
two quantities are estimated: the transport cost per ton
carried along it and its maximum capacity in tons per day.
Calculation of the former figure takes into account type of
road (paved, gravel, laterite) together with fixed overhead
charges, equipment charges and administrative expenses borne
by the road user; determination of the latter takes into account
the surface quality and geometry of the road concerned.   Given
this network information, Gauthier proceeds to determine the
potential for interaction between any pair of centres as
follows.   Let X and Y denote the location of two centres and
let d_{ij} be the straightline distance between them (Figure 2.12).
Determine the length of the least cost route between X and Y,
v_{ij}.   Extend the line XY by $(v_{ij} - d_{ij})/2$ in either direction
to reach S and T; the length of the line ST thus equals

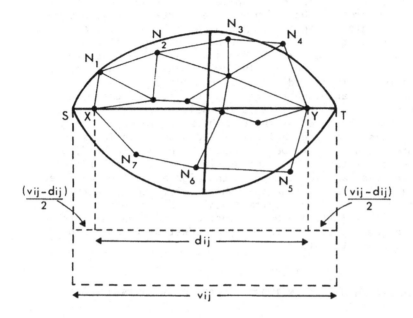

Figure 2.12   Definition of a Route System Linking Two Centres

From: GAUTHIER, H.L. (1968), Least Cost Flows in a Capacitated Network: A Brazilian Example in:
HORTON, F. (Ed.), Geographic Studies of Transportation
and Network Analysis, *Northwestern University Studies in Geography*, 16, 102-27.

Redrawn by permission.

v_{ij}. Construct the elipse which has SXYT as its major axis.
Note those nodes N_1, N_2, ... which lie closest to the edge of
this elipse and which together form a circuit from X to Y.
Consider the network bounded by this circuit. Gauthier
suggests that it is reasonable to assume that all flows
between X and Y will use this network for to use any link
outside it would involve an unacceptably long journey. Thus
it is suggested that a reasonable measure of the potential
for interaction between the two centres X and Y is given by
determining the maximum flow possible between them at least
cost on the network defined in the foregoing manner. Furthermore, it is suggested that the effects on this measure of
specified alterations to the transport network i.e. to flow
capacities and/or costs can be assessed by re-solving the
problem to yield a revised potential interaction level.
     Gauthier uses the out-of-kilter algorithm to determine
the potential for interaction between three pairs of centres:

São Paulo and the regional capital of Riberão Prêto which is 336 kilometres to the north *via* the shortest route; São Paulo and the regional capital of Bauru which is 360 kilometres to the north-west and, finally, between the regional capitals themselves which are 210 kilometres apart. The major result (Table 2.2) is the relatively favourable conditions both in terms of capacities and costs which exist for interaction between São Paulo and the regional capitals as compared to between the regional capitals themselves. It is suggested that this imbalance will need to be ameliorated if the attractiveness of the regional capitals as potential sites for future industry is to be increased. With this in mind, Gauthier proceeds to re-solve the problem twice, incorporating in each case an improvement to the highway system scheduled by Central Government which should improve the relative position of the regional capitals *vis a vis* each other. In both cases (Table 2.2), a dramatic increase in potential interaction levels is accompanied by a modest decrease in per unit transport costs.

TABLE   2.2

BRAZILIAN HIGHWAY NETWORK : LEAST COST MAXIMUM FLOWS

	Total Flow[1]	Cost[2]
A. SÃO PAULO - RIBERÃO PRÊTO (d_{ij} = 295 kms.)		
i) Present Network	12140	1.32
B. SÃO PAULO - BAURU (d_{ij} = 280 kms.)		
i) Present Network	14954	1.19
C. RIBERÃO PRÊTO - BAURU (d_{ij} = 180 kms.)		
i) Present Network	5766	1.50
ii) Addition: Paved Highway Bauru to Jau	9465	1.42
iii) Addition: Paved Highway São Carlos to Riberão Prêto	9799	1.40

1. Short Tons
2. Cruzeros per Ton-Kilometre

From GAUTHIER, H.L. (1968) as cited for Figure 2.12.

Reprinted by permission.

3

THE TRANSPORTATION AND RELATED PROBLEMS

3.1 INTRODUCTION

In this chapter, we discuss a number of related optimisation problems which have been used in a variety of contexts by geographers and planners. It will be shown that, in effect, many of them comprise some type of least cost flow problem with link capacity constraints and that they could therefore be tackled using the methods outlined in Section 2.4.2. In practice, this is not done; as will be seen, the models to be discussed possess special underlying mathematical structures which can be exploited to yield more straightforward solution approaches.

3.2 THE ASSIGNMENT PROBLEM

3.2.1 Formulation

Consider the case of a farmer who is about to harvest a crop from three equally sized fields A, B and C. The harvest is to be transported for storage in three barns X, Y and Z, one field being assigned to each barn. Given the distance from each field to each barn (Figure 3.1), which field's harvest should be assigned to which barn such that the total distance incurred in transporting the harvests to the barns is minimised?

The foregoing is an example of *the assignment problem*. In general, it comprises assigning n objects (e.g. harvests) to n facilities (e.g. barns) such that the total 'cost' of (e.g. distance involved in) the assignment is minimised. Succintly, the problem may be expressed as finding the pattern of assignments in order to:

Minimise: Total transport costs
s.t.   Each object assigned to one facility
         Each facility receives one object

DOI: 10.4324/9781003179030-3

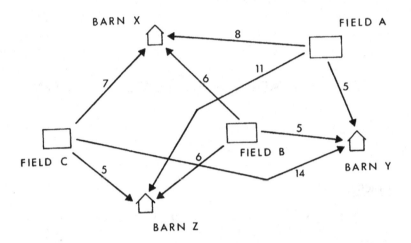

Figure 3.1 Assignment Problem: Input Data

The foregoing may be expressed mathematically as follows.
Let c_{ij} = The cost of assigning object i to facility j
(Fixed Variable)

X_{ij} = 1 if object i is assigned to facility j (Decision
Variable)
= 0 otherwise

The objective to minimise total costs is now given by:

$$\text{Minimise: } \sum_{i=1}^{n} \sum_{j=1}^{n} c_{ij} X_{ij} \qquad \text{---- (3.1)}$$

The constraint that the first object must be assigned to
one facility only is given by:

$$\sum_{j=1}^{n} X_{1j} = 1$$

Similarly, for the second object:

$$\sum_{j=1}^{n} X_{2j} = 1$$

or, summarising for all n objects:

$$\sum_{j=1}^{n} X_{ij} = 1 \quad \text{for } i = 1,\ldots,n \qquad \text{----(3.2)}$$

Similarly, summarising the condition that each of the n facilities mus t receive one object gives the constraints:

$$\sum_{i=1}^{n} X_{ij} = 1 \quad \text{for } j = 1,\ldots,n \qquad \text{----(3.3)}$$

The expressions (3.1)-(3.3) together provide a mathematical statement of the assignment problem. To the constraints, it might be imagined that the condition $X_{ij} = 0$ or 1 should be added; in fact, it can be shown that provided all of the c_{ij} terms are integers which can always be arranged for by multiplying them up by a suitable factor, one need merely specify that:

$$X_{ij} \geq 0 \quad \text{for all } i,j \qquad \text{----(3.4)}$$

(For a further comment on the validity of (3.4), see Section 3.3.6.) Before proceeding, it is worth noting that the foregoing mathematical formulation of the assignment problem follows the general guidelines for such formulations as expressed by (1.1)-(1.3) in Chapter One. The decision variables (X_{ij}'s) are denoted by upper case notation with the fixed variables (c_{ij}'s) in lower case. In addition to the major constraints, it is required that the decision variables be non-negative. Certain other features of the mathematical formulation should be noted also. First, in terms of the decision variables, both the objective and the constraints are linear, i.e. contain terms involving X_{ij} alone rather than (say) X_{ij}^2 or $X_{ij}/X_{k\ell}$. For this reason, the assignment problem comprises what is known as a *linear programming problem*. Second, it is to be noted that in the assignment problem, the constraints (3.2),(3.3) i.e. the equivalent of (1.2) in (1.1)-(1.3) are all equalities, that each right hand side value equals unity and that each coefficient of X_{ij} on the left hand sides is either one or zero. These latter mathematical properties allow the assignment problem to be solved in the rather straightforward manner now to be described.

3.2.2 Solution Method

A solution method for the assignment problem is now demonstrated using the crop-harvest example depicted in Figure 3.1. First, a table is prepared (Table 3.1(i)) which summarises the costs involved in assigning each object to each facility. Now, for each row in turn, the minimum of the cost values

TABLE 3.1

THE ASSIGNMENT PROBLEM : SOLUTION METHOD

(i)		To Barn				(ii)		To Barn			
		X	Y	Z				X	Y	Z	
From Field	A	8	5	11			A	3	0	6	-5
	B	6	5	6			B	1	0	1	-5
	C	7	14	5			C	2	9	0	-5

(iii)		X	Y	Z		(iv)		X	Y	Z
From Field	A	2	0	6			A		*	
	B	0	0	1			B	*		
	C	1	9	0			C			*
		-1						Optimal Solution		

is subtracted from each reading. Thus, in the case of the
first row, the value five is subtracted from eight, five,
eleven to yield the revised readings three, zero, six. The
value of five can be interpreted as the least amount of money
that will have to be paid in order to assign field A's harvest. The values subtracted from the second and third rows
are five and five respectively. Consider now the revised table
(Table 3.1(ii)). For each column in turn, the minimum cost
value in that column is subtracted from each reading. Thus in
the case of the first column, the value one is subtracted from
three, one, two to yield the revised readings two, zero, one
(Table 3.1(iii)). This value can be interpreted as the least
amount of money that will have to be paid in addition to
that subtracted in the case of the rows in order to ensure
that barn X receives an assignment. In this particular example,
the minimum values in the second and third columns are zero.
Thus nothing is subtracted from them. Consider now the resulting table (Table 3.1(iii)). Within it, a pattern of zeros
can be identified such that there is one zero in each row
and column (Table 3.1(iv)). This pattern represents the optimal pattern of assignments; the total cost (minimised) of
making these assignments is given by the sum of the individual costs involved. Thus, in the case of the example, the
optimal assignment pattern is:

$$A \rightarrow Y; \quad B \rightarrow X; \quad C \rightarrow Z$$

The total cost is given by:

$$6 + 5 + 5 = 16$$

The foregoing solution method obviously presupposes that the required pattern of zeros - one in each row/column - will be available after the prescribed subtractions have been performed i.e. in the equivalent of Table 3.1(iii). In practice, this does not always occur. An example is given in Table 3.2(i) - (ii). In this instance, one proceeds from the table

TABLE 3.2

ASSIGNMENT PROBLEM : REVISED PROBLEM SOLUTION

(i)

	W	X	Y	Z
A	1	4	6	3
B	8	7	7	9
C	4	5	8	7
D	6	7	8	5

(ii)

	W	X	Y	Z
A	0	3	5	2
B	-1	0	0	2
C	0	1	4	3
D	-1	2	3	0

(iii)

	W	X	Y	Z
A	0	2	4	1
B	2	0	0	2
C	0	0	3	2
D	2	2	3	0

(iv)

	W	X	Y	Z
A	*			
B			*	
C		*		
D				*

where the required pattern of zeros is not available as follows. Draw the smallest number of horizontal and vertical lines through the current cost table such that all the zero values are crossed out. Note the minimum of the uncrossed elements. Subtract this value from each of the uncrossed elements and add it to each element in a position where two lines cross. Inspect the resulting table for the required pattern of zeros. If this pattern is still absent, repeat the process.

   Applying the foregoing rules to Table 3.2(ii), three lines are required to delete the zero values. The minimum of the uncrossed values is one which when subtracted from each uncrossed element and added to each location where two lines cross yields the optimal assignment:

$$A \to W; \quad B \to Y; \quad C \to X; \quad D \to Z$$

The cost of this assignment equals 21.

3.2.3 Examples

The usual context in which the assignment problem has been

employed by geographers and planners is that of assigning
individuals e.g. school students to central facilities e.g.
school places. In the hypothetical case illustrated in
Figure 3.2, 100 school students living in the locations shown

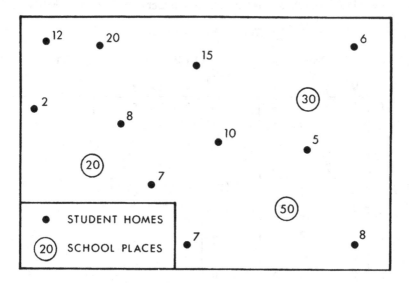

Figure 3.2 Hypothetical Assignment Problem

are each to be assigned to a place in one of three schools
which, between them, can supply 100 places. The assignment is
to be made in such a way that the total distance travelled by
students to reach schools is minimised. The problem could obviously be solved by applying the methods outlined in the
previous section to a table of 100 x 100 readings giving
the distance of each individual from each schoolplace. (In
practice, in this type of case, a less cumbersome technique
to be discussed in Section 3.3.2 is used.) Given the results,
the region to be served by each school could be delineated.
    Figure 3.3 shows the output from one school assignment
exercise carried out by Yeates (1963) in the context of
Grant County, Wisconsin. The actual school boundaries had ev-
olved on a trial and error basis through time. Yeates'
optimal solution to the corresponding assignment problem
shows that if about 18 per cent of the students were assigned
to different schools as illustrated, this would save nearly
$4000 per year in transport costs. Other studies which employ
the assignment problem include those of Maxfield (1972) who
considers the assignment of pupils to school places in the
Athens, Georgia school district, Goodchild and Massam (1969)
and Massam (1972) who deal with the assignment of individuals

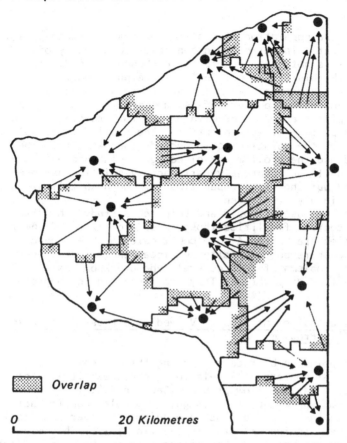

Figure 3.3 Changes in School Districts to Achieve a Least
    Distance Assignment
From:YEATES, M., (1968), An *Introduction to Quantitative Anal-
    ysis In Human Geography*, McGraw-Hill, New York, 112.
Redrawn by permission of the author.

to administrative centres in Southern Ontario (for a description see Section 7.7) and Cox (1965) who treats a similar type
of problem in the context of Scotland. A most interesting
discussion of the general issues underlying assignment can
be found in Morrill (1973).
    While the assignment problem is obviously an attractive
one in terms of the range of actual and potential applications, one feature which obviously limits its use must be
noted: both the capacities and the locations of the central
facilities e.g. schools must be known in advance. In practice, some latitude often exists concerning one or both of
these. Gould and Leinbach (1960) consider the problem of

serving the population of Western Guatemala with hospitals
to be located in three given centres. The capacity of each
hospital is not given but is to be chosen. In order to
deal with this situation, Gould and Leinbach begin by assuming that each hospital will have an equal capacity. Having
found the optimal pattern of assignments, the capacities of
the hospitals are altered with a view to obtaining a more
logical pattern of assignments and the problem is re-solved.
Once more, the solution is inspected, the capacity values are
altered and the problem re-solved again. The process continues until an apparently satisfactory solution has been
obtained but the final capacities for the hospitals are not
optimal in any strict sense.

In the case of Gould and Leinbach's study, the sites
of the central facilities (hospitals) are fixed and their
capacities are varied. A more complicated problem concerns
the case where both capacity and location may vary. Assignment problems of this general type are known as *loc-
ation-alloction problems*. They are discussed in Chapter
Seven.

3.2.4 The Assignment Problem Viewed as a Least Cost Maximum Flow Problem

A final point to be made concerning the assignment problem
(3.1)-(3.3) concerns the relationship between it and the
least cost maximum flow problem (Section 2.4.2). Although
it may not appear so, the assignment problem can in fact
be viewed and solved as such a problem. Consider once again
the harvest assignment example (Section 3.2.1). This may be
envisaged as a network linking two sets of three nodes each
(Figure 3.4). Each link has a cost value, c_{ij}, associated
with it. Imagine now that the nodes representing the fields
are linked back to a single source, S, by zero cost links
which have an upper capacity limit of one. In the same way,
imagine that the nodes representing the barns are linked
onwards to a single sink node, T, by zero cost links which
have an upper capacity limit of one. Imagine now solving
this problem as a least cost maximum flow problem. The maximum flow possible from S to T is obviously three units. Exactly one unit of flow will enter each of A, B, C and will
thus leave those nodes; exactly one unit of flow will leave
each of X, Y, Z and thus enter those nodes. The precise
routing of flows between A, B, C and X, Y, Z will depend
on the relative costs associated with the links. The links
used in the optimal solution will be those for which the
associated total travel 'cost' is minimised and will obviously correspond to the optimal assignment problem solution.

Because the assignment problem can be viewed as a
least cost maximum flow problem, it can be solved using the

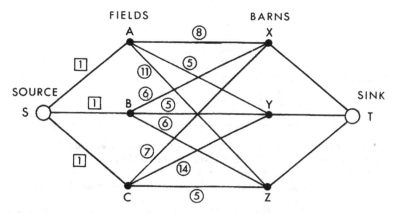

FIELDS   BARNS

Figure 3.4 The Assignment Problem as a Network Problem

① - 'Cost' associated with link   ▢ - Upper capacity of link

Figure 3.4 The Assignment Problem as a Network Problem

approaches outlined in Section 2.4.2 e.g. the out-of-kilter algorithm. In practice, the methods given in Section 3.2.2 are more straightforward and are therefore generally used.

3.3 THE TRANSPORTATION PROBLEM

3.3.1 Formulation

Consider the case of three factories A, B and C which are capable of producing 20, 35 and 50 units of a particular product per month. The product is to be delivered to three towns X, Y and Z whose monthly demand requirements are 45, 30 and 30 units respectively. If the cost of delivering a unit of product from each factory to each town is known (Table 3.3), the transportation problem involves determining the optimal pattern of deliveries from the factories to the towns which will minimise the total cost of transporting product. It is required that the solution be such that no factory is called upon to send out more product than it can supply and that each town receives its demand requirement.
 In general, for m origins and n destinations, *the transportation problem* or, as it is sometimes known, *the*

TABLE 3.3

THE TRANSPORTATION PROBLEM : TRANSPORT COSTS

Town

		X	Y	Z
	A	9	7	5
Factory	B	7	3	2
	C	2	1	1

Hitchcock-Koopmans transportation problem involves finding the pattern of product flows which will:

   Minimise: Total transport costs

   s.t.   Each origin sends out no more than it can
              supply
              Each destination receives its demand require-
              ment

For the present, it will be assumed, as is the case in the
numerical example that total supply available equals the
total demand required.(It will be shown later that this
assumption is not restrictive.) Thus each origin must send
out exactly what it can supply and each destination will
receive exactly what it demands. Mathematically, this may
be expressed as follows:

Let c_{ij} = The cost of transporting one unit of product from
      origin i to destination j

   X_{ij} = The number of units shipped from i to j (Decision
      Variable)

   s_i = The supply available at origin i, i = 1,...,m
   d_j = The demand requirement at destination j,
        j = 1,...,n

Now, following the logic used when formulating the assignment problem ((3.1)-(3.4)), the transportation problem can
be viewed as finding values for the X_{ij}'s which:

$$\text{Minimise: } \sum_{i=1}^{m} \sum_{j=1}^{n} c_{ij} X_{ij} \qquad \text{----(3.5)}$$

$$\text{s.t.} \qquad \sum_{j=1}^{n} X_{ij} = s_i; \ i = 1,...,m \quad \text{----(3.6)}$$

$$\sum_{i=1}^{m} X_{ij} = d_j, \ j = 1,...,n \quad \text{----(3.7)}$$

$$X_{ij} \geq 0 \text{ for all } i,j$$

The Transportation and Related Problems

Before proceeding, it should be noted that from a mathematical viewpoint, the transportation problem is a linear programming problem in the sense defined in Section 3.2.1. Indeed, the sole difference between it and the assignment problem is that the right hand sides of the constraints (3.6), (3.7) are integers rather than unity. It should be noted further that it can be shown that if all of the fixed variables (s_i, d_j, c_{ij}) are integers (which will be assumed here) the X_{ij}'s in the optimal solution will also be integers (except in one special circumstance to be discussed in Section 3.3.6).

3.3.2 Solution Method

As was the case with the assignment problem, the transportation problem can be solved in a relatively straightforward manner. The overall strategy is to begin with an arbitrary solution and to successively improve on it until the optimum is reached. The solution process commences by constructing a table (Table 3.4 (Top)) which lists the origins (factories) by row and the destinations(towns) by column. Each cell in the table thus represents one route which may or may not be used in a solution. It is divided by a diagonal line. The transport cost per unit of product for the route is inserted in the top left hand area while the amount of product to be shipped along the route will be inserted in the bottom right hand area. The production capacities for each origin are inserted to the right of each row while the requirements of each destination are placed below each column. Thus, when it comes to inserting flows on various routes, the requirement that (3.6) and (3.7) hold is equivalent to demanding that the individual flows are such that they total across each row and down each column to the stated totals.

Having drawn up the initial table, the next step involves finding an initial solution. This is most often achieved *via* the *northwest corner rule* which involves commencing with the top left hand (northwest) cell in the initial table and of successively assigning the maximum possible flow to each cell encountered thus satisfying each origin and destination in turn until the bottom right hand (southeast) cell is reached. Thus, for the example, the northwest cell represents the route A → X. The maximum flow that can be assigned to this route is 20 units which exhausts the the production capacity of factory A i.e. satisfies row one in the table. Thus factory B must deliver the remaining 25 units to X which satisfies column one in the table. The remaining capacity at B (10) must now be assigned to Y which satisfies row two. Y must receive the balance of its requirement (20) from C thus satisfying column two and leaving precisely 30 units to be assigned to Z. Note that because

TABLE 3.4

TRANSPORTATION PROBLEM : SOLUTION

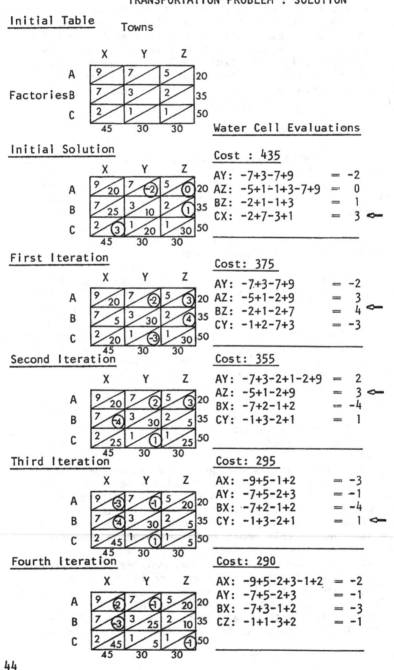

__Initial Table__   Towns

Initial Solution

First Iteration

Second Iteration

Third Iteration

Fourth Iteration

Water Cell Evaluations

Cost : 435

AY: −7+3−7+9	= −2
AZ: −5+1−1+3−7+9	= 0
BZ: −2+1−1+3	= 1
CX: −2+7−3+1	= 3 ⬅

Cost: 375

AY: −7+3−7+9	= −2
AZ: −5+1−2+9	= 3 ⬅
BZ: −2+1−2+7	= 4 ⬅
CY: −1+2−7+3	= −3

Cost: 355

AY: −7+3−2+1−2+9	= 2 ⬅
AZ: −5+1−2+9	= 3 ⬅
BX: −7+2−1+2	= −4
CY: −1+3−2+1	= 1

Cost: 295

AX: −9+5−1+2	= −3
AY: −7+5−2+3	= −1
BX: −7+2−1+2	= −4
CY: −1+3−2+1	= 1 ⬅

Cost: 290

AX: −9+5−2+3−1+2	= −2
AY: −7+5−2+3	= −1
BX: −7+3−1+2	= −3
CZ: −1+1−3+2	= −1

total supply equals total demand, the value to be placed in the final cell will always balance out the remaining supply and demand. The initial table represents one possible solution to the transportation problem. The total cost of this solution can be determined by summing the costs associated with each route which, for the example gives:

$$(9 \times 20) + (7 \times 25) + (3 \times 10) + (1 \times 20) + (1 \times 30) = 435$$

Having found an initial solution, we now wish to investigate whether it can be improved on by placing product on some route(s) not being used and by taking it off some that are being used. At all times, the flows must 'balance' in terms of the supply and demand totals. Within the context of a possible solution such as the initial solution in Table 3.4, routes which are being used currently (A → X; B → X; B → Y; C → Y; C → Z) are referred to as *stepping stones* while routes which are not in use currently (A → Y; A → Z; B → Z; C → X) are referred to as *water cells*. The method proceeds by evaluating the merit or otherwise of bringing each water cell into use i.e. of placing a flow on the route concerned. In order to perform this task for a given water cell, we proceed as follows:

1. Commencing at the water cell itself, identify a path which:
   (a) Involves moving in a clockwise direction
   (b) Involves stepping stones only
   (c) Involves changing ... row/column/row ... successively i.e. with no diagonal steps
   (d) Terminates back at the original water cell

It can be shown that there will always be exactly one such path associated with each water cell.

2. Having defined the path identified by 1. for a given water cell, list in the order in which they are encountered on the path the per unit transport costs associated with each cell starting with the water cell itself. Give the first of these (i.e. the per unit transport cost associated with the water cell itself) a negative sign, the next a positive sign, the next a negative sign and so on. Find the sum of these values. This sum gives a measure of the merit or otherwise of commencing to flow product along the route associated with the water cell. Insert the value in the water cell and circle it.

Considering 1. in the context of the example, focus attention on the water cell AY. The only path from AY which fulfills the criteria in 1. is:

AY → BY → BX → AX → (AY)

Another possibility might appear to be to move first from AY
to CY. However, having reached CY and bearing in mind that we
must now change column while continuing to move clockwise, the
only possible cell to which to proceed is AZ which is a water
cell and which is prohibited. Focus attention now on the
water call AZ. Here, the only possible first step is AZ → CZ;
then, being required to change column, the only possible step
is CZ → CY; continuing, the full path is:

$$AZ → CZ → CY → BY → BX → AX → (AZ).$$

The reader should satisfy himself that the unique paths associated with the remaining two water cells are:

$$BZ : BZ → CZ → CY → BY → (BZ)$$

$$CX : CX → BX → BY → CY → (CX)$$

Turning now to 2. and again to the water cell AY, the
per unit transport costs associated with the cells on the
unique path are 7(AY), 3(BY), 7(BX), 9(AX). Signing these as
stated previously and adding yields: .

$$- 7 + 3 - 7 + 9 = -2$$

The reader should verify that the summations for the other
cells are as given in Table 3.4. The result of each summation
is placed in a circle in the water cell in the initial solution table.
It was stated previously that the results of the foregoing summations give a measure of the merit or otherwise of
commencing to use a given water cell. In order to see why
this is so, consider again cell AY. Suppose that one unit of
flow is permitted from A to Y i.e. the route AY is brought
into use. How could this be permitted bearing in mind the
total supply/demand levels to which any solution must adhere
and assuming that the other water cells are to remain as
such? Having placed a unit of flow on the route AY, a unit of
flow would have to be removed from BY to ensure that Y still
receives its demand requirement; this latter step would
reduce the output of B by one unit and a unit of flow would
have to be added to route BX to ensure that B still sends out
its total production; now, X is getting one unit of flow in
excess of its demand; to counteract this, a unit of flow must
be taken from route AX which, given that a unit of flow was
added to route AY in the first place means that A is still
sending out its total production. To summarise, if a unit of
flow is placed on route AY, a unit of flow must be removed
from BY, added to BX and removed from AX to keep the complete
system balanced in terms of the total supplies and demands.
What would be the overall saving (if any) of adjusting the

solution in this way? To subtract a unit of flow from BY and
AX would cause a saving of +3 and +9 money units respectively
while to add a unit of flow to AY and BX would involve a
'saving' of -7 and -7 respectively. Thus the overall saving
on the complete operation would be:

$$- 7 + 3 - 7 + 9 = -2$$

which is in fact the precise calculation carried out already
by applying 1. and 2. Thus, the values emerging in 2.
represent the savings that can be made for each unit of flow
transferred on to the water cell route upon which attention
is being focussed whilst preserving the other water cells and
ensuring that the flows remain in balance with the total
supply and demand statistics. These values are referred to as
shadow costs. Note that in the case of cell AY the shadow
cost i.e. the saving if that route is brought in to use is
negative i.e. total transport costs would actually rise if
product was transferred on to this route. The route which
offers the greatest saving if brought into use (+3 money
units per unit of flow transferred) is CX.

   Recall that the objective underlying the transportation
problem is to find the flow pattern which minimises total
transport costs. Given that this is so, and given a particular solution which we are seeking to improve e.g. the initial
solution in Table 3.4, it obviously is most desirable to
divert flow on to that route which offers the greatest per
unit saving in transport costs i.e. on to that route with the
highest associated shadow cost value. As mentioned already,
this is CX in the case of the example. Now, bearing in mind
once again that the objective (3.5) implies making the greatest money saving possible and given that flow is to be placed
on route CX, it is presumably desirable to place as large
flow as possible on it i.e. to remove as large a flow as
possible from BX and CY and to add it to CX and BY. Quite
obviously, the largest flow that can be so transferred in
this case is the minimum of the current flows on BX and CY
i.e. 20 units. The revised solution obtained by transferring
20 units to CX and keeping the flow pattern balanced is shown
as the first iteration in Table 3.4. Notice that while CX
has now become a stepping stone, CY has been transformed to a
water cell; thus the total number of water cells and stepping
stones is as before. Notice too that the transportation cost
associated with the revised solution (375) is, as expected,
equal to the original cost (435) less the total number of
units shifted (20) multiplied by the cost saving per unit (3).

   Given a revised solution to a particular problem e.g.
the first iteration solution in Table 3.4, the method now
proceeds by evaluating the water cells in this solution using
1. and 2. Identifying the cell with the largest positive
shadow cost value (in case of a tie choose either cell) the

maximum flow possible is shifted on to the route concerned to yield yet another solution with a lower associated total transport cost. Then the process of evaluation and shifting is repeated again and continues until, on evaluation, no cell has an associated positive shadow cost. This indicates that no route exists which, if brought into use, will offer a money saving. Thus the least cost solution has been reached. The full calculations for the example are set out in Table 3.4. The reader is urged to study these in order to familiarise himself fully with the solution process.

Before leaving the *northwest corner stepping stone method* as this solution approach is usually called, it should be noted that the initial solution derived involved using five routes; at each stage of the solution process with the exchange of one water cell for a stepping stone and *vice-versa,* the number of routes in use remained at five. Thus, it was implicitly assumed from the outset, that the optimal solution would involve using five routes. In general, for m origins and n destinations, a total of m X n possible routes exist. Each solution generated will involve using (m + n - 1) of these. We leave until Section 4.8 an explanation of why from the outset it is reasonable to assume that the optimal solution to the transportation problem will generally involve using exactly (m + n - 1) routes; two situations in which this is not the case are described in Section 3.3.6.

3.3.3 Examples

Numerous examples of the transportation problem applied in a variety of contexts are available in the literature. Notable studies include those of Henderson (1958) (for a summary, see Hay (1977)) who deals with coal flows in the United States, Land (1957) who deals with the transport of coking coal in Great Britain, Cox (1965) who analyses interstate flows of aluminium bar in the United States, Rimmer (1968) who discusses cement flows in New Zealand and Osayimwese (1974) who considers the evacuation of groundnuts in Nigeria. Shaw (1970) examines optimal transport patterns for maincrop potato production in Britain while de Castro Lopo (1967) determines the extent to which actual migration patterns in Bihar, North India are similar to the patterns which would minimise total distance moved.

Within a context of declining energy resources, a particularly interesting application of the transportation problem is that described by Osleeb and Sheskin (1977) who consider the least cost flow patterns for natural gas in the United States and Canada for various years up to 1990. Estimates of available supplies were obtained for seventeen regions : eight onshore and five offshore regions in the United States and four regions in Canada. Demand estimates were available for each of the 48 contiguous states of the United States together

with Alaska and the Canadian provinces yielding 56 demand
regions in all. Each of the 17 X 56 links between supply and
demand regions had associated with it a cost (per million cubic
feet of gas transported) made up of the transport cost plus
production cost in the supply region. In this way, the varying
cost of producing natural gas in different regions was explicitly taken into account. Osleeb and Sheskin wished to
determine the least-cost flow pattern from supply to demand
regions. We focus here on their analysis for 1990.

Up to 1970, the supply of natural gas available in North
America exceeded total demand; since that time, the reverse
has been the case. Thus, in the context of the methods described in the previous section, the requirement that total
supply equals total demand does not hold. A divergence
between total supply and demand in a transportation problem
can be taken into account by modifying the methods discussed
in the previous section as follows. First, where total demand
exceeds total supply as in the current instance, create an
additional dummy or phantom origin with the ability of producing the shortfall in supply. Link it by routes with zero
associated transport costs to each destination. Solve the
transportation problem in the usual manner. Note the destinations served by the dummy source and the flow magnitudes
involved; in practice, these flows will not occur and the
relevant destinations will suffer a deficit. The strategy for
dealing with an excess of supply capacity over demand requirement is similar. A dummy or phantom destination with a
requirement for the excess production capacity is created.
Each link to this destination is given a zero associated transport cost. After solution in the previously described manner,
the flows to the dummy destination are noted. These do not
occur in reality and the corresponding origins underproduce by
the flow values.

Returning to Osleeb and Sheskin's study, Figure 3.5 shows
the projected least cost flow pattern for natural gas for 1990.
With the exception of the Canadian and Alaska supply regions,
the links used are generally short. Figure 3.6 shows the
destination regions in the United States which suffer a deficit
in the optimal solution. They comprise the east coast states
(excluding New England) together with the mid-west and the
south. Osleeb and Sheskin suggest that these are the regions
in which facilities for dealing with alternative supplies of
gas e.g. deliquifaction facilities for imported liquified
natural gas should be located.

A rather different application of the transportation
problem is that of Wheeler (1967) who considers intra-city work
trip patterns in Pittsburgh, Pennsylvania. (For a similar
study set within the context of Tulsa, Oklahoma see Wheeler
(1970).) The Pittsburgh Area Transportation Study subdivided
the Pittsburgh metropolitan area into 74 zones. For each zone,
the number of residents (origins) and the number of workplaces

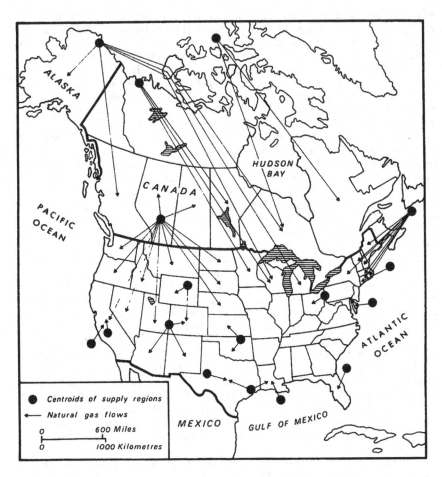

Figure 3.5 Projected Natural Gas Flows, 1990

From: OSLEEB, J.P. and SHESKIN, I.M., (1977), Natural Gas:
      a Geographical Perspective, *Geographical Review, 67,*
      71-85, Figure 4.

Redrawn by permission of the American Geographical Society.

(destinations) was known for a number of occupational categories e.g. managers and service workers. The average work
journey length for each occupational category was also known.
Given the distance between each pair of zones and using the
methods described in the previous section, Wheeler determines
for each occupational category the work trip pattern which
would minimise total distance travelled and the mean work
trip length associated with this. This latter statistic is

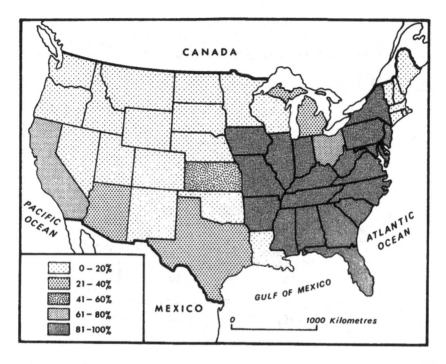

Figure 3.6 Projected Deficit Regions for Natural Gas Deliveries in the United States, 1990.

From: OSLEEB, J.P. and SHESKIN, I.M., (1977), Natural Gas:
à Geographical Perspective, *Geographical Review*, 67,
71-85, Figure 7.

Redrawn by permission of the American Geographical Society

then compared with the actual value to see to what extent
actual behaviour approaches that which minimises distance.
The conclusion is that while there is an overall tendency
towards trip patterns which minimise distance travelled, the
extent to which individual occupational categories approach
this varies.

3.3.4 An Alternative View of the Transportation Problem

Recall the final solution to the transportation problem
example discussed in Section 3.3.2 (Table 3.5). Consider now
the question of by how much the transport cost associated with
a particular water cell route i.e. a route which is unused at
optimality would have to be reduced in order for it to be used
in the optimal solution. Quite obviously, the reduction, X,
would have to be such as to cause the associated shadow cost
value to become positive i.e. would have to be at least the

51

TABLE 3.5

TRANSPORTATION PROBLEM : SHADOW PRICES

<u>THIRD ITERATION</u>

SHADOW PRICES

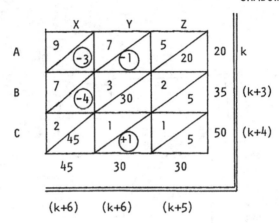

(k+6)　　(k+6)　　(k+5)

<u>FINAL</u>
<u>SOLUTION</u>

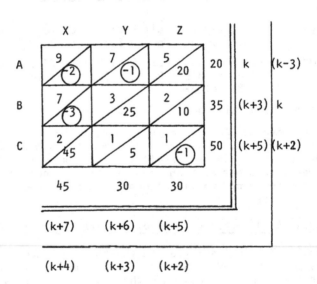

(k+7)　　(k+6)　　(k+5)

(k+4)　　(k+3)　　(k+2)

present shadow cost. To demonstrate, consider the specific case of cell BX. For this cell to be used as part of the optimal solution, its associated shadow cost would have to become positive which is equivalent to requiring that:

$$-(7-X) +3 - 1 + 3 > 0$$

i.e. that X exceed 3 which is the current shadow cost. To summarise therefore, the shadow cost associated with a water cell in the final solution table of a transportation problem may be interpreted as the amount by which the per unit transport cost associated with the route to which the shadow cost relates would have to be reduced in order for that route to be used in the optimal solution (assuming, of course, that the per unit transport costs associated with all the other routes remain the same).

Continuing to analyse the optimal solution table in Table 3.5, suppose now that if the product being manufactured in factory A was sold at the factory, it would fetch a price of k per unit sold. If this were so, what price would one expect a unit of product to fetch at each of the other factories (B,C) and towns (X, Y, Z) or, to put it another way, what would be the 'worth' of a unit of product at each of the other locations ? Factory A sends all of its product to town Z. The per unit transport cost incurred is five. Therefore the 'worth' of a unit of product at Z in terms of the price which should be paid for it is obviously (k + 5). Town Z also receives product from factory B at a per unit transport cost of two. Thus the 'worth' of a unit of product at factory B, given the price it can command at town Z, is (k + 3). Continuing the analysis, similar 'worth' values can be determined for town Y, factory C and town X in that order (Table 3.5). These values are referred to as the *shadow prices* or *dual variable values* associated with the optimal solution. By convention, the shadow prices for a set of origins are designated U_1, U_2, ... while the shadow prices for a set of destinations are designated V_1, V_2 ... .

Quite obviously, in the foregoing, the shadow prices arrived at for each origin and destination depended on the location of and the value chosen for the point where the analysis was initiated — factory A with a value of k in the example. Suppose now, that it is assumed that the shadow price at factory B is k. Determination of the remaining shadow prices yields the results in Table 3.5. Notice that their magnitudes relative to each other are the same as before. The reader should check that no matter what initial shadow price value is chosen and that no matter what point is designated as possessing that value, it will always be true for a particular transportation problem solution table that the difference between any two shadow price values will be constant.

How may the relative magnitudes of the differences between the shadow prices be interpreted ? Consider the case of factories A and B in the final solution table. Factory A with a shadow price of k is called upon in the optimal solution to deliver product to town Z *via* a route with an associated per unit cost of vie. This sets the shadow price at Z to (k + 5). Factory B also delivers to town Z but *via* a cheaper route. The shadow price at B, (k + 3), thus exceeds that at A which, in terms of the optimal solution, indicates that factory B is at a locational advantage over A : it is in a position to deliver *via* a relatively cheap route to a destination where the product commands a relatively high price. A precise measure of the locational advantage of B over A is given by the difference in shadow prices. Extending this reasoning to a set of m origins, with m associated shadow prices U_1, ..., U_m, it can be said that in terms of the optimal solution, the origins with the highest shadow prices are those in the most advantageous locations relative to the overall deliveries pattern. The locational advantage of any one origin over another is given by the shadow price difference. Returning now to the case of factories A and B, let us assume that the owners of these factories must pay a rent to occupy their sites. Given that factory B occupies a more favourable site, it should presumably pay a premium for so doing. A measure of what this premium or *location rent* should be is obviously given once again by the difference in the shadow price values associated with A and B i.e. by:

$$(U_A - U_B) = k - (k - 3) = 3.$$

Consider now the extension of this analysis to the destinations. By definition, a disadvantageous location will be one which receives its deliveries *via* a relatively high cost route and/or from an origin with a high shadow price i.e. will be one which has a high associated shadow price value. For n destinations with n associated shadow prices V_1, ..., V_n, it can be said that for a particular solution, the destinations with the highest shadow prices are in the most disadvantageous locations. Thus, in the case of the example, X is most disadvantageously located followed by Y and Z. Suppose now that when the product is delivered to a destination it is to be stored in a warehouse at that destination for which rent must be paid. Following the logic set out in the case of the origins, the rent that should be paid to (say) maintain a storage warehouse to store product at Z over and above the rent that should be paid for maintaining a similar warehouse at X is given by the shadow price difference i.e. by:

$$(V_X - V_Z) = (k + 7) - (k + 5) = 2.$$

Note that the direction of the subtraction in the case of the destinations is the opposite of that appropriate for the origins for, recall that in the case of the destinations, a low shadow price implies locational advantage.

Given our definition and interpretation of shadow prices, let us now extend the analysis one step further by imagining that in a system of m origins and n destinations, a single marketing organisation e.g. central government has decided to buy the total supply available at each factory, to ship it to the destinations and to sell it there. We consider how such an organisation would wish to organise the pattern of deliveries. Once again, interpreting the shadow prices at the origins as the 'worth' of each unit of product produced there, the total cost to the marketing organisation of buying each origin's output would be $\sum\limits_{i=1}^{m} s_i U_i$. Similarly, interpreting the shadow prices at the destinations as the 'worth' of each unit supplied there, the total receipts to the marketing organisation of selling the delivery at each destination would be $\sum\limits_{j=1}^{n} d_j V_j$. Assuming that the marketing organisation wishes to make as much money as possible on the complete operation of buying and selling, its objective would presumably be to choose a pattern of deliveries and thus a set of shadow prices such that the quantity:

$$\sum_{j=1}^{n} d_j V_j - \sum_{i=1}^{m} s_i U_i \qquad \text{----(3.8)}$$

is maximised.

Returning again to the final stage solution table, consider more explicitly the relationship between the various U_i and V_j values. First, in the case of a transport route in use (stepping stone) e.g. A → Z, the difference between the shadow price at the destination and origin exactly equals the per unit transport cost associated with the route. Mathematically, if the route from the i th origin to the j th destination is in use:

$$(V_j - U_i) = c_{ij} \qquad \text{----(3.9)}$$

Second, in the case of each route not being used e.g. B → X the difference between the shadow price at the destination and origin is less than the transport cost associated with the route or, mathematically, for the i th origin and the j th destination:

$$(V_j - U_i) < c_{ij} \qquad \text{----(3.10)}$$

Combining (3.9) and (3.10), it can be seen that at optimality, at least in the case of this example, the shadow prices are

55

such that:

$$(V_j - U_i) \leq c_{ij} \text{ for all } i, j \qquad \text{----(3.11)}$$

It will now be demonstrated that the condition (3.11) must
hold for the optimal solution to any transportation problem.

Considering once again a solution to the transportation
problem as viewed through the eyes of a single marketing
organisation, suppose that the organisation is trying to
decide whether to bring a particular route from i to j into
use will save money. If $(V_i - U_i)$ and c_{ij} are the shadow price
difference and per unit transport cost respectively, it will
obviously be profitable to bring the route into use if the
gain in the 'worth' of each unit of product as a result of
transport as expressed by the shadow cost difference more than
covers the transport cost involved. Consider the case of
route CY in the third iteration of the example (Table 3.5).
The current gain in 'worth' per unit of product transported
from C to Y as expressed by the shadow price difference is:

$$(k + 6) - (k + 4) = 2$$

The per unit transport cost associated with the route CY is 1
which is less than the shadow price difference. Thus, it is
profitable to commence using this route. Summarising mathematically, it is profitable to bring a route into use if:

$$(V_j - U_i) - c_{ij} > 0$$

$$\text{i.e. if } (V_j - U_i) > c_{ij} \qquad \text{----(3.12)}$$

Quite obviously, if (3.12) must hold for a route to be brought
into use, (3.11) expresses the condition that no further
routes can be brought into use i.e. that optimality has been
reached.

The objective (3.8) together with the constraints (3.11)
give an alternative formulation and interpretation for the
transportation problem. The reader may think that this view
has been arrived at *via* somewhat convoluted logic and that it
is of limited use. However, as shall be shown in Chapter
Five, it arises in a very natural way given the underlying
mathematics. A full discussion of this interpretation of the
transportation problem appears in Stevens (1961).

Turning once again to applications of the transportation
problem, one of the main reasons for determining the shadow
prices associated with an optimal solution is to identify and
usually map the origins and destinations which are in relatively advantageous and disadvantageous locations in terms of
the optimal delivery pattern. A particularly interesting
study in this context is that of O'Sullivan (1972, 1975) who,
given the supply and demand for each of thirteen different

freight commodity groups over 78 regions in Great Britain
determines for each commodity group the pattern of deliveries
which minimises distance. Having found this, the shadow
prices for the origins (U_i values) and destinations (V_i
values) are mapped. Figure 3.7 shows the result for one of

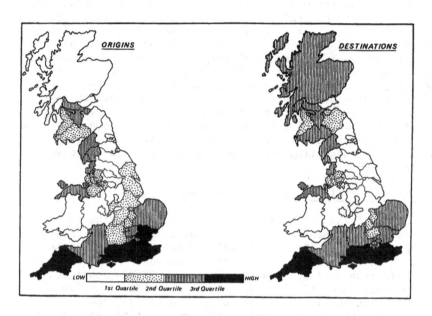

Figure 3.7 Origin and Destination Shadow Prices for Least
Distance Coal and Coke Flows in Great Britain

From: O'SULLIVAN, P., (1972), Linear Programming as a Forecasting Device for Interregional Freight Flows in
Great Britain, *Regional and Urban Economics*, 1,
383-96, Figure 1.

Redrawn by permission of the North Holland Publishing Company and the Author.

the commodities : coal and coke. First, for the shadow
prices for the origins and recalling that higher values of
U_i imply a more advantageous location for production, note
that the general pattern is for high prices in the south
where the demand for coal is reasonably high but supplies are
low with a decline towards the major coalfield areas. The
implication of the pattern is that, were further coal deposits
to be discovered, it would be most advantageous if these were
found in the south. Turning to the destination shadow prices
and recalling that higher values of V_j imply a more disadvantageous location for consumption, note that the general pattern
is once more for the highest values to occur in the south

57

where the relatively large number of consumers must receive their supplies from relatively far away with a fall-off towards the major production areas.

A major purpose in mapping shadow prices can be to provide a base from which planning recommendations can be made. One such study set within this context is that of Horton and Wittick (1969) who analyse work trips in Waco, Texas. The initial approach in the study follows that of Wheeler (1967) as discussed in Section 3.3.3. Having found the optimal pattern of least distance work trips, a map of the resultant U_i values and another of the V_j values is prepared. Horton and Wittick suggest that these may be looked at with a view to identifying areas which are particularly disadvantageously located in terms of, on the one hand, residential places available (low U_i values) and, on the other, job opportunities (high V_j values) and therefore that they may be used as **aids** for suggesting where new residences and/or jobs should be located.

3.3.5 More Efficient Starting Solutions

A criticism which can be levelled at the northwest corner rule for generating the initial solution to a transportation problem (Section 3.3.2) is that this solution is arrived at in an arbitrary manner. Presumably, if the various per unit transport cost values were taken into account at the outset and, in particular, an attempt was made to devise an initial solution in which many of the relatively low cost routes were being used,fewer iterations might be required in order to reach the optimum.

One way in which a (hopefully) more satisfactory initial solution can be obtained to a transport problem is *via* what is called the *least cost method*. The overall strategy comprises placing as large a flow as possible on the cheapest route, then as large a flow as possible on the next cheapest route that is available and so on until a possible solution has been arrived at. Taking the case of the previous example to illustrate (Table 3.6), there are two cheapest routes : CY and CZ with an associated transport cost of one. Arbitrarily choosing CY, the maximum flow that can be assigned to it is 30; this satisfies the demand at Y and deletes the routes AY and BY from further consideration. Of the remaining available routes, CZ is the cheapest. The maximum flow that can be assigned here is 20 which exhausts the production at C and thus deletes CX from further consideration. Of the remaining routes (AX, AZ, BX, BZ) the cheapest is BZ. Assigning the maximum possible flow to it (ten units) forces the remaining flows to be assigned to AX and BX as shown. The total cost associated with the revised initial solution is 425 which is a slight improvement on that obtained *via* the northwest corner method.

TABLE 3.6

TRANSPORTATION PROBLEM : REVISED INITIAL SOLUTIONS

LEAST COST METHOD

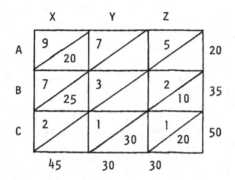

COST : 425

VOGEL APPROXIMATION METHOD

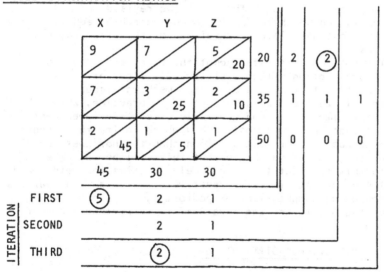

COST : 290

An alternative approach to obtaining a more satisfactory initial solution to a transportation problem is that known as the *Vogel Approximation Method*. Here, the overall strategy is to determine the cost penalty involved in not using the cheapest route currently available for each unsatisfied origin and destination and to assign the maximum flow possible to the

route with the largest associated penalty. Again, for the
example (Table 3.6), consider the routes available for shipp-
ing product from factory A. The associated per unit transport
costs are nine, seven and five respectively. Thus the cost
penalty which will be incurred by using the second cheapest
route (AY) rather than the cheapest route (AZ) for making
deliveries from A   is   two. The penalties associated
with each other origin and destination are entered on the
table. Of these maximum penalty (five) is that associated
with the route C → X which suggests that in a cost minimisation exercise, this route should be used if at all possible.
The maximum possible flow (45) is therefore assigned to it
which satisfies the demand at destination X and removes the
routes AX and BX from further consideration. Recalculating
the penalties for the other origins and destinations (in fact,
in this example, they do not change) there are now two cells
(CY, AZ) with the associated maximum penalty (two). Arbitrarily choosing AZ, the maximum amount that can be assigned here
is 20 units. Recalculating the remaining penalties leads to
an assignment of 5 units of flow to CY. The other flows must
then be 25 from B to Y and 10 from B to Z. The total transport cost associated with the resulting revised   initial
solution is 290 which represents a considerable reduction on
the total cost associated with either of the other two such
solutions.
     The foregoing results prompt the conclusion that the
Vogel Approximation method yields vastly superior initial
solutions to either of the other two methods discussed.
However, all that can be said is that in practice, while the
Vogel Approximation Method generally produces a lower cost
solution than the least cost method which in its turn generally produces a lower cost solution than the northwest corner
method, there is no guarantee that this will be so. When one
adds to this the fact that the Vogel Approximation Method and,
to a lesser extent, the least cost method require that various
time consuming computations be performed, it is often felt to
be advantageous to use the straightforward northwest corner
approach.

3.3.6 Computational Difficulties

Consider the problem and initial solution in Table 3.7. Two
routes are equal candidates to receive flows : AY and CX.
Arbitarily choosing CX, the associated stepping stone path is:

$$CX \rightarrow BX \rightarrow BY \rightarrow CY \rightarrow (CX)$$

The maximum amount of product that can be removed from BX and
CY for addition to CX and BY is 20 units which yields the
first iteration solution shown. Unfortunately, because the
initial solution flow on BX and CY happened to be equal, two

The Transportation and Related Problems

TABLE 3.7

TRANSPORTATION PROBLEM : DEGENERACY

INITIAL SOLUTION

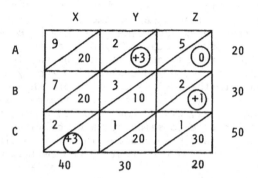

FIRST ITERATION

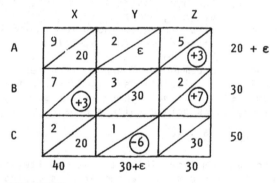

SECOND ITERATION

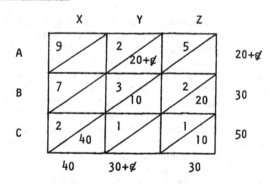

new water cells have been created. The solution process cannot continue as paths which conform to the rules given in Section 3.3.2 cannot be found for all water cells. The difficulty with the first iteration solution in Table 3.7 arises from the fact that fewer routes than expected possess flows i.e. fewer decision variables (the X_{ij}'s in the formulation in Section 3.3.1) than expected exceed zero. Such a condition is referred to as *degeneracy*. It may be catered for in the context of the transportation problem as follows. Choose any water cell and assign to it an arbitrarily small flow ε. Increment the origin and destination supply and demand associated with the cell by ε. (If more than one water cell must be transformed in order to create the requisite number of stepping stones, assign the required number of arbitrarily small flows, ε to selected water cells and increment the supply and demand values accordingly.) Continue the calculations in the usual manner treating the cell(s) with flows of ε as stepping stones. If at the end of any iteration setting some or all of the ε values to zero yields a solution with the requisite number of stepping stones, delete the ε values concerned from further consideration. If ε values exist in the final solution ignore them.

Returning to the first iteration solution in the example, one water cell must be transformed to a stepping stone. Arbitrarily choosing AY, a flow of ε is assigned to this cell and the supply at A and demand at Y are incremented by this amount. Continuing the calculations with AY being treated as a stepping stone yields the shadow cost values shown. The greatest value, +7, is associated with the path:

$$BZ \rightarrow CZ \rightarrow CX \rightarrow AX \rightarrow AY \rightarrow BY \rightarrow \quad (BZ).$$

Transferring the maximum flow yields the second iteration solution shown. Setting $\varepsilon = 0$, the number of stepping stones equals the number required. Thus the ε Values may be ignored in further calculations.

The condition of degeneracy represents a situation where, if it persists to the final iteration, the optimal solution involves fewer routes than expected being used. We now consider a case where the number of routes in use in an optimal solution can be greater than expected. Table 3.8 gives the final solution to the problem treated in Section 3.3.2 but with the per unit transport cost associated with the route A $\rightarrow$ Y reduced to six units. Notice that in the final iteration solution none of the shadow cost values are negative which suggests that no solution with a lower associated transport cost exists. Notice too, however, that the shadow cost associated with the cell AY equals zero which demonstrates that if product is shifted to this route, the total transport cost will not increase. This signals the existence of alternative optimal solutions. Proceeding in the same manner as before to

The Transportation and Related Problems

TABLE 3.8

TRANSPORTATION PROBLEM : ALTERNATIVE OPTIMAL SOLUTIONS

FINAL ITERATION

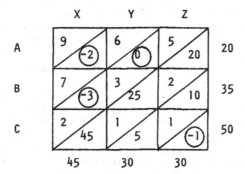

ALTERNATIVE SOLUTION

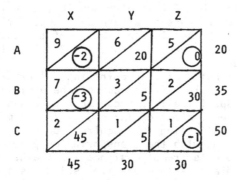

ANOTHER ALTERNATIVE SOLUTION

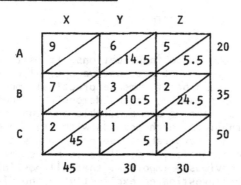

shift the largest possible volume of product among the routes corresponding to the relevant stepping stone path, the revised solution is given in Table 3.8. Notice that the total cost associated with this alternative is the same as before (290) and that the shadow cost associated with the newly created water cell, AZ, is zero thereby demonstrating that product could be shifted back to it. The two solutions are thus equally optimal. Furthermore, any intermediate allocation of product between the routes AY, AZ, BY, BZ which will involve a solution with only three water cells will also be optimal. One such solution is shown at the bottom of Table 3.8.

To summarise the foregoing, it can be said that in general, zero shadow costs in a final stage transportation problem solution table signal the existence of *alternative optimal solutions* which should be determined. Application of the methods discussed in Section 3.3.2 yields the 'extreme' solutions of a set of alternative optima e.g. the first two solutions in Table 3.8. Because flows can be shifted continuously between routes, an infinite number of intermediate alternative optima also exist many of which (e.g. the last solution in Table 3.8) will involve non-integer valued flow levels. Thus the presence of alternative optima represents a situation where the all integer nature of the optimal solution as stated at the end of Section 3.3.1 will not necessarily occur.

It should be noted at this point that alternative optimal solutions can also arise in the case of the assignment problem (Section 3.2). Specifically, it can be recognised *via* the existence in the equivalent of Table 3.1(iii) of more than one pattern of zeros fulfilling the required row/column condition (Section 3.2.2). As with the transportation problem this signals two or more 'extreme' assignments together with all possible intermediate assignments i.e. solutions involving partial assignments of objects to facilities. In these latter solutions, the condition:

$$X_{ij} = 0 \text{ or } 1 \quad \text{for all } i, j$$

will not hold.

Within the context of applications, it is to be noted that the identification of alternative optimal solutions *via* zero shadow costs can be of immense practical importance. First, in a planning sense, it can demonstrate that a number of alternative strategies are available and that apparently divergent alternatives, each perhaps with its own proponents, are actually equally desirable. Second, in a situation where the output from a particular model is to be compared with reality, it is obviously important that all possible alternative solutions be investigated explicitly in the first place — a point made for example by Barr and Smillie (1972) in their study of the transport patterns associated with the Soviet wood processing industry.

Finally, and still within the context of applications, it is to be noted that the structure of many assignment problems (Section 3.2) is such that they can be more conveniently solved using the methods given in Section 3.3.2 rather than those of Section 3.2.2. Consider once again the hypothetical assignment problem illustrated in Figure 3.2. In Section 3.2.3, it was envisaged that this problem would be solved by constructing a 100 X 100 table of distances from each origin (home) to each destination (schoolplace). Yet, because groups of students live at the same origins and the facilities (schoolplaces) are clustered at certain locations, the problem may be expressed more conveniently as a transportation problem with the supply points as the origins each with its capacity set to the number of pupils to be served and with the demand points as the destinations (schools) each with its requirement set to the number of places available. Proceeding in this manner in the case of the example would reduce the 100 X 100 assignment problem to a more manageable transportation problem involving eleven origins by three destinations.

3.3.7 The Transportation Problem Viewed as a Least Cost Maximum Flow Problem

As was the case with the assignment problem (Section 3.2.4), it is worth noting that the transportation problem can be viewed as a least cost maximum flow network problem and, therefore, that it can be solved using the approaches outlined in Section 2.4.2. e.g. the out-of-kilter algorithm. Consider once again the example in Section 3.3.2. Using the same approach as was employed in the case of the assignment problem (Figure 3.4), the origins (factories) A, B, C could be linked to the destinations (towns) X, Y, Z *via* a series of nine links each with the appropriate per unit transport cost. Now, as before, the origins could be linked back to a dummy source S and the destinations onwards to a dummy sink T. The upper capacities on these newly created links could be set to the production capacities of the three origins (factories) and the demand requirements of the three destinations (towns) respectively which in effect would constrain the flow outwards from each factory to equal its supply capacity and the flow inwards to each town to equal its demand requirement. In effect, this would ensure that the constraints (3.6) and (3.7) hold in the final solution which could now be obtained *via* the approaches outlined in Section 2.4.2. Furthermore, these could deal additionally with the so-called *capacitated transportation problem* where upper and/or lower limits are placed on the flows permitted on given origin-destination links.

3.4 THE TRANSHIPMENT PROBLEM

3.4.1 Formulation for One Intermediate Transhipment Point

In its most straightforward form, the transhipment problem (Figure 3.8) comprises a direct development of the transportation problem. m origins are linked to q intermediate or

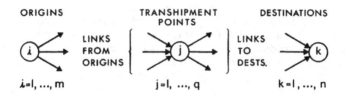

Figure 3.8 Transhipment Problem Where Each Unit of Product Passes Through One Intermediate Transhipment Point

transhipment points by routes with given per unit transport costs; the q transhipment points are linked onwards to n destinations by routes which also possess given per unit transport costs. It is assumed that the total supply of product available at the origins equals the total demand requirement at the destinations. (If total demand exceeds total supply, a dummy origin linked to each transhipment point *via* a zero cost route should be created; likewise, if total supply exceeds total demand, a dummy destination linked back to each transhipment point *via* a zero cost route should be created.) It is required that the pattern of deliveries which minimises total transport costs be found.

Mathematically, the transhipment problem in this form is:

$$\text{Minimise:} \quad \sum_{i=1}^{m} \sum_{j=1}^{q} c_{ij} X_{ij} + \sum_{j=1}^{q} \sum_{k=1}^{n} c_{jk} X_{jk} \quad \text{----(3.13)}$$

$$\sum_{j=1}^{q} X_{ij} = s_i; \quad i = 1, \ldots, m \quad \text{----(3.14)}$$

$$\sum_{j=1}^{n} X_{jk} = d_k; \quad k = 1, \ldots, n \quad \text{----(3.15)}$$

$$\sum_{i=1}^{m} X_{ij} - \sum_{k=1}^{n} X_{jk} = 0 \; ; j=1, \ldots, q \quad \text{----(3.16)}$$

$$X_{ij}, X_{jk} \geq 0 \text{ for all } i, j, k$$

The first term in the objective refers to the total cost of transporting product from the origins to the transhipment points while the second term refers to the total cost of transporting product onwards from the transhipment points to the destinations. The constraints require respectively that each origin ships out its total supply capacity, that each destination receives its total demand requirement and, finally, that each transhipment point ships out the total flow which enters it. Note that the transhipment problem is a linear programming problem in the sense defined in Section 3.2.1.

3.4.2 Solution Methods

The problem (3.13)-(3.16) may readily be solved by combining the methods in Sections 2.3.1 and 3.3.2. First, note that because no limits are placed on the level of flow on any link or on the level of flow passing through transhipment points, any flow between a particular origin and a particular destination will be routed *via* the shortest route as defined in Section 2.3.1. Thus solving the transhipment problem commences by determining the location and cost of the least cost route from each origin to each destination. These costs are then incorporated into an m x n transportation problem table which is solved in the usual manner. The optimal flows emerging are then assigned back to the links comprising the relevant least cost routes used.

As was the case with the assignment and transportation problems, the transhipment problem (3.13)-(3.16) can also be solved as a least cost maximum flow problem. The relevant network is derived by joining each origin back to a dummy source and each dstination onwards to a dummy sink. The new links are assigned capacities equal to the origin and destination capacities/requirements. Now, once again, the out-of-kilter algorithm or some related method can be used to obtain the optimal solution. Furthermore, upper and/or lower capacity constraints on the various origin-transhipment point and transhipment point-destination links can be taken into account if necessary.

3.4.3 Example

An insteresting application of the transhipment problem in the form(3.13)-(3.16) is that described by Maxfield (1969) who considers the optimal flow patterns for hard red spring wheat from the producing areas of the United States to various overseas markets. The transhipment points are the U.S. ports through which the wheat can be exported. Maxfield presents four different models which incorporate various assumptions concerning supplies available and transport costs and, in the case of each model, maps and comments on the relative magnitudes of the shadow price values in each of the producing regions.

3.4.4 Formulation With A Variable Number of Intermediate Transhipment Points

The transhipment problem formulation (3.13)-(3.16), refers to a situation where each origin is separated from each destination by a single transhipment point (Figure 3.8). An alternative version of the problem comprises a network of nodes and links where certain of the nodes act as sources, certain of the nodes act as sinks and the remaining nodes are transhipment points. A flow from a given source to a given sink could thus pass through any number of transhipment points. The least cost pattern of flows from source nodes to sink nodes is required.

Consider the network in Figure 3.9. Nodes one and six

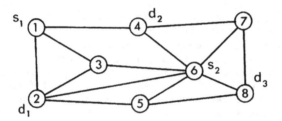

Figure 3.9 Transhipment Problem: Complex Case

are source nodes with supplies of product s_1, s_2 respectively; nodes two, four and eight are sink nodes with requirements d_1, d_2, d_3 respectively; nodes three, five and seven are transhipment points. Given the per unit transport cost associated with each link, the transhipment problem comprises finding the flow routings from the source nodes *via* transhipment nodes if appropriate to the sink nodes which minimise total transport costs.

The foregoing version of the transhipment problem can be solved *via* the methods discussed in Section 3.4.2. First, if total supply and demand are not balanced a dummy origin or destination as appropriate can be introduced. Now, the problem can be solved either by finding the cost of the least cost route between each source and sink and using the methods discussed in Section 3.3.2 or by introducing two additional nodes which are linked to the sources and sinks respectively *via* links of appropriate capacity and then by applying the methods of Section 2.4.2.

3.4.5 Volume Change At Transhipment Points

A logical and useful extension of the transhipment model depicted in Figure 3.8 is to the case where the transhipment points are envisaged as being intermediate points at which the commodity concerned is reprocessed in some way before being shipped onwards. This reprocessing involves a volume change by a factor of a_j which varies by transhipment point reflecting (say) the varying efficiency of the reprocessing facilities. (Thus, for example, $a_j = 0.80$ implies a volume reduction of twenty per cent at transhipment point j.) It is still required that the least cost pattern of deliveries from origins to transhipment points and onwards to destinations be found.

Formulating the problem mathematically, the objective, as before, is to determine the flows which

$$\text{Minimise :} \quad \sum_{i=1}^{m} \sum_{j=1}^{q} c_{ij} X_{ij} + \sum_{j=1}^{q} \sum_{k=1}^{n} c_{jk} X_{jk} \qquad ----(3.17)$$

A difficulty arises in the formulation of the constraints : because of the varying volume changes at each of the transhipment points, the condition that total supply equals total demand no longer holds. Thus, in the case of (3.14), it must merely be specified that the X_{ij}'s in the final solution are such that no origin is called to send out more than it can supply i.e.

$$\sum_{j=1}^{q} X_{ij} \leq s_i \; ; \; i = 1, \ldots, m \qquad ----(3.18)$$

while each destination must still receive its demand requirement i.e.

$$\sum_{j=1}^{q} X_{jk} = d_k \; ; \; k = 1, \ldots, n \qquad ----(3.19)$$

Finally, for each transhipment point, the volume of goods leaving must differ from that entering according to the factor a_j i.e.

$$\sum_{i=1}^{m} X_{ij} - \sum_{k=1}^{n} a_j X_{jk} = 0 \; ; \; j = 1, \ldots, q \qquad ----(3.20)$$

Also:

$$X_{ij}, X_{jk} \geq 0 \quad \text{for all i, j, k}$$

Taking the expressions (3.17)-(3.20) together, it is to be noted that this revised transhipment problem, which is

sometimes called the *Beckmann-Marschak problem*, still comprises a linear programming problem for, mathematically, the
objective and constraints are still linear expressions.
However, two complicating features which have not been encountered previously have entered the formulation. First, some of
the constraints (3.18) are in the form of inequalities.
Second, the coefficients of certain of the decision variables
in certain of the constraints, the X_{ik} terms in (3.20), are no
longer equal to unity. These two complexities together mean
that the problem can no longer be solved by adapting one of
the relatively straightforward approaches described in the
previous sections. The quest for a solution method which can
be used forms the subject of the next chapter.

3.4.6 Example

An example of a study which, in effect, involves solving
a transhipment problem with volume changes at the transhipment
points is that of Casetti (1966) who considers the optimal
location for (a) steel mills(s) serving the Quebec and Southern Ontario steel markets. Three major products must be
brought together in order to permit steel production : iron
ore, coal and limestone. Assuming the latter to be ubiquit-
ious and, therefore, discounting it from further consideration,
three potential types of site for a steel mill suggest themselves : at a source of iron ore to which coal will be shppped
and from which steel will be shipped to markets, at a source
of coal to which iron ore will be shipped and from which steel
will be shipped to markets and, finally, at a market to which
both ore and coal will be shipped. In the case of Quebec and
Southern Ontario in the early 1950's, the sole source of iron
ore was Northern Quebec from which ore is shipped by train to
the St. Lawrence at Seven Islands (S) and, in effect, is
available there for further use (Figure 3.10). The sole
source of coal was the United States which provides coal for
delivery to Canada at a number of Great Lakes ports ; for the
purpose of the study, all of this coal was assumed to be
available for further use at Ashtabula, Ohio (A). Finally,
the market for steel in Quebec and Southern Ontario effectively centred around two areas : Hamilton (H) in the west with a
demand requirement of 270 shiploads and Montreal (M) in the
east with a demand requirement of 120 shiploads. Given the
requirements for ore and coal per ton of steel produced and
the per unit transport costs associated with each type of
shipment possible (steel, ore, coal, empty) along each route,
Casetti wished to determine the optimal transport pattern for
ore and coal to steel mills and steel onwards to the markets
which would minimise total transport costs. He also wished to
see at which of the four possible locations - Seven Islands,
Hamilton, Montreal, Ashtabula - steel would actually be produced i.e. at which location(s) a steel mill should be

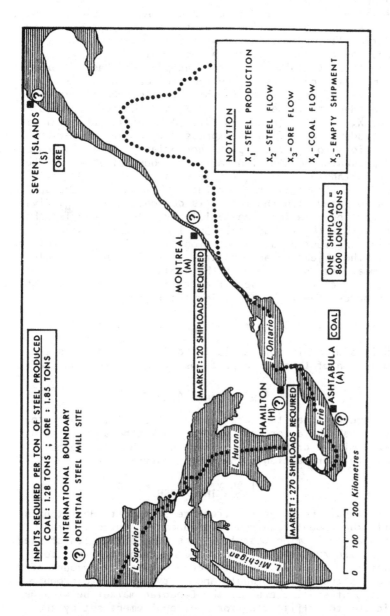

Figure 3.10 Inputs to Casetti's Study of Canadian Steel Production

constructed. One further complicating factor had to be taken
into account by the model : before the United States would
release coal from Ashtabula for use in Canada, a certain minimum amount of iron ore, k, had to be delivered to Ashtabula
for internal use by the United States. As part of his study,
Casetti wished to investigate how the optimal transport and
production pattern would vary with the amount of iron ore
demanded by the United States at Ashtabula.

In order to solve the foregoing problem, Casetti expresses it mathematically using the same approach as in (3.17)-
(3.20). In order to simplify the notation, the amount of
steel production is designated as X_1 and the four types of
flow as X_2, ..., X_5 (Figure 3.10). Any particular level of
steel production or flow is expressed by appending letter
designations to X_1, ..., X_5 as appropriate. Thus, for example,
X_{1A} represents the decision variable:amount of steel production at Ashtabula while X_{4AM} represents the amount of coal
shipped from Ashtabula to Montreal. The per unit transport
cost associated with the latter is designated as c_{3AM}. Given
the foregoing notation, the decision variables comprise those
listed across the top of Table 3.9 i.e. amount of steel produced at the four possible locations and all possible shipment
types. The objective and constraints making up the problem
are summarised in the body of the table where the numerical
values in each row represent the coefficients of the variables
listed across the top. The objective is thus:

$$\text{Minimise :} \quad 4.3X_{2AH} + 8.5X_{2AM} + \ldots + 3.2X_{5SM}$$

which is similar in form to (3.17) and which expresses the
minimisation of total transport costs. The first constraint
is:

$$X_{1A} - X_{2AH} - X_{2AM} = 0$$

which requires that the total amount of steel (if any) produced at Ashtabula for the Canadian market be shipped to
either Hamilton or Montreal. Certain of the constraints
deserve further mention. The fifth constraint i.e.

$$- 1.85 \, X_{1H} + X_{3SH} = 0$$

requires that the amount of iron ore shipped to Hamilton is
exactly the amount required to produce X_{1H} units of steel
there bearing in mind that 1.85 tons of coal per ton of steel
produced are required. In the same way, the previous constraint requires that the difference between the amount of
iron ore shipped to Ashtabula and that required to produce
X_{1A} units of steel there for the Canadian market be at least
sufficient to fulfill the iron ore requirement set by the
United States. The final three constraints are transport
conservancy constraints which in effect require that the

TABLE 3.9 : STEEL PRODUCTION FOR THE CANADIAN MARKET : OBJECTIVE AND CONSTRAINTS

CONSTRAINT NUMBER	STEEL PRODUCTION				STEEL SHIPMENTS						ORE SHIPMENTS		
c_{ij}	X_{1A} 0	X_{1H} 0	X_{1M} 0	X_{1S} 0	X_{2AH} 4·3	X_{2AM} 8·5	X_{2HM} 5·5	X_{2MH} 5·5	X_{2SM} 5·1	X_{2SH} 9·7	X_{3SM} 5·1	X_{3SH} 9·7	X_{3SA} 12·0
1		1			-1								
2			1			-1	-1						
3							-1	-1					
4				1					-1				1
5	-1·85												
6		-1·85											
7			-1·28										
8			-1·28										
9				-1·28									
10						1					1		
11								1				1	
12							-1		-1		-1	-1	-1
13										-1		-1	-1

CONSTRAINT NUMBER (CONT.)	COAL SHIPMENT					EMPTY SHIPMENTS										
c_{ij}	X_{4AH} 4·3	X_{4AM} 8·5	X_{4AS} 11·2	X_{5AH} 2·4	X_{5HA} 2·4	X_{5AM} 6·6	X_{5MA} 6·8	X_{5AS} 9·2	X_{5SA} 10·1	X_{5HM} 4·6	X_{5MH} 4·6	X_{5HS} 7·8	X_{5SH} 7·8	X_{5MS} 3·2	X_{5SM} 3·2	
1																= 0
2																≥ 270
3																≥ 120
4																= 0
5																= 0
6																= 0
7																= 0
8	1															= 0
9		1														= 0
10	1		1	1		1		1								= 0
11		1	1		-1		-1		-1	1	-1	1	-1			= 0
12									-1		-1			1	-1	= 0
13																= 0

From: CASETTI, E., (1966), Optimal Location of Steel Mills Serving the Quebec and Southern Ontario Steel Markets, *Canadian Geographer*, 10, 27–39, Table V.

Reprinted by permission of the Canadian Association of Geographers.

optimal pattern of flows be such that the total number of shipments arriving at any point equals the total number leaving it. Thus, for example, the last constraint:

$$-X_{2SM} - X_{2SH} - X_{3SM} - X_{3SH} - X_{3SA} + X_{4AS} + X_{5AS} - X_{5SA}$$
$$+ X_{5HS} - X_{5SH} + X_{5MS} - X_{5SM} = 0$$

requires that the total number of shipments into and out of Seven Islands be the same. The transport conservancy constraints are required to avoid a solution where (say) many ships commence their journeys at Seven Islands and complete them at one of the two markets. In this situation, if the optimal pattern of deliveries was to be repeated in (say) the following year it would be necessary to first transfer ships from the markets back to Seven Islands thereby incurring additional transport costs which would not have been incorporated explicitly in the model. The reader is urged to check each of the constraints in Table 3.9 and to satisfy himself as to its meaning.

Viewing the problem in Table 3.9 as a whole, it will be noted that it possesses the same characteristics as (3.17)-(3.20) : the objective and constraints are linear; certain of the latter involve left hand side coefficients which do not equal one and are in the form of inequalities. We therefore defer until the next chapter a description of how this problem can be solved mathematically and merely note here the results obtained by Casetti for two values of k : 320 shiploads and zero (Table 3.10). The salient feature of the solutions is that when the U.S. demand for Canadian ore is high, the total steel production for the Canadian market takes place at Seven Islands in part because the many ships transporting ore to the United States can conveniently return to Seven Islands with coal. When the U.S. demand for ore falls to zero, a proportion of the steel required by the Canadian market is produced at Ashtabula, in part because the ships which must call there to pick up coal, are programmed to bring ore from Seven Islands. Finally, in neither solution is steel produced at either of the two markets.

3.5 NETWORK DEVELOPMENT MODELS

Recall the capacitated transportation problem as defined in Section 3.3.7. Mathematically, it comprises the transportation problem (3.4)-(3.7) together with the additional constant sets:

$$X_{ij} \leq u_{ij} \quad \text{for some or all links i,j} \quad \text{----(3.21)}$$

TABLE 3.10

STEEL PRODUCTION FOR THE CANADIAN MARKET : SOLUTIONS

		SHIPLOADS	SHIPLOADS
U.S. ORE REQUIREMENT	k	320	-
STEEL PRODUCTION	X_{1A}	-	110
	X_{1S}	390	280
STEEL FLOWS	$(X_{2AH}$	-	110
	$(X_{2SM}$	120	120
	$(X_{2SH}$	270	160
ORE FLOW	X_{3SA}	320	204
COAL FLOW	X_{4AS}	507	264
EMPTY SHIPMENTS	$(X_{5HA}$	190	270
	$(X_{5HS}$	83	-
	$(X_{5MS}$	119	120
ALL OTHER ROUTES/FLOW TYPES		-	-

One Shipload equals 8600 Long Tons.

From: CASETTI, E., (1966), Optimal Location of Steel Mills Serving the Quebec and Southern Ontario Steel Market, *Canadian Geographer*, 10, 27-39, Table VII.

and/or $\quad X_{ij} \geq \ell_{ij} \quad$ for some or all links i,j $\quad$ ----(3.22)

where u_{ij} and ℓ_{ij} are upper and lower limits respectively placed on the flow permitted on the link from i to j at optimality.

We mention now two mathematical programming models which seek to extend the formulation $(3.4)-(3.7),(3.21/2)$ to permit improvements to the network to be carried out in some optimal manner. Quandt (1960) interprets these improvements in terms of investing a sum of money to be decided upon in each link which will raise its upper capacity limit u_{ij}. Specifically, if:

r_{ij} = The cost of raising the capacity of the link from i to j by one unit

ΔU_{ij} = The actual increase in capacity decided upon for this link (decision variable)

q $\quad$ = The total budget available

then the pattern of improvements and optimal flows must be such that:

$$\sum_{i=1}^{m} \sum_{j=1}^{n} r_{ij} \; \Delta U_{ij} \leq q \qquad \text{----(3.23)}$$

$$X_{ij} \leq u_{ij} + \Delta U_{ij} \text{ for all i, j pairs} \qquad \text{----(3.24)}$$

and $\quad X_{ij}$ and $\Delta U_{ij} \geq 0$ for all i, j pairs $\qquad$ ----(3.25)

i.e. the total budget spent on capacity improvements must not exceed that available and the optimal solution flows must not exceed the revised upper capacity limits. $(3.5)-(3.7)$ with $(3.23)-(3.25)$ now comprises an optimisation problem where the decision variables are the X_{ij} and the ΔU_{ij} values. It is to be noted that it comprises a linear programming problem in the sense defined in Section 3.2.1. However, as was the case with the transhipment problem with volume changes at the transhipment points, it involves inequalities and coefficients other than one in certain constraints which precludes solution *via* any of the methods discussed so far.

Another example of a network improvement model which has its origins in the transportation problem $(3.4)-(3.7)$ is that due to Garrison and Marble (1958) who present a formulation in which link capacity increases themselves cause changes to the supply capabilities and demand requirements at the various origins and destinations i.e. to the s_i and d_i values in (3.6) and (3.7). Once again, in terms of underlying mathematics, the problem turns out to comprise a linear programming problem. The reader is referred to the original publication or to the excellent review by MacKinnon and Barber (1977) for details.

4

LINEAR PROGRAMMING : THE SIMPLEX METHOD

4.1 INTRODUCTION

In the previous chapter, a linear programming problem was
defined as one in which the objective and constraints, when
expressed mathematically, turn out to be linear. The first
such problem expressed in full mathematically, the assignment
problem (Section 3.2.1), had certain special features : each
constraint was an equality, the coefficient of each decision
variable in the constraints was either zero or one and,
finally, the right hand side value of each constraint equalled
one. In the transportation problem (Section 3.3.1), the right
hand side value of each constraint could take any positive
value. In certain of the problems presented later in Chapter
Three e.g. (3.17)-(3.20) certain of the other special features
of the assignment problem were absent: some of the constraints
were inequalities and some of the coefficients of the decision
variables in the constraints were values other than zero or
one. In effect, these latter formulations represent a
progression towards a general linear programming problem of
the form :

$$\text{Optimise} : c_1 X_1 + c_2 X_2 + \ldots + c_n X_n$$

$$\text{s.t.} \quad a_{11} X_1 + a_{12} X_2 + \ldots + a_{1n} X_n \leq \text{ or } = \text{ or } \geq b_1$$

$$a_{21} X_1 + a_{22} X_2 + \ldots + a_{2n} X_n \leq \text{ or } = \text{ or } \geq b_2$$

$$\vdots$$

$$a_{m1} X_1 + a_{m2} X_2 + \ldots + a_{mn} X_n \leq \text{ or } = \text{ or } \geq b_m$$

$$X_1 \geq 0, \ X_2 \geq 0, \ \ldots, \ X_n \geq 0$$

or, more succintly :

DOI: 10.4324/9781003179030-4

$$\text{Optimise :} \quad \sum_{j=1}^{n} c_j \, X_j \qquad \qquad \text{---- (4.1)}$$

$$\text{s.t.} \quad \sum_{j=1}^{n} a_{ij} \, X_j \leq \text{ or} = \text{or} \geq b \; ; \; i = 1, \ldots, m$$

$$\text{---- (4.2)}$$

$$X_j \geq 0 \; ; \; j = 1, \ldots, n$$

$$\text{---- (4.3)}$$

(4.1)-(4.3) represent a general linear programming problem comprising n decision variables and m constraints. No limits are placed on the values the fixed variables (c_i's, a_{ij}'s; b_i's) have or on nature ($\leq$; $=$; $\geq$) of each of the constraints. An example of a general linear programming problem is :

$$\begin{array}{ll}
\text{Maximise :} & 3X_1 + 4X_2 \\
\text{s.t.} & 2X_1 + 3X_2 \leq 600 \\
& X_1 + X_2 \leq 225 \\
& 5X_1 + 4X_2 \leq 1000 \\
& X_1 \geq 0 \; ; \; X_2 \geq 0
\end{array} \quad \text{---- (4.4)}$$

Here : m = 3 ; n = 2

$$a_{11} = 2 \; ; \; a_{12} = 3 \; ; \; a_{21} = 1 \; ; \; a_{22} = 1 \; ; \; a_{31} = 5 \; ; \; a_{32} = 4$$

$$b_1 = 600 \; ; \; b_2 = 225 \; ; \; b_3 = 1000$$

$$c_1 = 3 \; ; \; c_2 = 4$$

4.2 SOME LINEAR PROGRAMMING FORMULATIONS

The purpose of this chapter is to describe a method known as *the simplex method* which can be used to solve problems of the type (4.1)-(4.3). At first sight, it might be expected that the number of geographical and planning problems which can be expressed in this format is low and therefore that the simplex method is of limited interest. Yet, the opposite is the case. Linear programming has been employed to investigate such diverse problems of health care services (Ware and Dickert (1976); Ittig (1978)), the choice of suitable irrigation techniques in a developing country (Soltani-Mohammadi (1972)), the placement of schools in an urban area (Trifon and Linvat (1973) and the choice of a site for a nuclear power station

(Anderson (1971)). In order to demonstrate the wide applic-
ability of linear programming, the formulation of linear
programming problems in five contrasting contexts is now
discussed. Some of the results obtained in actual studies
within these contexts are given in Section 4.7 after the
simplex method itself has been described.

4.2.1 Urban Landuse Design

An area of study within which linear programming has been
applied with considerable success is that of urban landuse
design. Consider an urban area subdivided into m subareas or
zones. The task of the urban landuse planner can be viewed
as deciding how much land within each zone should be allocated
to each of n landuse types in order to fulfill some objective
whilst obeying given planning criteria. An excellent description of how such models can be formulated in linear
programming terms is given in Laidlaw (1972) and Young (1972,
1974). In order to demonstrate the general approach, we
consider the model of Schlager (1965) - for a summary see
Chadwick (1971) and Reif (1973).
    The decision variables in Schlager's model comprise the
amount of land (acres) in Zone i to be allocated to each
landuse j. Specifically if :

X_{ij} = The amount of land in zone i to be allocated to
landuse j,

$i = 1, ..., m ; j = 1, ..., n$

and c_{ij} = The cost developing one acre of land in zone i for
use j

and if the objective is to minimise the total costs of development, then, following the approach of Section 2.5.1, this
can be written mathematically as :

$$\text{Minimise} : \sum_{i=1}^{m} \sum_{j=1}^{n} c_{ij} X_{ij} \qquad ---- (4.5)$$

The constraints may take various forms. First, the total
amount of land allocated between all uses in each zone must
not exceed the total acreage available. Specifically, if :

b_i = Total acreage available in zone i

and a_j = The service ratio associated with landuse j i.e. a
factor which inflates X_i to account for the service
area (streets etc) which must be provided per acre of
land allocated to use j

the acreage constraints are :

79

$$\sum_{j=1}^{n} a_j \, X_{ij} \leq b_i \; ; \; i = 1, \ldots, m \qquad\qquad ---- (4.6)$$

A further set of constraints might place a lower limit on the amount of land to be allocated to each landuse type. Specifically, if :

d_j = The lower limit on the amount of land to be allocated to use j these constraints would be of the form :

$$\sum_{i=1}^{m} X_{ij} \geq d_j \; ; \; j = 1, \ldots, n \qquad\qquad ---- (4.7)$$

Further constraints might concern the amount of land that may be allocated to one type of use relative to another either *in toto* as in :

$$\sum_{i=1}^{m} X_{ij} \leq g. \sum_{i=1}^{m} X_{ik}$$

$$\text{i.e.} \sum_{i=1}^{m} X_{ij} - g. \sum_{i=1}^{m} X_{ik} \leq 0 \qquad\qquad ---- (4.8)$$

where g is a constant expressing the amount of landuse k that may be provided relative to landuse j or on a zonal basis. Finally, it is obviously required that :

$$X_{ij} \geq 0 \; ; \; i=1, \ldots, m; \; j=1, \ldots, n \qquad\qquad ---- (4.9)$$

The formulation $(4.5)-(4.9)$ is highly generalised; the precise objective and constraints employed would vary from study to study. For the present, the most important point to note is that the mathematical form of both the objective and constraints is linear. The problem is therefore a specific version of $(4.1)-(4.3)$ and is solvable *via* the simplex method.

A somewhat more complicated landuse design model is that of Herbert and Stevens (1960). Summaries appear in Haggett *et al.* (1977), King (1972), Reif (1973) and Senior and Wilson (1974). The model concerns determining how households of various types will locate through a particular area. Specifically, m household groups are assumed. The first group might comprise single person households, the second middle income married couples with at least two children and so on. It is assumed that each household of a particular group has a known annual budget at its disposal. It is assumed further that the housing market offers a choice of distinct 'residential bundles' to potential buyers, a residential bundle being a particular combination of housetype, site, amenity level and travel pattern. Thus, one residential bundle might be a small apartment near the city centre while another might be a three bedroomed house in the outer suburbs. In all, it is assumed that there are n distinct residential bundles on offer to the household groups. It is further assumed that the amount of money a group j household would be prepared to allocate annually to living in a residential bundle of type k is known. This value is envisaged as being a function of the total household budget, the outgoings on non-residential items and the value a household of type j places on the characteristics of residential bundle type k. Thus, a single person might be prepared to allocate a relatively large sum of money to a one bedroomed apartment near the city centre but rather less to a three bedroomed house in the outer suburbs; the reverse would probably be true in the case of a middle income married couple with at least two children.

Consider an area e.g. a city subdivided into ℓ zones. Suppose that within a given time period, it is known that n_j households of group j, j=1, ..., m will locate through the area. The model seeks to determine the number of households of each group which will locate in each zone and residential bundle type. Let :

X^i_{jk} = The number of households of group j which are allocated to residential bundle type k in Zone i

b_{jk} = The amount of money a household of group j would be prepared to allocate annually to residential bundle type k

Suppose now that if a household of type j was to locate in Zone i and adopt residential bundle type k, the actual annual cost excluding rent payable for occupying the site would be c^i_{jk}. Consider the quantity :

$$(b_{jk} - c^i_{jk})$$

It represents the difference between what a household in group j would be prepared to pay for residential bundle k and what it will actually have to pay (exclusive of rent) if it adopts that residential bundle in Zone i. In a sense, therefore, it represents the savings to the household of adopting resident- ial bundle k in Zone i. It also represents the rent the household would be prepared to pay for a site in Zone i. Herbert and Stevens hypothesise that the households of various groups will allocate themselves to the residential bundles and among the zones in order to maximise their total savings i.e. to maximise their total rent paying ability. Mathematically, the objective thus involves finding the X^i_{jk} values which :

$$\text{Maximise :} \quad \sum_{i=1}^{\ell} \sum_{j=1}^{m} \sum_{k=1}^{n} (b_{jk} - c^i_{jk}) X^i_{jk} \quad \text{---- (4.10)}$$

This maximisation is subject to two conditions. First, the optimal values of X^i_{jk} must be such that the required number of households of each household group are located i.e.

$$\sum_{i=1}^{\ell} \sum_{k=1}^{n} x^i_{jk} = n_j \quad ; \quad j = 1, \ldots, m \quad \text{----}(4.11)$$

Second, the development pattern must be such that the total amount of land consumed in each zone does not exceed that available i.e.

$$\sum_{j=1}^{m} \sum_{k=1}^{n} s^i_k x^i_{jk} \leq a_i \quad ; \quad i=1, \ldots, \ell \quad \text{----}(4.12)$$

where : s^i_k = The acreage occupied by a single household of residential bundle type k in zone i

and a_i = The total acreage available for deveopment in zone i.

Finally, for obvious reasons, it is required that :

$$x^i_{jk} \geq 0 \quad \text{for all i, j, k.} \quad \text{----}(4.13)$$

The formulation (4.10) - (4.13) comprises a linear programming problem which, given the relevant fixed variable values, could be solved *via* the simplex method.

4.2.2 Regional and Interregional Development Problems

A subject area in which it has been suggested that linear programming could provide valuable insights is that of determining the levels at which various economic activities should operate in a region or set of regions in order to fulfill some objective. An excellent description of the types of model briefly summarised here is given in Isard (1958) and Stevens (1958).

Consider the case of an economy of a particular region which is independent of all other regions. Various distinct economic output activities can be defined as operating within the region. One purpose of these activities is to produce the various products required for consumption in the region e.g. foodstuffs, coal for domestic use, heavy industry products etc. Another purpose is to produce the inputs required by the other economic activities in order to enable them to achieve their outputs. Thus, for example, if heavy industry is to produce the output required of it, it will require a certain input of coal which must duly be produced by the coal production sector and which will be additional to the coal demanded from that sector for final consumption in domestic use. Certain economic activities must be undertaken within the economy for the sole purpose of supplying the inputs required by other activities. One such activity is the provision of transport : although it is not required in its own right, transport will be required by (say) the foodstuffs industry in order to enable that economic activity to produce what is demanded of it. An activity which operates solely to supply inputs to other sectors of the economy is known as an *intermediate activity*. If a list was to be drawn up of the various output activities in an economy, it would look like this :

<u>Output Activity</u>

```
                         (   1
                         (   .
                         (   i    Foodstuffs
        Products         (   .
        Demanded         (   .
        For Final        (   j    Heavy Industry
        Consumption      (   .
                         (   .
                         (   k    Coal
                         (   .
        ─────────────────(   .
                         (   .
                         (   .
        Intermediates    (   ℓ    Transport
                         (   .
                         (   .
                         (   .
                         (   M
```

Consider now the various inputs required to enable the economy to operate. First, there are the inputs from various economic activities which also produce final products for consumption e.g. coal. Second, there are the inputs from various intermediates e.g. transport. Finally, we shall envisage that there are various resources that are used up as the economy functions e.g. water and labour. If a list of the inputs to an economy were drawn up, it would look like this :

Input Activity

Products also	(1	
Demanded in Own	(:	
Right	(p	Coal

Intermediate (q Transport
Products

Resources (r Water

(s Labour

(T

The various inputs and outputs specified in the foregoing lists are set out as the rows and columns respectively in Table 4.1. There are M economic output activites and our interest is focussed upon the levels at which these must operate in order that the total economy produces the goods required for final consumption. Let these levels be X_1, ..., X_M respectively. Consider now the constraints under which the economy must operate. First, in the case of a product which is demanded for final consumption and is also required as an input to other activities e.g. coal, the total output of coal must be such as to meet the final demand and the required inputs to the other activities. Specifically, for product p (say, coal) if :

b_p = Final demand for consumption (of coal)

a_{pj} = The input of p (coal) required per unit output of sector j

the total output of p, X_p, must be such that :

$$X_p - \Sigma a_{ph} X_h \geq b_p \qquad\qquad ---- (4.14)$$

where the summation is over all products requiring an input of p. The constraint (4.14) is represented in a slightly different form in the pth row of Table 4.1. Here, multiplying each index by the corresponding decision variables yields :

$$\sum_{h=1}^{M} a_{ph} X_h \geq b_p \qquad\qquad ---- (4.15)$$

TABLE 4.1 : INPUTS AND OUTPUTS FOR A SINGLE REGION HYPOTHETICAL ECONOMY

OUTPUTS	PRODUCTS			INTS.			
INPUTS	FOODSTUFFS	HEAVY INDUSTRY	COAL	TRANS.			
e.g.	1 ... i ...	j ...	k	ℓ	M		
1	a_{11} ... a_{1i} ...	a_{1j}	a_{1k}	$a_{1\ell}$ ...	a_{1M}	$\geq b_1$
PRODUCTS ...						
COAL $\quad$ p	a_{p1} ... a_{pi} ...	a_{pj}	a_{pk} ...	$a_{p\ell}$ ...	a_{pM}	$\geq b_p$
INTERMEDIATES ...						
TRANS. $\quad$ q	a_{q1} ... a_{qi} ...	a_{qj}	a_{qk} ...	$a_{q\ell}$ ...	a_{qM}	$= 0$
...						
WATER $\quad$ r	a_{r1} ... a_{ri} ...	a_{rj}	a_{rk} ...	$a_{r\ell}$ ...	a_{rM}	$\geq -b_r$
RESOURCES ...						
LABOUR $\quad$ s	a_{s1} ... a_{si} ...	a_{sj}	a_{sk} ...	$a_{s\ell}$ ...	a_{sM}	$\geq -b_s$
... $\quad$ T	a_{T1} ... a_{Ti} ...	a_{Tj}	a_{Tk} ...	$a_{T\ell}$ ...	a_{TM}	$\geq -b_T$
DECISION VAR.^{s}	x_1 ... x_i ...	x_j ...	x_k	x_ℓ ...	x_M	

In order that (4.15) be the equivalent of (4.14), we interpret the a_{ph} coefficients in Table 4.1 as follows. First,
where the input (row) and output (column) are the same
product, $a_{ph} = 1$. Thus, in the case of the example, $a_{kk} = 1$.
Second, if the output activity is such that no input a_{pk} is
required, $a_{ph} = 0$. Thus, in the case of example, if the the
foodstuffs industry (i) requires no input of coal in order to
produce the output required of it, $a_{ci} = 0$. Finally, if the
output activity is such as to require an input from the row
activity, a_{ph} gives the volume of this input required per
unit output preceded by a negative sign e.g. in the case of
the example, if heavy industry (j) requires an input of coal
in order to produce its output, a_{cj} gives the volume of the
required input of coal per unit output of heavy industry
preceded by a negative sign.

Given this interpretation of the a_{ph} values in Table 4.1,
a constraint of the form (4.15) can be formed for each
product input. The same logic can be applied to the intermediate products. In this case, however, there is no final
demand : total production must be such as to satisfy the
input requirements of the other sectors. Thus, for each
intermediate, a constraint of the form :

$$\sum_{h=1}^{M} a_{qh} X_h = 0 \qquad \text{---- (4.16)}$$

must hold where a_{qh} has the same interpretation as before.
Finally, in the case of each resource, the levels of
economic activity as expressed by $X_1, \ldots, X_M$ must be such as
not to overuse that resource. Specifically for some resource
r, if a_{rh} represents the input of that resource required per
unit output in activity h preceded by a negative sign
($a_{rh} = 0$ implies no input of r is required) the condition :

$$\sum_{h=1}^{M} a_{rh} X_h \geq -b_r \qquad \text{----(4.17)}$$

must hold where b_r is the supply of resource r available.

To summarise, the constraints (4.15) - (4.17) together
with the obvious requirement that :

$$X_h \geq 0 ; h = 1, \ldots, M \qquad \text{----(4.18)}$$

constitute the constraints under which the economy must
operate. They are linear in the decision variables $X_1, \ldots,$
X_M and thus, if coupled with a suitable linear objective,
comprise a linear programming problem. Two such objectives
suggest themselves : cost minimisation and maximisation of
return. Specifically, if c_i is the cost of operating
activity i at unit level, we might wish to :

Linear Programming : The Simplex Method

$$\text{Minimise :} \quad \sum_{h=1}^{M} c_h X_h \qquad \text{---- (4.19)}$$

Again, if p_i is the return from operating activity i at unit level, we might wish to :

$$\text{Maximise :} \quad \sum_{h=1}^{M} p_h X_h \qquad \text{---- (4.20)}$$

The formulation (4.15)-(4.18) with (4.19) or (4.20) refers to a single region. The purpose is to determine the levels at which various economic activities should operate in order to fulfill the given objective. The methodology can be extended fairly readily to deal with a set of regions. The purpose becomes one of determining the levels at which various economic activities should operate within each of the regions and the pattern of product flows between the regions which will fulfill the given objective e.g. cost minimisation. Such models are called *interregional linear programming models*. The reader is referred to the references cited at the outset for details and to Hashim and Mathur (1975) for a specific example.

4.2.3 Agriculture

One of the main uses of linear programming in an agricultural context is to determine the acreages in an area (say a farm) which should be allocated to various uses in order to fulfill a stated objective while keeping within the bounds of given constraints. The general form of these models is similar to those relating to urban landuse design.

Consider the case of a farmer who wishes to determine the acreages of n crops which should be grown on his farm in order to maximise his return. If :

X_j = acreage of the jth crop grown ; j = 1, ..., n

and c_j = return per unit of the jth the crop grown

the objective is to find the values of X_j, j = 1, ..., n in order to :

$$\text{Maximise :} \quad \sum_{j=1}^{n} c_j X_j \qquad \text{---- (4.21)}$$

Growing an acre of a particular crop j uses up a certain amount of each of the (say m) resources available to the farmer in limited quantities. These resources include such entities as labour and water. Specifically if b_i units of the i th resource are available and one acre of crop j consume a_{ij} units of this resource, the optimal values of X_j must be such that :

$$\sum_{j=1}^{n} a_{ij} X_j \leq b_i ; i = 1, ..., m ; \qquad \text{---- (4.22)}$$

To these conditions must be added the obvious requirement that :

$$X_j \geq 0 ; j = 1, ..., n \qquad \text{---- (4.23)}$$

thereby yielding a linear programming problem.

A specific formulation of a linear programming problem in an agricultural context which will be discussed further in the next chapter is that of Henderson (1968). Henderson attempts to reproduce the decision making process of a farmer who at the end of a given year is deciding on the acreages X_j to allot to each of n crops for the following year. The return to be expected per acre of crop j, c_j, is known and the objective takes the form (4.21). Henderson hypothesises that a certain degree of inertia exists in the choice of crop acreages ; specifically, a farmer will not increase or decrease the acreage allotted to each crop from one year to the next by more than a certain amount. Given the acreage of each of the n crops grown in the current year, there are thus 2n constraints of the form :

$$X_j \leq b_j^{MAX} : j = 1, ..., n \qquad \text{---- (4.24)}$$

$$\text{and } X_j \geq b_j^{MIN} ; j = 1, ..., n \qquad \text{---- (4.25)}$$

where b_j^{MAX} and b_j^{MIN} are the maximum and minimum acreages respectively permitted for crop j next year. It is also required that the total acreage allotted to crops does not exceed that available on the farm i.e.

$$\sum_{j=1}^{n} X_j \geq a \qquad \text{---- (4.26)}$$

where a is the total acreage available. Imposition of the condition :

$$X_j \geq 0 ; i = 1, ..., n \qquad \text{---- (4.27)}$$

completes the linear programming formulation.

4.2.4 Diet Composition

One of the earliest applications of linear programming concerned the problem of determining the amounts of various foods which should make up a diet which fulfills given minimal nutritional requirements at least cost. The initial formulations concerned animal diets ; more recent studies have

88

investigated human diets. A summary of the structure of
linear programming problems as applied in this context is
given by Taylor (1977).

Suppose that a diet is to comprise some amount of each
of n foods, X_1, ..., X_n. If the cost per unit for each food
is known, c_j, $j = 1$, ..., n and if the objective is to choose
values for X_1, ..., X_n such that the total cost of the
resultant diet is minimised, this may be expressed mathematically as :

$$\text{Minimise} \quad \sum_{j=1}^{n} c_j X_j \qquad \qquad \text{---- (4.28)}$$

Suppose now that any diet must meet certain minimal
nutritional requirements as expressed by the minimum quantities of each of m entities which it must contain. These
entities might comprise such items as : calories, protein,
iron, calcium etc. Then, if the diet must contain b_i units
of the i th entity and a_{ij} is the amount of this entity con-
tained in a unit of food j, the amounts X_1, ..., X_n in the
final diet must be such that :

$$\sum_{j=1}^{n} a_{ij} X_j \geq b_i \; ; \; i = 1, ..., m \qquad \qquad \text{---- (4.29)}$$

Finally, it is obviously required that :

$$X_j \geq 0 \; ; \; j = 1, ..., n \qquad \qquad \text{---- (4.30)}$$

which completes the linear programming formulation.

4.2.5 Transport

In the previous chapter, a number of linear programming
problems relating to the general subject area of transportation were introduced. Certain of these e.g. the transportation
problem and the transhipment problem were solvable using
special mathematical methods. Others, by virtue of their more
complex mathematical structure e.g. the transhipment problem
with the volume changes at the transhipment points and the
network improvement problems were not. Reexamination of the
mathematical formulations of these latter problems (3.17)-
(3.20) and (3.5)-(3.7), (3.22)-(3.25) demonstrates that they
are in fact of the form (4.1)-(4.3) and can thus be solved
using the methods to be discussed in this chapter. One further
linear programming problem related to the general subject area
of transportation is discussed now.

Miller (1963) considers the task of assigning aircraft
of various types to the various routes in a system in order to
minimise the total cost of all flights in the system.
Specifically, if :

$$^j x^k_h \quad = \quad \text{The number of flights to be operated from j to k by aircraft type h}$$

and $^j c^k_h \;=\;$ The cost of operating a flight from j to k using aircraft type h

the objective is to :

$$\text{Minimise :} \qquad \sum_{h=1}^{q} \sum_{j=1}^{r} \sum_{k=1}^{s} \; {}^j c^k_h \; {}^j x^k_h \qquad\qquad \text{---- (4.31)}$$

the summation being over all origins, destinations and air-craft types of which there are q, r and s respectively. Turning to the constraints, the solution must be such that for each node and aircraft type, the number of incoming flights equals the number of outgoing flights i.e.

$$\sum_{k=1}^{s} \; {}^k x^j_h \; - \; \sum_{j=1}^{r} \; {}^j x^k_h \; = \; 0; \qquad \begin{array}{l} j=1, \; \ldots, \; r \\ h=1, \; \ldots, \; q \end{array} \text{---- (4.32)}$$

This constraint set is the equivalent of the flow conservancy constraints incorporated in Casetti's treatment of iron, coal and steel flows for the Canadian market (Section 3.4.6). Miller's second constraint set requires that the total hours of flying required on each aircraft type does not exceed that available. Specifically, if :

$$^j b^k_h \quad = \quad \text{Hours required to fly route jk in an aircraft of type h and}$$

$$t_h \quad = \quad \text{Total number of flying hours available on aircraft type h}$$

then the solution must be such that :

$$\sum_{j=1}^{r} \sum_{k=1}^{s} \; {}^j b^k_h \; {}^j x^k_h \; \leq \; t_h \; ; \; h=1, \; \ldots, \; q \text{ ---- (4.33)}$$

Finally it is required that the demand for transportation on each route be met. Specifically, if :

$$^j d^k \quad = \quad \text{The demand for transport from j to k}$$

and $^j a^k_h \;=\;$ The passenger carrying capability of an aircraft of type h over route jk

then the solution must be such that :

$$\sum_{h=1}^{q} \; {}^j a^k_h \; {}^j x^k_h \; \geq \; {}^j d^k \; ; \; \begin{array}{l} j=1, \; \ldots, \; s \\ k=1, \; \ldots, \; s \end{array} \qquad \text{---- (4.34)}$$

Linear Programming : The Simplex Method

It is also required that :

$$^{j}x^{k}_{h} \geq 0 \text{ for all } h, j, k \qquad \text{---- (4.35)}$$

The formulation $(4.31)-(4.35)$ comprises a linear programming problem with $(r-1)^2 q$ decision variables and :

$$qr + q + (r - 1)^2$$

constraints (excluding the non-negativity conditions). The nature of some of the solutions obtained by Miller in the context of an actual application is discussed in Section 4.9.

4.3 GRAPHICAL SOLUTION METHOD

We begin our description of solution methods for linear programming problems by introducing a simplified problem and solving it by drawing a graph. Consider the case of a house-builder who is about to develop a plot of land comprising 30 acres. Two types of house will built : Type One, the smaller of the two, sells for £30,000. Bearing in mind the size of gardens to be provided and the amount of land that must be set aside for roads etc., ten of these houses may be built per acre. In other developments where this housetype has been constructed, each house has been occupied by an average of five persons. Housetype Two, a larger house, sells for £40,000. 6 2/3 houses can be built per acre. On average, each house is occupied by four persons.

The housebuilder wishes to determine the number of houses of each type which should be built in order to maximise his return from sales. The numbers must be such that the area of land used does not exceed that available. In addition, in granting permission for the development, the local planning authority has made two stipulations : first, the total number of houses built must not exceed 225 and second, the total number of persons expected to settle in the development must not exceed 1000.

The problem facing the housebuilder may be expressed mathematically as a linear programming problem. The decision variables concern the number of houses of each type to be constructed. Letting these be X_1 and X_2 respectively and recalling that the price per house for the two types is £30,000 and £40,000, the builder's objective is to determine the values of X_1 and X_2 which :

$$\text{Maximise} : X_o = 3X_1 + 4X_2 \qquad \text{---- (4.36)}$$

where the coefficients of X_1 and X_2 are the return from sales per house for each housetype measured in ten thousand pound units.

Consider now the stipulation that the acreage used does not exceed that available (30 acres). If housetype one is developed at a density of ten houses per acre, each house requires 1/10 acres ; if X_1 houses of this type are built, they will occupy $1/10X_1$ acres. Similarly, if housetype two is developed at a density of 6 2/3 houses per acre, each house requires 3/20 acres ; if X_2 houses of this type are built, they will occupy $3/20 X_2$ acres. To require that the total development does not exceed 30 acres is thus equivalent to requiring that X_1 and X_2 are such that :

$$1/10 \ X_1 + 3/20 \ X_2 \leq 30$$

or :

$$2X_1 + 3X_2 \leq 600 \qquad\qquad \text{---- (4.37)}$$

where the right hand side of (4.37) gives the total acreage in twentieths of an acre. In mathematical terms, the requirement that the total number of houses built does not exceed 225 is obviously given by the condition :

$$X_1 + X_2 \leq 225 \qquad\qquad \text{---- (4.38)}$$

Finally, if an average of five people settle in each type one house, X_1 of these houses could be expected to house $5X_1$ persons; similarly, X_2 houses of type two could be expected to house $4X_2$ persons. To require that the development house less than 1000 persons is therefore equivalent to requiring mathematically that X_1 and X_2 are such that :

$$5X_1 + 4X_2 \leq 1000 \qquad\qquad \text{---- (4.39)}$$

Finally, for obvious reasons, it is required that :

$$X_1 \geq 0 \quad ;X_2 \geq 0 \qquad\qquad \text{---- (4.40)}$$

The formulation (4.36)-(4.40) comprises a linear programming problem of the form (4.1)-(4.3). (It is actually (4.4).) The optimal values of X_1 and X_2 can be found as follows.

Construct a graph on which the two axes represent respectively the two decision variables i.e. the number of houses of type one and type two to be built (Figure 4.1 (a)). Consider now the first constraint (4.37) i.e. concerning the total acreage consumed by the development. Suppose that the final solution is such that the total acreage is, in fact, used up. Then, X_1 and X_2 would have to be such that :

$$2X_1 + 3X_2 = 600 \qquad\qquad \text{---- (4.41)}$$

Leaving aside the other constraints, there are a number of

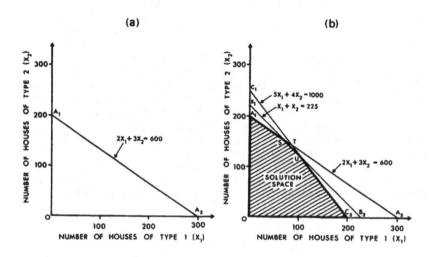

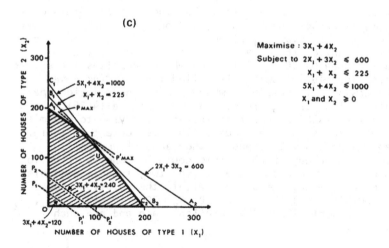

Figure 4.1 The Housebuilder Problem: Graphical Solution

ways in which the condition (4.41) could be achieved e.g. $X_1 =$ 300; $X_2 = 0$ (i.e. build 300 houses of type one and none of type two); $X_1 = 100$, $X_2 = 200$; $X_1 = 0$, $X_2 = 200$. Geometrically any solution which meets the condition (4.41) will plot out on the line of that equation. This line is shown as A_1A_2 on Figure 4.1(a) and it can be checked that the three solutions just mentioned do indeed plot on this line. Furthermore, any solution which underuses the total acreage available (e.g. $X_1 = 100$, $X_2 = 100$) will plot out below the line whilst any solution which overuses the acreage available and is thus not allowed by (4.37) (e.g. $X_1 = 200$, $X_2 = 200$) will plot out above the line. Thus the algebraic constraint condition (4.37) can be interpreted geometrically as requiring that the final values of X_1 and X_2 be such that when plotted graphically, the resultant point falls on or below the line A_1A_2.

The constraints (4.38) and (4.39) can be interpreted geometrically in the same manner : the optimal values for X_1 and X_2 must be such as when plotted to fall on or below :

$$X_1 + X_2 = 225$$

$$\text{and} \quad 5X_1 + 4X_2 = 1000$$

which are shown as B_1B_2 and C_1C_2 in Figure 4.1(b). Taking the conditions (4.37)-(4.39) together with the non-negativity conditions (4.40), it is obvious that the optimal values of X_1 and X_2 must be such that when plotted on the graph, they fall on or below A_1A_2, B_1B_2, C_1C_2, on or above the X_1 axis and on or to the right of the X_2 axis i.e. on the boundary of or within the area OA_1SUC_2. This area which comprises the set of all possible solution points is called the *solution space.*

We now seek to determine where within the solution space the values of X_1 and X_2 are such as to maximise (4.36). To commence this task, assume that instead of trying to maximise his return from sales, the housebuilder is content to achieve a given return - say 120 tens of thousands of pounds i.e. £1,200,000. One way in which this could be done is to build 40 houses of type one and none of type two; this is possible as the point $X_1 = 40$; $X_2 = 0$ plots within the solution space. Another possible solution is $X_1 = 0$; $X_2 = 30$. Indeed any X_1, X_2 values which plot within the solution space and are such that :

$$3X_1 + 4X_2 = 120 \qquad\qquad \text{---- (4.42)}$$

will yield the required profit. Geometrically, these points comprise all points on the line of equation (4.42) which fall within the solution space i.e. all points on P_1P_1' in Figure 4.1(c) which fall within OA_1SUC_2.

Suppose now that the housebuilder wishes to achieve a greater return, say 240. The values of (X_1, X_2) which enable

Linear Programming : The Simplex Method

this to be achieved are those on the line :

$$3X_1 + 4X_2 = 240$$

which plot within the solution space. This line is shown as
$P_2 P_2'$ in Figure 4.1(c). Note that the line relating to the
set of higher return solutions is parallel to that for the
lower return solutions and further removed from the origin.
Following the foregoing logic, if the housebuilder wishes to
achieve an even higher return, the set of possible solutions
would be located on a line parallel to $P_1 P_1'$ but yet further
removed from the origin. From this, it can be deduced that
the greatest return possible can be found by determining the
point(s) which lie on a line which is parallel to $P_1 P_1'$ and
$P_2 P_2'$, is as far removed from the origin as possible but which
still touches the solution space at at least one point. In
the case of the example, the line is $P_{MAX} P'_{MAX}$ (Figure 4.1
(c)) which touches the solution space at the single outer
point S. The coordinates of this point yield the optimal
solution i.e.

$$X_1 = 75 ; X_2 = 150$$

The return (maximised) associated with this building strategy
is :

$$3(75) + 4(150) = 825 \text{ i.e. } £8,250,000$$

Note that the optimal solution is such that the first two
constraints are exactly satisfied i.e. all the land available
is utilised and the maximum number of houses permitted is
built. The third constraint is not exactly satisfied : the
number of people who will settle in the development is expected to be :

$$5(75) + 4(150) = 975$$

which is somewhat below the upper limit permitted by (4.39).

Two characteristics of the foregoing solution method
should be noted. First, the method is obviously limited in
application : if, for example, there were three decision
variables e.g. three possible housetypes, a three dimensional
diagram would be necessary with the constraints being represented by planar surfaces. This would be difficult although
not impossible to draw. If, however, there were more than
three decision variables as is usually the case in real world
problems, it would not be possible to represent the objective
and constraints diagrammatically. For this reason, we must
seek an alternative method for solving such problems.
The second point to note in the foregoing problem is that

its structure is such that the optimal solution will (nearly) always lie at one of the outermost corners of the solution space. (We shall assume for the moment that this is always the case.) The importance of this observation is that for a given problem, it reduces the number of possible places where the optimal solution might lie : the solution space in Figure 4.1(c) comprises an infinite number of points but there are only five outer corner points 0, A_1, S, U and C_2. This in its turn suggests a method for seeking the optimal solution: the solution associated with the various outer corner points of the solution space should be examined in some logical order until such time as it is known that the corner point associated with the best solution has been reached. This is, in fact, the logic underlying the simplex method.

4.4   PRELIMINARIES TO THE SIMPLEX METHOD

Certain mathematical ideas required for an understanding of the simplex method are described in this section. For convenience, it is assumed that a maximisation problem with a number of 'less than or equals' constraints together with the usual non-negativity conditions is to be solved. The numerical example solved *via* the graphical method in the previous section is retained as the illustrative example.

4.4.1   Standard Form Representation

The simplex method comprises an algebraic method for finding the optimal solution to a linear programming problem. Given that most algebraic methods deal with equalities rather than inequalities, it is not surprising that the simplex method commences by restating the problem to be solved in terms of equations.
Reconsider the first constraint of the problem of the previous section i.e.

$$2X_1 + 3X_2 \leq 600 \qquad \text{---- (4.43)}$$

Because the left hand side of this equation is generally less than the right hand side, it is necessary to add a quantity to the left hand side to convert it to an equality. Denoting this quantity as S_1 gives the revised condition :

$$2X_1 + 3X_2 + S_1 = 600 \qquad \text{---- (4.44)}$$

A value for S_1 is fixed automatically if values for X_1 and X_2 are given; if $X_1 = X_2 = 100$, $S_1 = 100$; if $X_1 = 250$ and $X_2 = 10$, $S_1 = 70$. As can be seen, S_1 makes up the difference or 'slack' between the left and right hand sides of (4.43). For this reason, it is usually referred to as a *slack variable*.

Converting the three inequalities (4.37)-(4.39) to equations by inserting slack variables denoted S_1, S_2, S_3 respectively yields :

$$
\begin{aligned}
2X_1 + 3X_2 + S_1 \qquad\qquad &= 600) \\
&\qquad\qquad) \\
X_1 + X_2 \quad + S_2 \qquad\qquad &= 225) \qquad \text{---- (4.45)} \\
&\qquad\qquad) \\
5X_1 + 4X_2 \qquad\quad + S_3 \quad &= 1000)
\end{aligned}
$$

Consider now the objective (4.36) and the expression obtained by subtracting it from a quantity X_o and setting the resultant expression to zero i.e.

$$
X_o - 3X_1 - 4X_2 \qquad\qquad = 0 \qquad\qquad \text{---- (4.46)}
$$

Suppose that $X_1 = 30$ and $X_2 = 40$. Then for (4.46) to hold true, $X_o = 250$ which is in fact the value the objective would have for those values of X_1 and X_2 i.e. the return the housebuilder would receive if those numbers of each housetype were built. Again, suppose that $X_1 = 75$ and $X_2 = 150$ which is in fact the optimal solution as determined in the last section. Then, automatically, $X_o = 825$ which is in fact the optimal value of the objective. (4.46) is in fact defined in such a way that if X_1 and X_2 are known, X_o takes the value of the objective corresponding to those values of X_1 and X_2. Combining (4.45) and (4.46), the complete problem (4.36) $-$ (4.40) can be written in equation form as :

$$
\begin{aligned}
\text{SOLVE :} \quad X_o - 3X_1 - 4X_2 \qquad\qquad\qquad &= \quad 0) \\
&\qquad\qquad) \\
2X_1 + 3X_2 + S_1 \qquad\qquad &= 600) \\
&\qquad\qquad)\text{---- (4.47)} \\
X_1 + X_2 \quad + S_2 \qquad\qquad &= 225) \\
&\qquad\qquad) \\
5X_1 + 4X_2 \qquad\quad + S_3 &= 1000) \\
X_1, X_2 \ge 0 \qquad\qquad\quad &
\end{aligned}
$$

which comprises four equations, six variables and the non-negativity conditions. In general, a linear programming maximisation problem with all 'less than or equals' constraints of the form (4.1)-(4.3) i.e. comprising an objective, m inequalities, n decision variables and non-negativity conditions can be rewritten as :

$$\text{SOLVE :} \quad X_o - \sum_{j=1}^{n} c_j X_j = 0 \qquad\qquad)$$

$$\sum_{j=1}^{n} a_{ij} X_j + S_i = b_i \; ; \quad i=1, \ldots, m) \quad \text{----(4.48)}$$

$$X_j \geq 0 \; ; \qquad j=1, \ldots, n)$$

which involves $(m + 1)$ equations, $(m + n + 1)$ variables and the non-negativity conditions. A linear programming problem presented in the format (4.48) is said to be in *standard form*.

4.4.2 Solving Simultaneous Linear Equations

Expression of a linear programming problem in the form (4.48) suggests that in an algebraic sense, finding the optimal solution to such a problem involves finding the solution to a set of simultaneous linear équations. We now investigate certain aspects of this operation.

Consider the task of finding the values of X_1 and X_2 which simultaneously cause the equations :

$$2X_1 + 3X_2 = 7 \qquad)$$
$$\qquad\qquad\qquad\qquad\quad) \qquad \text{---- (4.49)}$$
$$4X_1 \quad 5X_2 = 13 \qquad)$$

to hold true. The usual approach is to multiply one or both equations across by (a) chosen constant(s) to create equal coefficients for one of the variables and then to subtract. Thus multiplying the first equation in (4.49) across by two yields :

$$4X_1 + 6X_2 = 14 \qquad)$$
$$\qquad\qquad\qquad\qquad) \qquad \text{---- (4.50)}$$
$$4X_1 + 5X_2 = 13 \qquad)$$

which on subtraction from the second equation gives :

$$4X_1 + 6X_2 = 14 \qquad)$$
$$\qquad\qquad\qquad\qquad) \qquad \text{---- (4.51)}$$
$$X_2 = 1 \qquad)$$

from which $X_2 = 1$. Therefore, from the first equation in (4.51), $X_1 = 2$. That these are in fact values of X_1 and X_2 that satisfy the equations (4.49) simultaneously can be checked by substitution which yields :

$$2(2) + 3(1) \overset{\checkmark}{=} 7$$
$$4(2) + 5(1) \overset{\checkmark}{=} 13$$

The foregoing example demonstrates the validity of two rules which may be applied when finding the values of X_1, X_2, ... which simultaneously satisfy a set of equations. First, any equation can be multiplied across by a constant; thus, in the example, if the first equation in (4.49) holds true, so too does the first equation in (4.50). Second, any equation can be subtracted from another to yield a revised equation; in the example, the second equation in (4.51) is the second equation in (4.50) with the first equation subtracted from it. (4.51) can be viewed as having been derived directly from (4.49) by applying the two foregoing rules simultaneously namely subtracting twice the first equation from the second.

We now view the task of finding the values of X_1 and X_2 which simultaneosuly satisfy (4.49) in a slightly different light. Suppose that the two foregoing rules were to be used in order to convert (4.49) to two equations of the form :

$$1.X_1 + 0.X_2 = ? \quad)$$
$$0.X_1 + 1.X_2 = ? \quad) \qquad ---- (4.52)$$

i.e. to create a coefficient of one and zero for X_1 in the first and second equations respectively and *vice versa* for X_2 If this were done, the right hand side values of (4.52) would be the required values of X_1 and X_2. How can the task of converting (4.49) to the format (4.52) be achieved? First, to create a coefficient of one for X_1 in the first equation, multiply across by 1/2:

$$1.X_1 + 3/2\ X_2 = 7/2 \quad)$$
$$4X_1 + 5\ X_2 = 13 \quad) \qquad ---- (4.53)$$

Next to create a coefficient of zero for X_1 in the second equation subtract four times the first equation from it :

$$1.X_1 + 3/2\ X_2 = 7/2 \quad)$$
$$0.X_1 - \quad X_2 = -1 \quad) \qquad ---- (4.54)$$

Next, to create a coefficient of one for X_2 in the second equation, multiply it across by minus one :

$$1.X_1 + 3/2\ X_2 = 7/2 \quad)$$
$$0.X_1 + 1.X_2 = 1 \quad) \qquad ---- (4.55)$$

Finally, to create a coefficient of zero for X_2 in the first equation, subtract the second equation multiplied across by 3/2 from it :

$$1.X_1 + 0.X_2 = 2 \quad)$$
$$0.X_1 + 1.X_2 = 1 \quad) \qquad ---- (4.56)$$

(4.56) gives the values of X_1 and X_2 obtained previously.

The task of solving a pair of equations *via* the methods described in (4.52)-(4.56) is cumbersome as compared with the approach of (4.49)-(4.51). It becomes advantageous, however, when a larger number of equations and unknowns are involved. Consider the task of finding the values of X_1, X_2, X_3, X_4 which simultaneously satisfy:

$$
\begin{aligned}
2X_1 + 3X_2 + 3X_3 + X_4 &= 13) \\
4X_1 + 5X_2 + 5X_3 + 2X_4 &= 24) \\
X_1 + X_2 + X_3 + X_4 &= 7) \\
X_1 + 3X_2 + 2X_3 + 4X_4 &= 19)
\end{aligned}
\qquad \text{---- (4.57)}
$$

Here it is not immediately clear as to how one should proceed to isolate the solution values for the particular variables. Thus the task is best viewed as using the two foregoing rules to rewrite (4.57) in the format:

$$
\begin{aligned}
1.X_1 + 0.X_2 + 0.X_3 + 0.X_4 &= ?) \\
0.X_1 + 1.X_2 + 0.X_3 + 0.X_4 &= ?) \\
0.X_1 + 0.X_2 + 1.X_3 + 0.X_4 &= ?) \\
0.X_1 + 0.X_2 + 0.X_3 + 1.X_4 &= ?)
\end{aligned}
\qquad \text{---- (4.58)}
$$

Given the format of the left hand sides in (4.58), the right hand sides are the required solution values. Conversion of (4.57) to (4.58) may be achieved as follows. First, to create a coefficient of one for X_1 in the first equation, divide it through by two :

$$
\begin{aligned}
1.X_1 + 3/2\, X_2 + 3/2\, X_3 + 1/2\, X_4 &= 13/2) \\
4X_1 + 5X_2 + 5X_3 + 2\, X_4 &= 24) \\
X_1 + X_2 + X_3 + X_4 &= 7) \\
X_1 + 3X_2 + 2X_3 + 4X_4 &= 19)
\end{aligned}
\qquad \text{---- (4.59)}
$$

Next, to create a coefficient of zero for X_1 in the second, third and fourth equations subtract four times, one times and one times the first equation from them respectively:

$$1.X_1 + 3/2\ X_2 + 3/2\ X_3 + 1/2\ X_4 = 13/2 \ )$$
$$)$$
$$0.X_1 - \quad X_2 - \quad X_3 + 0\ X_4 = -2 \ )$$
$$) \qquad ----\ (4.60)$$
$$0.X_1 - 1/2\ X_2 - 1/2\ X_3 + 1/2\ X_4 = 1/2 \ )$$
$$)$$
$$0.X_1 + 3/2\ X_2 + 1/2\ X_3 + 7/2\ X_4 = 25/2 \ )$$

Next, to create a coefficient of one for X_2 in the second equation, multiply it across by minus one. Then, to create coefficients of zero for X_2 in the first, third and fourth equations, subtract from them 3/2 times, -1/2 times and 3/2 times the second equation respectively. The method then involves creating a coefficient of one for X_3 in the third equation, a coefficient of zero for X_3 in the other equations, a coefficient of one for X_4 in the fourth equation and, finally, a coefficient of zero for X_4 in the other equations. The reader should check that the final solution is :

$$X_1 = 2\ ;\ X_2 = 1\ ;\ X_3 = 1\ ;\ X_4 = 3$$

4.4.3 Change of Basis Operations

A feature of the preceding two examples is that the number of equations equals the number of unknowns. Consider now the task of finding the values for X_1, X_2, X_3, X_4 which simultaneously satisfy :

$$2X_1 + 3X_2 + 1.X_3 + 0.X_4 = 8 \ )$$
$$) \qquad ----\ (4.61)$$
$$4X_1 + 5X_2 + 0.X_3 + 1.X_4 = 25 \ )$$

Because there are fewer equations than unknowns, this is impossible. Suppose however it is known that $X_1 = X_2 = 0$. Then (4.61) collapses to a system of two equations with two unknowns, X_3 and X_4, whose values could be determined. Indeed, given the form of (4.61) with coefficients of one and zero for X_3 in the first and second equations respectively and *vice versa* for X_4, the value of X_3 and X_4 if $X_1 = X_2 = 0$ can be seen directly to be eight and 25 respectively.

In the case of a set of equations where certain variables are known to be zero, these are referred to as the *non-basis variables*. The other variables are said to form the *basis*. Thus, in the preceding example, X_1 and X_2 are the non-basis variables while X_3 and X_4 form the basis.

Suppose now in the case of (4.61) that it is known that X_2 and X_3 are the non-basis variables and the value of the basis variables, X_1 and X_4 are required. How may these be conveniently obtained from (4.61) ? Following the logic of the previous section, the best approach would be to adjust

(4.61) so that the coefficient of X_1 is one in the first equation and zero in the second and *vice versa* (as is already the case) for X_4. This can be achieved by application of the two previously introduced rules. First, to create a co-efficient of one for X_1 in the first equation, multiply across by 1/2 :

$$1.X_1 + 3/2\ X_2 + 1/2\ X_3 + 0.X_4 = 4)$$
$$4\ X_1 + 5\ X_2 + 0.X_3 + 1.X_4 = 25) \qquad \text{---- (4.62)}$$

Next, to create a coefficient of zero for X_1 in the second equation, subtract four times the first equation from it :

$$1.X_1 + 3/2\ X_2 + 1/2\ X_3 + 0.X_4 = 4)$$
$$0.X_1 - 1X_2 - 2\ X_3 + 1.X_4 = 9) \qquad \text{---- (4.63)}$$

from which it can be immediately seen that if $X_2 = X_3 = 0$, $X_1 = 4$ and $X_4 = 9$.

A mathematical operation such as that outlined in (4.61)-(4.63) is referred to as a *change of basis operation*. Note that in such an operation, one variable enters the basis (X_1 in the case of the example) and another leaves it (X_2). The first step in such an operation is to create a coefficient of one for the coefficient of the variable entering the basis in the row in which the variable leaving the basis currently has a coefficient of one e.g. in the first row of (4.61). The equations are sometimes said to have been *pivotted* on this coefficient.

It is often convenient to represent a change of basis operation such as (4.61)-(4.63) in tabular form. In the case of (4.61), this gives :

BASIS	X_1	X_2	X_3	X_4	SOLUTION
X_3	[2]	3	(1)	0	8
X_4	4	5	0	(1)	25

The coefficients of the variables in each equation are listed by row with the right hand sides in a separate column entitled 'solution'. The basis variables are listed to the left and the coefficients of one which enable the values of these variables to be read off directly are circled. When a change of basis operation is to take place, a box is drawn around the coefficient about which the equations are to be pivotted. After this operation, the revised equations i.e. (4.63) would be represented in tabular form by :

BASIS	X_1	X_2	X_3	X_4	SOLUTION
X_1	①	3/2	1/2	0	4
X_4	0	-1	-2	①	9

4.4.4 Algebraic Characteristics of a Linear Programming Solution Space

Some interrelationships between the geometry of a linear programming solution space and the algebra of its constraints expressed in standard form are now considered. The housebuilder problem introduced in section 4.3 is used as an example. The first constraint of the problem written in standard form is :

$$2X_1 + 3X_2 + S_1 = 600 \qquad\qquad ---- (4.64)$$

Note that for any solution above the constraint line $S_1 < 0$, that for any solution exactly satisfying the constraint $S_1 = 0$ and that for any solution lying below the constraint $S_1 > 0$. Therefore to require geometrically that the final solution lie on or below $A_1 A_2$ (Figure 4.2) is equivalent to requiring

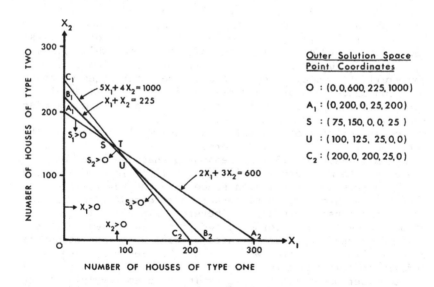

Outer Solution Space Point Coordinates

O : (0,0,600, 225, 1000)

A_1 : (0,200, 0, 25, 200)

S : (75, 150, 0, 0, 25)

U : (100, 125, 25, 0, 0)

C_2 : (200, 0, 200, 25, 0)

NUMBER OF HOUSES OF TYPE ONE

Figure 4.2 The Housebuilder Problem: Solution Space Characteristics

algebraically that $S_1 \geq 0$. Similarly, in the case of the second and third constraints, the final solution must be such that $S_2 \geq 0$ and $S_3 \geq 0$ respectively. It is also required that $X_1^2 \geq 0$ and $X_2^3 \geq 0$. Thus to summarise, the solution to (4.45), (4.46) must be such that :

$$X_1 \geq 0 \; ; \; X_2 \geq 0 \; ; \; S_1 \geq 0 \; ; \; S_2 \geq 0 \; ; \; S_3 \geq 0; \text{ ---- (4.65)}$$

Geometrically, the conditions (4.65) define the solution space for, by definition, to pass outside the solution space involves moving above one or more of the constraints which would cause one or more of S_1, S_2, S_3 to become negative or to the left of the X_2 axis which would cause X_1 to become negative or below the X_1 axis which would cause X_2 to become negative. In general, for a linear programming problem comprising n decision variables X_1, ..., X_n and m constraints with m associated slack variables S_1, ..., S_m, the final solution must be such that :

$$\left. \begin{array}{l} X_j \geq 0 \; ; \; j = 1, \ldots, n \;) \\ \\ S_i \geq 0 \; ; \; i = 1, \ldots, m \;) \end{array} \right\} \text{ ---- (4.66)}$$

Returning to the housebuilder problem, consider now the algebraic properties of a solution which lies on one of the outer edges of the solution space. By definition, the solution will lie on one of the following line segments (Figure 4.2) : OA_1, OC_2, A_1S, SU, UC_2. OA_1 is part of the X_2 axis along which $X_1 = 0$; OC_2 is part of the X_1 axis along which $X_2 = 0$; similarly, A_1S, SU and UC_2 are segments of the first, second and third constraints respectively along which $S_1 = 0$, $S_2 = 0$ and $S_3 = 0$ respectively. Thus, for a solution of the housebuilder problem lying on one of the outer edges of the solution space, one of the variables in (4.65) will equal zero. Similarly, for any linear programming problem comprising n variables and m constraints, a solution lying on one of the outer surfaces of the solution space will have one of the variables in (4.66) equal to zero.

Recall (Section 4.3) the reasoning that the solution to a linear programming problem will (generally) lie at one of the outer corners of the solution space. In the case of the housebuilder problem, these corners are formed by the junction of two constraints/axes. Therefore, in the solutions associated with these corners, two of the variables in (4.65) will equal zero. The coordinates of each corner solution are given in Figure 4.2 from which it can be seen that each does indeed contain two zero values.

Consider now a linear programming problem involving three decision variables and three constraints e.g. the housebuilder problem with an additional housetype included. Here the solution space would be three dimensional and bounded by planar constraints. The outer points of the solution space i.e. potential locations for the optimal solution, would occur at junctions formed by three constraints/axes. One would therefore expect that this solution would be such that three of X_1, X_2, X_3, S_1, S_2, S_3 would equal zero.

In general for a linear programming problem comprising n decision variables and m constraints, one is dealing with an n dimensional solution space where the outer points i.e. potential locations for the optimal solution occur at junctions formed by n constraints/axes. One would therefore expect this solution to be such that n of the (m+n) variables in (4.66) equal zero.

In order to appreciate the importance of these observations, consider again the housebuilder problem expressed in standard form (4.47). The problem comprises four equations and six variables and therefore cannot be solved for unique values of X_0, X_1, X_2, S_1, S_2, S_3. If, however, it were known that two of these variables equalled zero, the equations (4.47) would collapse to four equations with four unknowns which could be solved. It has now been shown that two variables do indeed equal zero at optimality. In general, for a linear programming problem comprising n decision variables and m constraints and written in standard form, there are when the objective is included (m+n+1) variables :

$$X_o, X_1, \ldots, X_n, S_1, \ldots, S_m \qquad \text{---- (4.67)}$$

but only (m+1) equations. If, however, it is known that n of the (m+n+1) variables equals zero at optimality as indeed has been argued to be the case, the system 'collapses' to (m+1) equations with (m+1) variables which can be solved for.

The overall implication of the foregoing comments is that if it were known when solving a linear programming problem which variables equalled zero in the optimal solution, the values of the remaining variables could be determined *via* the methods discussed in Section 4.4.2. The major difficulty is of course that in practice, one does not know initially which variables will equal zero at optimality. Thus the solution approach must be as follows. Arbitrarily set the requisite number of variables (e.g. two in the case of the housebuilder problem) to zero and solve for the remaining variables which will yield one possible optimal solution. Now see if this solution can be improved upon by allowing one of the variables currently equal to zero to become positive and, conversely, one of the variables currently of positive value to reduce to zero. Keep repeating this process on successive solutions until such time as no improvement over the current solution is possible. The optimal solution has then been obtained. Geometrically, it will be shown that this approach is in fact equivalent to examining the solution characteristics at various outer points of the solution space in turn as was suggested in Section 4.3. Algebraically, it corresponds to a series of change of basis operations. The appropriate mathematical methods are now described using the housebuilder problem as an illustration.

4.5 THE SIMPLEX METHOD

Reconsider the housebuilder problem expressed in standard form (4.47). Suppose that $X_1 = X_2 = 0$ and that the values the variables take when this is the case are required. Given the format in which (4.47) is presented, they can in fact be read off directly :

$$S_1 = 600 \ ; \ S_2 = 225 \ ; \ S_3 = 1000 \ ; \ X_0 = 0 \qquad \text{---- (4.68)}$$

Recalling the terminology in (4.43), the variables in (4.68) can be said to form the basis while X_1 and X_2 are the non-basis variables. Furthermore, following Section 4.43, the system of equations (4.47) can be represented in tabular form as :

BASIS	X_0	X_1	X_2	S_1	S_2	S_3	SOLN.	RATIO
X_0	(1)	-3	-4	0	0	0	0	
S_1	0	2	[3]	(1)	0	0	600	600/3
S_2	0	1	1	0	(1)	0	225	225/1
S_3	0	5	4	0	0	(1)	1000	1000/4

Note that as in the previous example, the variables are listed across the top with the variables forming the basis to the left. The coefficients of one which enable the solution values of the basis variables to be read off directly are circled. By convention, the objective row is separated by a horizontal line from the constraint rows ; also, by convention, the X_0 column, the X_1, X_2 ... columns and the slack variable columns are separated from each other by vertical lines. An additional column marked ratio, which may be ignored for the present, is placed to the right of the solution column. In the context of linear programming, a table such as this is usually referred to as a *simplex tableau*. In the simplex method, the initial solution and tableau considered is always that obtained directly from a representation of the problem in standard form.

   Consider the solution suggested by this tableau. It suggests that no houses be constructed $(X_1 = X_2 = 0)$ and that no return will accrue $(X_0 = 0)$. Presumably a more satisfactory solution could be found by permitting construction of houses of either type one or type two. Mathematically, this would involve allowing X_1 or X_2 to exceed zero i.e. to enter the basis. Which variable should enter the basis ? Viewed from the point of view of the housebuilder, which type of house would he prefer to begin constructing? Given that his object-ive is to maximise his return from sales, type two is the most logical choice as the return per house built is greater. This can be seen directly from the simplex tableau : scanning across the X_0 (objective) row the largest negative coefficient (i.e. positive coefficient in the original objective) occurs in the X_2 column.

Given that the housebuilder is going to construct houses of type two, how many should be build? Again, given that his objective is to maximise return from sales, he should build the maximum number possible. Quite obviously, this is not an infinite number : sooner or later, one of the three constr-aints will limit further development. Viewing each constraint in turn (Figure 4.1(b)), how many houses of type two can be built? First, in terms of the total acreage available, no more than 200 houses can be built. Second, in terms of total houses allowed, no more than 225 houses can be built. Finally, in terms of the constraint relating to population, no more than 250 houses can be built. Taking these results together, the severest restriction is imposed by the first constraint. The solution associated with making X_2 as large as possible is therefore :

$$X_0 = 800 \; ; \; X_1 = 0 \; ; \; X_2 = 200 \qquad \Big) $$
$$ S_1 = 0 \; ; \; S_2 = 25 \; ; \; S_3 = 200 \; \Big) \qquad \text{---- (4.69)}$$

Comparing this with the solution (4.68), it can be seen that if X_2 becomes positive, the constraints are such that S_1 is the variable which becomes zero i.e. which leaves the basis. We now consider how the foregoing calculations can be perform-ed in terms of the initial simplex tableau.

Given that X_2 is to enter the basis by virtue of being associated with the largest negative value in the X_0 row, the variable to leave the basis (i.e. which becomes zero in the revised solution) can be discovered as follows : for each constraint row in turn, determine the ratio of the value in the solution column to that in the column of the variable to enter the basis. Ignore ratios with negative denominators. The variable to leave the basis is that in the row associated with the smallest ratio. (In the case of a tie, choose either variable.)

The ratios for the sample problem have been duly calculat-ed and inserted in the column marked 'ratio' of the simplex tableau. The smallest value, 200, is associated with the S_1 row. Thus, this is the variable to leave the basis. Note that the three ratios obtained from the divisions and the resultant decision as to which variable should leave the basis correspond to those obtained when viewing the problem in terms of Figure 4.1(b).

We now wish to calculate the revised solution with X_2 in the basis and S_1 removed from it. Recalling Section 4.4.3, this may be achieved *via* a change of basis operation pivotting on the coefficient in the S_1 row and X_2 column of the current solution tableau which has therefore been squared. First, to create a coefficient of one for X_2 in the first constraint row, divide across by three which yields :

BASIS	X_0	X_1	X_2	S_1	S_2	S_3	SOLN.	RAT.
X_0								
X_1	0	2/3	①	1/3	0	0	200	
S_2								
S_3								

Next, multiply the revised row in turn by minus four, one and four and, to create zeros in the rest of the X_2 column, subtract from the X_0, S_2 and S_3 rows respectively which yields :

BASIS	X_0	X_1	X_2	S_1	S_2	S_3	SOLN.	RAT.
X_0	①	-1/3	0	4/3	0	0	800	
X_2	0	2/3	①	1/3	0	0	200	$200.\frac{3}{2}$
S_2	0	1/3	0	-1/3	①	0	25	25.3
S_3	0	7/3	0	-4/3	0	①	200	$200.\frac{3}{7}$

The revised solution can thus be read off as :

Basis variables : $X_0 = 800$; $X_2 = 200$; $S_2 = 25$; $S_3 = 200$

Non-basis
          variables : $X_1 = S_1 = 0$

which corresponds to (4.69).

The question must now be asked as to whether this revised solution can be improved upon further. Once more, scanning across the X_o row, note that the largest negative value occurs in the X_1 column. Thus, this variable should enter the basis. (If two or more variables tie in terms of largest negative values, that to enter the basis may be chosen arbitrarily.) The actual value of $-1/3$ indicates that in terms of the current solution, the housebuilder would make an additional profit of $1/3$ money units for every house of type one he builds, whilst adjusting the number of type two houses constructed to keep within the bounds of the constraints.

If X_1 enters the basis, which variable should leave? Calculating the ratios of the values in the solution and X_1 columns for each constraint and applying the foregoing rule indicates S_2 and thus the coefficient about which pivotting should take place. Multiplying the S_2 constraint row by three to create the necessary coefficient of one and multiplying the revised row by $-1/3$, $2/3$ and $7/3$ and subtracting from the X_o, X_2 and S_3 rows respectively yields the revised tableau:

BASIS	X_o	X_1	X_2	S_1	S_2	S_3	SOL.	RAT.
X_o	(1)	0	0	1	1	0	825	
X_2	0	0	(1)	1	-2	0	150	
X_1	0	(1)	0	-1	3	0	75	
S_3	0	0	0	1	-7	(1)	25	

which corresponds to the solution:

Basis Variables   : $X_o = 825$; $X_2 = 150$; $X_1 = 75$; $S_3 = 25$

Non-basis Variables   : $S_1 = S_2 = 0$

The question now arises as to whether this solution can be improved upon further. Once more, scanning across the X_o row, it can be seen that no negative values occur i.e. there is no non-basis variable which, if it were to enter the basis, would cause an increase in X_o. Thus the optimal solution has been reached, a point confirmed by the fact that the foregoing solution corresponds to that achieved using the graphical approach.

To summarise the foregoing, it can be seen that, as with certain other optimisation methods considered previously, the simplex method finds the optimal solution to a linear programming problem *via* a series of iterations. On each iteration, the variable to enter the basis and, given this variable, the variable to leave the basis are identified. A change of basis operation is then performed on the relevant simplex tableau.

A full summary of the procedure is given in Figure 4.3.

Two characteristics of the simplex procedure deserve special mention. First, in a geometrical sense in the case of a maximisation problem with all 'less than or equals' constraints, application of the simplex method involves commencing with a solution relating to the origin and of tracking successively from one outer point of the solution space to another until the optimal solution is reached. In the housebuilder example, the three solutions obtained correspond to the points 0, A_1 and S respectively in Figure 4.1(c). An implication of this characteristic of the solution process is that the speed with which the optimal solution might be reached in the case of a particular problem depends to some extent on the number of outer points the solution space associated with that problem has which in its turn is a function of the number of constraints. In general, a linear programming problem comprising many variables but few constraints will be solved more rapidly than one comprising few variables but with many constraints.

Second, it is to be noted that in contrast to the graphical approach, the simplex method could in theory be used to solve a linear programming problem comprising any number of variables and constraints. The sole implication for the foregoing methods would be that in the case of a problem with many variables and constraints the tableaux concerned would be larger and the actual calculations more tedious. However, because the simplex method comprises a series of exactly defined steps (Figure 4.3) it is readily amenable to solution using the computer. Most general purpose computer facilities will have a linear programming programme package available.

4.6   GENERALISATION OF THE SIMPLEX METHOD

The previous section elucidates how the simplex method can be used to solve a linear programming problem involving a maximisation objective with all 'less than or equals' constraints. We now consider the problems which arise and the ways in which the method may be adapted to cope with constraints of the 'greater than or equals' and 'equals' types and with a minimisation objective thereby providing a tool capable of solving any linear programming problem.

4.6.1 'Greater Than or Equals' Constraints

Consider the housebuilder problem introduced in Section 4.3 with one additional constraint:

Linear Programming : The Simplex Method

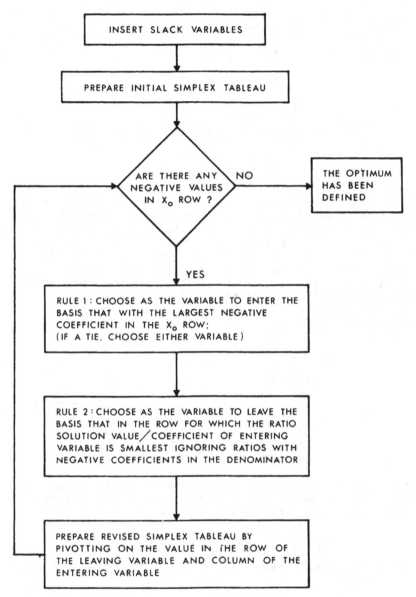

Figure 4.3 The Simplex Method for a Maximisation Problem With
All 'Less Than or Equals' Constraints

From: KILLEN, J.E. (1979), *Linear Programming: The Simplex
Method With Geographical Applications,* Concepts and
Techniques in Modern Geography Monograph Series
Number 24, Geo Abstracts, Norwich, Figure 2.

Redrawn by permission of the Author.

111

MAXIMISE : $3X_1 + 4X_2$

s.t. $2X_1 + 3X_2 \leq 600$

$X_1 + X_2 \leq 225$

$5X_1 + 4X_2 \leq 1000$ ---- (4.70)

$X_1 + 2X_2 \geq 150$

$X_1, X_2 \geq 0$

This additional constraint could represent (say) a stipulation by the local planning authority that the number of houses in the final development must be such that the number of smaller houses plus twice the number of larger houses exceeds 150.

Consider now the task of presenting (4.70) in standard form. Because the new constraint is of the 'greater than or equals' type, the slack variable introduced to convert it to an equality, S_4, must be such as to *reduce* the level of the left hand side to that of the right i.e. S_4 must have a negative sign. The complete standard form formulation is therefore:

SOLVE : $X_0 - 3X_1 - 4X_2 = 0$

$2X_1 + 3X_2 + S_1 = 600$

$X_1 + X_2 + S_2 = 225$ ---- (4.71)

$5X_1 + 4X_2 + S_3 = 1000$

$X_1 + 2X_2 - S_4 = 150$

The fact that S_4 is negatively signed in (4.71) has serious implications for the simplex method. Recall that in the previous problem, the initial solution (4.68) was given by:

$X_1 = X_2 = 0; S_1, S_2, S_3 > 0$

which corresponded geometrically to the origin. In this case, if $X_1 = X_2 = 0$:

$S_1 = 600; S_2 = 225; S_3 = 1000; S_4 = -150$ ---- (4.72)

i.e. S_4 is negative which demonstrates (recall (4.66)) that the origin now lies outside the solution space. This is confirmed by the geometrical representation of the revised problem (Figure 4.4): the origin no longer lies at a corner of the solution space. Because the simplex method operates by tracking from one corner of the solution space to another,

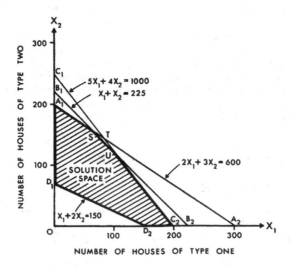

Figure 4.4 Linear Programming Problem With a 'Greater Than or Equals Constraint

a revised initial solution which does correspond to a corner point solution and from which one can proceed to solve (4.71) *via* a series of change of basis operations must be provided. One way in which this can be achieved is by what is known as the *Big-M method*.

Compare the problem (4.70) with:

$$
\begin{array}{lll}
\text{MAXIMISE :} & 3X_1 + 4X_2 - MR_4 & \\
\text{s.t.} & 2X_1 + 3X_2 & \leq 600 \\
& X_1 + X_2 & \leq 225 \\
& 5X_1 + 4X_2 & \leq 1000 \\
& X_1 + 2X_2 + R_4 & \geq 150 \\
& X_1, X_2, R_4 & \geq 0
\end{array}
\qquad \text{---- (4.73)}
$$

In the case of (4.73), an additional variable, R_4, has been introduced. The coefficient of R_4 is plus one in the 'greater than or equals' constraint and $-M$ where M is envisaged as being a very large number, say one million, in the objective. Consider now the value R_4 would be expected to have in the optimal solution of (4.73). If R_4 was positive,

113

even a very small number, the value of the objective would be very much reduced because of the large negative coefficient associated with R_4 in it. Thus, it is virtually certain that the optimal value of R_4 in (4.73) will be zero i.e. R_4 will be a non-basis variable. If this is so, the solution to (4.73) will be the same as for (4.70) for, substituting $R_4 = 0$ in (4.73) yields (4.70). Thus, in fact, R_4 has been introduced into (4.73) in such a way as to ensure its disappearance. The advantage it confers is that it permits an initial solution simplex tableau to be generated without difficulty.

Representing (4.73) in standard form with R_4 in the initial basis yields:

$$
\begin{array}{llllll}
\text{SOLVE}: & X_o - 3X_1 - 4X_2 & & + MR_4 & = 0 &)\\
& & & & &)\\
& 2X_1 + 3X_2 & +S_1 & & = 600 &)\\
& & & & &)\\
& X_1 + X_2 & +S_2 & & = 225 &) \quad ---- \quad (4.74)\\
& & & & &)\\
& 5X_1 + 4X_2 & +S_3 & & = 1000 &)\\
& & & & &)\\
& X_1 + 2X_2 - S_4 & & + R_4 & = 150 &)
\end{array}
$$

Representing this by a simplex tableau yields:

BASIS	X_o	X_1	X_2	S_4	S_1	S_2	S_3	R_4	SOL.	RATIO
	1	-3	-4	0	0	0	0	M	0	
	0	2	3	0	1	0	0	0	600	
	0	1	1	0	0	1	0	0	225	
	0	5	4	0	0	0	1	0	1000	
	0	1	2	-1	0	0	0	1	150	

The format of this tableau is such that S_1, S_2, S_3, R_4 could be considered as the initial basis with one exception: the coefficient of R_4 in the X_o row is M; yet it should be zero if R_4 is a basis variable. This can be corrected by multiplying the fourth constraint row across by M and subtracting from the X_o row which yields:

BASIS	X_0	X_1	X_2	S_4	S_1	S_2	S_3	R_4	SOL.	RATIO
X_0	①	-3-M	-4-2M	M	0	0	0	0	-150M	
S_1	0	2	3	0	①	0	0	0	600	600/3
S_2	0	1	1	0	0	①	0	0	225	225/1
S_3	0	5	4	0	0	0	①	0	1000	1000/4
R_4	0	1	[2]	-1	0	0	0	①	150	150/2

The solution associated with this tableau is:

Basis Variables : X_0 = -150M; S_1 = 600; S_2 = 225; S_3 = 1000; R_4 = 150

Non-Basis
  Variables   : X_1 = X_2 = S_4 = 0

Note that this solution is as would be expected in the case of
a linear programming problem with three original variables
(X_1, X_2, R_4) and four constraints : three variables equal zero
and the condition (4.66) holds. Note too that a negative
value for X_0 is in fact allowed for by (4.66); indeed, as was
explained (4.46), the value for X_0 is fixed automatically by
the values the other variables in the objective expression
take.

    The preceding tableau places the problem (4.74) in a
format amenable to solution using the simplex method. Recalling that M stands for one million and scanning across the X_0
row, the variable with the largest associated negative
coefficient is X_2. Thus this variable enters the basis.
Calculation of the ratio between the solution and X_2 columns
indicates that R_4 leaves. The change of basis operation
yields:

BASIS	X_0	X_1	X_2	S_4	S_1	S_2	S_3	R_4	SOL.	RATIO
X_0	①	-1	0	-2	0	0	0	2+M	300	
S_1	0	1/2	0	3/2	①	0	0	-3/2	375	$375.\frac{2}{3}$
S_2	0	1/2	0	1/2	0	①	0	-1/2	150	150.2
S_3	0	3	0	2	0	0	①	-2	700	$700.\frac{1}{2}$
X_2	0	1/2	①	-1/2	0	0	0	1/2	75	-ve

i.e. Basis Variables: $X_0 = 300$; $X_2 = 75$; $S_1 = 375$; $S_2 = 150$; $S_3 = 700$

Non-Basis
Variables: $X_1 = S_3 = R_4 = 0$

Note that R_4 has left the basis and thus that the problem
(4.74) has in effect become (4.70). The revised solution
corresponds to the point D_1 in Figure 4.4 which is indeed an
outer point of the solution space of (4.70). The reader
should check that the optimal solution is reached in two
further iterations and is:

Basis Variables : $X_0 = 825$; $X_1 = 75$; $X_2 = 150$; $S_3 = 25$; $S_4 = 225$

Non-basis
variables: $S_1 = S_2 = R_4 = 0$

    The preceding example involves adjusting a linear pro-
gramming problem to deal with one 'greater than or equals'
constraint. When a number of these constraints occur, a set
of variables of the form R_i, one for each constraint, must be
introduced. The solution method then proceeds as before. An
example involving three 'greater than or equals' constraints
is given in Section 4.6.3.

4.6.2 Equality Constraints

Consider a linear programming problem with a constraint of
the form:

$$a_{i1} X_1 + a_{i2} X_2 + \ldots + a_{in} X_n = b_i \qquad \text{---- (4.75)}$$

Because (4.75) is in the form of an equality, no slack variable needs to be introduced on conversion to standard form
which raises complications concerning an initial basis
solution. These complications may be circumvented by noting
that if (4.75) holds true, then so too must the two conditions:

$$a_{i1} X_1 + a_{i1} X_2 + \ldots + a_{in} X_n \leq b_i \qquad \text{---- (4.76)}$$

$$a_{i1} X_1 + a_{i1} X_2 + \ldots + a_{in} X_n \geq b_i \qquad \text{---- (4.77)}$$

(4.76) and (4.77) are inequalities which can be dealt with
using the methods discussed previously. They thus replace
(4.75) for application of the simplex method.

4.6.3 Minimisation Objective

The presence of an objective involving minimisation rather
than maximisation has implications both for the way in which
variables of the form R_i are incorporated into a problem with

'greater than or equals' constraints and for the rule to be used to choose the variable to enter the basis on each iteration of the simplex method. In order to demonstrate the changes required, consider the problem:

$$\text{Minimise} : 600Y_1 + 225Y_2 + 1000Y_3$$

$$\begin{array}{llll}
\text{s.t.} & 2Y_1 + & Y_2 + & 5Y_3 & \geq 3) \\
& 3Y_1 + & Y_2 + & 4Y_3 & \geq 4) \\
& 5Y_1 + & Y_2 + & 4Y_3 & \geq 2) \\
& Y_1 \geq 0 \; ; \; Y_2 \geq 0 &&&
\end{array}$$

$$\text{---- (4.78)}$$

There are three 'greater than or equals' constraints. Thus one R_i variable must be introduced for each constraint. Let these be R_1, R_2, R_3 respectively. Recall that each variable R_i must also be incorporated into the objective multiplied by an arbitrarily large number, M. Recall too that these new terms are given a sign such that all the R_i variables should equal zero in the final solution. Just as a negative sign is appropriate in the case of a maximisation problem for MR_i, a positive sign is appropriate in the case of minimisation for, consider:

$$\text{Minimise} : 600Y_1 + 225Y_2 + 1000Y_3 + MR_1 + MR_2 + MR_3$$

$$\begin{array}{lllll}
\text{s.t.} & 2Y_1 + & Y_2 + & 5Y_2 + R_1 & & \geq 3) \\
& 3Y_1 + & Y_2 + & 4Y_2 & + R_2 & \geq 4) \\
& 5Y_1 + & Y_2 + & 4Y_3 & + R_3 & \geq 2) \\
& Y_1 \geq 0 \; ; \; Y_2 \geq 0 &&&&
\end{array}$$

$$\text{---- (4.79)}$$

In (4.79), the values of R_1, R_2, R_3 in the optimal solution can be expected to equal zero for if any of these variables achieved even a small positive value, the value of the objective (to be minimised) would rise by a considerable amount. If $R_1 = R_2 = R_3 = 0$, the problem (4.79) reduces to (4.78).
    Introducing slack variables S_1, S_2, S_3 into (4.79) and representing the problem *via* a simplex tableau with R_1, R_2, R_3 as the initial basis yields:

BASIS	Y_o	Y_1	Y_2	Y_3	S_1	S_2	S_3	R_1	R_2	R_3	SOL.	RAT.
	1	+600	-225	-1000	0	0	0	-M	-M	-M	0	
	0	2	1	5	-1	0	0	1	0	0	3	
	0	3	1	4	0	-1	0	0	1	0	4	
	0	5	1	4	0	0	-1	0	0	1	2	

With the exception of the '-M' values in the R_1, R_2, R_3 columns of the X_o row, the problem possesses the desired format. These values may be eliminated by adding M times the first, second and third rows to the X_o row which yields the revised tableau:

BASIS	Y_o	Y_1	Y_2	Y_3	S_1	S_2	S_3	R_1	R_2	R_3	SOL.	RAT.
Y_o	①	-600 +10M	-225 +3M	-1000 +13M	-M	-M	-M	0	0	0	9M	
R_1	0	2	1	5	-1	0	0	①	0	0	3	3/5
R_2	0	3	1	4	0	-1	0	0	①	0	4	4/4
R_3	0	5	1	[4]	0	0	-1	0	0	①	2	2/4

Consider now the variable which should enter the basis. Recall that in the case of a maximisation problem, the variable chosen was that whose increase from zero allowed *the greatest increase* in the objective i.e. the variable with the *largest negative coefficient* in the X_o row. Obviously, in the case of minimisation, we seek the variable whose increase from zero allows *the greatest decrease* in the object- ive i.e. the variable with the *largest positive coefficient* in the objective row. Scanning across the Y_o row of the preceding tableau, the variable to enter the basis is there- fore Y_3. Applying the same ratio rule as before, the variab- le to leave is R_3 yielding:

BASIS	Y_o	Y_1	Y_2	Y_3	S_1	S_2	S_3	R_1	R_2	R_3	SOL.	RAT.
Y_o	①	650 $-25/4M$	25$-$ 1/4M	0	$-M$	$-M$	$-250+$ 9/4M	0	0	250$-$ 13/4M	500+ 5/2M	
R_1	0	$-17/4$	$-1/4$	0	-1	0	$\boxed{5/4}$	①	0	$-5/4$	1/2	$\frac{1}{2} \cdot \frac{4}{5}$
R_2	0	-2	0	0	0	-1	1	0	①	-1	2	2/1
Y_3	0	5/4	1/4 ①	0	0	$-1/4$	0	0	0	1/4	1/2	$-$ve

S_3 now enters the basis with R_1 leaving. The reader should check that the optimal solution is reached after three iterations and is:

BASIS	Y_o	Y_1	Y_2	Y_3	S_1	S_2	S_3	R_1	R_2	R_3	SOL.
Y_o	①	0	0	-25	-75	-150	0	75$-$M	150$-$M	0	825
S_3	0	0	0	-2	2	-3	①	-2	3	-1	4
Y_1	0	①	0	-1	1	-1	0	-1	1	0	1
Y_2	0	0	①	0	-3	2	0	3	-2	0	1

4.7   SOME LINEAR PROGRAMMING STUDY RESULTS

A number of actual linear programming applications set within certain of the contexts discussed in Section 4.2 are now described. Each problem was solved using the methods discussed in the preceding sections.

4.7.1   Urban Landuse Design

An excellent example of a relatively straightforward application of a model of general form (4.5)-(4.9) is that described by Heroux and Wallace (1975) (for another example, see Day (1973)) who consider the case of a developer developing 11,147 acres of land in upstate New York for residential and associated purposes. Of the total area, 5385.6 acres were to be set aside for road construction, open space, a reservoir etc., leaving 5761.4 acres to be allocated by the model. Some mix of nine dwelling types was to be built. Each dwelling of a particular type was expected to house a given number of persons and to occupy a given acreage. The number of persons expected to seek educational facilities and employment was

known for each dwelling type. The constraints required that
the development be such that:

(i) The number of dwellings of each type constructed be such
     as to house a given total population (similar to 4.39 but
     with a 'greater than or equals' inequality)
(ii) The acreage zoned for industrial land, commercial land,
     educational facilities, service buildings, health
     facilities, recreational facilities, cultural facilities,
     cemeteries and churches be such as to meet the needs of
     the population housed e.g. in the case of educational
     facilities, if:

X_j = Acreage assigned to housetype j,   j=1, ..., n

X_k = Acreage assigned to educational facility type k,
     k =1, ..., q

d_j = Density of development of housetype j (e.g. houses
     per acre)

p_{jk} = Average number of persons in the house of type j
     requiring a place in an educational facility of
     type k

r_k = Number of places provided per acre allocated to
     educational facility type k

then, in the final landuse plan:

$$\sum_{j=1}^{n} p_{jk}\, d_j\, X_j \;\leq\; r_k\, X_k \qquad k=1, \ldots, q \qquad \text{---- (4.80)}$$

i.e. the number of places provided in educational facilities
of each type must be sufficient to meet the projected demand.

(iii) The total acreage zoned does not exceed that available
      as in (4.6).

   The developer's objective was taken as maximising total
profit as given by an expression of the form (4.20). The per
unit profit values in the objective associated with such landuses as educational facilities, service buildings, health
facilities etc were negative as these are landuses the
developer is forced to provide *via* constraints of the type
(4.80) at his own expense. Table 4.2 summarises the results
obtained by Heroux and Wallace. The model allocates more than
half of the land available to dwelling types one and three;
five dwelling types are not constructed at all.
   One of the limitations of landuse design *via* linear programming is illustrated by the results in Table 4.2 : while
the model gives the acreages to be allocated to each landuse,
it gives no indication of how these should be juxtaposed in a

TABLE 4.2

RESULTS OBTAINED IN A LANDUSE DESIGN STUDY

LANDUSE	NATURE OF PROFIT TO DEVELOPER	PROPORTION OF ACREAGE ASSIGNED	ACTUAL ACREAGE ASSIGNED
Dwellings			
- Type One	+ve	)	741
- Type Three	+ve	) 0.55213	2441
- Type Six	+ve	) 0.03773	217
- Type Nine	+ve	0.01350	78
Manufacturing	+ve	0.06023	347
Schools	-ve	0.09513	548
Commercial	+ve	0.06345	365
Public Services	-ve	0.00634	36.5
Health Services	-ve	0.00803	46.3
Parks/Recreation	-ve	0.14455	833
Cultural Fac- ilities	-ve	0.00150	8.6
Cemeteries	-ve	0.00418	24
Churches	-ve	0.01324	76

From: HEROUX, R.L. and WALLACE, W.A., (1975), New Community Development With The Aid of Linear Programming in:

SALKIN, H. and SAHA, J., *Studies in Linear Programming*, North Holland Publishing Company, Amsterdam, 309-22, Table 2.

desirable manner. Thus a considerable input is still required from the individual planner in producing the final detailed plan. Another point to be made in connection with results such as these is that they relate to a problem conceived with a precisely defined objective and constraints. In practice, the true objective underlying a particular planning exercise can seldom be defined precisely in terms of a single entity e.g. profit maximisation. Thus the results emerging in a particular programming study must often be treated merely as a general guide to what might be done. Quite often, in an actual planning situation, a given problem is solved for a number of objectives to see by how much and in what ways the resultant optimal plans differ. This is the approach adopted by Bammi and Bammi (1975) in a study of landuse planning for Du Page County, Illinois. An alternative approach is to construct a complex objective which incorporates a number of elements e.g. cost minimisation, profit maximisation etc. in some weighted manner, thereby approximating more accurately what the true objective of the planning process actually is. An example of this approach is that discussed by Ben-Shahar *et al.* (1969) who view the planning process as maximising a function entitled 'welfare' which is made up of various individual items.

Another feature of urban design linear programming formulations e.g. that of Heroux and Wallace is that they take no account of the effect that certain of the programmed developments e.g. concerning transport might themselves have on further development. Thus, for example, Heroux and Wallace presume that a certain proportion of land in their area of study will be allocated to transport facilities; yet, the provision of these facilities will of itself affect the nature and extent of landuse development in the areas through which they pass. Two notable models which go some way towards attempting to bridge the gap between landuse and transportation planning are those of Ochs (1969) and Dickey and Azola (1972).

4.7.2 Recreational Landuse

A subject area in which it has been suggested that linear programming could be used to advantage is that concerning the acquisition and use of land for recreational purposes. An early application by Meier (1968) (for a summary see Daellenbach and Bell (1970)) concerns maximising the total recreational benefit gained in one or more regions through a land acquisition programme which does not oversupply the demand for such land or overspend the available budget.

Cheung and Auger (1976) consider a situation where recreational landuse competes with other potential landuses in a set of areas. Specifically, there are four areas A, B, C and D with four potential uses for each area or part thereof

TABLE 4.3

RECREATIONAL LANDUSE : MODEL INPUTS/OUTPUTS

VARIABLE - LANDUSE	RETURN ACRE^{-1}	VALUE IN OPT. SOL.
Region A (300 Acres)		
X_1 - White spruce production	-1.86	0
X_2 - Barley production	-9.95	0
X_3 - Hunting	-1.86	0
X_4 - White spruce production and hunting	0.14	0
Region B (80 Acres)		
X_5 - White spruce production	0.24	0
X_6 - Potato production	-73.75	0
X_7 - Camping	0.20	0
X_8 - White spruce production and camping	1.44	80
Region C (268 Acres)		
X_9 - White spruce production	-4.08	0
X_{10}- Wheat production	10.00	268
X_{11}- Fishing	10.00	0
X_{12}- White spruce production and fishing	-0.08	0
Region D (1046 Acres)		
X_{13}- Poplar production	-0.16	0
X_{14}- Potato production	-92.5	0
X_{15}- Hunting	-0.16	0
X_{16}- Poplar production and hunting	0.64	1042

From: CHEUNG, H.K. and AUGER, J.A., (1976), Linear Programming and Land Use Allocation, *Socio-Economic Planning Sciences, 10,* 43-5.
Reprinted by permission of the Pergamon Press Limited.

(Table 4.3). Each use has an associated return per acre and the objective is to find the acreage which should be allocated to each use in each region in order to maximise the total return. The per acre cost and the per acre consumption of labour for each landuse possibility in each region are known and, following the format of (4.22), the first two constraints require that the values of $X_1, \ldots, X_{16}$ are such that the total labour and capital available is not overused. The final four constraints require that the total acreage used in each region does not exceed that available e.g. for region A:

$$X_1 + X_2 + X_3 + X_4 \leq 300 \qquad\qquad ---- \quad (4.81)$$

The optimal solution is given in Table 4.3. No land in region A is utilised; region B is devoted in its entirely to white spruce production and camping while wheat is allocated to all of region C. Virtually all of region D is allocated poplar production and hunting. The optimal solution uses the total labour supply available i.e. the labour constraint holds exactly at optimality but does not spend the entire budget. In the case of the acreage constraints, the second and third of these hold exactly at optimality.

4.7.3 Agriculture

A straightforward application of the model (4.21)-(4.23) is that described by Puterbaugh *et al.* (1957) who discuss determining the mix of eight possible activities which should be carried on a farm in central Indiana (Table 4.4). Four constraints are involved : the amounts of land and labour available must not be overused, the requirement by livestock for hay must not exceed that available on the farm and, finally, a certain amount of corn is available while any additional corn required may be purchased on the open market for 10¢ more. The crop growing activities $(X_1, \ldots, X_4)$ and the corn buying activity (X_8) are carried on solely to provide animal feed and thus have negatively signed per unit return coefficients in the objective; yet, the third and fourth constraints force certain of these activities to enter the optimal solution.

The optimal solution obtained by Puterbaugh *et al.* is set out in Table 4.4. Two crop rotation activities are engaged in to serve a sole livestock enterprise - hog raising. The optimal solution fully utilises the land, labour and corn availability.

An extremely interesting yet straightforward application of linear programming in an agricultural context which differs somewhat from that discussed above is that of Heady and Egbert (1962) who consider the amounts of six crops which should be produced in each of 104 regions in the United States in order to maximise total profits over all regions

TABLE 4.4

FARM MANAGEMENT PROBLEM : MODEL INPUTS/OUTPUTS

VARIABLE - AGRICULTURAL ACTIVITY	RETURN ACRE^{-1}	VALUE IN OPT. SOL.
Crop Production for Animals*		
X_1 - C C C C O M	-23.40	0
X_2 - C C C O M	-23.06	292.91
X_3 - C	-32.34	12.08
X_4 - M	-16.04	0
Livestock Enterprises		
X_5 - Beef cows herd	81.85	0
X_6 - Two litter hog enterprise	458.06	100.04
X_7 - Calf feeding programme	110.50	0
Direct Purchase		
X_8 - Corn	-1.30	0

$S_1 = 0$; $S_2 = 0$; $S_3 = 134.28815$; $S_4 = 0$; $X_o = 40828.4$ dollars

* C - Corn ; O - Oats ; M - Maize

From : PUTERBAUGH, H.L., KEHRBERG, E.W. and DUNBAR, J.O., (1957), Analyzing The Solution Tableau of a Simplex Linear Programming Problem in Farm Organization, *Journal of Farm Economics*, 39, 478-89.

Reprinted by permission of the Editor

Linear Programming : The Simplex Method

i.e. to:

$$\text{Maximise} : \sum_{i=1}^{104} \sum_{j=1}^{6} c_{ij} \, X_{ij} \qquad \text{---- (4.82)}$$

where: X_{ij} = The amount of the jth crop produced in the ith region

c_{ij} = The profit per unit of the jth crop produced in the ith region.

The six crops considered by Heady and Egbert are : wheat for human consumption and wheat, corn, oats, barley and grain sorghum all for animal consumption. The 104 regions were drawn up so as to be as homogeneous as possible in terms of soil type etc. The model is constrained by 106 constraints. First, for each region in turn:

$$\sum_{j=1}^{6} a_{ij} \, X_{ij} \leq s_i \qquad \text{---- (4.83)}$$

where a_{ij} = The acreage required in region i to grow one unit of crop j

and s_i = The total acreage available in region i.

Next, the production of wheat for human consumption must be such that a given national requirement, b_1 is met i.e.

$$\sum_{i=1}^{104} X_{i1} \geq b_1 \qquad \text{---- (4.84)}$$

Finally, the production of the remaining five crops must be such that a given national requirement for animal foodstuffs expressed as the total livestock nutrition value, b_2, is met i.e.

$$\sum_{i=1}^{104} \sum_{j=2}^{6} e_{ij} \, X_{ij} \geq b_2 \qquad \text{---- (4.85)}$$

where e_{ij} = livestock nutrition value of a unit of crop j produced in region i.

Heady and Egbert present results for various runs of the model e.g. for $b_1 = 678$ and $b_2 = 3549$ million bushels and for $b_1 = 800$ and $b_2 = 4000$. The former figures are the actual demands for wheat for human production and for animal foodstuffs in 1954. Thus the optimal production pattern (which is mapped by Heady and Egbert) should approximate the actual production pattern in that year while the optimal pattern for $b_1 = 800$, $b_2 = 4000$ (which is also mapped) indicates those areas which should be brought into production and those where the nature of production should alter when demand increases.

Yet another relatively straightforward application of linear programming to an agricultural problem is that of Connolly (1974) who investigates the optimal number of cattle and sheep which should be grazed on a meadow of a particular botanical makeup. The reader is referred to the original paper for details.

4.7.4 Diet

Four studies which describe the results emerging from an application of linear programming in the context of (4.28)-(4.30) are those of Gould and Sparks (1969), De Castro and Lauritz (1967), Kearney (1971) and Griffiths and Conniffe (1974/5). The former two models relate to human diets and the latter two to animal diets.

In its most straightforward form, Gould and Sparks' model involves using the formulation (4.28)-(4.30) to determine the amount of each of forty foods to be included in a least cost diet which meets nine dietary requirements. The problem is set within the context of Southern Guatemala where, in fact, the per unit cost of each food varied between each of 24 town locations. Thus a linear programming problem of the form (4.28)-(4.30) was solved 24 times i.e. for each town location in turn with the relevant cost values in the objective function thereby giving the cost and composition of the least cost diet at each place. The spatial variation in these costs is shown in Figure 4.5. The most notable feature is the increased cost of the least cost diet in the larger urban centres reflecting the higher food prices there caused by higher demands.

4.8 SOME RELATIONSHIPS BETWEEN THE NORTHWEST CORNER STEPPING STONE METHOD FOR SOLVING THE TRANSPORTATION PROBLEM AND THE SIMPLEX METHOD

Consider once again the transportation problem solved *via* the northwest corner stepping stone method in Section 3.3.2. Writing the objective of this problem in the form (4.46), the complete formulation is:

$$
\begin{aligned}
\text{Solve}: X_o - 9X_{11} - 7X_{12} - 5X_{13} - 7X_{21} - 3X_{22} - 2X_{23} - 2X_{31} - X_{32} - X_{33} &= 0 \\
X_{11} + X_{12} + X_{13} &= 20 \\
X_{21} + X_{22} + X_{23} &= 35 \\
X_{31} + X_{32} + X_{33} &= 50 \\
X_{11} + X_{21} + X_{31} &= 45 \\
X_{12} + X_{22} + X_{32} &= 30 \\
X_{13} + X_{23} + X_{33} &= 30
\end{aligned}
$$

$$X_{ij} \geq 0 \quad i,j = 1, \ldots, 3 \qquad \text{---- (4.86)}$$

127

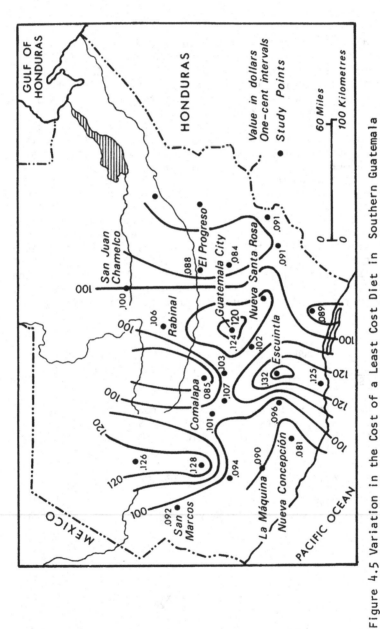

Figure 4.5 Variation in the Cost of a Least Cost Diet in Southern Guatemala

From: GOULD, P.R. and SPARKS, J.P., (1969), The Geographical Context of Human Diets in Southern
Guatemala, *Geographical Review*, 59, 58-82, Figure 3.
Redrawn by permission of the American Geographical Society.

There are six constraints and ten decision variables. However, given that the problem is balanced in terms of total supply and demand as is indicated by the equalities in the constraints, one of the latter is in fact redundant : if the first five constraint conditions in (4.86) hold, the last condition will hold automatically. Thus, in effect, the problem comprises five constraints and ten decision variables. The final constraint is dropped from further consideration.

The problem (4.86) is in fact somewhat similar in mathematical form to a linear programming problem expressed in standard form (4.48). If in fact it was such a problem so expressed and if it was solved using the simplex method, it would be expected (Section 4.4.4) that at optimality, X_o and five of the other X_{ij} decision variables would exceed zero i.e. form the basis. Interestingly enough, this is indeed the case (Table 3.5) : furthermore, recall (Section 3.3.2) that the northwest corner stepping stone method proceeds from the outset in such a way as to assume implicitly that this will be the case.

A further similarity between the northwest corner stepping stone calculations and the simplex method can be seen by noting the solutions at successive iterations of the former. Specifically (Table 3.4) the first iteration solution is:

$$X_o = 435; \ X_{11} = 20; \ X_{21} = 25; \ X_{22} = 10; \ X_{32} = 20; \ X_{33} = 30$$
$$X_{12}, X_{13}, X_{23}, X_{31} = 0 \qquad \text{---- (4.87)}$$

while the second iteration solution is:

$$X_o = 375; \ X_{11} = 20; \ X_{21} = 5; \ X_{22} = 30; \ X_{31} = 20; \ X_{33} = 30$$
$$X_{12}, X_{13}, X_{23}, X_{32} = 0 \qquad \text{---- (4.88)}$$

Note that one variable of positive value in the solution (4.87) has become zero in the solution (4.88) - X_{32} - while another variable of zero value in the solution (4.87) has become positive in (4.88) - X_{31}. This is equivalent to what occurs in a change of basis operation in the simplex method. Finally, recall in the case of the northwest corner stepping stone method how the decision was made as to which route should accept a flow : the route chosen was that with the largest associated savings value i.e. that associated with the water cell of largest positive shadow cost value. Again, there is a parallel with the simplex method where, in the case of a minimisation problem the variable chosen to enter the basis is that with the largest positive coefficient in the X_o row of the current tableau.

We now demonstrate that the northwest corner stepping stone and simplex methods are in fact equivalent to each other.

129

Consider the initial solution to the transportation problem (4.87) as given in Table 3.4. The variables X_o, X_{11}, X_{21}, X_{22}, X_{32}, X_{33} are positive and thus, in a sense, form the basis. If this solution was to be presented as a simplex tableau the format of the equations (4.86) would have to be:

BASIS	X_o	X_{11}	X_{12}	X_{13}	X_{21}	X_{22}	X_{23}	X_{31}	X_{32}	X_{33}	SOL.	RAT.
X_o	①	0	*	*	0	0	*	*	0	0	*	
X_{11}	0	①	*	*	0	0	*	*	0	0	*	
X_{22}	0	0	*	*	0	①	*	*	0	0	*	
X_{33}	0	0	*	*	0	0	*	*	0	①	*	
X_{21}	0	0	*	*	①	0	*	*	0	0	*	
X_{32}	0	0	*	*	0	0	*	*	①	0	*	

where * is any number. Quite obviously the equations (4.86) are not in this format but they could be easily so converted by judicious use of the operations described in Section 4.4.2. The reader should check that this yields the tableau:

BASIS	X_o	X_{11}	X_{12}	X_{13}	X_{21}	X_{22}	X_{23}	X_{31}	X_{32}	X_{33}	SOL.	RAT.
X_o	①	0	-2	0	0	0	1	3	0	0	435	
X_{11}	0	①	1	1	0	0	0	0	0	0	20	∞
X_{22}	0	0	1	1	0	①	1	-1	0	0	10	-ve
X_{33}	0	0	0	1	0	0	1	0	0	①	30	∞
X_{21}	0	0	-1	-1	①	0	0	1	0	0	25	25
X_{32}	0	0	0	-1	0	0	-1	☐1	①	0	20	20

which indeed does correspond to the initial solution in Table 3.4. Notice too that the coefficients of the non-basis variables in X_o row correspond to the shadow costs obtained for the water cells in the northwest corner stepping stone method. Thus the numerical information in the tableau replicates that in the initial solution table in every respect. Choosing the variable with the largest positive value in the X_o row to enter the basis (X_{31}) and calculating the relevant ratio demonstrates that X_{32} is the variable to leave. Pivotting on the required coefficient (squared) yields:

BASIS	X_o	X_{11}	X_{12}	X_{13}	X_{21}	X_{22}	X_{23}	X_{31}	X_{32}	X_{33}	SOL.
X_o	①	0	-2	3	0	0	4	-3	0	0	375
X_{11}	0	①	1	1	0	0	0	0	0	0	20
X_{22}	0	0	1	0	0	①	0	0	0	0	30
X_{33}	0	0	0	-1	0	0	1	0	0	①	30
X_{21}	0	0	-1	0	①	0	1	0	-1	0	5
X_{31}	0	0	0	-1	0	0	-1	①	1	0	20

which corresponds to the first iteration solution in Table 3.4
thereby demonstrating that the simplex method replicates the
results obtained using the northwest corner stepping stone
approach. The reader is invited to complete the simplex calculations checking that the results obtained at each stage do
indeed correspond to the successive iterations in Table 3.4.

4.9   SPECIAL CASES

Up to this, it has been assumed that for any linear programming problem comprising n decision variables and m constraints
thereby generating a total of (m + n + 1) variables in the
standard form formulation, a unique optimal solution exists in
which exactly (m + 1) of the (m + n + 1) variables exceed zero.
Some situations in which this turns out not to be the case are
now described and their implications for the simplex solution
approach discussed.

4.9.1   Alternative Optimal Solutions

Reconsider the housebuilder problem introduced in Section 4.3
and suppose that the two housetypes sell for £40,000 and
£60,000 respectively. This yields the revised problem:

$$
\begin{aligned}
\text{Maximise}: \quad & 4X_1 + 6X_2 & &)\\
\text{s.t.} \quad & 2X_1 + 3X_2 \leq 600 & &)\\
& X_1 + X_2 \leq 225 & &) \qquad \text{----(4.89)}\\
& 5X_1 + 4X_2 \leq 1000 & &)\\
& X_1 \geq 0; \; X_2 \geq 0 & &)
\end{aligned}
$$

The graphical solution is depicted in Figure 4.6. As can be
seen, the slope of the profit line is such that it touches an
outer line segment of the solution space (A_1S) rather than a

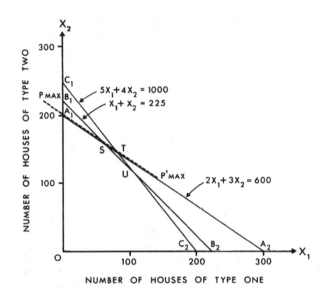

Figure 4.6 Alternative Optimal Solutions

single point. Thus any values of $(X_1 X_2)$ which plot on this line segment will achieve the maximum return i.e. there is a set of alternative optimal solutions.

In order to see how this situation may be identified *via* the simplex method, consider the initial tableau for (4.89):

BASIS	X_o	X_1	X_2	S_1	S_2	S_3	SOLUTION	RATIO
X_o	①	-4	-6	0	0	0	0	
S_1	0	2	③	①	0	0	600	600/3
S_2	0	1	1	0	①	0	225	225/1
S_3	0	5	4	0	0	①	1000	1000/1

On the first iteration, X_2 enters the basis while S_1 leaves which yields:

BASIS	X_o	X_1	X_2	S_1	S_2	S_3 .	SOLUTION	RATIO
X_o	①	0	0	2	0	0	1200	
X_2	0	2/3	①	1/3	0	0	200	200.3/2
S_2	0	[1/3]	0	-1/3	①	0	25	25.3
S_3	0	7/3	0	-4/3	0	①	200	200.3/7

which corresponds to the point A_1 in Figure 4.6. Scanning
across the X_o row, there are no negative values which suggests
that the optimal solution has been reached. Notice however
that one of the non-basis variables, X_1, has a coefficient of
zero in the X_o row which indicates that while permitting this
variable to enter the basis will not effect an improvement in
the current solution, there will be no deterioration either.
Permitting the relevant change of basis operation yields:

BASIS	X_o	X_1	X_2	S_1	S_2	S_3	SOLUTION	RATIO
X_o	①	0	0	2	0	0	1200	
X_2	0	0	①	1	-2	0	150	
X_1	0	①	0	-1	3	0	75	
S_3	0	0	0	1	-7	①	25	

which corresponds to the point S in Figure 4.6. Notice that,
as expected, the value of X_o in this solution is still 1200.
Note also that the non-basis variable S_2 now has a coefficient
of zero in the X_o row. If it were permitted to enter the
basis, the first iteration simplex tableau would be obtained
once more. Thus these two solutions, together with all those
occurring on the line segment joining them are equally optimal.
    To summarise, the presence of alternative optimal solut-
ions can be recognised in the simplex method through the
existence of zero values for non-basis variables in the X_o row
of the initial optimal solution; the range of equally optimal
solutions may be seen by permitting the non-basis variables
with associated zero coefficients to enter the current basis.
    Recall how the recognition and identification of
alternative optima in the case of the transportation problem
was carried out (Section 3.3.6): a water cell with an associated shadow cost of zero at optimality suggested the existence
of alternative optimal solutions which were duly calculated by
permitting a flow in the water cell concerned. The method of
recognition and calculation is in effect exactly the same here

133

thereby demonstrating once more the equivalence of the simplex
and northwest corner stepping stone methods.

As was mentioned in Section 3.3.6, the full identification of alternative optimal solutions (e.g. a range of equally
desirable landuse sets in an urban, recreational or agricultural context) should they exist, is of immense practical
importance for they offer the planner leeway in terms of the
final recommended plan. They can also permit considerations
not included explicitly in the objective to be taken into
account. Miller (1963) in an application of the model (4.31)-
(4.34) to aircraft movements in the United States encountered
alternative optimal solutions. For one run of the model
dealing with four aircraft types - Boeing 707, Boeing 720,
Lockheed Electra and Viscount - operating a route system
encompassing New York, Chicago, Miami, Los Angeles, Washington,
San Francisco, Detroit and Boston in 1963 and assuming a 95
per cent occupany rate of aircraft, it was found that Boeing
707 or Boeing 720 aircraft could equally well be allocated to
the New York to Chicago route. Faced with this range of
possible solutions, an airline company might choose the actual
solution e.g. to fly Boeing 707 aircraft on the basis of
factors not accounted for directly by the model e.g. prestige.

4.9.2 Degeneracy

As defined in Section 3.3.6, the term degenerate applies to a
linear programming solution in which the number of zero valued
variables is greater than expected. Recall again (Section
4.4.4) that in the case of a linear programming problem
involving n decision variables and m constraints, it is to be
expected that at optimality, X_0 and m of the other variables
(decisions and slacks) will have non-zero values. Degeneracy
thus occurs when fewer than m of these variables have non-zero
values. In terms of the optimal solution, degeneracy causes
no problems of interpretation. However, as will be discussed
in the next chapter, the presence of a degenerate optimal
solution does cause difficulties when interpreting certain
other aspects of a linear programming problem.

In order to see how degeneracy may be recognised and
dealt with *via* the simplex method, consider the revised housebuilder problem:

$$
\begin{aligned}
\text{Maximise :} \quad & 3X_1 + 4X_2 \\
& 2X_1 + 3X_2 \leq 600 \\
& X_1 + X_2 \leq 225 \\
& 3X_1 + 5X_2 \leq 1000 \\
& X_1 \geq 0 \; ; \; X_2 \geq 0
\end{aligned}
\qquad ---- \ (4.90)
$$

the solution space for which is depicted in Figure 4.7. The

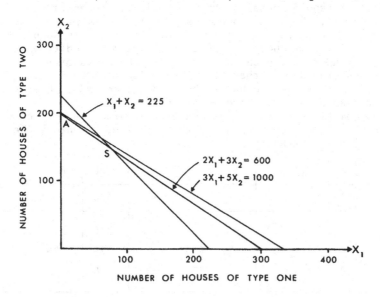

Figure 4.7 Degeneracy

initial simplex tableau is:

BASIS	X_o	X_1	X_2	S_1	S_2	S_3	SOL.	RAT.
X_o	①	-3	-4	0	0	0	0	
S_1	0	2	③	①	0	0	600	600.1/3
S_2	0	1	1	0	①	0	225	225.1
S_3	0	3	5	0	0	①	1000	1000.1/5

X_2 is the variable to enter the basis. Both S_1 and S_3 tie as candidates to leave. Abritrarily choosing S_1 yields:

BASIS	X_o	X_1	X_2	S_1	S_2	$-S_3$	SOL.	RAT.
X_o	①	-1/3	0	4/3	0	0	800	
X_2	0	2/3	①	1/3	0	0	200	200.3/2
S_2	0	1/3	0	-1/3	①	0	25	25.3
S_3	0	-1/3	0	-5/3	0	①	0	0

135

Note that in this solution, S_3, in addition to the non-basis variables X_1 and S_1 equals zero which signals degeneracy. Geometrically, the solution corresponds to the point A in Figure 4.7. Because the first and third constraints happen to meet at this point, both S_1 and S_3 equal zero in addition to X_1. The reader should check that if, on the basis of the ratios associated with the initial solution tableau S_3 had been forced to leave the basis then, in the revised table, the basis variable S_1 would have equalled zero.

Mathematically, the existence of degeneracy in this case need cause no problem. On the next iteration, X_1 enters the basis while S_3 leaves to yield:

BASIS	X_o	X_1	X_2	S_1	S_2	S_3	SOL.	RAT.
X_o	①	0	0	3	0	-1	800	
X_2	0	0	①	-3	0	2	200	200.1/2
S_2	0	0	0	-2	①	☐1	25	25
X_1	0	①	0	5	0	-3	0	-ve

This solution is still degenerate and still refers to the point A. However, on the next iteration S_3 enters the basis and S_2 leaves, which yields:

BASIS	X_o	X_1	X_2	S_1	S_2	S_3	SOL.	RAT.
X_o	①	0	0	1	1	0	825	
X_2	0	0	①	1	-2	0	150	
S_3	0	0	0	-2	1	①	25	
X_1	0	①	0	-1	3	0	75	

which is the optimal solution and corresponds to S in Figure 4.7.

The preceding example demonstrates what is known as *temporary degeneracy* : although certain of the intermediate solutions encountered during the simplex process are degenerate, the optimal solution is not. The existence of a degenerate optimal solution is denoted by a tableau in which one or more of the basis variables are zero whilst all of the objective row coefficients of the non-basis variables exceed zero (maximisation) or are less than zero (minimisation).

In the case of the foregoing example, the presence of degeneracy caused no problem for the operation of the simplex method. In certain rare instances (which we do not elaborate on here), this is not the case : the solution process becomes 'stuck' generating successively the same intermediate degenerate solution with alternating basis variables. The technique used to avoid this involves altering the original problem by changing (a) chosen right hand side value(s) of (a) certain constraint(s) by an abritrarily small value, ε. It should be noted that this is similar to the approach used to deal with degeneracy in the case of the transportation problem (Section 3.3.6).

4.9.3 Constraint Contradiction

Consider the linear programming problem:

$$
\begin{aligned}
\text{MAXIMISE} : \quad & 3X_1 + 4X_2 & & \\
\text{s.t.} \quad & 2X_1 + 3X_2 & \leq\ & 600 \\
& X_1 + X_2 & \leq\ & 225 \\
& 5X_1 + 4X_2 & \leq\ & 1000 \\
& 2X_1 + X_2 & \geq\ & 500 \\
& X_1 = X_2 \geq 0 &
\end{aligned}
\qquad \text{----(4.91)}
$$

The solution space for the first three constraints is as shown in Figure 4.1(b). However, the additional fourth constraint requires that the solution lies above the line:

$$2X_1 + X_2 = 100$$

i.e. the line joining $(0,100)$ and $(50,0)$ which, in terms of the first three constraints, is obviously impossible. The constraints thus contradict one another; there is no solution space and no optimal solution.

In order to see how this situation may be recognised *via* the simplex method, proceed as in Section 4.6 to introduce an additional variable R_4 associated with the final constraint which yields the revised problem:

$$
\begin{aligned}
\text{MAXIMISE} : \quad & 3X_1 + 4X_2 - MR_4 & & \\
\text{s.t.} \quad & 2X_1 + 3X_2 & \leq\ & 600 \\
& X_1 + X_2 & \leq\ & 225 \\
& 5X_1 + 4X_2 & \leq\ & 1000 \\
& 2X_1 + X_2 + R_4 & \geq\ & 500 \\
& X_1 \geq 0\ ;\ X_2 \geq 0 &
\end{aligned}
\qquad \text{----(4.92)}
$$

Incorporating slack variables and adjusting to create zero values in the X_o row for each basis variable yields:

137

BASIS	X_o	X_1	X_2	S_4	S_1	S_2	S_3	R_4	SOL.	RAT.
X_o	①	$-3-2M$	$-4-M$	M	0	0	0	0	$-500M$	
S_1	0	2	3	0	①	0	0	0	600	$600.1/2$
S_2	0	1	1	0	0	①	0	0	225	225
S_3	0	$\boxed{5}$	4	0	0	0	①	0	1000	$1000.1/5$
R_4	0	2	1	-1	0	0	0	①	500	$500.1/2$

X_1 is the variable to enter the basis with S_3 leaving which yields :

BASIS	X_o	X_1	X_2	S_4	S_1	S_2	S_3	R_4	SOL.
X_o	①	0	$-8/5+3/5M$	M	0	0	$3/5+2/5M$	0	$600-100M$
S_1	0	0	$7/5$	0	①	0	$-2/5$	0	200
S_2	0	0	$1/5$	0	0	①	$-1/5$	0	25
X_1	0	①	$4/5$	0	0	0	$1/5$	0	200
R_1	0	0	$-3/5$	-1	0	0	$-2/5$	①	100

i.e. Basis variables : $X_o=600-100M$; $X_1= 200$: $S_1= 200$; $S_2= 25$; $R_1= 100$

Non-basis
  variables   : $X_2= S_3= S_4 = 0$

By virtue of positive coefficients in the X_o row, this is in fact the optimal solution. Note that in this instance the variable R_4, introduced in such a way as to apparently ensure its disappearance, is in fact in the final basis which causes the optimal value of R_4 to be a large negative number. In general, it can be shown that whenever one or more R_i variable occurs in the basis of a final solution to a linear programming problem, the problem actually involves a constraint contradiction. Thus there is in fact no optimal solution.

The existence of contradictions within constraints is one that is often encountered in actual linear programming applications. Indeed, in many real world applications, the major purpose of the first run of a linear programming model is to see whether the various constraints do indeed permit a solution. Consider once again the regional economy problem discussed in Section 4.2.2. The constraints (4.15) require that certain demands for products be met and are of the 'greater than or equals' type; conversely, the constraints (4.17) require that certain resources are not overused and are thus in effect of the 'less than or equals' type. In the case of a situation where the demands are such as cannot be supplied given the resources available, the constraint sets (4.15) and (4.17) will contradict and R_i variables will appear in the final basis solution to (4.14)-(4.18). One example of this occurring within the foregoing methodological framework is described by Jenkins and Robson (1974) who attempt to determine the least cost construction programme for houses, roads, educational facilities, shopping etc. which will meet a number of targets e.g. concerning employment provided, population catered for, housing and services supplied whilst not overusing current resources e.g. workers available. On initial runs of the model, the constraints turned out to contradict one another i.e. the targets set were unachieveable given the resources available. Jenkins and Robson proceed to relax the targets until a feasible solution (which is discussed in further detail in Section 5.3) emerges.

4.9.4 Infinite Solution Space

Consider the linear programming solution space formed by the constraints:

$$X_1 - X_2 \leq 100 \quad)$$
$$X_1 \qquad \leq 300 \quad) \qquad \text{---- (4.93)}$$
$$X_1 \geq 0; \; X_2 \geq 0 \quad)$$

Unlike the solution space associated with all of the problems considered so far, that associated with this problem (Figure 4.8) is not completely enclosed which suggests that for certain objectives, the optimal solution will lie at infinity. Specifically, in the present case, if the objective is:

$$\text{MAXIMISE} : 2X_1 - X_2 \qquad \text{---- (4.94)}$$

the solution lies at A; whereas in the case of:

$$\text{MAXIMISE} : 2X_1 + X_2 \qquad \text{---- (4.95)}$$

it lies at infinity.
   Within the context of the simplex method, the existence of an infinite solution space and a check of whether the corresponding optimal solution lies at infinity can be carried out as follows. First, in the case of (4.94), (4.93), the

139

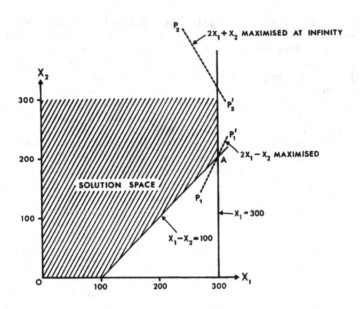

Figure 4.8 Infinite Solution Space

initial simplex tableau is :

BASIS	X_o	X_1	X_2	S_1	S_2	SOL.	RATIO
X_o	①	-2	1	0	0	0	
S_1	0	1	0	①	0	300	300
S_2	0	☐ 1 -1		0	①	100	100

Note that unlike any problem treated so far, the coefficients
of one of the decision variables (X_2) in the constraint rows
are all equal to or less than zero. This signifies that the
solution space is open ended in terms of this variable, i.e.
X_2 can increase to infinity. In general, for any decision
variable X_1, ..., X_n at any stage of the solution process,
if the constraint row coefficients associated with that
variable are all less than or equal to zero, that variable
may increase to infinity; the situation happens to occur in
the initial tableau in the case of this particular example.
    Given the finding that X_2 may increase to infinity, it
should be checked immediately as to whether X_2 equals infinity
comprises the optimal solution. Substituting X_2 equals
infinity in (4.94) yields the solution:

$$X_o = - \infty$$

which, given that the objective involves maximisation, is obviously not the optimal solution. Thus the simplex process continues in the normal manner. Notice however that in the case of the objective (4.95), substituting X_o equals infinity yields:

$$X_o = \infty$$

which, in this case, obviously does comprise the optimal solution.

5

LINEAR PROGRAMMING : SENSITIVITY
ANALYSIS AND THE DUAL

5.1 SENSITIVITY ANALYSIS

The last chapter discussed methods by which the optimal
solution to any linear programming problem can be obtained.
Very often, within the context of an actual problem and once
this solution has been determined, we wish to investigate how
(if at all) it alters for given changes in the original formulation e.g. in certain of the coefficients of the objective
and/or the right hand sides of given constraints. The conduct
of such an investigation is referred to as *sensitivity
analysis*.

   For a particular linear programming problem, sensitivity
analysis can obviously provide answers to questions of immense
practical importance. The landuse design planner for example
is always extremely interested in the effect on his current
plan of (say) altering various of the planning requirements
as (say) expressed by   constraints of the type (4.8). An
individual farmer will be most anxious to assess how his
production pattern should change in the event of given alterations in the per unit prices he receives for various outputs
i.e. for given changes in the objective coefficients of (4.21).
In the case of an economy, central government would certainly
wish to assess the effect on the total production required of
each sector of a given technological change in a particular
sector which would alter its demands from the other sectors
i.e. alter the coefficients of the constraint relating to
that sector (Section 4.2.2).

   From a mathematical point of view, an obvious way in
which the effect of given changes in a   given problem
could be calculated would be to reformulate it and re-solve it
using the methods of the previous chapter. The major disadvantage is that this is time consuming especially if the
effect of a large number of different changes to the original
problem are to be evaluated in turn. We thus seek ways by
which sensitivity analyses can be conducted without completely

DOI: 10.4324/9781003179030-5   143 re-solving the problem. A major advantage of the simplex method and, in particular, of the format of the optimal solution tableau it produces is that the sensitivity of this solution to changes of various types can be assessed relatively easily.

For a particular linear programming problem and its optimal solution, five major types of question concerning the sensitivity of this solution may be asked namely, how would it change if :

(i) The right hand sides of certain of the constraints (b_i values in (4.2)) in the original problem change in a specified manner

(ii) The coefficients of the objective (c_i values in (4.1)) in the original problem change in a specified manner

(iii) The coefficients of certain of the constraints (a_{ij} values in (4.2)) in the original problem change in a specified manner

(iv) A new activity enters the original problem

(v) A new constraint enters the original problem.

Mathematical methods by which each of the questions (i)-(v) can be answered solely by reference to the original problem and to its optimal solution tableau are now discussed. The overall approach is the same for each case: first, a check is made to see if the proposed change in the original problem is such as to cause the current optimal solution to alter; if it is, the revised solution is then calculated.

5.2 THREE MATHEMATICAL PROPERTIES

Three mathematical properties of simplex tableaux which together permit the sensitivity questions posed in the previous section to be investigated relatively easily are now stated without proof. In order to dmonstrate these properties, consider the linear programming problem:

$$\text{MAXIMISE} : 3X_1 + 4X_2 + 2X_3$$

$$\text{s.t.} \quad \left. \begin{array}{rcl} 2X_1 + 3X_2 + 5X_3 & \leq & 600 \\ X_1 + X_2 + X_3 & \leq & 225 \\ 5X_1 + 4X_2 + 4X_3 & \leq & 1000 \\ X_1 \geq 0 \; ; \; X_2 \geq 0 \; ; \; X_3 \geq 0 \end{array} \right\} \quad \text{---- (5.1)}$$

This is in fact the housebuilder problem (4.36)-(4.40) with the possibility of building a third housetype incorporated. The final solution tableau is :

BASIS	X_o	X_1	X_2	X_3	S_1	S_2	S_3	SOL.
X_o	①	0	0	4	1	1	0	825
X_2	0	0	①	3	1	-2	0	150
X_1	0	①	0	-2	-1	3	0	75
S_3	0	0	0	2	1	-7	①	25

Notice that the final solution is the same as before (Section 4.3). The properties of the third housetype are such that it is not part of the optimal solution; X_3 is not in the final basis and there is a positive value (four) in the X_3 column of the X_o row. Notice also that as before, the first two constraints are fully satisfied at optimality ($S_1 = S_2 = 0$) whereas the third is not ($S_3 = 25$). For convenience in what follows, the formulation (4.36)-(4.40) will be referred to as the *original housebuilder problem* while the formulation (5.1) will be referred to as the *revised housebuilder problem*.

For any simplex solution tableau, we refer to the readings in the X_o row and in the columns beneath the initial basis variables with M set to zero as *the simplex multipliers*. Recall the final solution tableau for the problem solved in Section 4.6.3:

BASIS	Y_o	Y_1	Y_2	Y_3	S_1	S_2	S_3	R_1	R_2	R_3	SOL.
Y_o	①	0	0	-25	-75	-150	0	75-M	150-M	0	825
S_1	0	0	0	-2	2	-3	①	-2	3	-1	4
Y_1	0	①	0	-1	1	-1	0	-1	1	0	1
Y_2	0	0	①	0	-3	2	0	3	-2	0	1

The initial basis was R_1, R_2, R_3. The values in the X_o row

145

and beneath these variables with M =0 are 75, 150, 0 which are therefore the simplex multipliers. The simplex multipliers associated with the optimal solution tableau of the revised housebuilder problem are 1, 1, 0. By convention, the simplex multipliers are usually represented by a column matrix*. Thus, the two preceding sets of multipliers are:

$$
\begin{pmatrix} 75 \\ \\ 150 \\ \\ 0 \end{pmatrix} \quad \text{and} \quad \begin{pmatrix} 1 \\ \\ 1 \\ \\ 0 \end{pmatrix} \quad \text{respectively.}
$$

In addition to the matrix of simplex multipliers, we can define an m X m matrix comprising the values in the constraint rows and beneath the simplex multipliers. Referring to this matrix as A, we have for the problem of Section 4.6.3 :

$$
A = \begin{pmatrix} -2 & 3 & -1 \\ -1 & 1 & 0 \\ 3 & -2 & 0 \end{pmatrix}
$$

and for the revised housebuilder problem:

$$
A = \begin{pmatrix} 1 & -2 & 0 \\ -1 & 3 & 0 \\ 1 & -7 & 1 \end{pmatrix}
$$

Given for any simplex solution tableau the matrix of simplex multipliers and the matrix A, it can be shown that the following properties will always hold true:

PROPERTY ONE

$$
A \cdot \begin{pmatrix} \text{Initial Constraint Right} \\ \text{Hand Sides Expressed as} \\ \text{A Column Matrix} \end{pmatrix} = \begin{pmatrix} \text{Current Values} \\ \text{of Basis Variables} \end{pmatrix}
$$

Thus in the case of the problem of Section 4.6.3 :

$$
\begin{pmatrix} -2 & 3 & -1 \\ -1 & 1 & 0 \\ 3 & -2 & 0 \end{pmatrix} \begin{pmatrix} 3 \\ 4 \\ 2 \end{pmatrix} \overset{\checkmark}{=} \begin{pmatrix} 4 \\ 1 \\ 1 \end{pmatrix}
$$

---

*For a summary of matrix algebra, see Appendix A.1

Linear Programming : Sensitivity Analysis and the Dual

and for the revised housebuilder problem:

$$\begin{pmatrix} 1 & -2 & 0 \\ -1 & 3 & 0 \\ 1 & -7 & 1 \end{pmatrix} \begin{pmatrix} 600 \\ 225 \\ 1000 \end{pmatrix} \leqq \begin{pmatrix} 150 \\ 75 \\ 25 \end{pmatrix}$$

PROPERTY TWO

$$A \cdot \begin{pmatrix} \text{Coefficients in} \\ \text{Column } j \text{ of} \\ \text{Initial Tableau} \end{pmatrix} = \begin{pmatrix} \text{Coefficients in} \\ \text{Column } j \text{ of} \\ \text{Current Tableau} \end{pmatrix}$$

Thus for column X_1 of the revised householder problem:

$$\begin{pmatrix} 1 & -2 & 0 \\ -1 & 3 & 0 \\ 1 & -7 & 1 \end{pmatrix} \begin{pmatrix} 2 \\ 1 \\ 5 \end{pmatrix} = \begin{pmatrix} 0 \\ 1 \\ 0 \end{pmatrix}$$

and again, for column X_3:

$$\begin{pmatrix} 1 & -2 & 0 \\ -1 & 3 & 0 \\ 1 & -7 & 1 \end{pmatrix} \begin{pmatrix} 5 \\ 1 \\ 4 \end{pmatrix} = \begin{pmatrix} 3 \\ -2 \\ 2 \end{pmatrix}$$

PROPERTY THREE

(Coefficients in the) (Simplex   )   (Coeff. in) (Coeff.)
(ith Column of initial) (Multipliers) − (ith Col.) = (in ith)
(Tableau Expressed as)   (of X Row)   (Col. of)
(a Row Matrix   )   (of Init-) (X Row)
                                        (ial Tabl.) (of   )
                                                     (Current)
                                                     (Tableau)

Thus for the X_2 column of the revised housebuilder problem:

$$(3 \quad 1 \quad 4) \begin{pmatrix} 1 \\ 1 \\ 0 \end{pmatrix} + (-4) = (0)$$

while for the X_3 column :

147

$$(5 \quad 1 \quad 4) \begin{pmatrix} 1 \\ 1 \\ 0 \end{pmatrix} + (-2) \overset{\checkmark}{=} (4)$$

Finally, for the Y_3 column of the problem solved in Section 4.6.3,

$$(5 \quad 4 \quad 4) \begin{pmatrix} 75 \\ 150 \\ 0 \end{pmatrix} + (-1000) \overset{\checkmark}{=} (-25)$$

5.3 CHANGES IN RIGHT HAND SIDE COEFFICIENTS

Reconsider the original housebuilder problem as depicted in Figure 4.1, i.e.

$$
\begin{aligned}
\text{Maximise : } & 3X_1 + 4X_2 \\
\text{s.t.} \quad & 2X_1 + 3X_2 \leq 600 \\
& X_1 + X_2 \leq 225 \\
& 5X_1 + 4X_2 \leq 1000 \\
& X_1 \geq 0; \ X_2 \geq 0
\end{aligned}
\qquad \text{---- (5.2)}
$$

Suppose now that the right hand side of the first constraint is 601 i.e. that an additional 1/20 acre of land is available to the housebuilder. How would the optimal solution change? Graphically, the effect of the revised right hand side in the first constraint would be to move the constraint line A_1A_2 in Figure 5.1 slightly further outwards from the origin. The optimal solution would occur at the junction of the lines:

$$2X_1 + 3X_2 = 601$$
$$X_1 + X_2 = 225$$

i.e. at : $X_1 = 74$; $X_2 = 151$. The value of the objective associated with this point is given by:

$$X_o = (3)(74) + (4)(151) = 826$$

The foregoing calculations thus demonstrate that should 1/20 acre of additional land become available, the housebuilder should build one less house of Type One and one more house of Type Two; overall, his total return will increase by one money unit i.e. £10,000. It can thus be said that from the housebuilder's point of view, the 'worth' of an additional unit of land is one money unit. Viewed in yet another way, it can be said that the builder should be prepared to pay up to one

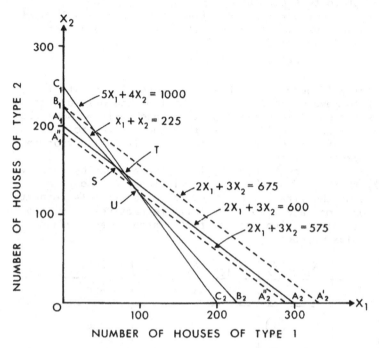

Figure 5.1 Revised Housebuilder Problem

money unit i.e. £10,000 in order to obtain and develop one extra unit i.e. 1/20 acre of land.

Consider now how the solution to (5.2) changes if the right hand side of the second constraint increases by one. The revised optimal solution lies at the junction of the lines:

$$2X_1 + 3X_2 = 600$$

$$X_1 + X_2 = 226$$

and is:

$$X_0 = 826; \quad X_1 = 78; \quad X_2 = 148$$

Thus if one additional house was permitted in the development, the housebuilder should construct three more houses of Type One and two less of Type Two thereby increasing his total return by one money unit. Thus the 'worth' to the builder of permission to construct one extra house is one money unit; he would presumably be prepared to pay up to one money unit in order to obtain this permission.

Finally, consider how the optimal solution to (5.2) would change if the development was permitted to house one extra person i.e. if the third constraint was:

$$5X_1 + 4X_2 \leq 1001$$

Geometrically (Figure 5.1), this would cause the constraint line C_1C_2 to move slightly further out from the origin; the optimal solution would still lie at S whose position would be unchanged. Thus it could be said that the 'worth' to the housebuilder of permission to house one additional person in the development is zero.

To summarise the foregoing, it has been found by re-solving (5.2) that the 'worth' of a unit increase in the right hand sides of the first, second and third constraints respectively is one, one and zero money units respectively. Consider now the optimal solution tableau to the problem as produced by the simplex method:

BASIS	X_o	X_1	X_2	S_1	S_2	S_3	SOL.
X_o	(1)	0	0	1	1	0	825
X_2	0	0	(1)	1	-2	0	150
X_1	0	(1)	0	-1	3	0	75
S_3	0	0	0	1	7	(1)	25

and note in particular the values of the simplex multipliers; they are one, one and zero respectively. Thus in the case of this example at least, the simplex multipliers give the sensitivity of X_o to unit changes in the right hand sides of the corresponding constraints. In fact, it can be shown mathematically that this will always be the case. Thus the simplex method is such as to yield information concerning the first type of sensitivity question posed in the previous section directly *via* the optimal solution tableau.

It should be noted that the interpretation of the simplex multipliers in terms of the 'worth' of a unit change in the right hand side of the corresponding constraints matches the expected format of the optimal simplex solution tableau in a logical manner. In the case of a maximisation problem and for a constraint which is fully utilised at optimality, the slack variable associated with that constraint equals zero; thus the slack variable will not be in the final basis and will therefore have a positive associated simplex multiplier i.e. a positive associated 'worth' which one would indeed expect in the case of 'resource' which is fully used.

Linear Programming : Sensitivity Analysis and the Dual

Conversely, for a constraint which is not fully utilised at optimality, the corresponding slack variable will be in the basis of the final solution tableau and will therefore have a zero associated simplex multiplier i.e. a zero associated 'worth' which again, one would indeed expect in the case of a 'resource' of which there is a surplus. A similar interpretation applies in the case of a minimisation problem. Here, however, each of the simplex multipliers will be zero or negative at optimality and will give the amount by which X_o will decrease for a unit decrease in each constraint right hand side. For reasons to be discussed later, simplex multipliers are often referred to as *shadow prices* or *dual variable values*. The reader may recall that these terms were also introduced in the context of the transportation problem (Section 3.3.4).

We now draw attention to an important condition which must be attached to the foregoing interpretation of the simplex multipliers. Reconsider the problem (5.1) and what happens to the optimal solution value X_o as the right hand side value of the first constraint increases continuously i.e. as the acreage available for development becomes greater and greater. Geometrically (Figure 5.1), this is equivalent to assessing how the location of the optimal solution point S moves as the constraint line A_1A_2 moves further and further away from the origin. As this occurs, the point S moves along the line segment A_1S with, as expected, X_o increasing by one unit for each unit increase in the right hand side of the constraint. Eventually with:

$$2X_1 + 3X_2 = 675$$

the constraint line occupies the position B_1A_2' and the optimal solution is:

$$X_o = 1000; \quad X_1 = 0; \quad X_2 = 225$$

Now consider what would happen if the available acreage increased further thus removing the constraint line $B_1 A_2'$ yet further from the origin. The optimal solution would remain at B_1 being constrained by the X_2 axis and the second constraint and would be of the form:

$$X_o = 1000; \quad X_1 = 0; \quad X_2 = 225$$

$$S_1 > 0 \quad ; \quad S_2 = 0 \quad S_3 > 0$$

$S_1 > 0$ implies that the solution is no longer constrained by the first constraint; thus, once the acreage available exceeds 675 units the 'worth' of additional units of acreage falls to zero. At this point, the basis of the optimal solution changes with X_1 leaving and S_3 entering.

151

Consider now how the optimal solution to (5.2) changes as the acreage available to the housebuilder decreases i.e. as the right hand side of the first constraint becomes smaller Just as the 'worth' of a unit increase in acreage is one money unit, it is to be expected that the 'cost' of a unit decrease in acreage is one money unit which indeed turns out to be the case. Geometrically, as A_1A_2 moves closer to the origin, the optimal solution moves along the line segment SU with X_0 decreasing by one for each unit decrease in acreage. Eventually, with the total available acreage at 575 $(A_1''A_2'')$, the optimal solution lies at U for which:

$$X_0 = 800; \quad X_1 = 100; \quad X_2 = 125$$

Now if the acreage available decreases further, the optimal solution moves along the line segment UC_2 being constrained by the first and third constraints. The form of the solution is thus:

$$X_0 > 0; \quad X_1 > 0; \quad X_2 > 0$$

$$S_1 = 0; \quad S_2 > 0; \quad S_3 = 0$$

Once again, the basis has changed (S_2 entering; S_3 leaving) and so too therefore have the simplex multipliers. For each unit decrease in acreage, the decrease in X_0 i.e. the relevant simplex multiplier is now 1 1/7.

To summarise the foregoing, it has been shown graphically that 'worth' of a unit of acreage in the current optimal solution as indicated by the relevant simplex multiplier is one and that this remains valid provided the total acreage available lies between 575 and 675 and, of course, the other constraints are unchanged; once the acreage available to the housebuilder passes outside these limits, the basis of the optimal solution together with the simplex multipliers changes. The general implication of this for interpreting an optimal solution simplex tableau is that *the foregoing sensitivity interpretation of simplex multipliers remains valid only within the range of right side values of the corresponding constraint for which the current solution basis remains unchanged.* We now show how this range can be determined mathematically.

Reconsider the problem (5.2) with the right hand side of the second constraint written as:

$$2X_1 + 3X_2 \leq 600 + \Delta_1 \qquad\qquad ---- (5.3)$$

It has been shown graphically that the current basis and simplex multipliers remain valid within the range:

$$-25 \leq \Delta_1 \leq 75 \qquad\qquad ---- (5.4)$$

Consider now the first property of Section 5.2. Writing the first constraint of (5.2) in the form (5.3), the property yields:

$$\begin{pmatrix} 1 & -2 & 0 \\ -1 & 3 & 0 \\ 1 & -7 & 1 \end{pmatrix} \begin{pmatrix} 600 + \Delta_1 \\ 225 \\ 1000 \end{pmatrix} = \begin{pmatrix} \Delta_1 + 150 \\ -\Delta_1 + 75 \\ \Delta_1 + 25 \end{pmatrix} \qquad ---- (5.5)$$

Recalling that the right hand side of (5.5) gives the values of the current basis variables and recalling too that by definition, these values must remain positive if the current basis variables are to remain valid, Δ_1 must be such that:

$$\begin{array}{l} \Delta_1 + 150 \geq 0 \ \text{i.e.} \ \Delta_1 \geq -150 \\ -\Delta_1 + 75 \geq 0 \ \text{i.e.} \ \Delta_1 \leq 75 \\ \Delta_1 + 25 \geq 0 \ \text{i.e.} \ \Delta_1 \geq -25 \end{array} \qquad ---- (5.6)$$

Taking the conditions (5.6) together yields the overall condition:

$$-25 \leq \Delta_1 \leq 75 \qquad ---- (5.7)$$

which corresponds to (5.4).

Using the same methods to determine the range of values over which the right hand side of the second constraint (Δ_2) may vary without altering the basis yields:

$$\begin{pmatrix} 1 & -2 & 0 \\ -1 & -3 & 1 \\ 1 & -7 & 1 \end{pmatrix} \begin{pmatrix} 600 \\ 225 + \Delta_2 \\ 1000 \end{pmatrix} = \begin{pmatrix} 150 - 2\Delta_2 \\ 75 + 3\Delta_2 \\ 25 - 7\Delta_2 \end{pmatrix}$$

from which:

$$\begin{array}{l} 150 - 2\Delta_2 \geq 0 \quad \text{i.e.} \ \Delta_2 \leq 75 \\ 75 + 3\Delta_2 \geq 0 \qquad \quad \Delta_2 \geq -25 \\ 25 - 7\Delta_2 \geq 0 \qquad \quad \Delta_2 \leq 25/7 \end{array}$$

which gives the overall condition:

$$-25 \leq \Delta_2 \leq 25/7$$

i.e. provided the number of houses permitted within the development lies between 200 and 228 4/7 the nature of the optimal solution in terms of the current basis and simplex multipliers remains the same. The reader should check that for the right hand side of the third constraint, the range through which this can change without changing the optimal solution is :

$$\Delta_3 \geq -25$$

The foregoing methods provide a means of determining the interval over which each constraint right hand side can vary without altering the current solution basis. Consider now the task of determining the effect on the current optimal solution of a specific hypothesised change. Suppose, for example, that the first constraint in the initial house-builder problem is altered to :

$$2X_1 + 3X_2 \geq 650$$

How will this affect the optimal solution tableau as presented at the outset of this section? Applying Property One yields:

$$
\begin{pmatrix} 1 & -2 & 0 \\ & & \\ -1 & 3 & 0 \\ & & \\ 1 & -7 & 1 \end{pmatrix}
\begin{pmatrix} 650 \\ \\ 225 \\ \\ 1000 \end{pmatrix}
=
\begin{pmatrix} 200 \\ \\ 25 \\ \\ 75 \end{pmatrix}
$$

Note that as expected from (5.7), each of the revised solution values is positive which confirms that the current basis is still valid. The revised value of X_0 is 875 and the new solution tableau is:

BASIS	X_0	X_1	X_2	S_1	S_2	S_3	SOL.
X_0	①	0	0	1	1	0	875
X_2	0	0	①	1	-2	0	200
X_1	0	①	0	-1	3	0	25
S_3	0	0	0	1	-7	①	75

Suppose now that the first constraint in the initial housebuilder problem is:

$$2X_1 + 3X_2 \leq 700$$

Proceeding as before to use Property One to calculate the revised solution values yields:

$$
\begin{pmatrix} 1 & -2 & 0 \\ & & \\ -1 & 3 & 0 \\ & & \\ 1 & -7 & 1 \end{pmatrix} \begin{pmatrix} 700 \\ \\ 225 \\ \\ 1000 \end{pmatrix} = \begin{pmatrix} 250 \\ \\ -25 \\ \\ 125 \end{pmatrix}
$$

i.e. X_2 250; X_1 -25; S_3 125 from which X_o 925. The revised solution tableau is:

BASIS	X_o	X_1	X_2	S_1	S_2	S_3	SOL.
X_o	①	0	0	1	1	0	925
X_2	0	0	①	1	-2	0	250
X_1	0	①	0	[-1]	3	0	-25
S_3	0	0	0	1	-7	①	125
RATIO				1/-1	1/3		

Quite obviously, with X_1 negative, this solution is not feasible; the negative value for X_1 indicates that the current basis is no longer appropriate which could have been predicted in advance from (5.6).

Given that the current solution basis is no longer appropriate, we require a method for determining the revised basis and optimal solution. This can be achieved most easily *via* what is known as the *dual-simplex method* which, like the simplex method, operates *via* a (series of) change of basis operation(s). The rules for choosing the variables to leave/ enter the basis are as follows. First, choose as the variable to leave the basis that with the largest associated negative value in the solution column; in the case of a tie, choose either variable. Second, to choose the variable to enter the basis, calculate for each non-basis variable column in turn the ratio between the value in the X_o row and that in the row of the variable to leave the basis. Ignore ratios with zero or positive denominators. Choose as the variable to enter the basis that with the smallest associated ratio (minimisation) or with the smallest absolute value of the associated ratios (maximisation); in the case of a tie, choose either variable. If all of the denominators are zero or positive, the revised problem has no feasible solution.

Applying the dual-simplex rules to the foregoing tableau, X_1 leaves the basis and S_1 enters. Pivotting on the appropriate coefficient in the usual manner yields the revised optimal solution:

BASIS	X_o	X_1	X_2	S_1	S_2	S_3	SOL.
X_o	①	1	0	0	4	0	900
X_2	0	1	①	0	1	0	225
S_1	0	-1	0	①	-3	0	25
S_3	0	1	0	0	-4	①	100

which, as can be checked graphically, is the correct revised solution.

Two final points concerning the foregoing methods should be noted. First, in conjunction with an optimal solution simplex tableau, they permit any type of sensitivity question concerning constraint right hand sides to be answered without having to re-solve the problem 'from scratch'. This underlines the previously mentioned major advantage of the simplex method: the format of the final solution tableau is such as to enable sensitivity questions to be answered relatively easily. Second, it should be noted that the methods could be used equally readily to assess the effect on an optimal solution of simultaneous changes to a number of constraint right hand sides; once more, it would merely be necessary to apply Property One followed, if required, by the dual-simplex method.

A number of the studies described in Section 4.7 quote dual variable/simplex multiplier values although rather fewer of them discuss the ranges within which these are valid. Recall for example (Section 4.7.2) the study of recreational landuse by Cheung and Auger (1976). There were six constraints relating respectively to the total capital and labour and the land available in four regions A, B, C and D. Recall too that at optimality, the total labour supply was fully used (S_1 =0) as was the land available in regions B and C (S_4, S_5 = 0). Thus these constraints have positive associated dual variable values. In the case of the labour constraint, this value is $1.20 i.e. an increase/decrease in the supply of labour by one man-day would cause an increase/decrease in the total return of $1.20. Furthermore this value remains valid i.e. the basis of the solution in Table 4.3 remains the same provided the total supply of labour lies between 147 man-days and 702 man-days. Given that in the formulation of the problem to which Table 4.3 refers 700 man-days of labour were assumed, it can now be seen that the policy suggested by this solution should change in a fundamental way if there was even a slight increase in labour supply.

Recall (Section 4.9.3) the summary of the linear programming application of Jenkins and Robson (1974) concerning the devising of a construction programme to meet given targets

whilst minimising total costs. Table 5.1 summarises the
initial feasible solution calculated by them having relaxed
the targets set. The associated dual variable values show for
example that if the total population to be catered for was to
increase by one, the increase in cost would be 0.14 money
units; conversely, if the right hand side of the constraints
associated with the provision of housing was to be relaxed by
one unit, the reduction in cost would be 4.87 money units.
Jenkins and Robson point to the possibility of determining the
ranges over which the various dual variable values remain
valid but do not present actual results.

Turning again to the agricultural application of
Puterbaugh *et al.* (1957) (Section 4.7.3) and recalling that
the model involved four constraints concerning land availability, labour availability, hay and corn, Table 4.4 indicates
that at optimality, the first, second and fourth constraints
hold exactly. The dual variable values associated with their
right hand sides are 45.03, 4.51 and 0.085 respectively. Thus,
for example, in the case of land, an additional available acre
would result in an increased return to the farmer of $45.03
assuming that the basis of the revised optimal solution
remained the same. Thus, given the current optimal solution,
this figure represents the 'worth' of an additional acre of
land to the farmer and therefore the rent he would presumably
be prepared to pay for it.

5.4 CHANGES IN OBJECTIVE COEFFICIENTS

Recall the revised housebuilder problem (5.1) whose objective
was:

$$\text{Maximise} : 3X_1 + 4X_2 + 2X_3$$

and the final solution tableau which was:

BASIS	X_o	X_1	X_2	X_3	S_1	S_2	S_3	SOL.
X_o	①	0	0	4	1	1	0	825
X_2	0	0	①	3	1	-2	0	150
X_1	0	①	0	-2	-1	3	0	75
S_3	0	0	0	2	1	-7	①	25

Questions concerning the sensitivity of the coefficients in an
objective arise in two different contexts. First, for a
decision variable which is not included in the optimal

TABLE 5.1

REGIONAL DEVELOPMENT MODEL : INITIAL SOLUTION (PART OF) AND DUAL VARIABLE VALUES

	1.	Optimal Sol. Value	Dual Variable Value
Objective			
Cost (Minimised)		£3623 million	
Demographic Targets			
Total population	$\geq$	3 328 000	0.14
Total employment	$\geq$	1 311 000	1.21
Net outward migration	$\leq$	78 600	0.14
Total unemployment	$\leq$	55 300	1.14
Construction Targets			
New housing (av. units)	$\geq$	60 600	4.87
Primary schools (no. places)	$\geq$	65 500	0.48
Roads (1/4 mile lengths)	$\geq$	248	87.9
Shopfloor space ('000 ft^2)	$\geq$	4 375	8.0
Office floor space ('000 ft.^{2})	$\geq$	4 227	12.9

1. Direction of relevant constraint. Thus, for example, it was required that the amount of new housing provided be > a given value; the optimal solution value was 60600 with an associated dual value of 4.87.

From: JENKINS, P.M. and ROBSON, A., (1974), An Application of Linear Programming Methodology for Regional Strategy Making, *Regional Studies, 8* , 267-79, Table 1.

Reprinted by permission of the Cambridge University Press.

solution basis e.g. X_3 in the revised housebuilder problem, by what amount would the coefficient of this variable in the objective have to increase in the case of a maximisation problem or decrease in the case of a minimisation problem in order for it to be so included? In the case of X_3 in the revised housebuilder problem, this is equivalent to determining the price at which the third housetype would have to sell in order for it to at least partially replace the first and/or the second types in the planned development. The second type of sensitivity question concerns the range within which an objective coefficient associated with a variable which is in the final solution basis may vary without causing a change in that solution. Thus, for example, in the case of X_1 in the revised housebuilder problem, we might require the range over which the price of a Type One house could vary without causing the current optimal policy of building 75 type one houses and 150 type two houses to change.

Considering the case of a non-basis variable first, suppose that the price of a Type Three house is to be increased by some amount Δ_3 in order to ensure that some of these houses will be built i.e. that X_3 will be in the revised optimal solution basis. The revised objective function is:

$$\text{Maximise} : 3X_1 + 4X_2 + (2 + \Delta_3) X_3$$

which will appear in the X_o row of the initial simplex tableau as:

BASIS	X_o	X_1	X_2	X_3	S_1	S_2	S_3	SOL.
X_o	1	-3	-4	$-2-\Delta_3$	0	0	0	0

As the simplex method proceeds, constants will be added to/ subtracted from the term $(-2-\Delta_3)$ which will in fact leave the term '$-\Delta_3$' untouched. Thus the X_o row of the final solution tableau will be:

BASIS	X_o	X_1	X_2	X_3	S_1	S_2	S_3	SOL.
X_o	1	0	0	$4-\Delta_3$	1	1	0	825

We are now seeking the conditions under which Δ_3 is such as to cause X_3 to enter the basis. In order for this to happen, the coefficient associated with X_3 in the X_o row must become less than or equal to zero i.e.

$$4 - \Delta_3 \leq 0$$

i.e. $\Delta_3 \geq 4$. Thus in the case of the revised housebuilder problem, houses of Type Three will be included in the optimal

159

plan only if those houses sell for six or more money units i.e. £60,000 or more. If this happens, the revised optimal solution can be determined via a further change of basis operation on the current optimal solution simplex tableau with the relevant X_o row coefficient duly adjusted.

It should be noted that the preceding analysis leads to a direct interpretation of the coefficients of the non-basis decision variables in the X_o row of the final simplex solution tableau: they represent the amounts by which the relevant co-efficients in the original objective would have to change (increase in the case of a maximisation problem and decrease in the case of a minimisation problem) in order for them to enter the optimal solution basis i.e. in order for the relevant X_j value in (4.1)-(4.3) to become positive at optimality. They are often referred to as the $shadow$ $costs$.

Recall (Section 3.3.2) that the term shadow cost was used previously to refer to the savings/costs associated with the water cells in the transportation problem and in particular (Section 3.3.4) that at optimality, these values give for each unused route (water cell) the reduction in the per unit transport cost i.e. c_{ij} value in the original objective (3.5) necessary if that route is to be brought into use in the optimal solution i.e. if the variable X_{ij} in (3.4)-(3.7) is to be positive at optimality. It can now be noted that this interpretation of the shadow cost values matches that given in this section exactly.

We now consider how the range over which the objective row coefficient of a variable which is in the optimal solution basis can vary without changing that solution. Taking house-type one in the revised housebuilder problem as an example, we wish to determine the interval through which the price of a house of this type can vary without altering the current policy to build 75 Type One houses and 150 Type Two houses. Specifically, if the price of a Type One house is $(3 + \Delta_1)$, the revised objective is:

$$\text{Maximise} : (3 + \Delta_1) \, X_1 + 4X_2 + 2X_3$$

Again, following the same logic as in the previous case, the revised optimal solution tableau will be:

BASIS	X_o	X_1	X_2	X_3	S_1	S_2	S_3	SOL.
X_o	1	$-\Delta_1$	0	4	1	1	0	825
X_2	0	0	1	3	1	-2	0	150
X_1	0	1	0	-2	-1	3	0	75
S_3	0	0	0	2	1	7	1	25

In this instance, because X_1 is a basis variable, the tableau is no longer in the required format : the coefficient of X_1 in the X_0 row is not zero. This situation may be rectified by adding Δ_1 times the second constraint row to the X_0 row which yields the revised tableau:

BASIS	X_0	X_1	X_2	X_3	S_1	S_2	S_3	SOL.
X_0	①	0	0	$4-2\Delta_1$	$1-2\Delta_1$	$1+3\Delta_1$	0	$825 + 75\Delta_1$
X_2	0	0	①	3	1	-2	0	150
X_1	0	①	0	-2	-1	3	0	75
S_3	0	0	0	2	1	7	①	25

We are seeking the range of values which Δ_1 may take without altering the current basis. Given that this is a maximisation problem, the basis will remain the same provided Δ_1 is such that the coefficient of each non-basis variable in the X_0 row remains positive i.e.

$$4 - 2\Delta_1 \geq 0 \quad \text{i.e.} \; \Delta_1 \leq 2 \quad)$$
$$1 - \Delta_1 \geq 0 \quad \text{i.e.} \; \Delta_1 \leq 1 \quad)$$
$$1 + 3\Delta_1 \geq 0 \quad \text{i.e.} \; \Delta_1 \geq -1/3)$$

---- (5.8)

Taking the conditions (5.8) together yields the overall condition:

$$-1/3 \leq \Delta_1 \leq 1$$

i.e. the price of a Type One house can vary between £26,667 and £40,000 without altering the current basis solution policy of building 75 Type One houses and 150 Type Two houses. If, in fact, the price of a Type One house varies outside these limits, the revised optimal solution can be determined by substituting the appropriate value for Δ_1 in the preceding tableau and carrying out the necessary change of basis operation. Thus, for example, if $\Delta_1 = -1$ i.e. the price of a Type One house falls by £10,000, the revised X_0 row of the optimal solution tableau is:

BASIS	X_0	X_1	X_2	X_3	S_1	S_2	S_3	SOL.
X_0	1	0	0	6	2	-2	0	750

By virtue of a negative coefficient, S_2 enters the basis while X_1 leaves. The reader should check that the revised optimal

Linear Programming : Sensitivity Analysis and the Dual

solution is :

Basis Variables   : $X_o = 800$; $X_2 = 200$; $S_2 = 25$; $S_3 = 200$
Non-basis Variables : $X_1 = X_3 = S_1 = 0$

Within the context of applications, a sensitivity analysis
on the coefficients of the objective of a linear programming
problem is often carried out. This reflects the fact that
these coefficients generally relate to such entities as costs
and returns which, in reality, vary frequently. A further use
of this type of sensitivity analysis can be to provide an
estimate of the cost of forcing certain variables into the
final solution because their inclusion is considered to be
desirable for other reasons. Recall for example the landuse
planning study of Heroux and Wallace (1971) (Section 4.7.1)
and, in particular, the finding (Table 4.2) that only four of
the nine possible dwelling types should be included in the
optimal plan. Heroux and Wallace proceed to determine the
amounts by which the returns on the five excluded dwelling
types would have to increase in order for them to be included
and find them to be $89, $6323, $2905, $1960 and $1230 per
unit for the second, fourth, fifth, seventh and eighth types
respectively. These therefore are the costs involved in
forcing these housetypes into the final plan.
       A linear programming application which pays particular
attention to the sensitivity of the objective coefficients is
that of Kearney (1971) who considers the optimal composition
for a pig feed diet appropriate to Irish conditions. The
problem formulation is as in (4.28)-(4.30); some combination
of seventeen foods is to fulfill twelve dietary requirements
at least cost. The optimal solution is given in Table 5.2.
For each food not included in the diet i.e. not in the basis
of the optimal solution, the degree to which the per unit cost
of that food would have to reduce in order for it to be so
included as extracted from the X_9 row of the optimal solution
is given. For each food included in the diet, the range over
which its price can vary without altering the current solution
is given. Kearney uses these results to identify those foods
which would enter and leave the optimal diet given relatively
small cost changes : barley, pollard (N), milo and soyabean
meal and discusses in particular the role of foods which are
not readily available in Ireland but must be imported.
       Another study which deals in some detail with the sensit-
ivity of linear programming objective coefficients is that of
Gould and Sparks (1969) who, recall (Section 4.7.4), solve a
problem of the form (4.28)-(4.30) for each of 24 locations in
Guatemala. For various foods not included within the least
cost diet, Gould and Sparks note the cost reduction required
for it to be so included. These values vary from optimal
solution to optimal solution i.e. from location to location and

TABLE 5.2

PIG FEED FORMULATION : OPTIMAL SOLUTION AND OBJECTIVE
COEFFICIENT SENSITIVITIES

INGREDIENT	PRICE TON^{-1} (£)	LEVEL OF INCLUSION (PROPORTION)	DEGREE OF COST REDUCTION[1] or ALLOWABLE COST RANGE[2]
Wheat	31.0	0.183	29.484 - 31.008
Oats	30.0	-	5.028
Barley	31.0	-	1.673
Pollard (N)	27.0	0.539	26.968 - 30.016
Pollard (F)	31.0	-	10.501
Beet Pulp	23.5	0.045	18.761 - 23.524
Maize	34.0	-	4.226
Milo	31.3	0.148	31.291 - 32.935
Soyabean Meal	50.0	0.026	49.961 - 54.615
Groundnut Meal	54.0	-	26.341
Fishmeal	96.0	0.047	79.432 - 96.100
Meat & Bone Meal	52.0	-	9.852
Dried Skim	95.0	-	34.674
Grass Meal	32.0	-	7.793
Limestone Flour	5.0	0.010	4.474 - 30.968
Diacalcic Phosphate	37.0	-	35.127
Salt	13.0	0.002	5.402 - 538.891

[1]For a non-basis variable   [2]For a basis variable

From: KEARNEY, B., (1971), Linear Programming and Pig Feed
Formulation, *Irish Journal of Agricultural Economics
and Rural Sociology*, 3, 145-55, Tables 2 and 3.

can be mapped to give what Gould and Sparks call a reduced-cost surface. Figure 5.2 shows the reduced cost surface for

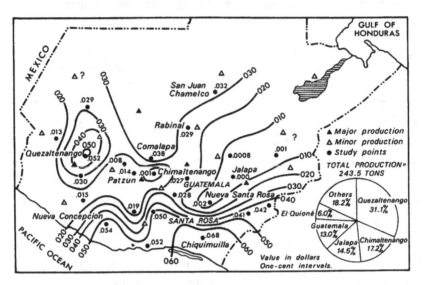

Figure 5.2 Reduced Cost Surface for Apples

From: GOULD P.R. and SPARKS, J.P., (1969), The Geographical
Context of Human Diets in Southern Guatemala,
Geographical Review, 59, 58-82, Figure 14.

Redrawn by permission of the American Geographical Society.

apples. Jalapa is a high production area for this product;
thus they are cheap enough relative to other foods to enter
the least cost diet and their associated shadow cost value is
zero. The shadow costs increase to peaks in the Quezaltenango
and Chiqumuilla regions which indicates that in these areas,
apples are particularly non-comeptitive as potential diet
ingredients.

5.5 OTHER TYPES OF SENSITIVITY ANALYSIS

The final three types of sensitivity question posed in Section
5.1 are now discussed. Within the context of actual applications, these types of sensitivity analyses are carried out less
frequently than those described in the previous two sections.
Thus the discussion is briefer.

Linear Programming : Sensitivity Analysis and the Dual

5.5.1   Changes in Constraint Coefficients

As in the case of the objective row coefficients (Section 5.4), the mathematical methods required to deal with changes in the constraint coefficients of variables inside and outside the current optimal solution basis differ. The former case is mathematically complex and will not be considered further. In order to demonstrate the methods appropriate to dealing with a non-basis variable, reconsider the revised housebuilder problem where the coefficient of X_3 in the first constraint has altered by some amount Δ_{13}. (This is equivalent to supposing that the density at which the third housetype will be built has altered.) We wish to see whether this alteration will cause the optimal solution to change with X_3 entering the basis. As far as the simplex calculations are concerned and bearing in mind that these involve adding/subtracting rows in each tableau, the effect of adding Δ_{13} to the term in the X_3 column of the first constraint row in the initial solution tableau will be to alter all the terms in the X_3 column of the final solution tableau.

The sensitivity analysis proceeds by first calculating the revised term in the X_3 column of the X_o row in the optimal   tableau using Property Three which yields:

$$(\ (5 + \Delta_{13}) \quad 1 \quad 4) \begin{pmatrix} 1 \\ \ \\ 1 \\ \ \\ 0 \end{pmatrix} + (-2) = (4 + \Delta_{13}) \quad\quad ---- (5.9)$$

By definition, bearing in mind that we are dealing with a maximisation problem, if this revised term in the X_o row is positive i.e. Δ_{13} is such that:

$$(4 + \Delta_{13}) > 0$$

the current optimal solution is unchanged and the sensitivity investigation ceases. If, however, Δ_{13} is such that the revised term in the X_3 column of the X_o row is negative then, by definition, the basis will change and we wish to calculate the revised optimal solution. In order to do this we calculate first the revised readings in the X_3 column of the constraint rows using Property Two which, in this case, yields:

$$\begin{pmatrix} 1 & -2 & 0 \\ -1 & 3 & 0 \\ 1 & -7 & 1 \end{pmatrix} \begin{pmatrix} 5 + \Delta_{13} \\ 1 \\ 3 \end{pmatrix} = \begin{pmatrix} 3 + \Delta_{13} \\ -2 - \Delta_{13} \\ 1 + \Delta_{13} \end{pmatrix} \quad\quad ----(5.10)$$

Considering (5.9) and (5.10) together, the incorporation of

Δ_{13} in the first constraint of the problem leads to the revised optimal solution tableau:

BASIS	X_o	X_1	X_2	X_3	S_1	S_2	S_3	SOL.
X_o	①	0	0	$4+\Delta_{13}$	1	1	0	825
X_2	0	0	①	$3+\Delta_{13}$	1	-2	0	150
X_1	0	①	0	$-2-\Delta_{13}$	-1	3	0	75
S_3	0	0	0	$1+\Delta_{13}$	1	-7	①	25

which can be re-solved with X_3 entering the basis after substitution of Δ_{13}.

The foregoing methods can be used equally well if each of the constraint coefficients associated with a given variable change. Thus, if the revised housebuilder problem becomes:

MAXIMISE : $3X_1 + 4X_2 + 2X_3$

s.t. $2X_1 + 3X_2 + (5+\Delta_{13}) X_3 \leq 600$

$X_1 + X_2 + (1+\Delta_{23}) X_2 \leq 225$

$5X_1 + 4X_2 + (4+\Delta_{33}) X_3 \leq 1000$

$X_1 \geq 0 ; X_2 \geq 0 ; X_3 \geq 0$

application of Property Three shows the revised X_o row coefficient of X_3 in the optimal tableau to be:

$$((5 + \Delta_{13}) (1 + \Delta_{23}) (4 + \Delta_{33})) \begin{pmatrix} (1) \\ ( ) \\ (1) \\ ( ) \\ (0) \end{pmatrix} + (-2) = (4+\Delta_{13}+ \Delta_{23})$$

which is negative if Δ_{13} and Δ_{23} are such that:

$$\Delta_{13} + \Delta_{23} \leq -4$$

Assuming that this is so, the revised constraint coefficients are given by:

$$\begin{pmatrix} 1 & -2 & 0 \\ -1 & 3 & 0 \\ 1 & -7 & 1 \end{pmatrix} \begin{pmatrix} 5 + \Delta_{13} \\ 1 + \Delta_{23} \\ 3 + \Delta_{33} \end{pmatrix} = \begin{pmatrix} 3 + \Delta_{13} - 2\Delta_{23} \\ -2 - \Delta_{13} + 3\Delta_{23} \\ 1 + \Delta_{13} - 7\Delta_{23} + \Delta_{33} \end{pmatrix}$$

whose values given Δ_{13}, Δ_{23} and Δ_{33} can be duly calculated and substituted in the current final solution tableau which can then be re-solved.

From the point of view of applications, sensitivity testing of one or more of the constraint coefficients associated with a particular decision variable usually arises within the context of testing the effects of technological change. Thus, in the case of a regional economy and a linear programming problem of the form (4.15)-(4.19), a change of technology in a given sector, j, would alter the input requirements per unit output for that sector i.e. the column values a_{ij}, $i = 1, \ldots, T$ in Table 4.1. Again, in the case of an agricultural linear programming problem of the type (4.21)-(4.23), a change in the production method for some activity would alter the per unit input requirements of the activity for the various resources thereby once again changing the relevant a_{ij} constraint coefficients associated with the relevant decision variable. Indeed, when viewed in this context, the a_{ij} values in a linear programming formulation are often referred to as the *technological coefficients*.

5.5.2 Addition of A New Decision Variable

One example of noting the effect of incorporating an additional decision variable in a linear programming problem has been treated already. Reconsider the formulation of the original housebuilder problem (4.36)-(4.40) and of the revised housebuilder problem (5.1). In the revised problem, an additional activity (X_2) has been incorporated. A comparison of the optimal solution tableaux of the initial and revised problems (Sections 4.5 and 5.1 respectively) demonstrates that in this case, the nature of the new activity is such that it does not alter the optimal solution. We now demonstrate how this can be shown *via* the rules introduced in Section 5.2 and how the revised solution can be calculated in those cases where the nature of the additional activity is such as to cause it to enter the optimal solution basis.

In the case of the initial housebuilder problem, consider the effect of introducing an additional activity, X_3 to yield the revised problem:

$$\text{Maximise : } 3X_1 + 4X_2 + \Delta_3 X_3$$

$$\text{s.t.} \quad 2X_1 + 3X_2 + \Delta_{13} X_3 \leq 600$$

$$X_1 + X_2 + \Delta_{23} X_3 \leq 225 \qquad \text{----(5.11)}$$

$$5X_1 + 4X_2 + \Delta_{33} X_3 \leq 1000$$

$$X_1 \geq ; X_2 \geq 0 ; X_3 \geq 0$$

We first wish to seek whether the coefficients of X_3 are such as to cause it to enter the optimal solution basis which is equivalent to determining whether, when it is incorporated in the current solution tableau, the coefficient of X_3 in the X_o row turns out to be negative (maximisation problem) or positive (minimisation problem) as appropriate. As in the previous section, the value of this coefficient may be obtained via Property Three and is :

$$(\Delta_{13} \ \Delta_{23} \ \Delta_{33}) \begin{pmatrix} 1 \\ ( ) \\ (1) \\ ( ) \\ (0) \end{pmatrix} + (-\Delta_3) = (\Delta_{13} + \Delta_{23} - \Delta_3)$$

Thus the new variable, X_3, will enter the basis if Δ_3, Δ_{13}, Δ_{23} and Δ_{33} are such that :

$$\Delta_{13} + \Delta_{23} - \Delta_3 \leq 0 \qquad \text{----(5.12)}$$

In the specific case of the revised housebuilder problem, $\Delta_3 = 2$, $\Delta_{13} = 5$, $\Delta_{23} = 1$ and $\Delta_{33} = 4$ which yields a value of 4 for (5.12). Thus, in this instance, X_3 does not enter the basis; the current optimal solution remains valid which confirms the previous result.

Suppose now that $\Delta_3 = 2$, $\Delta_{13} = 1/2$, $\Delta_{23} = 1$ and $\Delta_{33} = 4$. In this case, the left hand side of (5.12) is $-1/2$; the value in the X_3 column of the objective row of the revised simplex tableau is thus negative which indicates that the activity X_3 will enter the basis yielding a revised optimal solution. In order to calculate this revised solution, the values in the X_3 column of the constraint rows of the current solution are required. As in the previous section, these can be calculated via Property Two which yields:

$$\begin{pmatrix} 1 & -2 & 0 \\ (-1 & 3 & 0 \\ 1 & -7 & 1 \end{pmatrix} \begin{pmatrix} \Delta_{13} \\ \Delta_{23} \\ \Delta_{33} \end{pmatrix} = \begin{pmatrix} \Delta_{13} - 2\Delta_{23} \\ -\Delta_{13} + 3\Delta_{23} \\ \Delta_{13} - 7\Delta_{23} + \Delta_{33} \end{pmatrix}$$

which with $\Delta_{13} = 1/2$, $\Delta_{23} = 1$, $\Delta_{33} = 4$ yields:

$$\begin{pmatrix} -3/2 \\ \\ 5/2 \\ \\ -5/2 \end{pmatrix}$$

The complete revised current solution tableau is thus :

BASIS	X_o	X_1	X_2	X_3	S_1	S_2	S_3	SOL.
X_o	①	0	0	-1/2	1	1	0	825
X_2	0	0	①	-3/2	1	-2	0	150
X_1	0	①	0	5/2	-1	3	0	75
S_3	0	0	0	-5/2	1	7	①	25

upon which the necessary change of basis operation can be performed.

5.5.3 Imposition of An Additional Constraint

As has been the case with the other types of sensitivity analysis, the incorporation of (an) additional constraint(s) may or may not cause the current optimal solution to a given problem to change. For a specific case, we therefore test first whether the new constraint is such as to alter the current solution; if it is, we proceed to determine the revised solution.

Reconsider the initial housebuilder problem and suppose that the additional constraint:

$$3X_1 + 2X_2 \leq 600 \qquad\qquad ----(5.13)$$

is imposed. A check against the graphical representation of the solution space (Figure 5.1) demonstrates that the new constraint is not binding : the optimal solution is unchanged. However, in the case of the additional constraint:

$$3X_1 + 2X_2 \leq 300 \qquad\qquad ----(5.14)$$

the new condition is binding ; the optimal solution alters with the optimal value of the objective decreasing.

The mathematical methods by which the nature of an additional constraint can be checked and (where appropriate) the revised optimal solution can be calculated, are as follows.

Taking the case of the original housebuilder problem with (5.13) added, the additional constraint is appended to the current optimal solution tableau as it would appear in an initial solution tableau. Designating the slack variable associated with it as S_4, this yields :

BASIS	X_o	X_1	X_2	S_1	S_2	S_3	S_4	SOL.
X_o	1	0	0	1	1	0	0	825
X_2	0	0	1	1	-2	0	0	150
X_1	0	1	0	-1	3	0	0	75
S_3	0	0	0	1	-7	1	0	25
S_4	0	3	2	0	0	0	1	600

Viewing this tableau as a whole, it is not in the required format : the coefficients of X_1 and X_2 in the final constraint row should be zero. Zero coefficients can be created here by subtracting two times the first and three times the second constraint row from the final constraint row which yields the revised tableau :

BASIS	X_o	X_1	X_2	S_1	S_2	S_3	S_4	SOL.
X_o	①	0	0	1	1	0	0	825
X_2	0	0	①	1	-2	0	0	150
X_1	0	①	0	-1	3	0	0	75
S_3	0	0	0	1	-7	①	0	25
S_4	0	0	0	1	-5	0	①	75

i.e. Basis Variables : $X_o = 825$; $X_1 = 75$; $X_2 = 150$; $S_3 = 25$; $S_4 = 75$

Non-basis Variables : $S_1 = S_4 = 0$

Thus the third constraint is such that the slack variable associated with it is positive in the current optimal solution i.e. this solution lies below it. Thus it is not binding.

Consider now the case of incorporating (5.14) in the original housebuilder problem. Repeating the preceding steps, the revised simplex tableau is :

BASIS	X_o	X_1	X_2	S_1	S_2	S_3	S_4	SOL.
X_o	(1)	0	0	1	1	0	0	825
X_2	0	0	(1)	1	-2	0	0	150
X_1	0	(1)	0	-1	3	0	0	75
S_3	0	0	0	1	-7	(1)	0	25
S_4	0	0	0	1	$\boxed{-5}$	0	(1)	-225
RATIO				1/1	1/-5			

A negative value for S_4 indicates that the additional constraint to which this slack variable relates is such as to
lie below the current optimal solution point i.e. excludes it
from the revised solution space. We therefore seek the revised optimal solution which may be determined *via* the dual-
simplex method outlined in Section 5.3. S_4 enters the basis
with S_2 leaving which yields the revised solution tableau :

BASIS	X_o	X_1	X_2	S_1	S_2	S_3	S_4	SOL.
X_o	(1)	0	0	6/5	0	0	1/5	780
X_2	0	0	(1)	3/5	0	0	-2/5	240
X_1	0	(1)	0	$\boxed{-2/5}$	0	0	3/5	-60
S_3	0	0	0	-2/5	0	(1)	-7/5	340
S_2	0	0	0	-1/5	(1)	0	-1/5	45
RATIO				6/5 / -2/5			1/5 / 3/5	

X_1 now leaves the basis with S_1 entering which yields the
revised optimal solution :

BASIS	X_o	X_1	X_2	S_1	S_2	S_3	S_4	SOL.
X_o	(1)	3	0	0	0	0	2	600
X_2	0	3/2	(1)	0	0	0	1/2	150
S_1	0	-5/2	0	(1)	0	0	-3/2	150
S_3	0	-1	0	0	0	(1)	-2	400
S_2	0	-1/2	0	0	(1)	0	-1/2	75

Within the context of applications, the incorporation of additional constraints generally relates to an attempt to improve the realism of an initial problem formulation by taking additional factors into account. Thus in the case of Gould and Sparks' study of human diets in Guatemala, the initial model run for each of the 24 locations (Section 4.7.4) involved 40 foods and nine constraints. Gould and Sparks conclude that no matter what the costs, few, if any, people would be prepared to accept this diet. Therefore, to make it more realistic, they incorporate further constraints in their model to ensure that one-third of the protein comes from animal sources and that at least fifteen tortillas and one portion of black beans are included. Later on in their study, certain other foods are forced into the diet *via* further constraints and an attempt is made to take account of the tastes of persons of different ethnic backgrounds.

In addition to the foregoing type of practical application, the treatment of additional constraints can also be of use in a purely computational sense. Very often for a specific linear programming problem, one can identify certain constraints at the outset (known as *secondary constraints*)which it is felt will not be binding on the optimal solution. A convenient approach to solving problems where secondary constraints can be identified is to omit these from the initial formulation; having solved a smaller linear programming problem, one then proceeds *via* the preceding methods to check in turn that each secondary constraint is in fact non-binding on the solution. If a binding constraint is encountered, the revised optimal solution must be determined and each of the other secondary constraints must then be checked against it.

5.6. PARAMETRIC LINEAR PROGRAMMING

Each of the preceding types of sensitivity analysis involves determining the effect (if any) on the current optimal solution of a linear programming problem of a single discrete change in some aspect of it e.g. a unit change in the right hand side of a given constraint or a change of k units in a given objective row coefficient. In certain instances, we wish to assess the effect of a continuous change in some aspect or aspects of a given problem e.g. how the optimal solution alters as a given objective row coefficient varies over the range zero to infinity and/or as a given constraint right hand side varies in a similar manner. A description of the mathematical methods by which such continuous sensitivity assessments may be conveniently made lies outside the scope of this text; they fall within what is known as *parametric linear programming*.

Two examples of studies involving parametric linear programming are those of Mandell and Tweeten (1971) and

Granholm and Ohlsson (1975). The former focusses on the optimal production pattern for cotton in the United States. For each of 234 areas, a linear programming problem of the type (4.21)-(4.23) is solved. In each case, the decision variables represent the crops which could possibly be grown in the area concerned while the constraints represent the resources available. The output of cotton in each optimal solution thus reflects not only its suitability in terms of the area's resources but also its success in competing against the other crops which can be grown there. Mandell and Tweeten proceed to test for each solution how the optimal acreage of cotton in each area alters as the price received for it as given by the relevant objective coefficient increases in a continuous manner. A summary of the results aggregated into four major regions is shown in Figure 5.3.

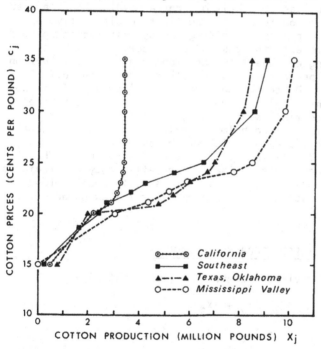

Figure 5.3 Relationship Between Cotton Production and Price for Given Regions in the United States

Redrawn by permission. P.I. Mandell and Luther G. Tweeten, "The Location of Cotton Production in the United States under Competitive Conditions: A Study of Crop Location and Comparative Advantage." Geographical Analysis, vol. 3 (October 1971), pp. 334-53. Copyright © by the Ohio State University Press.

As can be seen, cotton production is least sensitive to price changes in California where production remains stable once the price reaches a little over 20 cents per pound; it is more sensitive to price changes in the Mississippi Valley.

Granholm and Ohlsson's study involves determining the investment which should be made in each of eight sectors and 24 regions of Sweden's economy in the period 1965-80. The total material investment costs are to be minimised. The constraints require that the pattern of investment be such that a given production level is achieved in each sector, that certain employment targets are met and that the change in each sector's output in each region falls below a stated maximum level. A final constraint requires that the investment pattern be such that the largest difference in value added per person i.e. between the 'richest' and 'poorest' regions be less than or equal to a certain value u. The case of $u \to 0$ is referred to as the equalisation alternative and corresponds to a policy of raising the poorest region up to the level of richest; the case of $u \to \infty$ corresponds to a policy of having no regard to the final regional distribution of value added per person and is referred to as the efficiency alternative. Quite obviously as u is allowed to increase from zero to infinity i.e. the right hand side of the final constraint is continuously relaxed, the optimal value of the objective declines. Granholm and Ohlsson present the actual result obtained *via* parametric methods by means of a graph (Figure 5.4). The difference in the optimal value of the objective between the equalisation and efficiency alternatives is no less than 31 per cent. Thus this difference represents the price which would have to be paid for following an equalisation policy.

5.7 THE DUAL LINEAR PROGRAMMING PROBLEM

Reconsider the revised housebuilder problem (5.1) :

$$
\begin{aligned}
\text{MAXIMISE :} \quad & 3X_1 + 4X_2 + 2X_3 \\
\text{s.t.} \quad & 2X_1 + 3X_2 + 5X_3 \leq 600 \\
& X_1 + X_2 + X_3 \leq 225 \\
& 5X_1 + 4X_2 + 4X_3 \leq 1000 \\
& X_1 \geq 0 \; ; \; X_2 \geq 0
\end{aligned}
$$
----(5.15)

and the problem (4.78) of the previous chapter :

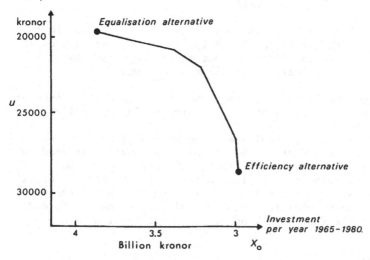

Largest difference in value added per employee between two provinces in 1980.

Figure 5.4 Relationship Between Investment Level and Largest Difference in Value Added per Employee for Sweden

From: GRANHOLM, A. and OHLSSON, O., (1975), A Note on Distribution Analysis in a Linear Programming Model, *Regional Science and Urban Economics*, 5, 483-91, Figure 1.

Redrawn by permission of the North Holland Publishing Company and the Authors.

$$\text{MINIMISE:} \quad 600\,Y_1 + 225\,Y_2 + 1000\,Y_3$$

$$\text{s.t.} \quad 2\,Y_1 + Y_2 + 5\,Y_3 \leq 3$$

$$3\,Y_1 + Y_2 + 4\,Y_3 \leq 4$$

$$5\,Y_1 + Y_2 + 4\,Y_3 \leq 2 \quad \text{---(5.16)}$$

$$Y_1 \geq 0;\ Y_2 \geq 0;\ Y_3 \geq 0$$

In a sense, one problem is the 'reverse' of the other because:

(i) The sense of the optimisation is opposite - maximisation in (5.15) and minimisation in (5.16)

(ii) The sense of the constraints is opposite - 'less than or equals' in (5.15) and 'greater than or equals' in (5.16)

(iii)   The coefficients of X_1, X_2, X_3 respectively in the objective of (5.15) form the right hand sides of the first, second and third constraints respectively in (5.16) and *vice versa*

(iv)   The coefficients of X_1, X_2, X_3 respectively in the i th constraint of (5.15) form the coefficients of Y_i in the first, second and third constraints respectively in (5.16) and *vice versa*

It should finally be noted that the usual condition concerning the non-negativity of the decision variables applies in both cases.

By definition, the linear programming problem (5.16) is said to form *the dual* of (5.15) which is usually referred to as *the primal*. In general, for any linear programming problem involving maximisation with all 'less than or equals' constraints or, conversely, minimisation with all 'greater than or equals' constraints, the dual problem can be formed by use of the four preceding rules. Thus for the primal problem :

$$\text{MINIMISE :} \quad \sum_{j=1}^{n} c_j \; X_j$$

$$\text{s.t.} \quad \sum_{j=1}^{n} a_{ij} \; X_j \geq b_i \; ; \; i = 1, \ldots, m$$

$$X_j \geq 0 \; ; \; j = 1, \ldots, n$$

$$\text{----(5.17)}$$

the corresponding dual problem is :

$$\text{MAXIMISE :} \quad \sum_{i=1}^{m} b_i \; Y_i$$

$$\sum_{i=1}^{m} a_{ij} \; Y_i \leq c_j \; ; \; j = 1, \ldots, n$$

$$Y_1 \geq 0 \; ; \; i = 1, \ldots, m$$

$$\text{----(5.18)}$$

A particular point to note concerning the foregoing inter-relationships is that they are such as to cause the number of constraints in the primal problem to equal the number of decision variables in the dual and *vice versa*. Thus (5.17) comprises m constraints and n decision variables while (5.18) comprises m decision variables and n constraints. Very often, when formulating a dual linear programming problem from a primal, it is convenient to envisage each dual variable Y_i as relating back to the i th constraint in the primal. Note that in each dual constraint in (5.18), j=1, ..., n, Y_i is multiplied by the coefficient of X_j in the i th constraint of the primal; the coefficient of Y_i in the dual objective comprises the right hand side of the i th constraint in the primal.

Consider now the task of formulating the dual of :

MAXIMISE : $3X_1 + 4X_2$ Corresp. Dual Vars.

s.t. $2X_1 + 3X_2 \leq 600$ Y_1

            $X_1 + 2X_2 \geq 150$ Y_2

            $X_1 + X_2 = 225$ Y_3

$$----(5.19)$$

Designating the dual variables corresponding to the three constraints as Y_1, Y_2, Y_3 respectively, there are difficulties: the second constraint is of the 'greater than or equals' type while the third constraint is an equality. These difficulties may be circumvented as follows. First, multiplying the second constraint across by minus one yields :

$$-X_1 - 2X_2 \leq -150 \qquad ----(5.20)$$

i.e. a constraint of the required 'less than or equals' type. Second, we note without proof (for which see for example Taha (1976), Section 4.2.2) that when a primal problem constraint is in the form of an equality, the corresponding dual variable should be unrestricted in sign. Taking the foregoing two points together, the dual of (5.19) is thus :

MINIMISE : $600Y_1 - 150Y_2 + 225Y_3$

s.t. $2Y_1 - Y_2 + Y_3 \geq 3$

             $3Y_1 - 2Y_2 + Y_3 \geq 4$

             $Y_1 \geq 0 \; ; \; Y_2 \geq 0 \; ; \; Y_3$ Unrestricted

The foregoing rules together permit the formulation of the dual of any linear programming problem.

Given the existence of a precise interrelationship between a primal linear programming formulation and its dual, one would expect that there might also be an interrelationship between their optimal solutions. In order to investigate the nature of this interrelationship, reconsider the solution to (5.15) as given in Section 5.2 i.e.

BASIS	X_o	X_1	X_2	X_3	S_1	S_2	S_3	SOL.
X_o	(1)	0	0	4	1	1	0	825
X_2	0	0	(1)	3	1	-2	0	150
X_1	0	(1)	0	-2	-1	3	0	75
S_3	0	0	0	2	1	-7	(1)	25

and the solution to the dual problem (5.16) which was presented in Section 4.6.3 :

BASIS	Y_o	Y_1	Y_2	Y_3	S_1'	S_2'	S_3'	R_1	R_2	R_3	SOL.
Y_o	(1)	0	0	-25	-75	-150	0	75-M	150-M	0	825
S_3'	0	0	0	-2	2	-3	(1)	-2	3	-1	4
Y_1	0	(1)	0	-1	1	-1	0	-1	1	0	1
Y_2	0	0	(1)	0	-3	2	0	3	·-2	0	1

Certain similarities between the two foregoing solutions which it can be proved will always hold true between a primal and its dual can be noted. First, the optimal value of the objective is the same in both problems i.e.

$$X_o = Y_o = 825$$

Second, the optimal values of the decision variables in one problem are the same as the simplex multipliers in the other (hence the alternative term dual variable values for these multipliers). Thus, in the primal, the optimal solution is : $X_1 = 75$; $X_2 = 150$; $X_3 = 0$ which are indeed respectively the simplex multipliers in the dual ; likewise, in. the dual, the optimal decision variable values are : $Y_1 = 1$, $Y_2 = 1$, $Y_3 = 0$ which once more are indeed the simplex multipliers in the primal.

Third, the optimal values of the slack variables in one problem are the same when appropriately signed as the shadow costs in the other. Thus, in the primal, the optimal slack variable values : $S_1 = 0$; $S_2 = 0$; $S_3 = 25$ are indeed (with a negative sign for Y_1') the shadow costs associated with Y_1, Y_2, Y_3 respectively in the dual; likewise, in the dual, the optimal slack variable values are $S_1' = 0$; $S_2' = 0$; $S_3' = 4$ which

178

are indeed the shadow costs associated with X_1, X_2, X_3 respectively in the primal.

The overall implication of the foregoing similarities between the optimal primal and dual solutions is that the optimal solution tableau for one of them automatically yields the optimal solution to the other together with two important pieces of information concerning sensitivity : the simplex multipliers and the shadow costs. Thus it can be seen that, instead of solving a linear programming problem directly, we may if we wish formulate the corresponding dual problem, solve it and then note from the final solution tableau the optimal solution, simplex multipliers and shadow costs associated with the primal. One computational situation in which this seemingly roundabout procedure can offer advantage in terms of speed of solution is when the primal problem comprises few variables but many constraints. Recall (Section 4.5) the argument that such a problem might prove time consuming to solve. Note too that the corresponding dual problem would by definition comprise many variables but, more important, few constraints and therefore that it could probably be solved very much more quickly.

5.8 INTERPRETATION OF THE DUAL

Possible greater speed in obtaining the optimal solution to a particular linear programming problem represents just one reason as to why the dual is of interest. Another and indeed more important reason as to why it is of interest relates to the fact that in many instances, when it is formulated, the dual itself turns out to possess a particular interpretation which, when applied, throws further light on the complete structure of the problem being solved. The precise nature of this interpretation and its usefulness varies from case to case. The overall approach is now discussed.

5.8.1 The Dual of a Maximisation Problem

Isard (1958) offers an excellent interpretation of the dual of a linear programming problem using the following example. Within a given region, two economic activities may take place. The return per unit output from each of these activities is one money unit and the objective is to find the levels at which the activities should operate (X_1 and X_2) in order to maximise the total return. Given quantities of four resources water, land, labour and capital, are available in the region. Each unit of production of X_1 and X_2 uses up given amounts of the four resources. The optimal values of X_1 and X_2 must be such that no resource is overused.

Following the logic of the previous chapter and given the relevant data (Table 5.3) the requisite linear

TABLE 5.3

RESOURCE USE PROBLEM : INPUT DATA

Resource	Requirement Per Unit Output		Availability
	Activity One	Activity Two	
Water	0.5	0.6	6
Land	0.2	0.15	1.8
Labour	0.4	0.2	3
Capital	3.0	2.0	24

From : ISARD, W., (1958), Interregional Linear Programming :
An Elementary Presentation and A General Model,
Journal of Regional Science, 1, 1-59, Table 1.

Reprinted by permission of the Editor and the Author.

programming formulation is :

$$\text{MAXIMISE :} \quad X_1 + X_2$$

$$\text{s.t.} \quad 0.5X_1 + 0.6X_2 \leq 6$$
$$0.2X_1 + 0.15X_2 \leq 1.8$$
$$0.4X_1 + 0.2X_2 \leq 3 \qquad \text{----(5.21)}$$
$$3.0X_1 + 2.0X_2 \leq 24$$

$$X_1, X_2 \geq 0$$

Designating the slack variables associated with the four constraints as S_1, ..., S_4 respectively, the optimal solution is:

$$X_o = 10.5 \ ; \ X_1 = 3 \ ; \ X_2 = 7.5$$

$$S_1 = 0 \ ; \ S_2 = .075; \ S_3 = 0.3; \ S_4 = 0$$

The associated simplex multipliers are :

$$(1.25 \quad 0 \quad 0 \quad .125)$$

Following the rules of the previous section and introducing
the dual variables Y_1, ..., Y_4 to correspond to the first,

..., fourth constraints in (5.21), the dual problem is :

$$\text{MINIMISE :} \quad 6Y_1 + 1.8Y_2 + 3Y_3 + 24Y_4 \qquad \text{----(5.22)}$$

$$\left. \begin{array}{l} 0.5Y_1 + 0.2Y_2 + 0.4Y_3 + 3.0Y_4 \leq 1) \\ 0.6Y_1 + 0.15Y_2 + 0.2Y_3 + 2.0Y_4 \leq 1) \end{array} \right\} \text{----(5.23)}$$

$$Y_1 \geq 0; Y_2 \geq 0; Y_3 \geq 0; Y_4 \geq 0 \text{ ----(5.24)}$$

From the foregoing primal solution and designating the slack variables associated with the constraints (5.23) as S_1' and S_2' respectively, the optimal solution to (5.22)-(5.24) is :

$$Y_0 = 10.5 \; ; \; Y_1 = 1.25 \; ; \; Y_2 = 0 \; ; \; Y_3 = 0 \; ; \; Y_4 = 0.125$$

$$S_1' = 0 \; ; \; S_2' = 0$$

We now seek an interpretation for the problem (5.22)-(5.24) in its own right.

In order to approach this interpretation, suppose that within the region there are a number of firms which will engage in the optimal mix of activities one and two. The four resources required to do this: water, land, labour and capital are controlled by a number of entrepreneurs who will sell them to the firms at prices to be fixed by themselves. We wish to focus attention on the levels these prices will take. Let them be designated Y_1, Y_2, Y_3 and Y_4 respectively.

Consider first the case of a firm which decides to consider engaging in one unit of activity one. From Table 5.3, this will involve consuming 0.5, 0.2, 0.4 and 3.0 units of water, land, labour and capital respectively. If the per unit costs of these resources are Y_1, ..., Y_4 respectively, the total cost to the firm of purchasing the resources required to engage in one unit of economic activity one will be :

$$0.5Y_1 + 0.2Y_2 + 0.4Y_3 + 3.0Y_4 \qquad \text{---- (5.25)}$$

Recall now that the return to the firm engaging in one unit of activity one is one money unit. Given that this is the case and given the values of Y_1, Y_2, Y_3, Y_4 as fixed by the entrepreneurs, the firm could find itself in one of three situations when it calculates the price it will have to pay for the resources necessary to engage in one unit of economic activity one. First, Y_1, ..., Y_4 could be such that :

$$0.5Y_1 + 0.2Y_2 + 0.4Y_3 + 3.0Y_4 < 1 \qquad \text{---- (5.26)}$$

Here the return to the firm having engaged in a unit of economic activity one more than covers the cost of purchasing the necessary resources ; thus the firm would presumably be prepared to engage in this activity. Second, $Y_1, \ldots, Y_4$ could be such that :

$$0.5Y_1 + 0.2Y_2 + 0.4Y_3 + 3.0Y_4 = 1 \qquad\qquad ---- (5.27)$$

This represents a marginal situation for the firm; it is just feasible to engage in the activity. Finally, $Y_1, \ldots, Y_4$ could be such that :

$$0.5Y_1 + 0.2Y_2 + 0.4Y_3 + 3.0Y_4 > 1 \qquad\qquad ---- (5.28)$$

Here the return to the firm having engaged in a unit of economic activity one does not even cover the cost of purchasing the necessary resources ; thus the firm would presumably not be prepared to engage in this activity.

Let us now consider the matter of fixing $Y_1, \ldots, Y_4$ from the point of view of the entrepreneurs who, recall, are envisaged as making this decision and who wish to maximise their returns. Suppose first that $Y_1, \ldots, Y_4$ are such that (5.26) is true i.e. the firms engaging in activity one can more than pay for the resources consumed. The entrepreneurs will see an opportunity for raising their prices and increasing their return; indeed, from their point of view, they would wish that if the firms engage in economic activity one at all, $Y_1, \ldots, Y_4$ are such that (5.27) holds true which corresponds to a situation where they reap the total return the firm gains for having engaged in the activity. The entrepreneurs would not be immediately worried if $Y_1, \ldots, Y_4$ were such that (5.28) holds true i.e. economic activity one is precluded from taking place. They merely wish to maximise their returns and have no interest in which economic activities are actually engaged in by the firms. Taking the preceding two points together and viewing the matter of resource pricing from the point of view of the entrepreneurs, they would wish $Y_1, \ldots, Y_4$ to be such that either (5.27) or (5.28) holds true i.e.

$$0.5Y_1 + 0.2Y_2 + 0.4Y_3 + 3.0Y_4 \geq 1 \qquad\qquad ---- (5.29)$$

which is in fact the first constraint of the dual linear programming problem (5.22)-(5.24). The meaning of the second constraint can be argued in the same manner.

Continuing to view the problem from the point of view of the entrepreneurs, consider now the total return they will receive from the sale of the resources. First, in a situation where each resource is totally used, this return will be:

$$6Y_1 + 1.8Y_2 + 3Y_3 + 24Y_4 \qquad\qquad ---- (5.30)$$

In practice, for a given solution, certain resources will not be fully used up. (The optimal solution to (5.21) indicates that neither land nor labour are fully used in the case of the current example.) Faced with a surplus of a given resource, the entrepreneurs will be prepared to successively undercut each other in selling it to the firms. Under conditions of perfect competition, its price will fall to zero i.e. $Y_1 = 0$. Given therefore that the entrepreneurs will only receive a return from those resources which are fully used up at optimality, the expression (5.30) gives the total return to the entrepreneurs in all conditions : the Y_1 values associated with the underused resources are zero which causes the relevant terms in (5.30) to disappear. Recalling again that neither land nor labour are used fully in the present example, $Y_2 = Y_3 = 0$ and (5.30) becomes :

$$6Y_1 + 1.8(0) + 3(0) + 24Y_4$$

which is indeed an expression for the total return accruing to the entrepreneurs in these circumstances.

Given that the entrepreneurs wish to maximise their total return, one might suspect that maximisation of (5.30) subject to the constraints (5.23), (5.24) would represent a valid pricing problem from their point of view. Inspection of (5.22) shows however that the direction of the optimisation is to minimise (5.30). We now show why this is in fact appropriate.

Still viewing the matter of price fixing from the point of view of the entrepreneurs, let us suppose that they arbitrarily decide to fix the per unit price of each resource at one money unit i.e. $Y_1 = Y_2 = Y_3 = Y_4 = 1$. Their hope would be that these prices would be such as to cause all of the resources to be fully utilised; if this did turn out to be the case, their return would be by substitution in (5.30):

$$6(1) + 1.8 (1) + 3 (1) + 24 (1) = 34.8 \qquad \text{---- (5.31)}$$

We shall refer to this quantity as the *fictitious return* to the entrepreneurs. Consider now what would actually happen if Y_1, Y_2, Y_3, Y_4 equalled one. Checking against the constraints ('5.23), it would not be profitable for either activity one or activity two to be engaged in by the firms. Thus no production would take place, no resources would be consumed and the *actual return* to the entrepreneurs would be zero.

Quite obviously, the foregoing situation would be unsatisfactory from the point of view of both the firms and the entrepreneurs. In order to stimulate some production and thus generate a financial return to themselves through resource consumption, the entrepreneurs would presumably be prepared to reduce their prices. Specifically, suppose they halve these i.e. $Y_1 = Y_2 = Y_3 = Y_4 = 0.5$. This will reduce the fictitious returns to the entrepreneurs to 17.4; checking against the constraints (5.23), the actual returns will remain at zero. Thus, the entrepreneurs will presumably adjust the resource prices again to (say) :

$$Y_1 = 0.5 \; ; \; Y_2 = 0.5 \; ; \; Y_3 = 0.5 \; ; \; Y_4 = 0.2625 \qquad \text{---- (5.32)}$$

This reduces the fictitious returns to the entrepreneurs to 11.7; checking against the constraints it is still not feasible for a firm to engage in activity one but it is now feasible to engage in activity two. Presumably, through the region, this activity will now be engaged in to the maximum extent possible, i.e. (from (5.23)) $X_2 = 10$ which will consume 6, 1.5, 2 and 20 units of water, land, labour and capital respectively yielding an actual return to the entrepreneurs of:

$$(0.5)(6) + (0.5)(1.5) + (0.5)(2) + (0.2625)(20) = 10 \quad \text{--(5.33)}$$

A comparison of this solution with those preceding it shows that while the fictitious returns to the entrepreneurs have decreased yet again, the actual returns have increased. This raises the obvious question concerning the values to which $Y_1, \ldots, Y_4$ must be reduced in order to maximise the actual return to the entrepreneurs. Consider the solution values emerging from solving (5.22)-(5.24) i.e. the simplex multipliers associated with the optimal solution to (5.21):

$$Y_1 = 1.25 \; ; \; Y_2 = 0 \; ; \; Y_3 = 0 \; ; \; Y_4 = 0.125 \qquad \text{---- (5.34)}$$

Here the fictitious returns to the entrepreneurs are 10.75 - a reduction from the previous solutions. Checking against the constraints (5.23) indicates that both economic activities will be engaged in, presumably to the maximum extent permitted by the constraints in (5.21) i.e. $X_1 = 3$; $X_2 = 7.5$ thereby consuming 6, 11.85, 3.45 and 24 units respectively of water, land, labour and capital. The actual return to the entrepreneurs in supplying these resources will be:

$$(6)(1.25) + (11.85)(0) + (3.45)(0) + (24)(0.125) = 10.5$$

which is higher than in each of the previous cases and actually equals the fictitious return.

That the actual return achieved by (5.34) is in fact the maximum possible can be verified by noting how it would alter if any of $Y_1, \ldots, Y_4$ were to be changed. First, a decrease in any of $Y_1, \ldots, Y_4$ would cause a decrease in the fictitious returns to the entrepreneurs. Quite obviously, the actual returns cannot exceed the fictitious returns ; thus these will decrease also. Second, an increase in any of $Y_1, \ldots, Y_4$ will increase the fictitious returns; however, it will also cause certain (in this case both) of the dual constraints (5.23) which currently hold as equalities to be broken thereby causing firms to cease certain (in this case both) economic activities; thus the actual returns to the entrepreneurs will be reduced (in this case to zero). We therefore reach the important conclusion that from the point of view of the entrepreneurs, minimisation of fictitious returns is equivalent to maximisation of actual returns. Thus the direction of the optimisation in (5.22) is appropriate.

In general, for any linear programming problem involving maximisation, the overall form of the primal is to choose levels for each of a set of activities in order to :

MAXIMISE :   Some quantity e.g. profit

s.t.   Each resource not overused

The general form of the dual is then to choose per unit prices for the resources in order to :

MINIMISE :   Fictitious returns (equivalent to maximising actual returns)

s.t.   Prices are such as to absorb all profits accruing to the resource purchasers

It is to be noted that the interpretation given here for Y_1, ..., Y_m i.e. as prices paid for resources accords exactly with that given in Section 5.3 where, recall, the simplex multipliers or dual variable values in a maximisation problem i.e. Y_1, ..., Y_m were interpreted as the per unit 'worths' of each resource to the consumer of it.

5.8.2   The Dual of a Minimisation Problem

The logic underlying the interpretation of the dual of a linear programming minimisation problem follows that for a maximisation problem closely. By way of example, consider the following straightforward diet composition problem (Section 4.2.4) which is discussed by Gould and Sparks (1969) at the outset of their previously cited study.

Three foods : eggs, oranges and tortillas are available to form a diet at costs per one hundred grammes of nine, three and one cents respectively. The final diet must be such as to yield a given minimum intake level of calories, protein and vitamin C. If these levels together with the contribution per one hundred grammes of the various foods are as given in Table 5.4, then, following the logic of Section 4.2.4, the appropriate minimum cost diet problem is :

Linear Programming : Sensitivity Analysis and the Dual

$$\text{Minimise :} \quad 9X_1 + 3X_2 + X_3$$

$$\text{s.t.} \quad 160X_1 + 69X_2 + 201X_3 \geq 2700$$

$$11.3X_1 + 0.8X_2 + 5.5X_3 \geq 65 \quad \text{----(5.35)}$$

$$X_1 + 200X_2 + 0X_3 \geq 2000$$

$$X_1 \geq 0; \ X_2 \geq 0; \ X_3 \geq 0$$

where X_1, X_2, X_3 are the levels of eggs, oranges and tortillas respectively to be included in the diet. Following the rules

---

TABLE 5.4

HUMAN DIET PROBLEM : INPUT DATA

	Yield Per 100 Grammes			Minimum Diet Requirement
	Eggs	Oranges	Tortillas	
Calories	160	69	201	2700
Protein	11.3	0.8	5.5	65
Vitamin C	1	200	0	2000

From: GOULD, P.R. and SPARKS, J.P., (1969), The Geographical Context of Human Diets in Southern Guatemala, *Geographical Review*, 59, 58-82, Table II.

Reprinted by permission of the American Geographical Society.

---

of the previous section, the dual problem is :

$$\text{Maximise :} \quad 2700Y_1 + 65Y_2 + 2000Y_3$$

$$\text{s.t.} \quad 160Y_1 + 11.3Y_2 + Y_3 \leq 9$$

$$69Y_1 + 0.8Y_2 + 200Y_3 \leq 3 \quad \text{----(5.36)}$$

$$201Y_1 + 5.5Y_2 + 0Y_3 \leq 1$$

$$Y_1 \geq 0 \ ; \ Y_2 \geq 0; \ Y_3 \geq 0$$

We now seek an interpretation for (5.36).
Recall (Section 5.7) that Y_1, Y_2, Y_3 are in fact the

simplex multipliers associated with (5.35) and therefore that they represent the effect on X_0 of a unit change in the right hand sides of the first, second and third constraints respectively (Section 5.3). Thus, for example, Y_1 gives the increase in the cost of the least cost diet if the calorie requirement increases from 2700 to 2701. Suppose now that the foods to compose the least cost diet is being paid for *via* a subsidy being donated by central government ; Y_1 then gives the amount by which this subsidy would have to increase if the requirement for calories was increased from 2700 to 2701.

Retaining this interpretation of Y_1, Y_2, Y_3 as the subsidies payable per calorie, per unit of protein and per unit of vitamin C purchased for the diet, consider the problem of formulating the diet from the point of view of those who provide the subsidy. First, in the case of 100 grammes of oranges, these, if purchased will provide 160 calories, 11.3 units of protein and one unit of vitamin C. The total subsidy payable will thus be:

$$160Y_1 + 11.3Y_2 + Y_3 \qquad\qquad ----(5.37)$$

The cost of one hundred grammes of oranges is nine cents. The subsidy levels could be such that this cost is not met i.e.

$$160Y_1 + 11.3Y_2 + Y_3 < 9 \qquad\qquad ----(5.38)$$

in the which case oranges will not be purchased or just met i.e.

$$160Y_1 + 11.3Y_2 + Y_3 = 9 \qquad\qquad ----(5.39)$$

in the which case the subsidy levels are such as to just permit the purchase of oranges or met with a surplus i.e.

$$160Y_1 + 11.3Y_2 + Y_3 > 9 \qquad\qquad ----(5.40)$$

in the which case the subsidy levels are such as to permit the purchase of oranges and leave a surplus for those who do this. From the point of view of the donors of the subsidy, the situation (5.40) is undesirable : hence the imposition of the condition (5.38), (5.39) as the first constraint in (5.36). Hence also the logic underlying the other constraints. Given the total requirement of the diet, the total subsidy payable is:

$$2700Y + 65Y_2 + 2000Y_3 \qquad\qquad ----(5.41)$$

Following the logic of the previous section, this is in fact the fictitious subsidy payable; minimisation of the actual subsidy payable will be equivalent to the maximisation of the fictitious subsidy which does indeed form the objective of (5.36).

It is to be noted that as might be expected, the

interpretation of the dual variables in the case of a primal involving maximisation is opposite in sense to the case of a primal involving minimisation : in the former case, $Y_1, \ldots, Y_m$ are 'prices' whereas in the latter they comprise 'subsidies'. The general form of a primal problem involving minimisation is to choose the levels for each of a set of activities in order to :

> MINIMISE :   Some quantity e.g. costs
>
>   s.t.   Certain required standards met

The general form of the dual is to choose a series of subsidy values per unit of each requirement in order to :

> MAXIMISE :   Fictitious subsidy payable (equivalent to minimising actual subsidy)
>
>   s.t.   Subsidies paid are just sufficient to cover the costs of the activities/goods actually engaged in/purchased

5.9   DUAL FORMULATIONS : FURTHER EXAMPLES

5.9.1   Henderson (1968)

Recall (Section 4.2.3) the agricultural landuse problem of Henderson (1968) : (4.21), (4.24)-(4.26). Multiplying (4.25) across by minus one and introducing the dual variables R_j^{MAX}, $j = 1, \ldots, n$; R_j^{MIN}, $j = 1, \ldots, n$ and R to correspond to the constraints (4.24),(4.25) and (4.26) respectively, the dual problem is :

$$
\begin{aligned}
\text{MINIMISE :} \quad & \sum_{j=1}^{n} b_j R_j^{MAX} - \sum_{j=1}^{n} b_j R_j^{MIN} + R \\
\text{s.t.} \quad & R_j^{MAX} - R_j^{MIN} + R \geq c_j \\
& j = 1, \ldots, n \\
& R_j^{MAX}, R_j^{MIN} \geq 0; \; j=1,\ldots,n \; ; R \geq 0
\end{aligned}
$$

$$---- (5.42)$$

Henderson interprets the dual from the point of view of entrepreneur land owners who rent land to the farmers. R gives the 'worth' to the farmer of an extra acre of land and, therefore, from the point of view of the landowners, represents the rent an acre of land will fetch. R_j^{MAX} gives the worth to the farmer of a unit increase in the upper limit of crop j acreage permitted. Therefore, from the point of view of the land-owners, it represents an additional sum per acre that can be added to the overall rent R when land is devoted to use j. Finally, $R_{j\ MIN}$ gives the worth (negative) to the farmer of a unit increase in the lower limit of crop j permitted. There-fore, from the point of view of the landowners, it represents a subsidy per acre that must be subtracted from the overall rent R when land is devoted to use j.

From the point of view of the landowners, the objective in (5.42) relates to a minimisation of the fictitious returns received from rent which is equivalent to a maximisation of actual returns. The constraints fix the rent levels in such a way that for crop j, the rent per acre of crop j grown payable by the farmer will either equal or exceed his return. Where the rents are such as to cause the latter to be the case, crop j will not be grown.

5.9.2 Herbert and Stevens (1960)

Recall (Section 4.2.1) the residential landuse model of Herbert and Stevens (1960) : (4.10)-(4.13). Multiplying the constraint (4.11) across by minus one and reversing the order of (4.11) and (4.12) yields the problem:

$$\text{MAXIMISE} : \sum_{i=1}^{\ell} \sum_{j=1}^{m} \sum_{k=1}^{n} (b_{jk} - c_{jk}^{i}) \, X_{jk}^{i}$$

$$\text{s.t.} \quad \sum_{j=1}^{m} \sum_{k=1}^{n} s_{k}^{i} \, X_{jk}^{i} \leq a_{i} \; ; \; i = 1, \ldots, \ell$$

$$\sum_{i=1}^{\ell} \sum_{k=1}^{n} X_{jk}^{i} = - n_{j} \; ; \; j = 1, \ldots, m$$

$$X_{jk}^{i} \geq 0 \text{ for all } i, j, k$$

Following Section 5.7 and recalling that for an equality con-straint in the primal the corresponding dual variable is unrestricted in sign, the dual problem is :

$$\text{MINIMISE} : \sum_{i=1}^{\ell} a_{i} \, U_{i} - \sum_{j=1}^{m} n_{j} \, V_{j}$$

$$\text{s.t.} \quad s_{k}^{i} \, U_{i} - V_{j} \geq (b_{jk} - c_{jk}^{i}) \text{ for all } i, j, k$$

$$U_{i} \geq 0 \; ; \; i = 1, \ldots, \ell$$

$$V_{j} \text{ unrestricted}$$

where the dual variables U_i, $i=1, \ldots, \ell$ and V_j, $j=1, \ldots, m$ correspond to the first and second constraint sets respectively in the primal.

Proceeding in the same manner as before, U_i represents the change in the objective for a unit change in the right hand side of the corresponding constraint in the primal which in this instance would be the increase in total rent paying ability achieved by a unit increase in the area of zone i, i.e. the 'worth' of an acre of land in zone i. From the point of view of the owners of the land in zone i, U_i thus represents the rent per acre that could be charged for land in that zone.

The interpretation of the variables V_j may best be understood by examining the dual constraint set. Recalling that s_k is the acreage occupied by a single household of residential bundle type k in zone i, the quantity $s_k U_i$ gives the rent which will be payable by this household. Recalling that $(b_{ik} - c_{ik}')$ represents the rent paying ability of such a household, the quantity V_j gives the difference between these two quantities and is thus the subsidy (positive) or surplus (negative) required by/achieved by that type of household in that zone within the optimal solution. The need for subsidies to certain household types arises from the fact that the first constraint set requires that all households be located. The objective involves minimising the total fictitious returns from rents adjusted by the subsidy values i.e. maximising the actual returns. The reader is referred to the original paper for further details and, in particular, for an in-depth discussion of the precise role of the V_j values.

5.9.3. Miller (1963)

Recall (Section 4.2.5) the aircraft scheduling model of Miller (1963) (4.31)-(4.35). Introducing the dual variables $^j V_h$, $j = 1, \ldots, r$; W_h, $h = 1, \ldots, q$ and $^j U^k$, $j = 1, \ldots, r$; $k = 1, \ldots, s$ to correspond to the constraints (4.32), (4.33) and (4.34) respectively and multiplying (4.33) across by minus one to yield all 'greater than or equals' constraints, the dual problem is :

$$\text{MAXIMISE :} \quad -\sum_{h=1}^{q} s_h W_h + \sum_{j=1}^{r} \sum_{k=1}^{s} {}^{jk}d \cdot {}^{jk}U \quad \text{----(5.43)}$$

$$\text{s.t.} \quad {}^kV_h - {}^jV_h - {}^j b_h^k W_h + {}^j a_h^k {}^j U^k \leq {}^j c_h^k \quad \text{----(5.44)}$$

$$^j V_h \text{ unrestricted}$$

$$W_h \geq 0 \; ; \; h = 1, \ldots, q$$

$$^j U^k \geq 0 \; ; \; j = 1, \ldots, r \; ; \; k = 1, \ldots, s$$

Linear Programming : Sensitivity Analysis and the Dual

The dual variables may be interpreted in the usual manner. First, ^jV_h gives the change in the value of the objective in altering (4.32) to:

$$\sum_{k=1}^{s} {}^kx_h^j - \sum_{k=1}^{s} {}^jx_h^k = 1 \text{ for a given j and h}$$

i.e. the change in the total costs when it is required that the final schedule be such that one aircraft of type h be placed at j. If ^jV_h is positive, i.e. total costs increase when it is required that one aircraft of type h be placed at j, ^jV_h gives the subsidy that should be paid to the airline for adopting this course of action; if on the other hand ^jV_h is negative, it represents the rent the aircraft company could afford to pay for being permitted to place an aircraft of type h at location j.

The dual variables W_h give the sensitivity of the optimal solution to a unit change in the right hand side of (4.33) multiplied across by minus one i.e. to a unit change to t_h in:

$$-\sum_{j=1}^{r} \sum_{h=1}^{q} {}^jb_h^k \, {}^jx_h^k \geq - t_h \quad \text{for a given h} \quad ----(5.45)$$

A unit increase in t_h in (5.45) is equivalent to decreasing by one hour the flying time available in aircraft of type h. The corresponding W_h value thus gives the 'worth' of an hour of such flying time to the airline company and thus the rent the company would be prepared to pay per hour for such an aircraft. Finally, and following the same logic, the dual variables $^ju^k$ give the increase in total cost to the airline company of carrying an additional passenger from j to k and therefore the 'subsidy' or 'fare' the company should receive for so doing.

Given the foregoing interpretations of the dual variables, the complete dual problem can now be interpreted as determining rents/subsidies associated with each location, rental costs per hour for each aircraft type and per passenger cost levels for each route. The constraints require that for each route and aircraft type, those who fix the levels of the various foregoing costs/subsidies do so in such a way that the return to the company in making a flight on a route ($^ja_h^k \, ^ku^k$) less the rental cost for the aircraft ($^jb_h^k \, W_h$) and adjusted to account for the change in potential rental costs caused by moving the aircraft ($^kV_h - {}^jV_h$) is less than or equal to the actual cost to the company of making the movement. If the overall return to the company as given by the left hand side of (5.44) is less than the actual cost involved, the corresponding aircraft route movement will not in fact take place. The objective concerns the maximisation of the fictitious subsidy (fare) paid to the airline (as given

by the second term in the objective) less the return for
rental of aircraft which, following the logic of previous
sections is equivalent to the minimisation of actual subsidies
adjusted for rental returns. Note that because the actual
number of aircraft kept at each location equals zero (4.32),
the rents/subsidies associated with each location i.e. the
$^J V_h$ values do not occur explicitly in the objective.

5.10 A FURTHER NOTE ON PRIMAL-DUAL INTERRELATIONSHIPS

Recall (Section 4.9.1) the manner in which the existence of
alternative optimal solutions to a particular linear programming problem was signalled via the format of the final simplex
solution tableau : (a) certain non-basis variables(s) possess-
ed (a) zero value(s) in the X_o row. Consider now the
implications of such a situation for the corresponding dual
solution. Taking the last solution tableau in Section 4.9.1
i.e.

BASIS	X_o	X_1	X_2	S_1	S_2	S_3	SOLUTION
X_o	①	0	0	2	0	0	1200
X_2	0	0	①	1	-2	0	150
X_1	0	①	0	-1	3	0	75
S_3	0	0	0	1	-7	①	25

as an example, consider now the nature of the corresponding
dual solution. Recall (Section 5.7) that the simplex multipliers in the primal give the dual variable values whilst the
shadow costs give the corresponding slack variable values.
Designating the three dual variables as Y_1, Y_2, Y_3 and the
slack variables as S_1' and S_2' respectively, the dual solution
corresponding to the preceding tableau is :

$$Y_o = 1200 \; ; \; Y_1 = 2 \; ; \; Y_2 = 0 \; ; \; Y_3 = 0)$$
$$S_1 = 0 \; ; \; S_2 = 0 \qquad) \qquad \text{----} (5.46)$$

A point to note concerning this solution is that it contains
more zero valued variables than would be expected on the basis
of Section 4.4.4 ; it is thus degenerate in the sense of
Section 4.9.2. In fact, the dual solution corresponding to
any primal solution involving alternative optima will always
be degenerate because, by definition, the solution tableau of
the latter will always contain more zero values than expected

in the X_ρ row of the final simplex tableau. The same reasoning can be used to show that where the solution to a primal problem is degenerate, the corresponding dual solution will involve alternative optima.

From the point of view of actual applications, the existence of alternative optimal solutions and/or degeneracy in the primal can somewhat restrict the amount of information generated by the dual. Reconsider the dual of Miller's aircraft scheduling problem discussed in the previous section. Presumably, within the context of an actual application, great interest would focus on the ${}^J V_h$, W_h and ${}^J U^k$ values emerging as these would give for example the relative merits of using various locations for storing aircraft of different types and the relative 'worths' of the various aircraft types. However, in solving the primal formulation (4.31)-(4.35) Miller encountered both alternative optima (as was discussed in Section 4.9.1) and degeneracy. Thus both degeneracy and, more important, alternative optima i.e. alternative values for ${}^J V_h$, W_h and ${}^J U^k$ exist in the dual solution which obviously severely restricts the drawing of any precise conclusions on the basis of their relative magnitudes e.g. concerning the relative merits of different aircraft types and storage locations.

5.11   THE DUAL OF THE TRANSPORTATION PROBLEM

Recall (Section 3.3.1) the transportation problem (3.5)-(3.7). Introducing the dual variables U_i, $i=1, \ldots, m$ to correspond to the origin constraints (3.6) and V_j, $j=1, \ldots, n$ to correspond to the destination constraints (3.7) and multiplying the former across by minus one, the corresponding dual problem is :

$$\text{MAXIMISE :} \quad \sum_{j=1}^{n} d_j V_j - \sum_{i=1}^{m} s_i U_i \qquad \text{----(5.47)}$$

$$\text{s.t.} \qquad V_j - U_i \leq c_{ij} \qquad \text{----(5.48)}$$

$$U_i, V_j \text{ unrestricted in sign} \text{ ----(5.49)}$$

Note that in fact, this formulation corresponds to the alternative view of the transportation problem presented in Section 3.3.4 : (3.8), (3.11). Notice too that the interpretation of the problem as given in Section 3.3.4 corresponds closely to that which would be obtained following the logic set out in Section 5.8. The U_i and V_j values represent the current 'worth' of a unit of product at each origin and destination respectively. The objective involves maximising the fictitious increase in total worth achieved as a result of transportation which is equivalent to minimising the actual increase i.e. to minimising total transport costs. The constraints require that the increase in 'worth' be less or equal to the transportation costs involved. If, in fact, (5.48) holds as an inequality for a particular origin and destination, transportation will not take place on the route concerned. Once more, this confirms the interpretation presented in Section 3.3.4.

Recall (Section 4.8) that when expressed in the form (3.5)-(3.7), one constraint in the transportation problem is redundant. It can be shown that if the problem is solved *via* the simplex method as set out in Section 4.8 but with the redundant constraint included, the resultant solution will be degenerate. Recall from the previous section that this signals the existence of alternative optimal solutions for the dual variables i.e. for $U_1, \ldots, U_m$ and $V_1, \ldots, V_n$. Recall too (Section 3.3.4) that such alternative solutions do indeed exist : a set of shadow cost values for a particular solution e.g. in Table 3.5 could only be deduced after one of these had been abritrarily set. Thus, once more, the methods introduced to deal with the transportation and other related problems in Chapter Three replicate the results obtainable *via* the more general approaches presented in this and the previous chapter.

6

INTEGER PROGRAMMING

6.1 INTRODUCTION

An *integer programming* problem comprises a problem of the
form (1.1)-(1.3) with an additional condition appended,
namely that the values of each of the decision variables
comprising the optimal solution be integer valued. If only
certain of the decision variables are to be integer valued
at optimality, the problem is said to involve *mixed integer
programming*. In this text, we shall consider *integer linear
programming* problems only i.e. linear programming problems of
the form (4.1)-(4.3) to which the integer condition has been
added.

A review of the examples presented in the previous two
chapters suggests a number of situations in which non-integer
solution values are inappropriate; within the context of an
urban landuse study for example (Section 4.2.1, 4.7.1), a
recommendation that (say) 1.37 schools be built has little
meaning. A good example of an integer linear programming
formulation is that of Evans (1972) who considers a problem
posed initially by Bacon (1971). The problem involves finding the number of trips a consumer should make within a given
time period to each of n shopping centres in his area in
order to minimise his total trip costs whilst providing at
least a given number of opportunities to buy each of m given
goods. Formally, if:

c_j = The cost of a trip to shopping centre j, $j=1, \ldots, n$
and

X_j = The number of trips undertaken to shopping centre j in
the time period under consideration

the objective is to:

Minimise : $\sum\limits_{j=1}^{n} c_j X_j$ ----(6.1)

DOI: 10.4324/9781003179030-6

Now, if:

n_i = The minimum number of opportunities which must be provided to buy good i, i=1, ..., m

and a_{ij} = 1 if good i is available in shopping centre j and equals zero otherwise

the optimal values of X_j must be such that:

$$\sum_{j=1}^{n} a_{ij} X_j \geq n_i \; ; \; i = 1, \ldots, m \qquad \text{----(6.2)}$$

Finally and obviously, it is required that each X_j be non-negative and integer valued which completes the formulation.

Within the context of applications, it is interesting to note that the transportation problem (Section 3.3) is in fact an integer programming problem. It can be shown that if all of the s_i, d_i and c_{ij} values in (3.5)-(3.7) are integers, so too will be the optimal values for X_{ij} (except where there are alternative optimal solutions i.e. where flows can be shifted continuously between sets of routes (Section 3.3.6)).

Turning to possible solution methods for integer programming problems, one approach which immediately suggests itself is to solve the problem to hand as a straightforward linear programming problem using the simplex method and then to round the non-integer optimal solution values downwards in the case of maximisation and upwards in the case of minimisation. Unfortunately, while this approach often yields the correct solution especially if the optimal values of X_j are large, this is not always the case. Consider the problem:

$$\text{Maximise} : 5X_1 + 8X_2$$
$$\text{s.t.} \quad 7X_1 + 8X_2 \leq 28 \qquad \text{----(6.3)}$$
$$X_1 + 2X_2 \leq 6$$
$$X_1 \; X_2 \text{ are non-negative integers} \qquad \text{----(6.4)}$$

whose solution space is depicted in Figure 6.1 (OB_1SA_2). Solving (6.3) as a linear programming problem i.e. with (6.4) replaced by:

$$X_1, X_2 \geq 0 \qquad \text{----(6.5)}$$

yields the optimal solution:

$$X_o = 25^{1/3}; \; X_1 = 1^{1/3}; \; X_2 = 2^{1/3}$$

which suggests the optimal integer solution:

$$X_o = 21 \; ; \; X_1 = 1 \; ; \; X_2 = 2$$

In fact, the optimal integer solution is:

$$X_O = 24 \; ; \; X_1 = 0 \; ; \; X_2 = 3$$

Given that 'rounding off' the corresponding optimal linear programming decision variable values does not necessarily yield the appropriate integer programming optimal solution, we seek other methods for finding this. Two general approaches are available : *cutting plane methods* and *branch and bound methods*. A specific version of each of these is now presented.

6.2   CUTTING PLANE METHODS : THE FRACTIONAL ALGORITHM

Reconsider the problem (6.3) with (6.4) or (6.5). Figure 6.1 shows the solution space (OB_1SA_2) and the optimal solution

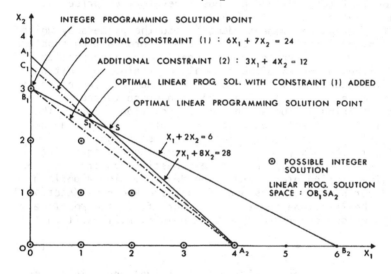

Figure 6.1 Integer Programming Problem

point (S) for the linear programming problem. Also shown are those points within or on the boundary of this solution space where X_1 and X_2 are integers. These comprise the set of possible solution points for (6.3), (6.4) of which one (assuming the absence of alternative optima) will be optimal.

Consider now the task of solving (6.3), (6.5) with the constraint C_1A_2 in Figure 6.1 added. The geometry of this constraint is such that it reduces the linear programming solution space while not excluding any potential integer solution point. Within the context of integer programming, such an additional constraint is referred to as a *cutting plane*. Solving a linear programming problem with (a) cutting plane constraint(s) added can give rise to one of two results: either the revised solution will be integer valued and must therefore be the required integer programming solution or the revised solution will be non-integer valued. In the latter case, the new solution must at least be 'closer' to the required integer programming solution. The solution to (6.3), (6.5) with C_1A_2 added (which is given by S_1 in Figure 6.1) is non-integer valued. Thus, all that can be said is that this revised solution must be closer to the required integer programming solution. Consider now the task of solving (6.3), (6.5) with the cutting plane B_1A_2 added. Notice that B_1A_2 is more restrictive than C_1A_2 excluding from consideration a larger area of the original solution space OB_1SA_2. Solution of (6.3), (6.5) with B_1A_2 added yields $X_1 = 0$; $X_2 = 3$. This solution is integer valued and must therefore comprise the optimal solution to (6.3), (6.4).

The foregoing comments demonstrate the process by which cutting plane methods for solving integer programming problems work. First, the corresponding linear programming problem is solved. Then a series of additional constraints or cutting planes is successively introduced. Each new cutting plane is such as to reduce the original solution space further in area whilst retaining all possible integer solution points. The first all integer solution encountered after imposing a new cutting plane gives the required optimal solution.

Quite obviously, when solving an integer programming problem using cutting planes, a key question concerns how the successive cutting planes are to be derived. The algorithm to be described here makes use of what are known as *fractional parts*. The fractional part of a number, f, is the *positive* fraction which is obtained when the number, N, is written in the form:

$$N = I + f \qquad\qquad ----(6.6)$$

where I is an integer (positive or negative) and f is a positive fraction. Thus for N = 3 1/5:

$$3\ 1/5 = 3 + 1/5$$

and thus f = 1/5. Again for N = -3 1/5:

$$-\ 3\ 1/5 = -4 + 4/5$$

and thus f = 4/5. Notice that because f must be positive while I may be positive or negative, the fractional part associated with -3 1/5 is + 4/5 and not -1/5.

In order to see how fractional parts may be used to construct successive cutting plane constraints, reconsider the problem (6.3), (6.5). The optimal solution as obtained using the simplex method is:

BASIS	X_o	X_1	X_2	S_1	S_2	SOLUTION
X_o	①	0	0	1/3	8/3	76/3
X_1	0	①	0	1/3	-4/3	4/3
X_2	0	0	①	-1/6	7/6	7/3

Neither of the decision variables is integer valued. We thus identify the decision variable possessing the largest associated fractional part. In the case of a tie (as exists here) either variable may be chosen. Arbitrarily choosing X_2, we note the corresponding constraint equation in the current tableau i.e.

$$X_2 - 1/6 \ S_1 + 7/6 \ S_2 = 7/3 \qquad \text{----(6.7)}$$

Rewriting the coefficients in (6.7) in the form of the right hand side of (6.6) yields:

$$X_2 + (-1+5/6) \ S_1 + (1+1/6) \ S_2 = 2' + 1/3$$

i.e. $\qquad X_2 - S_1 + S_2 + 5/6 \ S_1 + 1/6 \ S_2 = 2 + 1/3 \quad \text{----(6.8)}$

Now, if it is required that each of X_2, S_1, S_2 in (6.8) be integer valued, the first three terms in (6.8) will be integer valued. Thus, in order to maintain the veracity of (6.8) and recalling that S_1, $S_2 > 0$, the sum of the remaining terms must equal 1/3 or 1 1/3 or 2 1/3 or ... etc. i.e.

$$5/6 \ S_1 + 1/6 \ S_2 = I_1 + 1/3 \qquad \text{----(6.9)}$$

where I_1 is a non-negative integer. Rearrangement of (6.9) yields:

$$-5/6 \ S_1 - 1/6 \ S_2 + I_1 = -1/3 \qquad \text{----(6.10)}$$

which, in terms of the simplex method can be viewed as a new constraint with a basis variable I_1. Appending this additional constraint to the current optimal solution tableau yields:

BASIS	X_o	X_1	X_2	S_1	S_2	I_1	SOLUTION
X_o	①	0	0	1/3	8/3	0	76/3
X_1	0	①	0	1/3	-4/3	0	4/3
X_2	0	0	①	-1/6	7/6	0	7/3
I_1	0	0	0	-5/6	-1/6	①	-1/3
RATIO				1/3 8/3 -5/6 -1/6			

A negative value for I_1 demonstrates that the solution is no longer optimal; the additional constraint is such as to exclude the current optimal solution from the revised solution space. The dual-simplex method (Section 5.3) can be used to obtain the revised solution. I_1 leaves the basis whilst S_1 enters which yields:

BASIS	X_o	X_1	X_2	S_1	S_2	I_1	SOLUTION
X_o	①	0	0	0	13/5	2/5	126/5
X_1	0	①	0	0	-7/5	2/5	6/5
X_2	0	0	①	0	6/5	-1/5	12/5
S_1	0	0	0	①	1/5	-6/5	2/5

The revised optimal value is lower than before. Unfortunately, imposition of the condition (6.10) has not been such as to cause X_1 or X_2 to take integer values.

Before proceeding, it is worth examining the precise nature of the newly imposed condition (6.10) in more detail. In terms of the initial starting solution:

$$S_1 = 28 - 7X_1 - 8X_2$$

$$S_2 = 6 - X_1 - 2X_2$$

Thus, when expressed in terms of X_1 and X_2, (6.10) becomes:

$$-5/6 \ (28-7X_1-8X_2) - 1/6 \ (6-X_1- 2X_2) + I_1 = - 1/3$$

which reduces to:

$$6X_1 + 7X_2 + I_1 = -24 \qquad \text{---- (6.11)}$$

or, envisaging I_1 as a slack variable:

$$6X_1 + 7X_2 \leq 24 \qquad \text{---- (6.12)}$$

The constraint (6.12), is in fact that plotted as A_1A_2 in Figure 6.1. As discussed previously, it forms a cutting plane. The original optimal solution point, S, is excluded from the solution space. The optimal solution now lies at S_1 which is indeed specified by the last simplex tableau.

It has now been demonstrated that for this example, the methods (6.7)-(6.10) provide a cutting plane. In fact, it can be shown that these methods when applied to a simplex tableau will always yield such a plane. Thus, except in exceptional circumstances which we do not elaborate on here, successive applications of the foregoing methods i.e. successive introductions of tighter and tighter cutting planes will ultimately yield the required integer optimal solution.

To continue with the calculations and returning to the last simplex tableau, the value of X_2 possesses the largest fractional part. The corresponding constraint statement:

$$X_2 + 6/5S_2 + -1/5I_1 = 12/5 \qquad \text{----(6.13)}$$

yields the cutting plane condition:

$$-1/5S_2 - 4/5I_1 + I_2 = -2/5 \qquad \text{----(6.14)}$$

which when appended to the tableau gives:

BASIS	X_0	X_1	X_2	S_1	S_2	I_1	I_2	SOLUTION
X_0	①	0	0	0	13/5	2/5	0	126/5
X_1	0	①	0	0	-7/5	2/5	0	6/5
X_2	0	0	①	0	6/5	-1/5	0	12/5
S_1	0	0	0	①	1/5	-6/5	0	2/5
I_2	0	0	0	0	-1/5	-4/5	①	-2/5
Ratio					$\dfrac{13/5}{-1/5}$	$\dfrac{2/5}{-4/5}$		

Application of the dual-simplex method shows that I_2 leaves the basis with I_1 entering which yields:

BASIS	X_o	X_1	X_2	S_1	S_2	I_1	I_2	SOL.
X_o	①	0	0	0	5	0	1/2	25
X_1	0	①	0	0	-3/2	0	1/2	1
X_2	0	0	①	0	5/4	0	-1/4	5/2
S_1	0	0	0	①	1/2	0	-3/2	1
I_1	0	0	0	0	1/4	①	-5/4	1/2

Although X_1 is now integer valued, X_2 is not. Thus, presumably, the foregoing methods must be applied yet again which will involve introducing yet another constraint row and another variable in the simplex tableau. Indeed, it would appear that in the case of a problem involving many iterations, one would be dealing with a large tableau by the conclusion.

Fortunately, in practice, this will not be the case. Consider the last iteration in the foregoing calculations. I_2 has left the basis while I_1 has entered. Recall (6.10)-(6.12) that in effect, I_1 is a slack variable associated with the first cutting plane imposed. The fact that I_1 has entered the basis on the second iteration demonstrates that the new solution is no longer bound by this cutting plane. Given that the method proceeds by imposing stricter and stricter cutting planes, once one particular plane becomes non-binding i.e. its associated I variable re-enters the basis, it will never become binding again. Thus the corresponding constraint row can be dropped from further calculations. In the case of the last simplex tableau, this means that the final row can be ignored to yield as input to the third iteration:

BASIS	X_o	X_1	X_2	S_1	S_2	I_2	SOLUTION
X_o	①	0	0	0	5	1/2	25
X_1	0	①	0	0	-3/2	1/2	1
X_2	0	0	①	0	5/4	-1/4	5/2
S_1	0	0	0	①	1/2	-3/2	1

In general, for an integer programming problem comprising n variables and m constraints, it can be shown that the number of constraint rows to be considered in the relevant simplex tableaux will never exceed (m + n). Whilst this exceeds the m rows involved in linear programming solutions, it still comprises a manageable size for most problems.

We leave it as an exercise for the reader to continue the cutting plane calculations on the preceding tableau. The optimal solution which does indeed correspond to that noted at the end of the previous section is obtained after two further iterations.

To conclude, certain features of the cutting plane approach for solving integer programming problems as exemplified by the foregoing example deserve mention. Barring exceptional mathematical circumstances, the method will always yield the required optimal solution eventually but there is no way of telling in advance how many iterations will be required. This can be disadvantageous especially when the problem concerned is being run on a computer facility where time is limited. Unfortunately, if the calculations are terminated before the optimal solution has been found, the method is such as to not even yield an all integer suboptimal solution : the calculations are such that the first all integer solution which is generated is the optimum.

Within the context of a particular problem, the speed at which the optimal solution will be reached depends on two factors : the method used to choose the variable and constraint from which the cutting plane will be derived and the way in which the cutting plane is constructed. Concerning the former, the approach used here was to choose the decision variable with the largest associated fractional part and, in the case of a tie, to choose arbitrarily. The reader should check that if at the first iteration in the preceding calculations X_1 had been chosen, the optimal solution would have emerged at the end of the second iteration. Concerning the latter, the method (6.6)-(6.10) represents but one way in which cutting planes can be derived mathematically; others exist which for some problems, will yield the optimal solution more rapidly. Unfortunately, within the context of both methods for choosing variables/constraints and methods for constructing cutting planes, no one technique has emerged which has been found to be universally the most efficient. Rather, each of the various techniques which have been suggested has been used to advantage in solving certain problems.

6.3   BRANCH AND BOUND METHODS : DAKIN'S ALGORITHM

We shall demonstrate a specific version of the second major method for solving integer programming problems, branch and bound, by using it to solve the formulation (6.3)-(6.4). For a maximisation problem, the method commences by defining a feasible (i.e. all integer) solution which has an associated objective value, below which it is known the optimum does not lie. In the absence of any other information, a suitable initial feasible solution for the example which fulfills the foregoing condition is:

$$X_1 = 0 \; ; \; X_2 = 0$$

for which $X_o = 0$. This value for X_o is referred to as the *current lower bound* (L.B.).

Once a lower bound for X_o and its associated solution has been defined, the branch and bound procedure commences (as did the cutting plane approach) by solving the equivalent linear programming problem i.e. (6.3), (6.5). The solution, together with the foregoing current lower bound value for X_o is summarised as Problem One in Figure 6.2. If this solution

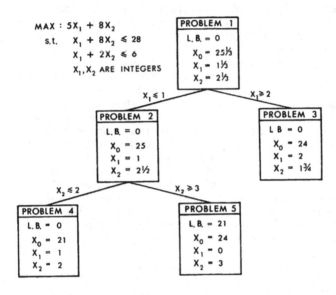

MAX : $5X_1 + 8X_2$

s.t. $X_1 + 8X_2 \leqslant 28$

$X_1 + 2X_2 \leqslant 6$

X_1, X_2 ARE INTEGERS

PROBLEM 1

L.B. = 0

$X_0 = 25\frac{1}{3}$

$X_1 = 1\frac{1}{3}$

$X_2 = 2\frac{1}{3}$

$X_1 \leqslant 1$

$X_1 \geqslant 2$

PROBLEM 2

L.B. = 0

$X_0 = 25$

$X_1 = 1$

$X_2 = 2\frac{1}{2}$

PROBLEM 3

L B = 0

$X_0 = 24$

$X_1 = 2$

$X_2 = 1\frac{3}{4}$

$X_2 \leqslant 2$

$X_2 \geqslant 3$

PROBLEM 4

L.B. = 0

$X_0 = 21$

$X_1 = 1$

$X_2 = 2$

PROBLEM 5

L.B. = 21

$X_0 = 24$

$X_1 = 0$

$X_2 = 3$

Figure 6.2 Dakin's Branch and Bound Algorithm

was integer valued it would comprise the required optimum; because it is not, the branch and bound procedure is invoked.

Consider one of the non-integer valued variables in Problem One e.g. X_1. If $X_1 = 1$ 1/3 in the linear programming solution it is obvious that in the integer programming solution either:

$$X_1 \leq 1 \qquad\qquad ----(6.15)$$

or $\qquad X_1 \geq 2 \qquad\qquad ----(6.16)$

In general, for any linear programming solution with $X_j = b_j$ at optimality where b_j is non-integer valued, either:

$$X_j \leq [b_j] \qquad \qquad ----(6.17)$$

$$X_j \geq [b_j] + 1 \qquad \qquad ----(6.18)$$

in the corresponding integer programming problem where $[b_j]$ is the largest integer less than or equal to b_j. Imposition of (6.15) and (6.16) in turn on (6.3), (6.4) yields two new linear programming problems which are labelled as Problems Two and Three respectively in Figure 6.2. Because these can be looked upon as having been derived directly from Problem One *via* the imposition of (6.15) and (6.16) in turn, they are represented as such by two branches emanating from that problem. Solving them in turn using the methods discussed in Section 5.5.3 yields the solutions shown. Unfortunately, neither is all-integer valued. Thus the method must proceed.

Two possibilities for continuing present themselves. First, one could obtain two new linear programming problems from Problem Two by imposing the additional conditions:

$$X_2 \leq 2 \; ; \; X_2 \geq 3 \qquad \qquad ----(6.19)$$

Second, one could impose the additional conditions:

$$X_2 \leq 1 \; ; \; X_2 \geq 2 \qquad \qquad ----(6.20)$$

on Problem Three. Within the context of Figure 6.2, the squares representing Problems Two and Three are said to constitute *active nodes* because each contains at least one non-integer valued variable which thus could be used to generate two additional linear programming problems. From which of these two active nodes should the branching process be performed first? The logical answer to this question can be seen by noting that the branching process involves the imposition of additional constraints on a currently solved linear programming problem. Thus, in the case of a maximisation objective, each derived problem possesses a lower X_o value than that from which it is descended. We are seeking an optimal solution where X_o is as large as possible but each X_i is integer valued and, in the absence of any other information, it is logical to guess that such a solution is most likely to be found to a problem emanating from the currently active node where X_o is greatest. Thus, in the case of the example and viewing the X_o values for Problems Two and Three, we branch on Problem Two.

Solving the left hand branch as Problem Four (Figure 6.2) yields the solution:

$$X_1 = 1 \; ; \; X_2 = 2 \; ; \; X_o = 21 \qquad \text{----}(6.21)$$

This is an all-integer solution and vastly superior to that corresponding to the current lower bound value. Thus it is retained and L.B. (i.e. the value below which the optimal value of X_o in (6.3), (6.4) cannot lie) is set to 21. Because the solution to Problem Four is integer valued, no further linear programming problems can be derived from it by imposing conditions of the form (6.17), (6.18). In terms of Figure 6.2, Problem Four is said therefore to comprise a *terminal node*.

Continuing with the solution process and solving the right hand branch problem (Problem Five) yields:

$$X_1 = 0 \; ; \; X_2 = 3 \; ; \; X_o = 24 \qquad \text{----}(6.22)$$

Once more, this is integer valued. Thus, in terms of Figure 6.2, Problem Five comprises a terminal node. Comparison of the X_o value in Problem Five and that corresponding to L.B. (Problem Four) shows that the former is superior. Thus it is retained and L.B. is set to 24.

Referring once more to Figure 6.2, there is now but one active node — that associated with Problem Three. Thus, two further linear programming problems could be derived by branching from it. However, given that $X_o = 24$ for this node, the X_o values for any problem derived from it will be less than this. Given that the current value of L.B. is 24, any solutions associated with problems derived from Problem Three will obviously be suboptimal and thus they need not be evaluated explicitly. Thus the solution (6.22) is the required optimum.

To summarise the foregoing, in the case of a maximisation problem, the branch and bound procedure commences by setting a lower bound to the optimal solution. Then, commencing with the optimal linear programming solution, the method proceeds iteratively, branching on each iteration on the node for which X_o is greatest. Whenever an all-integer solution for which X_o exceeds L.B. is encountered, this is retained and L.B. is set to X_o. The procedure ceases when there is no active node for which $X_o >$ L.B.

The branch and bound approach can be adapted readily to solve a minimisation problem. First, an initial upper bound all-integer solution is defined e.g.

$$X_1 = X_2 \; \ldots \; = X_n = M \; ; \; X_o = \text{U.B.}$$

where M is a very large number. At each iteration, branching is performed on the node for which X_o is smallest. Whenever an all-integer solution for which X_o is less than U.B. is encountered, this is retained and U.B. is set to X_o. The procedure ceases when there is no active node for which

$X_0 <$ L.B.

The numerical example demonstrates certain features of the branch and bound approach which merit specific comment. First, in common with the cutting plane approach, branch and bound involves making a number of arbitrary decisions. These include the choice of the node at which branching is to take place, the method of branching (the approach of (6.17), (6.18) represents but one possibility) and the variable on which branching is to occur. Concerning the latter, the reader should check that if X_2 had been used as the branching variable in Problem One in the example, the optimal solution would have been encountered at once. Concerning the choice of the node from which branching is to take place, the reader should check that if in the example branching on X_2 from Problem Three had been carried out before branching on X_2 from Problem Two, two further linear programming problems would have had to have been solved. A difficulty which surrounds these arbitrary decisions is that in common with the decisions underlying the cutting plane approach, no one method has been found which universally yields the optimal solution most rapidly. Thus a number of branch and bound algorithms exist of which that discussed here is but one example. The reader is referred to a specialist text e.g. Salkin (1975) for other examples.

One feature of branch and bound methods is that they commence by fixing a lower (maximisation)/upper (minimisation) bound on the optimal solution. Very often, especially in the case of a problem involving many variables, the number of computations required can be reduced considerably if an efficient bound i.e. a solution for which L.B. is high (maximisation)/U.B. is low (minimisation) can be determined at the outset or at least early on in the calculations. In the case of a maximisation problem for example, if L.B. is high, then, for many nodes, the condition $X_0 <$ L.B. will hold which will obviate the requirement to solve problems descended from them. A number of methods exist for determining an efficient initial bound for an integer programming problem; the reader should consult a specialised text for details.

One feature of the branch and bound approach which offers an advantage over the cutting plane approach is that 'good' all-integer solutions emerge before the optimal solution. Thus, within the context of computer operations, an early termination of the calculations can still provide a 'good' solution. A major disadvantage of the branch and bound approach over the cutting plane approach is that the number of active nodes each comprising a linear programming formulation and its solution which will have to be retained at each stage of the calculations is not predictable in advance and may become very large thus taxing available computer space. This potential difficulty underlines the importance of determining an efficient bound as early on in the calculations as

207

possible. It is to be noted that difficulties concerning storage space do not arise in the case of the cutting plane approach where, recall, the calculations focus on successive simplex tableaux with a maximum of (m+n) constraint rows.

Despite potential storage space difficulties which can reach serious proportions in the solution of real-world problems, the branch and bound approach has generally proved more useful for solving large problems of the type most commonly encountered by geographers and planners. This is because the cutting plane approach often requires an unrealistically large number of iterations in order to achieve the optimal solution. For this reason, its use has tended to be confined to mixed integer problems where only a small number of variables are required to be integer valued at optimality.

7

ZERO — ONE   PROGRAMMING

7.1 INTRODUCTION

In this chapter, we discuss mathematical programming models of the form (1.1) - (1.3) where some or all of the decision variables are required to equal zero or one at optimality. Problems in which all of the decision variables are required to equal zero or one a,re called *zero-one programming problems;* those in which certain variables only are so constrained are called *mixed zero-one programming problems.* If in a mixed zero-one programming problem the non zero-one variables are required to be integer valued at optimality, the problem comprises a *mixed integer zero-one programming problem.*

At first sight, the potential usefulness of zero-one programming models in real-world situations might appear to be limited. Yet, as the wide range of examples to be presented will show, this is far from being the case. Zero-one decision variables provide a means of incorporating decisions of the 'Yes/No' type e.g. to locate or not to locate into mathematical programming models. One of the main contexts within which mathematical programming is used by geographers and planners is to answer questions of this type in an optimal manner.

By way of an introductory example, consider once again the transportation problem (3.4)-(3.7). Suppose now that in order to meet the demand d_j at each of $j = 1, \ldots, n$ destinations, factories are to be built at some of $i = 1, \ldots, m$ available sites. If the decision is taken to construct a factory at site i, setup costs, f_i, will be incurred. The capacity of the factory will be s_i. It is required that the sites at which the factories should be built together with the origin-destination flow pattern which minimises the sum of setup and flow costs be found. Formally, if:

c_{ij} = per unit transport cost from factory (origin) i to destination j

DOI: 10.4324/9781003179030-7

$Y_i = 1$ if a factory is built at site i

$ = 0$ otherwise

$X_{ij} =$ the flow of product from factory (origin) i to destination j

the problem is to:

$$\text{MINIMISE: } \sum_{i=1}^{m} \sum_{j=1}^{n} c_{ij} X_{ij} + \sum_{i=1}^{m} f_i Y_i \qquad \text{-----(7.1)}$$

$$\text{s.t.} \quad \sum_{i=1}^{m} X_{ij} = d_j \; ; \; j = 1, \ldots, n \; \left.\right)$$

$$\sum_{j=1}^{n} X_{ij} \leq s_i Y_i \; ; \; i = 1, \ldots, m \; \left.\right) \qquad \text{----(7.2)}$$

$$X_{ij} \geq 0; \; Y_i = 0 \text{ or } 1 \quad \left.\right)$$

The first constraint set is as in the transportation problem while the second set ensures that no product is shipped from a site where a factory is not built and that no factory ships out more product than it can produce. A number of versions of the foregoing model which is called *the transportation problem with setup costs* have been suggested (for a summary, see for example Salkin and Balinsky (1973)). The important point to note here is the manner in which the zero-one variables Y_i, $i=1, \ldots, m$ have been used to incorporate decisions of the Yes/No type into the transportation problem. The formulation (7.1), (7.2) comprises a mixed zero-one programming problem.

Within the general context of applications, it is interesting to note that the assignment problem (Section 3.2) is in fact a zero-one programming problem. It can be shown that the optimal X_{ij} values in (3.1)-(3.4) will all equal zero or one (except where alternative optimal solutions exist when, recall, fractional values are possible - Section 3.3.6).

7.2 SOLUTION METHODS FOR ZERO-ONE PROGRAMMING PROBLEMS

Consider the following problem taken from Scott (1971a) (for a general discussion see also Scott (1969b)):

$$\text{Minimise : } \quad 2X_1 + 12X_2 + 9X_3 + 3X_4 + 5X_5 \quad \left.\right)$$

$$\text{s.t.} \quad 3X_1 + 8X_2 + 6X_3 + 4X_4 + 2X_5 \geq 8 \left.\right) \quad \text{----(7.3)}$$

$$X_1, X_2, X_3, X_4, X_5 = 0 \text{ or } 1 \quad \left.\right)$$

Zero-One Programming

At the outset, it is to be noted that zero-one programming problems can be solved *via* the methods discussed in the previous chapter. In the case of (7.3), replacement of the final constraint set by the conditions:

$$X_i \leq 1, \; i = 1, \ldots, 5$$

and application of the simplex method will yield an optimal solution with:

$$0 \leq X_i \leq 1 \; ; \; i = 1, \ldots, 5$$

The cutting plane or branch and bound approaches can now be applied to those variables which do not equal zero or one. In practice, the simplex method allied with branch and bound is often applied, especially if it is known in advance that solution of the initial linear programming problem *via* the simplex method will yield an optimal solution in which many of the decision variables will equal zero or one i.e. a solution containing relatively few variables upon which branching may have to be performed.

Looking at the overall structure of a given zero-one programming problem e.g. (7.3), it possesses one important property which is absent from the integer programming equivalent : because, at optimality, each decision variable must equal either zero or one, the number of possible solutions of which one (assuming the absence of alternative optima) will be optimal is limited. Specifically, for a problem involving n decision variables, there are 2^n possible solutions i.e. unique combinations of values of zero or one for $X_1, \ldots, X_n$. In effect, when seeking the optimal solution to a zero-one programming problem, we are seeking that combination of zeros and ones for the decision variables for which the objective is optimised whilst maintaining feasibility in terms of the constraint(s). When viewed in this manner, zero-one programming problems are often said to involve *combinatorial programming*.

A number of solution methods have been devised for zero-one programming problems which make use of the foregoing characteristics and, in particular, of the fact that there are a limited number of possible solutions. One such method is the *partial enumeration algorithm* or, as it is sometimes called, the *additive algorithm*. It is based on the branch and bound approach of the previous chapter (Section 6.3) but involves performing a series of additions/subtractions at each stage rather than solving linear programming problems. The initial node of the tree (i.e. the equivalent of Problem One in Figure 6.2) comprises the set of all possible solutions. The method proceeds at each stage by setting a particular decision variable value, X_j, to zero (left hand branch) and one (right hand branch) thereby moving one step towards a fully defined solution i.e. all X_j values specified. The rules for branching are such (for a full explanation see for example Wagner (1969)) that the optimal solution should be encountered relatively quickly.

Recall (Section 6.3) that a major disadvantage of the branch and bound method and thus of the partial enumeration algorithm is that it requires that a (sometimes unmanageably large) number of problems and their associated solutions be stored simultaneously. We now describe a solution approach for zero-one programming problems, *backtrack programming*, which, while employing the notion of a tree, obviates the need to retain large numbers of solutions simultaneously.

The set of possible solutions to a zero-one programming problem can be envisaged as comprising a tree such as that in Figure 7.1 which relates to the problem (7.3). The 'base' node (node one) represents the solution where all the decision variables are zero valued; the first column of nodes (nodes two to six) represents the set of solutions where the variable stated in brackets is unity while the other variables are zero valued; the next column of nodes (nodes seven to sixteen) represent the set of solutions where the two variables stated in brackets are unity while the others are zero and so on. The nodes can be looked upon as having been derived from each other *via* the links as follows: designating the decision variables as $X_1, \ldots, X_n$, the node relating to the solution where some combination of decision variables $X_i, \ldots, X_j$ equal unity has immediately descended from it the nodes where:

$$X_i, \ldots, X_j, X_{j+1} ; \qquad X_i, \ldots, X_j, X_{j+2} ; \qquad \ldots ;$$
$$X_i, \ldots, X_j, X_n$$

respectively equal unity. Note that this rule for node descent gives rise to a tree where each possible solution occurs once and only once: the 32 nodes in Figure 7.1 represent the $2^n = 2^5 = 32$ possible solutions to (7.3).

Given a tree of possible solutions to a given zero-one programming problem, the backtrack programming solution approach proceeds by examining these by proceeding clockwise around the tree, backtracking as necessary. In the case of Figure 7.1, a clockwise path about the tree is achieved by visiting in turn nodes:

$$1 \to 2 \to 7 \to 17 \to 27 \to 32 \to (27) \to (17) \to 28 \to (17)$$
$$\to (7) \to 18 \to 29 \to (18) \to (7) \to 19 \to (7) \to (2) \to 8 \to 20$$
$$\to \ldots$$
$$\to (14) \to (4) \to 15 \to (4) \to (1) \to 5 \to 16 \to (5) \to (1) \to 6$$

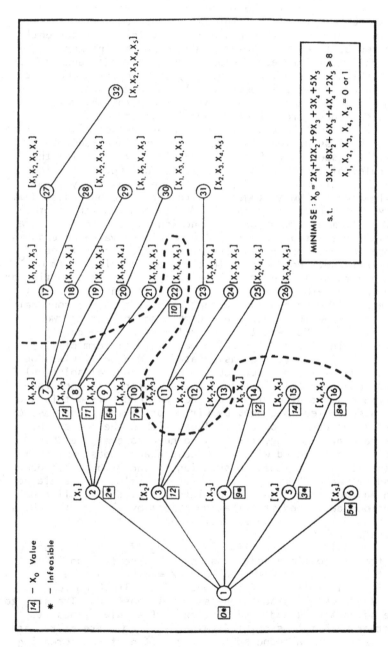

Figure 7.1 Zero-One Programming Formulation : Tree of Possible Solutions

213

Nodes in brackets denote a backtrack movement. One way in which the problem (7.3) could be solved would be to examine the solution nodes in the foregoing order retaining at all times the best feasible solution encountered so far in the process. After every node had been examined, the currently retained best feasible solution would be the optimum.

While this procedure represents the overall approach of the backtrack method, a further key idea concerns the fact that in practice, all possible solution nodes need not be examined explicitly. Rather, given the method by which the solution nodes were derived from each other and the mathematical form of the problem, certain of the solutions will be known to be suboptimal in advance and will not require explicit inspection. Returning to Figure 7.1, notice that the rules of descent are such that for any node for which some combination of the X_j, $j=1$, $\ldots$, n equal unity, that combination of the X_j together with certain other X_js equal unity in the descendant nodes. Notice too that the mathematical form of the objective function is such that if in a particular solution, a zero-valued decision variable changes to one (as happens in the case of descendant nodes) then X_o must increase. Notice also that the mathematical form of the constraint left hand side is such that if in a particular solution, a zero-valued decision variable changes to one (as happens in the case of descendant nodes), then the constraint left hand side must increase. Combining the latter two points, it can be seen that the rules of node descent as exhibited in Figure 7.1 and the mathematical form of (7.3) are such that if the solution associated with a particular node (which may or may not turn out to be the optimal solution) is found to be feasible in terms of the constraint, then the solutions associated with the nodes descended from this node will also be feasible but, by virtue of having higher associated X_o values, suboptimal. Thus, within the context of backtrack programming, there is no need to evaluate the solutions associated with these descendant nodes explicitly. Furthermore, if a feasible solution to the problem has been found for which $X_o = k$, then, if for the solution associated with another node, feasible or infeasible, $X_o > k$, all the solutions descended from that node must by virtue of possessing higher X_o values be suboptimal and can therefore be ignored.

Reconsider now the task of solving (7.3) by inspecting the tree of possible solutions in clockwise fashion. For the solution associated with node one, $X_o = 0$ but this solution is not feasible in terms of the constraint. Tracking to node two, $X_o = 2$ but this solution is also infeasible. Tracking to node seven $X_o = 14$ and the solution is feasible. Thus it, together with the associated value of X_o, 14, are stored as the best solution found so far. By virtue of the foregoing properties, all solutions associated with the nodes descended from node seven will be suboptimal. Thus they may be ignored. Furthermore, if any node for which $X_0 > 14$ is encountered later on, it, together with its descendants, may be ignored. We now backtrack to node two and onwards to node eight. The solution associated with this node is feasible. Because the associated value of X_0, 11, is lower than the current best solution value (14), this solution replaces the current best solution. We leave as an exercise for the reader the task of evaluating the remaining nodes. The optimal solution (node 22) is:

$$X_0 = 10 \; ; \; X_1 = 1 \; ; \; X_2 = 0 \; ; \; X_3 = 0 \; ; \; X_4 = 1 \; ; \; X_5 = 1$$

The foregoing calculations demonstrate two important properties of the backtrack programming approach which were alluded to earlier. First, in terms of computer operations, the storage requirements are minimal : at any stage in the calculations, it is only the best current solution which must be retained. Second, the number of solutions which must be examined explicitly is less than the total number possible (2^n) and will hopefully be small. In the current example, only the 14 solutions to the left of the dotted line in Figure 7.1 i.e. 43.75 per cent of the total had to be so examined.

It is to be emphasised that the facility for ignoring certain solutions during backtrack programming derives specifically from the fact that the form of the objective and the left hand side(s) of the constraint(s) are such that when any decision variable increases in value (i.e. from zero to one) so too does the corresponding objective value and constraint left hand side(s). Formally, the objective and constraint left hand sides are said to be *monotonically increasing*.

The foregoing tree of possible solutions is used here within the context of a minimisation problem but it could be employed equally well to solve a maximisation problem with (a) monotonically increasing 'less than or equals' constraint(s). In this case, the initial solution (node one) would be feasible but non-optimal ($X_0 = 0$). Branching would take place outwards with each successive solution offering a better value for X_0. Backtracking would take place from any node for which the associated solution was infeasible. By definition, solutions associated with nodes descended from infeasible solution nodes would also be infeasible and therefore would not require explicit inspection.

The type of tree of possible solutions given in Figure 7.1 represents but one method for setting out all such solutions. An alternative, in effect the reverse of Figure 7.1, involves defining the base node solution as that where all of the decision variables equal unity; the derivatives comprise solutions where successive variables take zero values.

One context within which it has been suggested that back-track programming might be employed to advantage is in solving the optimal network problem which, recall (Section 2.2.2) involves finding for a set of nodes the set of connecting links which should be constructed in order to minimise total user costs whilst keeping the length of network provided below some maximum ℓ_{MAX}. The problem is a combinatorial programming problem in the sense that the combination of links which should be constructed is required. Formally if:

d_{ij} = The distance *via* a direct link (if constructed) from node i to node j

and X_{ij} = 1 if a link from i to j is constructed

= 0 otherwise

the constraint in (2.1) can be rewritten in terms of zero-one variables as:

$$\sum_{i=1}^{n-1} \sum_{j=i+1}^{n} d_{ij} \, X_{ij} \leq \ell_{MAX} \qquad \text{----(7.4)}$$

Following the example presented by Scott (1969a) but with modified notation, consider the four nodes ABCD (Figure 7.2) which are to be connected by some or all of the links shown. A tree comprising all possible solutions can be constructed by taking as the base node the network comprising all allowable links. Each successive node involves the deletion of one further link with the numbering of the links being used in the same manner as the subscripting of the X_j's in (7.3) to insure that each possible solution occurs once and only once. As in the case of the preceding numerical example, the backtrack method branches outwards until a feasible solution in terms of (7.4) is found; all networks beyond the node corresponding to this solution possess fewer links and therefore higher associated user costs. Therefore they are suboptimal and need not be considered explicitly.

The potential advantage of the backtrack approach over the heuristic methods presented in Chapter Two for solving the optimal network problem is that it leads to the optimal solution. Against this must be weighed the considerable drawback that even for problems comprising relatively small numbers of nodes, the tree of possible solutions and thus the time required to inspect this can be very large. Scott (1969a) reports on the results obtained for five ten node problems, six nine node problems, seven eight node problems and eight seven node problems. Computer solution times for these fairly modest formulations varied from under one minute to well over one hour in one case with the majority of

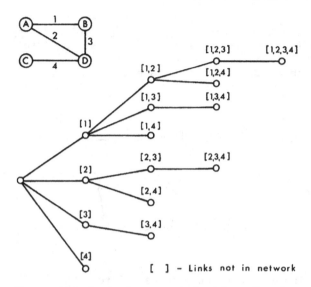

Figure 7.2 Optimal Network Problem: Permitted Links and Set
of Possible Solutions

Based on: SCOTT, A.J., (1969), The Optimal Network Problem:
Some Computational Procedures, *Transportation
Research*, 3, 201-10, Figure 1.

Adapted by permission of the Pergamon Press .

networks requiring a solution time of several minutes.
    An interesting alternative attempt to solve the optimal
network problem exactly using a branch and bound approach
(Section 6.3) is reported by Boyce *et al.* (1973). Applying
logic similar to that underlying the implicit enumeration
algorithm, the base node of the branch and bound tree comprises the set of all possible networks. Branching takes
place by specifically excluding a specified link from (left
hand branch) or including it (right hand branch) in the final
solution thereby moving one step further towards a fully
defined solution. Boyce *et al.* report solving ten node 45
link networks in less than 400 seconds of computer time which
suggests that their algorithm is superior to that of Scott
(1969a). Nevertheless, for large problems, it would still
appear that heuristic approaches of the type discussed in
Section 2.2.2 provide the only means of obtaining solutions.

7.3 THE TRAVELLING SALESMAN PROBLEM

A zero-one programming problem which has attracted consider-able attention is *the travelling salesman problem* which for n nodes e.g. cities involves determining the shortest complete circuit route among the nodes such that each node is visited once. Figure 7.3 shows the solution obtained for a

Figure 7.3 Travelling Salesman Route for a Thirteen Node
    Problem

thirteen node problem.
    Mathematically, for n points, the travelling salesman problem can be expressed as a zero-one programming problem by defining:

X_{ij}= 1 if the optimal route includes a link from node i
    to node j

= 0 otherwise

d_{ij}= Distance from node i to node j *via* a direct link

Now, for n nodes, the objective of minimising the total route distance is given by:

$$\text{Minimise :} \quad \sum_{\substack{i=1 \\ i \neq j}}^{n} \sum_{j=1}^{n} d_{ij} \, X_{ij} \qquad \text{----(7.5)}$$

The requirement that each node be visited just once by the route can be expressed by two constraint sets which require respectively that each node has one route entering it and one route leaving i.e.

218

$$\sum_{i=1}^{n} X_{ij} = 1 \; ; \; j = 1, \ldots, n$$

$$\sum_{j=1}^{n} X_{ij} = 1 \; ; \; i = 1, \ldots, n$$

$$\text{----} (7.6)$$

It is to be noted that the formulation (7.5), (7.6) (the condition $i \neq j$ on the summation in the objective can be dropped if d_{ii} is set arbitrarily to infinity) together with the condition:

$$X_{ij} \geq 0 \qquad \qquad \text{----} (7.7)$$

actually comprises an assignment problem of the form (3.1)-(3.4). Thus, if (7.5)-(7.7) offered a complete specification of the travelling salesman problem, this could be solved *via* the methods presented in Chapter Three. In order to see why (7.5)-(7.7) does not offer a complete specification of the travelling salesman problem, consider the following solution obtained to a five node problem which is illustrated in Figure 7.4:

$$X_{23} = 1 \; ; \; X_{34} = 1 \; ; \; X_{42} = 1 \; ; \; X_{15} = 1 \; ; \; X_{51} = 1$$

$$\text{All other } X_{ij} = 0 \qquad \qquad \text{----} (7.8)$$

While this solution fulfills the conditions (7.6) and is indeed a valid assignment problem solution, it is not a feasible travelling salesman problem solution for the route specified by it involves two subtours rather than one complete circuit. In order to prevent such subtours arising in solutions, additional constraints must be appended to (7.6) e.g.

$$X_{15} + X_{51} \leq 1$$

$$X_{23} + X_{34} + X_{42} \leq 2 \qquad \qquad \text{----} (7.9)$$

which would prevent the two subtours shown in Figure 7.4. Unfortunately, even for a relatively small problem e.g. concerning five nodes, the number of possible subtours and thus the number of additional constraints of the form (7.9) which must be added to ensure an optimal solution which comprises a single circuit is very great. Thus, only the smallest travelling salesman problems can be specified in full and solved directly.

One approach which, it has been suggested, can be used to solve larger travelling salesman problems is that of branch and bound (Section 6.3). Wagner (1969) demonstrates three versions of the branch and bound approach using the five node problem with the inter-nodal distances given in Table 7.1 as a demonstration. Two of these approaches are summarised here.

Figure 7.4 Travelling Salesman Problem : Hypothetical Solution
for a Five Node Problem

The first method, *the method of excluded subtours,* commences by defining by inspection a possible solution e.g.

$$X_{12} = X_{23} = X_{34} = X_{45} = X_{51} = 1 \; ; \; \text{all other} \; X_{ij} = 0 \quad ----(7.10)$$

for which X_0 =65. This value places an upper bound on the
optimal solution i.e. UB. 65. The problem is now solved as an
assignment problem of the form (7.5)-(7.7). If this solution
comprises a complete circuit, it obviously comprises the
optimal solution. In the event of subtours emerging, branching is initiated. The optimal solution to the problem referred to in Table 7.1 is in fact (7.8) i.e. that depicted in
Figure 7.4. X_0 for this solution equals 60. Branching is
initiated by choosing the smallest subtour i.e. 1 → 5 → 1.
Now, obviously either $X_{15} = 0$ and/or $X_{51} = 0$ at optimality.
Thus two new problems are created with $c_{15} = \infty$ (left hand
branch) and $c_{51} = \infty$ (right hand branch). These
revised values for c_{15} and c_{51} are such
as to force X_{15} and X_{51} respectively to zero which destroys
the subtour. Re-solving the original problem with each of
the new constraints appended yields two further solutions
whose X_0 values exceed 60. If either of these solutions comprises a complete circuit with an associated X_0 value below
65, this solution is stored as the best currently available
and UB. is set to X_0. Branching then takes place from the
solution including a subtour for which X_0 is lowest (and less
than UB). The process continues until such time that there is
no solution comprising subtours for which $X_0 <$ UB. Once this
occurs, the solution currently associated with UB. is known to
comprise the optimal solution.

A disadvantage of the method of excluded subtours is that
it involves solving an assignment type linear programming
problem at each node of the branch and bound tree. An alternative branch and bound method which obviates this necessity is
the method of partial tours. Once again, an intiial feasible
solution is determined e.g. (7.10) for the problem in Table
7.1 for which recall UB. = 65. Now attention is focussed on a
specific chosen node e.g. node one. Quite obviously, in the

TABLE 7.1

INTER-NODAL DISTANCES FOR A FIVE NODE TRAVELLING SALESMAN
PROBLEM

		TO	NODE				
	FROM		1	2	3	4	5
NODE	1			10	25	25	10
	2		1		10	15	2
	3		8	9		20	10
	4		14	10	24		15
	5		10	8	25	27	

From: Harvey M. Wagner, PRINCIPLES OF OPERATIONS RESEARCH:
With Applications to Managerial Decisions, © 1969,
p.472. Reprinted by permission of Prentice-Hall Inc.,
Englewood Cliffs, N.J.

optimal solution either X_{12} or X_{13} or X_{14} or X_{15} must equal
unity with the other three variables equalling zero. These
four mutually exclusive possibilities comprise the four
initial branches of the branch and bound tree (Figure 7.5)
and, for each, the minimum possible value that X_o could
ultimately take given the route whose use is being insisted
upon can be calculated. (We do not present here the method
by which this statistic is determined but merely remark that
it involves applying techniques similar to those employed in
the Vogel Approximation Method (Section 3.3.5) to the data in
Table 7.1.) We now proceed to branch on the branch and bound
node for which the lowest value possible for X_o is lowest and
less than U.B. which, in the case of the example is that corresponding to use of the route from node one to node five. If
this link is used, one of three links can radiate from node
five : in terms of the decision variables one of X_{52}, X_{53}, X_{54}
must equal one with the others equalling to zero.
This gives rise to three further branches in Figure 7.5 for
which the minimum value possible for X_o if the relevant routes
are used can be calculated. Once again, branching takes place
on the tree node for which the minimum possible value for X_o
is lowest and less than U.B. Eventually, after three

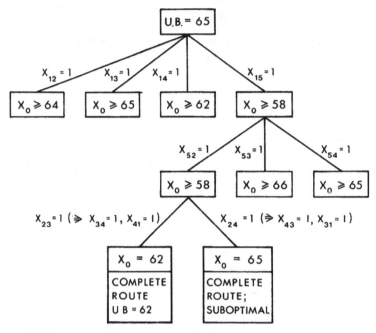

OPTIMAL SOLUTION : $X_{15} = X_{52} = X_{23} = X_{34} = X_{43} = 1; X_0 = 62$

Figure 7.5 The Travelling Salesman Problem : Solution *via* the Method of Partial Tours

From: Harvey M. Wagner, PRINCIPLES OF OPERATIONS RESEARCH: With Applications to Managerial Decisions, © 1969, p.479. Reprinted by permission of Prentice-Hall Inc., Englewood Cliffs, N.J.

branchings in a five node problem, a complete route together with its associated X_0 value is specified. If this X_0 value falls below U.B., U.B. is set to X_0 and the relevant solution is stored as the best currently available. The branching process continues until there is no branch and bound tree node for which the minimum value X_0 could ultimately take is less than U.B. The solution associated with U.B. is then known to comprise the optimal solution.

Recall that the main reason for utilising the branch and bound approach to solve the travelling salesman problem centres on its ability to deal with larger problems than could be formulated exactly at the outset. Despite this ability, consideration of the two foregoing approaches suggests that even branch and bound would be unsuitable for solving problems with very large numbers of nodes because the relevant branch and bound trees and, in particular, the number of solutions to be retained at any one time, would become unmanageably large. For this reason, large travelling salesman problems must be solved heuristically. Two heuristic methods discussed by Scott (1971a) are those of Karg and Thompason and of Lin. The former commences by joining some two adjacent nodes. Then, the node nearest to one of the two end nodes is linked to the network. This process continues until all n points are joined *via* (n-1) links at which time the two end points are connected. The algorithm of Lin commences with a possible solution such as that obtained *via* the Karg and Thompson approach and attempts to successively improve upon this by successively deleting and replacing subsets of links in a systematic manner.

A problem which is a direct development of the travelling salesman problem is the *chromatic travelling salesman problem*. Here, a number of nodes are to be partitioned into subgroups, each with its associated travelling salesman circuit. The objective is to minimise the number of circuits i.e. the number of salesmen required whilst ensuring that no route exceeds a specified maximum permissible length. Harvey *et al.* (1974a) discuss solving the chromatic travelling salesman problem within the context of sparsely populated rural areas of Sierra Leone. Salesmen were to be assigned to each area such that each node (market place) was visited once on a circuit and no circuit involved more than forty hours to complete. The number of salesmen (circuits) was to be minimised. A discussion of certain related but more complex travelling salesman type problems appears in Boye (1965).

7.4 THE TOTAL COVER PROBLEM

We consider in this and in the five sections which follow a set of related location problems which comprise zero-one programming formulations. The general theme involves locating central facilities e.g. fire stations, schools in some optimal manner in order to serve a set of demand nodes e.g. population centres sited at given locations. The zero-one variables generally denote whether a central facility will be located at a particular location. Excellent general reviews of these models are provided by White and Case (1974) and by Hodgart (1978).

The *total cover problem* (which has also been called the *location set covering problem*) considers the task of servicing m demand nodes at known locations by central facilities which may be located at some or all of n given sites. Certain or all of these sites may coincide with demand nodes. The objective is to locate the minimum number of central facilities possible whilst ensuring that each demand node is within some distance, d, or travel time, t, of a facility. Toregas and Revelle (1972, 1973) suggest that solutions to this problem would be of interest when locating facilities within a context of financial stringency where some minimum level of service as measured by maximum permissible distance (d) or travel time (t) must be achieved. They suggest also that the model could be used to partition an area into regions each possessing one central facility. An aspect of practical importance within the context of an actual application would be the rate at which the number of facilities required increases with decreasing d or t which could be determined by solving the problem for varying d or t values.

The total cover problem can be expressed in zero-one programming terms as follows. For $i = 1, ..., m$ demand (population) nodes and $j = 1, ..., n$ possible facility sites let:

$d_{ij} =$ The distance from demand node i to facility site j

$X_j = 1$ if facility site j is used

$= 0$ otherwise

The problem is then:

$$\text{Minimise}: \sum_{j=1}^{n} X_j$$

$$\sum_{j=1}^{n} a_{ij} X_j \geq 1, \; i=1, ..., m \quad \text{----(7.11)}$$

where $a_{ij} = 1$ if, given d (or t), demand node i can be served by a facility at j

$= 0$ otherwise

This problem could be solved *via* the methods in Chapter Six e.g. using the simplex method and branch and bound or as a combinatorial problem (Section 7.2). Toregas and Revelle suggest an alternative approach which involves determining first for each demand node the facility sites from which it could be served. A graphical method is then used to reduce the number of facility sites actually used to a minimum. They note that the total cover problem can be readily extended to treat a situation where certain central facilities are pre-located by appending constraints of the form:

$$X_j = 1$$

7.5 THE PARTIAL COVER PROBLEM

The *partial cover problem* (which has also been called the *maximal covering location problem*) is set within the same context as the total cover problem. Not more than k central facilities are to be located amongst n ($\geq$k) possible sites such that as large a proportion as possible of m demand nodes are within a given distance, d, (or time, t) of a facility. Formally, using the notation introduced in the preceding section, the problem is:

$$\begin{array}{ll} \text{Maximise :} & \displaystyle\sum_{i=1}^{m} \; \underset{j}{\text{Max}} \; \{ a_{ij} \, X_j \} \\[3ex] \text{s.t.} & \displaystyle\sum_{j=1}^{n} \; X_j \leq k \end{array} \right) \quad ----(7.12)$$

The constraint requires that no more than k facilities be located. Within the objective, if demand point i is within a distance d (time t) of some facility, the appropriate values of a_{ij} and X_{ij} and thus of their product will be unity. For a demand point which is served by at least one demand point, Max $\{a_{ij} X_j\}$ will equal unity. The objective thus expresses
$\quad j$
the requirement that the total number of demand nodes which can be served by at least one central facility be maximised. As in the case of the total cover problem, the pre-location of certain of the central facilities can be guaranteed by the imposition of additional conditions of the form:

$$X_j = 1$$

The formulation (7.12) highlights the difference between the total and partial cover problems. In the former, the minimum permissible level of service to be provided expressed as the maximum permitted distance (time) between any central facility and demand node is given and the number of central facilities supplied is to be minimised; in the latter, the number of central facilities to be supplied is given and the level of service as expressed by the proportion of demand nodes within some given distance (time) of a central facility is to be maximised. If in the partial cover problem the number of central facilities to be located is incremented one at a time i.e. (7.12) is solved with k=1, then with k=2 etc., the solution with the minimum value of k for which all nodes are served represents the optimal solution to the total cover problem. Viewed in this manner, the total cover problem represents a special case of the partial cover problem.

Church and ReVelle (1974) discuss methods for solving the partial cover problem and report on computational experience. First, using an alternative formulation to (7.12), linear programming with branch and bound is employed. In almost 80 per cent of the problems solved, the initial linear programming optimal solution comprised all zero-one values thus obviating the necessity to activate branch and bound. For larger problems, two heuristic approaches are suggested. The *greedy adding algorithm* picks for the first central facility the site which serves the largest proportion of the demand nodes, for the second the site which serves the largest proportion of demand nodes unserved by the first facility and so on. The *greedy adding with substitution algorithm* is similar but seeks after each additional central facility has been located to re-locate the other facilities one by one thereby increasing the proportion of demand nodes served.

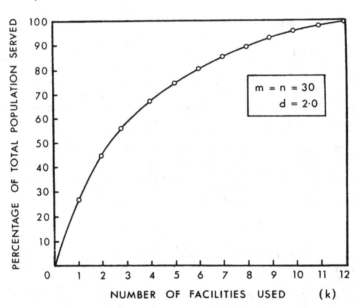

Figure 7.6 Solutions to a Partial Cover Problem

From: CHURCH, R. and REVELLE, C., (1974), The Maximal Covering Location Problem, *Papers of the Regional Science Association*, *32*, 101-18, Figure 1.

Redrawn by permission of the Regional Science Association

Figure 7.6 summarises the results obtained by Church and Revelle for a partial cover problem involving 30 demand nodes and with central facilities permitted to locate at any of these. With $d = 2.0$ and $k = 1$ in (7.12), less than thirty per cent of the demand nodes were served. This rose to one hundred per cent for $k = 12$ which therefore represents the solution to the equivalent total cover problem. Within the context of Section 5.6, Figure 7.7 gives a parametric programming analysis on k in (7.12).

7.6 THE p-MEDIAN PROBLEM

In its most straightforward form as discussed by ReVelle and Swain (1970), the *p-median problem* (which has also been called the *generalised partial cover problem* and the *location-allocation problem on a graph*)considers m demand nodes whose populations are p_i, i = 1, ..., m. Central facilities are to be placed at n ($<$ m) of these demand nodes and each will serve the requirement of the node itself together with those surrounding unserved nodes to which it is nearest. Labelling the central facilities as j = 1, ..., n, the p-median problem involves determining the n demand nodes at which central facilities should be located in order to minimise the total distance the complete population will have to travel in order to reach the nearest central facility.

In order to express the p-median problem mathematically, let:

X_{ij}= 1 if demand node i is served by a facility at j i.e. if the nearest facility to i is located at j

= 0 otherwise

p_i= The population of demand node i

d_{ij}= The distance from node i to node j

If a facility is located at some node, j, then, for that node, X_{jj}= 1 and d_{jj}= 0. Now, the problem is:

$$\text{Minimise :} \quad \sum_{i=1}^{m} \sum_{j=1}^{n} p_i \, d_{ij} \, X_{ij} \qquad \text{----(7.13)}$$

$$\text{s.t.} \quad \sum_{j=1}^{n} X_{ij} = 1 \; ; \; i=1, ..., m \qquad \text{----(7.14)}$$

$$\sum_{j=1}^{n} X_{jj} = n \; ; \; j=1, ..., n \qquad \text{----(7.15)}$$

$$X_{jj} \geq X_{ij}; \; i,j=1, ..., m \text{ ----(7.16)}$$

which require respectively that each demand point be assigned to one facility, that the number of faciltiies located be n and that no demand node (i) be assigned to another node (j) which does not assign to itself i.e. possess a facility. In addition, Rojeski and ReVelle (1970) impose additional constraints to ensure that each demand node is indeed assigned to the central facility nearest it in the optimal solution.

The formulation (7.13)-(7.16) comprises a zero-one programming problem. ReVelle and Swain (1970) suggest that it
can be conveniently solved *via* linear programming with branch
and bound applied to the non zero-one valued decision variables at optimality. It is suggested also that large problems
could be solved initially with the constraint set (7.16)
omitted in order to ease the computational burden; after the
initial optimal solution is obtained, specific conditions of
the form (7.16) could be added iteratively to prevent assignments to nodes where no facility exists until such time that
all the demand nodes are indeed assigned to nodes where
facilities are located. In terms of computational experience
for a series of trial problems, ReVelle and Swain report that
non zero-one solutions to the initial linear programming
problem (7.13)-(7.15) were the exception rather than the rule.

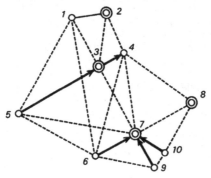

O   Community which does not assign to itself
◎   Community which self - assigns
    Arrows indicate assignments
    Arrows and dashed lines indicate road network

Figure 7.7 Optimal Solution for a p-median Problem With
       m = 10; n = 4.

Figure 7.7 shows the optimal solution obtained to a ten node,
four facility problem after 34 iterations i.e. additions of
constraints of the form (7.16).
    While ReVelle and Swain view the p-median problem as a
linear programming problem with zero-one decision variables,
it can also be viewed as a combinatorial programme as defined
in Section 7.2 : specifically, the objective can be viewed as
finding the combination of n of the m possible central
facility sites which minimise total travel distance.

Following the approach set out in Section 7.5 large problems can be solved heuristically. In common with the logic underlying the greedy adding with substitution algorithm for solving the partial cover problem, White and Case (1974) describe a method due to Ignizio for solving the p-median problem which proceeds by allocating facilities to sites one at a time and which, after each iteration, employs a routine which removes from the solution any assigned facility which is no longer justified due to subsequent assignment.

An interesting example of the p-median problem applied within a practical context is that discussed by Harvey *et al.* (1974b) who were interested in determining where central places of various orders should be located in certain reasonably densely populated regions in Sierra Leone. (For sparsely populated regions, it was felt that the provision services should be in the form of periodic markets as generated by the chromatic travelling salesman problem as discussed in Section 7.3 — Harvey *et al.* (1974a).) Specifically, for each of five regions and given the numbers of central places of various order to be located and a network of the type depicted in Figure 7.7, a p-median solution algorithm was used to locate the places in such a way as to minimise (7.13). The reader is referred to the original publication for details.

It is interesting to note that the p-median problem (7.13)-(7.16) is related to the transportation problem with setup costs (7.1), (7,2) in the following manner. Suppose in the latter problem that any factory which is built has an infinite capacity, that the setup costs at any site are zero and that the number of factories to be constructed is given. Under these conditions the first constraint set in (7.2) vanishes, the second constraint set comprises equalities and the terms $f_i Y_i$ disappear from the objective. An additional constraint concerning the number of factories to be constructed must be added. Noting that under these conditions, each demand point will obviously be served by the nearest factory, the revised problem comprises a p-median problem.

7.7 DEVELOPMENTS OF THE p-MEDIAN PROBLEM

Due to the potentially large number of practical applications within the subject of Geography and Planning, the p-median problem has received considerable attention in the literature and a number of extensions to the basic model have been suggested. Rojeski and ReVelle (1970) suggest that the constraint (7.15) which places a limit on the number of central facilities to be located be replaced by one which takes into account the setup and operating costs for a central facility at each potential location. Specifically, if:

f_j = The setup cost for a facility at node j

b_j = The operating cost per person served at node j

c = The total budget available

it is suggested (7.15) be replaced by:

$$\sum_{j=1}^{n} f_j X_{jj} + \sum_{j=1}^{n} b_j \sum_{i=1}^{n} p_i X_{ij} \leq c \qquad \text{----(7.17)}$$

One potential drawback of a solution to a particular real-world problem is that a particular demand node may be placed at an unacceptably large distance from a central facility. In the case of the solution illustrated in Figure 7.7, node five is relatively and perhaps unacceptably far removed from the central facility to which it is assigned (at node three). In order to avoid optimal solutions to the p-median problem where certain population nodes are placed at unacceptably large distances away from the central facilities to which they are assigned and following the logic underlying the total and partial cover problems (Section 7.4 and 7.5), it has been suggested that the constraint set:

$$d_{ij} X_{ij} \leq d \text{ for all } i, j \qquad \text{----(7.18)}$$

be appended to (7.13)-(7.16) where d is the maximum permitted distance between a node and the facility to which it is assigned. This revised problem is known as the *p-median problem with a maximum distance constraint*. Two heuristic approaches for its solution are described by Khumawala (1973). (For a description of an alternative approach, see Church and Meadows (1977).) In the first of these, the *delta method*, it is assumed initially that central facilities exist at each of the demand nodes. Facilities are then successively closed until the number of facilities remaining is equal to that permitted (n). At each iteration, the facility closed is that which increases the value of (7.13) by the smallest amount possible without contravening (7.18). The second method, the *omega method*, proceeds by successively opening facilities, activating on each occasion the facility which leads to the greatest reduction in travel distance whilst taking account of (7.18). It is worth noting that the delta and omega methods for solving the p-median problem with a maximum distance constraint are similar in approach to the backwards and forwards heuristic algorithms respectively for solving the optimal network problem (Section 2.2.2) : recall that the former commences with an 'optimal' but non-feasible solution whilst the latter commences with a non-optimal solution. In an interesting postscript to his work, Khumawala (1975) describes a method by which given the delta and omega solutions to a particular problem, a special routine is applied to improve these further. The final heuristic solution is the better of these two revised solutions i.e. that associated with the lower value of (7.13).

An interesting additional insight into the p-median problem with a maximum distance constraint is that provided by Church and Meadows (1977). As expressed by (7.13)-(7.16), the p-median problem involves determining some subset of n out of m nodes at which central facilities should be located. The d_{ij} values input to (7.13) presumably relate to the shortest inter-nodal distances along (say) a pre-existing road network e.g. such as is shown in Figure 7.7. In the absence of a constraint of the form (7.18) i.e. for the p-median problem in its basic form (7.13)-(7.16) it can be shown that the set of n central facility locations *on this network* which minimises (7.13) will indeed correspond to n of the m nodes. Thus, a solution approach to the p-median problem (7.13)-(7.16) which considers only the nodes themselves as potential solution points (as do those of Rojeski and ReVelle (1970) and that due to Ignizio - White and Case (1974)) is valid. Church and Meadows show that where a set of constraints of the form (7.18) is appended, there are now possible candidate locations for central facilities (which they call *network intersect points*) which lie on the links joining the initial nodes. They present a method for identifying these and for taking them into account when solving the problem heuristically. Taking these additional potential solution points into account yields more satisfactory solutions than the approaches of Khumwala (1973, 1975) who, recall, only considers the nodes themselves as potential locations for the central facilities.

The foregoing algorithms for solving the p-median problem with a maximum distance constraint presuppose that a solution can indeed be found for which (7.18) holds i.e. that a feasible solution to (7.13)-(7.16), (7.18) exists. In practice, a situation could easily arise akin to the partial cover problem (Section 7.5) in which no placement of n central facilities places every demand node within a distance d of a facility. This situation is considered by Holmes *et al.* (1973) within the context of locating day-care facilities in Columbus, Ohio. Their approach involves in effect subsuming the constraints (7.18) into the objective (7.13) to yield:

$$\text{Maximise} : \sum_{i=1}^{m} \sum_{j=1}^{m} p_i (d - d_{ij}) X_{ij} \qquad ----(7.19)$$

where the notation is as before. The objective comprises two terms: the first, $p_i d X_{ij}$, offers a measure of the total demand served (recall that d is a constant); the second, $p_i d_{ij} X_{ij}$ gives the total amount of travel required by the solution. In effect, maximisation of (7.19) involves counter-balancing a maximisation of the number of persons served against the distances which must be travelled by them to reach the central facilities. This general notion of counterbalancing distances travelled and population served is extended further by Goodchild (1978) who discusses a number of approaches to the p-median problem which explicitly assume that the level of demand which will be catered for by a particular solution is related to various characteristics of that solution e.g. concerning distances to be travelled to central facilities, characteristics of those facilities and frequencies of use.

ReVelle *et al.* (1976) consider three further extensions to the basic p-median problem. First, demands are assumed to occur continuously along network links rather than merely at nodes occurring at link junctions. Second, and in the spirit of the travelling salesman problem (Section 7.3), a mobile unit is assumed to depart from some node(s) to be chosen, thereby serving the demand along certain links. Ultimately the mobile unit arrives at and services a facility at some distant point. (ReVelle *et al.* discuss this particular development within the context of providing ambulances which depart from despatching stations and ultimately serve hospitals.) A final development suggested by ReVelle *et al.* involves a generalisation to deal with changing demand patterns through time. The reader is referred to the original article for details. Some further general ways in which the p-median problem can be extended are discussed at the end of Section 7.9.

7.8 THE LOCATION-ALLOCATION PROBLEM

In its most usual form, the *location-allocation problem* considers m demand nodes whose populations are p_i, $i = 1, ..., m$. Central facilities are to be placed at n (<m) locations through the area in which the demand nodes exist. Each central facility will serve the population of the demand nodes to which it is nearest. Labelling the central facilities as $j = 1, ..., n$, the location-allocation problem involves determining where these should be placed in order to minimise the total distance the population will have to travel to reach the nearest central facility.

The location - allocation problem is similar to the p-median problem. The major difference is that in the case of the location-allocation porblem, central facilities are not constrained to locate at some combination of pre-specified points e.g. the demand nodes but rather may locate anywhere in continuous space. Thus the location-allocation problem is not essentially combinatorial in its underlying structure — a feature which has fairly severe implications for its formulation and solution.

In order to understand the complexity underlying the location-allocation problem, consider first the task of optimally locating a single central facility to serve all of the m demand nodes. The solution of this problem known as the *generalised Weber problem* involves finding the so-called *point of minimum aggregate travel* or *median point*. It is to be noted that solution of the special case involving three points of equal importance (population) has been discussed already (Section 2.2.3) : the point of minimum aggregate travel lies at the Steiner point. For a problem involving m demand nodes, suppose that the location of the i th node is given by the coordinates (X_i, Y_i) (Figure 7.8). Now suppose

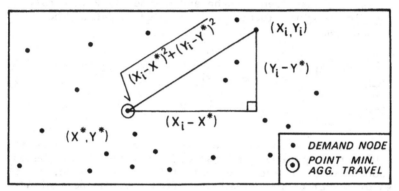

Figure 7.8 Location-Allocation Problem Involving One Central Facility

that the location of the point of minimum aggregate travel has actually been found and is given by the coordinates $(X*, Y*)$. From the theorem of Pythagoras, the distance from the ith node to the point of minimum aggregate travel is:

$$\{(X_i - X*)^2 + (Y_i - Y*)^2\}^{\frac{1}{2}} \qquad ----(7.20)$$

and the total amount of travel involved in transferring the population of the i th demand node, p_i, to $(X*, Y*)$ is:

$$p_i \{(X_i - X*)^2 + (Y_i - Y*)^2\}^{\frac{1}{2}} \qquad ----(7.21)$$

Generalising to cover all nodes, the total amount of travel involved in transferring the population of every node to $(X*, Y*)$ is:

$$\sum_{i=1}^{m} p_i \{(X_i - X*)^2 + (Y_i - Y*)^2 \}^{\frac{1}{2}} \qquad ----(7.22)$$

233

Thus, the objective underlying the single facility location-allocation problem can be viewed as finding $(X*, Y*)$ in order to minimise (7.22).

In terms of underlying mathematics, the objective (7.22) is unlike any of those encountered so far in this text; it is nonlinear (recall the definition of linearity given in Section 3.2.1) in terms of the decision variables $X*$, $Y*$. Furthermore, in contrast to all of the other models considered so far in this chapter, these variables are not of the zero-one type. Some further mathematical characteristics of the objective (7.22) are considered in Section 8.3.2. It can simply be remarked here that its form is such as to force us to solve the generalised Weber problem heuristically. One possible method is that described by Kuhn and Kuenne (1962). First, the coordinate of the location of the *mean centre* of the demand nodes as given by:

$$\bar{X} = \frac{\sum\limits_{i=1}^{m} P_i \, X_i}{\sum\limits_{i=1}^{m} P_i} \quad ; \quad \bar{Y} = \frac{\sum\limits_{i=1}^{m} P_i \, Y_i}{\sum\limits_{i=1}^{m} P_i} \qquad ----(7.23)$$

is found. (This is in fact the point whose location minimises the sum of the square of the distances travelled by the demand node populations to reach the central facility.) Then, *via* a series of iterations, this point shifted towards the median centre. Cooper (1968) generalises the objective (7.22) to that of minimising:

$$\sum\limits_{i=1}^{m} P_i \{ (X_i - X*)^2 + (Y_i - Y*)^2 \}^{k/2} \qquad ----(7.24)$$

and shows that provied $k \geq 1$ as is the case in (7.22), Kuhn and Kuenne's method will always tend towards the required point of global minimum travel.

A study which involved determining median points and which was cited in Section 3.2.3 within the context of the assignment problem is that of Goodchild and Massam (1969) who consider the siting of administrative centres to serve the population of Southern Ontario, Canada. Initially, eight centres together with the percentage of the total population that each could serve (Figure 7. 9(a)) were defined. The population was distributed among 590 townships of which 504 were occupied. Assuming that each township's population was located at its centre, the population was assigned to administrative centres using the assignment/transportation problem algorithm (Chapter Three) thereby yielding the regions served by each centre. As can be seen, certain administrative centres lay towards the edge of the areas they served and

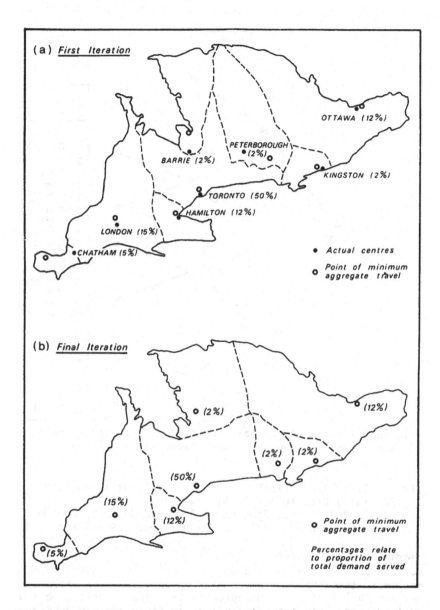

Figure 7.9 Initial and Final Iteration Solutions For the Assignment of Townships to Administrative Centres in Southern
Ontario, Canada.

From: GOODCHILD, M.F. and MASSAM, B.H., (1969), Some Least-
Cost Models of Spatial Administrative Systems in
Southern Ontario, *Geografiska Annaler*, 52B, 86-94.

Redrawn   by permission.

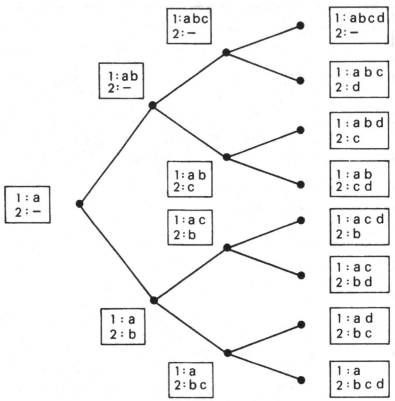

Figure 7.10 Tree of Possible Solutions for a Location-Allocation Problem Involving Four Demand Nodes and Two Central Facilities

From: SCOTT, A.J., (1969), On the Optimal Partitioning of Spatially Distributed Point Sets   in:
SCOTT, A.J. (Ed.), *Studies in Regional Science*, London Papers in Regional Science, Pion, London, 57-72, Figure 1.

Redrawn by permission.

could presumably be located more conveniently. Taking each region in turn, Goodchild and Massam determined the median centre (point of minimum aggregate travel) appropriate to the region. Then, given these revised locations for the administrative centres, the assignment exercise was repeated and the optimal regional boundaries redrawn. Then, once more, the median centres were recalculated. Repetition of the process of assignment followed by relocation through a number of iterations yielded a final stable solution (Figure 7. 9 (b)).

The preceding discussion involves locating a single central facility in order to serve a series of demand nodes

236

and the foregoing application by Goodchild and Massam essentially involves applying this process to each of a set of independent pre-specified regions at the end of each iteration. Recall that as defined at the outset, the location-allocation problem involves determining *simultaneously* the locations at which n central facilities should be sited. Mathematically and following (7.22), the general problem can be viewed as finding the coordinates of the n central facility location points $(X*_1, Y*_1)$, $(X*_2, Y*_2)$, ..., $(X*_n, Y*_n)$ which:

$$\text{Minimise:} \quad \sum_{i=1}^{m} \sum_{j=1}^{n} p_i \lambda_{ij} \{(X_i - X_j*)^2 + (Y_i - Y_j*)^2\}^{\frac{1}{2}} \quad ----(7.25)$$

where $\lambda_{ij} = 1$ if demand node i is served by central facility j
i.e. is nearest to central facility j

$= 0$ otherwise

and where:

$$\sum_{j=1}^{n} \lambda_{ij} = 1$$

i.e. each demand node is assigned to a central facility (which, given the nature of (7.25) will, in fact, be the nearest facility). It is thus to be noted that in common with the models discussed earlier in this chapter, the general location-allocation problem contains zero-one variables and therefore that it is to some extent a combinatorial problem : it is required that the combination of demand nodes to be served by each facility (together with the best locations for the latter) be found.

Scott (1969c) suggests a method by which this combinatorial property can be used together with backtrack programming (Section 7.2) to solve relatively small location-allocation problems exactly. Consider a case where m=4 and n=2. Labelling the four demand nodes as a, b, c, d and the two facilities as '1' and '2', a tree of all possible solutions is given in Figure 7.10. The base node denotes the solution where demand node a is allocated to facility one. Now, considering the addition of demand node b, it may be assigned either to facility one or two as designated by the upper and lower branches respectively. The third and fourth branches assign nodes c and d respectively and the set of all possible solutions is given by the nodes associated with the outermost branches. Now, a value of (7.25) can be calculated for each possible solution in Figure 7.10. Thus, for example, for the solution 1 : ac ; 2 : d, the value of (7.25) is given by the total travel involved in locating central facility one at the median point associated with demand nodes a and c (which can be determined *via* the Kuhn and Kuenne (1962) method) and central

237

facility two at node d. Furthermore, because each branching involves incorporating another demand node into the solution, the value of (7.25) must increase for successive descendant nodes just as X_o did for the example (7.3). Therefore the optimal solution can be determined *via* backtrack programming. Hopefully, a 'good' solution will emerge early on in the process thereby obviating the necessity to examine many nodes explicitly.

The notion of solving location-allocation problems explicitly *via* a tree of the type in Figure 7.10 is taken up by Kuenne and Soland (1972) who employ branch and bound rather than backtrack programming. On the first iteration, branching takes place on the base node and the two resultant solutions are stored. Thereafter, on each iteration, branching takes place on the node for which the value of (7.25) is lowest while nodes for which the value of (7.25) exceeds that for the best feasible solution currently available are classed as terminal. Recall (Section 6.3) that one of the disadvantages of the branch and bound approach is that the number of active node solutions which must be retained at any one time can become unacceptably large ; Kuenne and Soland found that a problem with $m=23$; $n=3$ required storage space in excess of that available on an IBM360/91 computer.

The major conclusion to be drawn from the foregoing comments is that while relatively small location-allocation problems can be solved exactly (for another approach for dealing with the case where $n=2$, see Ostresh (1975)), larger problems must be tackled heuristically. Tornqvist *et al.* (1971) suggest a possible procedure which is succinctly summarised by Horner (1980). First, the area under study is overlain by a series of grid cells. The total demand (population) within each cell is assumed to be located at its centre. An arbitrary starting solution i.e. locational pattern for the n central facilities is defined and the resultant value of (7.25) is determined. Now, each central facility location is considered in turn and, while all other locations are held fixed, it is moved to see if a new position lowers (7.25). Movement takes place first along the x-axis (first to the west, then, if that raises the value of (7.25) to the east); then, when a new position for the x-coordinate has been identified, along the y-axis, first south and then, if necessary, north. Movements are made *via* a series of steps the length of which can be set and adjusted by the researcher and continue until the facility is sited at a location where no further movement will reduce (7.25). Each iteration of the heuristic involves applying the foregoing re-location process to the first, second, ..., n th central facilities in turn. The process concludes when a solution which offers no further reduction in (7.25) by re-locating facilities emerges. Hopefully, this will represent the global optimum but there is no guarantee of this. One method by which confidence in a particular final solution can be increased is by solving a given problem a number of times, starting on each occasion with a different initial solution; if a certain final solution emerges frequently, one can be reasonably confident that it represents the true optimum.

The output from the foregoing heuristic process comprises the optimal value of (7.25) together with the final locations of the n central facilities. Given that persons are to be served by the nearest central facility, a map of the regions to be served by each such facility can be drawn. Figure 7.11 shows the optimal facility locations and regions where three

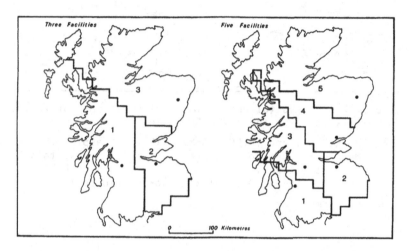

Figure 7.11 Optimal Locations and Hinterlands For Three and Five Facilities to Serve the Population of Scotland

From: ROBERTSON, I.M.L., (1974), Scottish Population Distribution: Implications for Locational Decisions, *Transactions of the Institute of British Geographers*, *63*, 111-24, Figure 5.

Redrawn by permission.

and five facilities respectively are to be sited serve the population of Scotland (Robertson (1974a))while Figure 7.12 compares the location and regions for twelve hospitals in the Irish Republic produced by application of the preceding methods with those recommended in a Government report (Horner and Taylor (1979)). Further examples of similar outputs include those of Tonqvist *et al.* (1971) who consider the location of cement block factories and warehouses in Sweden,

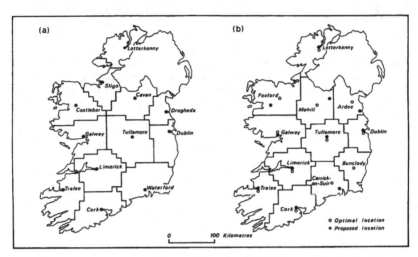

Figure 7.12 Proposed (a) and Optimal (b) Locations for Twelve
Hospitals to Serve the Irish Republic

From: HORNER, A.A. and TAYLOR, A-M., (1979), Grasping the
Nettle - Locational Strategies for Irish Hospitals,
Administration. (Journal of the Institute of Public
Administration, Dublin) 27, 348-70, Figure 1.

Redrawn by permission.

Robertson (1978) who investigates optimal locations for recreation centres in Glasgow and Horner (1980) who deals with
the siting of airports in Ireland.

Before proceeding, it is worth pausing to consider the
relationship between location-allocation problem solutions
of the type just discussed and assignment problem solutions
of the type discussed in Section 3.2.3 e.g. that of Yeates
(1963) — Figure 3.3. In each problem type, the location and
population of a set of demand nodes are given. In the
location-allocation problem, the optimal locations for n
central facilities are to be found. The level of demand to
be serviced by each central facility i.e. its required
capacity is generated in the solution *via* the fact that the
objective (7.25) requires that each demand node be served by
the nearest central facility. Thus a solution could emerge
where a particular central facility is called upon to handle
an unacceptably large demand. In contrast to this, in the
assignment problem, the locations and capacities of the
central facilities are fixed and the optimal allocation is to

be determined. This allocation will not necessarily involve each demand node being serviced by the nearest central facility. Quite obviously, underlying both of the foregoing problems, there is a more general optimisation problem which involves simultaneously determining the optimal number, location and capacities for a set of central facilities in order to fulfill some complex objective e.g. of the type discussed in Section 4.7.1. Some steps towards solving this more general type of problem together with other developments of the location-allocation problem are now mentioned.

7.9 DEVELOPMENTS OF THE LOCATION-ALLOCATION PROBLEM

Recall (Figure 7.11) the optimal locations for three and five central facilities to serve the population of Scotland. In later publications, Robertson (1974b, 1976) suggests that use of the objective (7.25) employing as it does straight line distance measurements, is not appropriate in a situation where the road network is sparse and circuitous and where, for example, long inlets effectively separate adjacent locations. In order to take account of these features, Robertson recasts the location-allocation problem in a form where the grid square populations as input to the heuristic procedure of Tornqvist *et al.* (1971) are arranged along a graph whose links designate the presence of an actual connection between adjacent cells. The heuristic procedure is suitably adjusted to deal with this revised input which, in effect, comprises a p-median type of problem.

Recall (Section 3.4.5) the transhipment problem with a volume change at the transhipment points. Scott (1970) cites the problem where the locations of the transhipment points are to be found in addition to the optimal flows. Formally, if $(X_1, Y_1), \ldots, (X_m, Y_m)$ are the coordinate locations of m origins and $(X_1', Y_1'), \ldots, (X_n', Y_n')$ are the coordinate locations of n destinations, it is required that the coordinate locations of q transhipment points $(X*_1, Y*_1), \ldots, (X*_q, Y*_q)$ together with the optimal flows be found which:

$$\text{Minimise} : \sum_{i=1}^{m} \sum_{j=1}^{q} \{ (X_i - X*_j)^2 + (Y_i - Y*_j)^2 \}^{\frac{1}{2}} X_{ij}$$

$$+ \sum_{j=1}^{q} \sum_{k=1}^{m} \{ (X*_j - X_k)^2 + (Y*_j - Y_k)^2 \}^{\frac{1}{2}} X_{jk} \quad ----(7.26)$$

subject to the constraints (3.18)-(3.20).

Two further versions of the location-allocation problem which have been suggested are the *hierarchical location-allocation* problem and the *stepwise location-allocation*

problem. The former considers the location of central
facilities which are hierarchical in nature : each facility
offers first order services e.g. health centre services but
only n' (<n) offer second order services e.g. hospital
services and so on. The objective is to locate the hier-
archy of central facilities such that the total distance
travelled from demand nodes to nearest facilities and, where
necessary, onwards to facilities of higher order is minimised.
Two papers which treat versions of this problem are those of
Dokmeci (1973) and Narula and Ogbu (1979). Ostresh (1979)
considers the related problem of locating central facilities
where the objective is to minimise the total distance involved in travelling to these facilities from given demand nodes
(as given by (7.25)) together with the distance involved in
making given transfers between the facilities themselves.
The stepwise location-allocation problem involves determining
the optimal order in which central facilities should be
located in a situation where (say) one facility is to be
located at a time e.g. in each year. A discussion of this
problem is offered by Ostresh (1978) while an example set
within the context of a programming method which has yet to
be discussed appears in Section 9.4.2.

Two important assumptions underlie the location-allocation
problem (7.25) and, indeed, most of the formulations discussed in Sections 7.4-7.9. First, concerning the central
facilities to be located, it is assumed that their number is
known in advance, that all potential locations are equally
desirable in terms of setup costs etc and that the capacities
of the facilities will be such as to serve the needs of all
those allocated to them i.e. nearest them. Second, it is
assumed that all persons will use the nearest facility. In
practice, in many instances, these assumptions are unrealistic. From the point of view of the locator of the central
facilities, the number of these is generally not specified in
advance. Indeed, a key question concerns their number and
capacities. From the point of view of the user of the central
facilities, the nearest facility will not necessarily be
used; instead, there might be perceived to be an advantage
in using a more distant facility e.g. if the nearest facility
tends to be congested. A further point concerning the view-
points of the locators and users of central facilities
within the general location-allocation problem framework is
that they are essentially opposed : the former would presumably prefer to locate as few facilities as possible while the
latter would presumably prefer a facility to be located at
every demand point.

Much recent research into location-allocation problems
and related models has concentrated on developing more
general mathematical formulations which take the foregoing
types of issue into account. Two excellent general discussions are those offered by Beaumont (1979) and Leonardi

(1981a,b). A specific example of a location-allocation formulation which does not require that individuals be served by the nearest central facility is mentioned in Section 8.5.1.

7.10 FURTHER EXAMPLES OF PROGRAMMING FORMULATIONS INCORPORATING ZERO-ONE VARIABLES

7.10.1 Scheduling Planning Projects : Tourist Development in Turkey

Swart *et al.* (1975) consider determining for each of a set of regions in Turkey the subset of tourist projects which should be adopted in order to maximise the total benefit accruing whilst not over-spending the budget available or disregarding given precedences of certain projects over others. Consider a particular region i for which eight projects have been proposed and suppose that the precedence that these are to take over each other is as shown in Figure 7.13: project

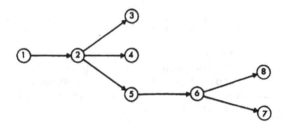

Figure 7.13 Project Precedence Relationships for Some Region i

From: SWART, W.W., GEARING, C., VAR, T and CANN, G., (1975), Investment Planning for the Tourism Sector of a Developing Country With the Aid of Linear Programming in: SALKIN, H.M. and SAHA, J. (Eds.), *Studies In Linear Programming*, North Holland, Amsterdam, 227-49, Figure 1.

Redrawn by permission of the North Holland Publishing Company and the authors.

seven can only be undertaken if project six is completed which, in its turn can only be undertaken if project two is completed and so on. Now, let:

X_{ij} = 1 if project j is undertaken in region i

= 0 otherwise

c_{ij} = The cost of completing project j in region i

b_{ij} = The benefit accruing if project j is completed in region i

k = The total budget available for spending over all projects and regions

The objective of maximising total benefit is given by:

Maximise: $\sum_i \sum_j b_{ij} X_{ij}$ $\qquad$ ----(7.27)

where the summations are over all regions and projects within each region respectively. The constraint that the total budget available not be overspent is given by:

$$\sum_i \sum_j c_{ij} X_{ij} \leq k \qquad ----(7.28)$$

The required precedence relationships can be incorporated *via* a further series of constraints. For region i (Figure 7.13), the precedence of project six over project seven, project five over project six and of project two over project five may be guaranteed *via* the conditions:

$$\left.\begin{array}{ll} X_{16} \geq X_{17} & \text{i.e.} \quad X_{16} - X_{17} \geq 0 \\ X_{15} \geq X_{16} & X_{15} - X_{16} \geq 0 \\ X_{12} \geq X_{15} & X_{12} - X_{15} \geq 0 \end{array}\right\} \qquad ----(7.29)$$

After a detailed discussion of how the b_{ij} values may be measured meaningfully, Swart *et al.* present results for a four region model for Turkey. The formulation (7.27)-(7.29) comprises a zero-one programming model and solutions could be obtained *via* the methods discussed in Section 7.2. In fact, Swart *et al.* proceed by using the simplex method and then by adjusting k to obtain all zero-one solutions.

7.10.2 Plant Location and Air Quality Management

Guldmann and Shefer (1977) consider an area e.g. a city comprising p residential zones labelled r=1, ..., p and s industrial subareas labelled i=1, ..., s. n polluting plants labelled k=1, ..., n are considered. Certain of these are located already in industrial subareas and the others are to be so located. One of the m pollution abatement techniques labelled j=1, ..., m is to be applied to each plant. (One of these techniques can be to do nothing.) It is required that a location (where necessary) and a pollution abatement strategy be determined for each plant which will minimise the total pollution abatement cost whilst not overusing the available land in any industrial subarea or exceeding a maximum level of pollution permitted in each residential zone.

Formally, if:

X_{ijk} = 1 if plant k is located in industrial subarea i and pollution abatement technique j is applied to it

= 0 otherwise

the objective is to determine the values of X_{ijk} which:

$$\text{Minimise} \quad \sum_{i=1}^{s} \sum_{j=1}^{m} \sum_{k=1}^{n} c_{jk} X_{ijk} \qquad \text{----(7.30)}$$

where c_{jk} = The cost of applying pollution abatement strategy j to plant k

Now, each plant must locate somewhere i.e.

$$\sum_{i=1}^{s} \sum_{k=1}^{n} X_{ijk} = 1 \; ; \; j=1, ..., m \qquad \text{----(7.31)}$$

If some plant k is already located in some subarea i, it is required that:

$$\sum_{j=1}^{m} X_{ijk} = 1 \text{ for the relevant i and k} \qquad \text{----(7.32)}$$

Now, letting:

s_k = The land requirement (acres) of plant k

a_i = The acreage available in industrial subarea i

it is required that:

$$\sum_{j=1}^{m} \sum_{k=1}^{n} s_k X_{ijk} \leq a_i \; ; \; i=1, ..., s \qquad \text{----(7.33)}$$

Finally, if:

p_k = The pollution output from plant k before any abatement

r_{km} = The proportional reduction in pollution output from plant k if pollution abatement technique m is applied (r_{km} = 1 implies no reduction, r_{km} = 0.80 implies a 20% reduction etc.)

a_{ir} = The proportion of pollution output in industrial sub-area r which affects residential area r (as determined by climate etc.)

it is required that:

$$\sum_{i=1}^{s} \sum_{j=1}^{m} \sum_{k=1}^{n} p_k \, r_{km} \, a_{ir} \, X_{ijk} \leq c_r; \; r=1, \ldots, q$$

$$---- (7.34)$$

where c_r = Maximum permitted pollution level in residential zone r

The formulation (7.30)-(7.34) comprises a zero-one programming problem. Guldman and Shefer proceed to develop the basic model in order to permit pre-located plants to move and to permit economies of scale where the same pollution abatement technique is applied to plants in the same industrial subarea. The model is demonstrated for Haifa, Israel which is divided into seven industrial subareas and six residential zones. Four plants are pre-located and two new ones are to be located. Two pollution abatement techniques are available. The resultant model formulation involves 56 zero-one decision variables and is solved using branch and bound.

7.10.3 Some Network Development Models

Recall the network development models discussed in Section 3.5. Another model set within this general context is that due to Ridley (1968, 1969) which is summarised by Scott (1971a). Reconsider the type of transhipment problem discussed in Section 3.4.4 i.e. comprising a series of arcs and nodes where certain of the latter are sources and sinks while the remainder are transhipment points. Suppose that the travel time associated with each arc, t_{ij}, is known and that the transhipment problem has been solved to yield the optimal flow pattern i.e. the X_{ij} values which minimise the total travel time involved in transporting product from sources to sinks.

Suppose now that a sum of money, q, is available for investment in the network and that spending some given amount of this total, c_{ij}, on the link (i,j) will reduce the travel time on that link from t_{ij} to r_{ij} where:

$$r_{ij} = (t_{ij} - r.c_{ij}) \qquad\qquad \text{----(7.35)}$$

i.e. where r is a constant giving the reduction in travel time on a link per unit of money invested in it. Now, letting:

$Y_{ij} = 1$ if an investment is made in link (i,j)

$\quad = 0$ otherwise

The revised travel time on link (i,j) is given by:

$$r_{ij} = (b_{ij} - r. c_{ij} Y_{ij}) \qquad\qquad \text{----(7.36)}$$

The objective of determining the links in which investment should be made and the optimal flows which yield the lowest revised value of total travel time is given by:

$$\text{Minimise} \quad \sum_{\text{LINKS}} r_{ij} X_{ij}$$

i.e. Minimise $\quad \sum_{\text{LINKS}} (t_{ij} - r.c_{ij} Y_{ij}) X_{ij} \qquad \text{----(7.37)}$

s.t. $\qquad\qquad\qquad \sum_{\text{LINKS}} c_{ij} Y_{ij} \leq q \qquad\qquad \text{----(7.38)}$

i.e. the budget available is not overspent and subject to constraints of the form (3.14), (3.15) and (3.16) on the sources, sinks and transhipment points respectively.

The foregoing formulation comprises a mixed zero-one programming formulation in the sense defined in Section 7.1 for certain of the decision variables i.e. the Y_{ij} are required to equal either zero or one at optimality. Thus the problem can be viewed as a combinatorial problem in the sense defined in Section 7.2 : it is required that the combination of links in which investment should occur in order to minimise (7.37) be found. The solution method discussed by Ridley utilises this combinatorial interpretation.

Two further studies which cast network development problems within the context of mixed zero-one programming are those of Barber (1975, 1977a) who considers the road networks of Colombia and South Sulawesi, Indonesia respectively. One feature which Barber incorporates into his models is that of determining the optimal ordering through time of link improvements/additions. An example of this type of problem but set within the context of a programming method yet to be discussed appears in Section 9.4.1. A general discussion of various other network investment models can be found in Steenbrink (1974).

8

NONLINEAR PROGRAMMING

8.1 INTRODUCTION

8.1.1 Nonlinear Programming Models

Virtually all of the formulations discussed so far in this book have involved some version of the general linear programming model (4.1)-(4.3) which is so named (recall Section 3.2.1) because the objective and constraints, when expressed mathematically, turn out to be linear. In this chapter we consider *nonlinear programming* models i.e. models in which the objective and/or constraints are nonlinear. In its most general form, a nonlinear programming problem can be expressed as:

$$\text{Optimise}: f(X_1, \ldots, X_n) \qquad \text{----(8.1)}$$

$$\text{s.t.} \quad g_i(X_1, \ldots, X_n) \leq \text{ or } = \text{ or } \geq b_i; \ i=1, \ldots, m$$

$$\text{----(8.2)}$$

and where, generally, the condition :

$$X_j \geq 0 \ ; \ j = 1, \ldots, n \qquad \text{----(8.3)}$$

is not imposed explicitly. $f(X_1, \ldots, X_n)$ and $g_i(X_1, \ldots, X_n)$ represent mathematical expressions involving the decision variables. Some or all of (8.1), (8.2) are non-linear. An example of a nonlinear programming problem is:

$$\text{Maximise}: 4X_1 + 6X_2 - 2X_1^2 - 2X_1 X_2 - 2X_2^2 \quad \left.\begin{array}{r} \\ \\ \end{array}\right)$$
$$X_1 + 2X_2 \qquad\qquad \leq 2 \left.\begin{array}{r}\\\end{array}\right) \ \text{----(8.4)}$$
$$X_1, X_2 \geq 0 \qquad\qquad \left.\begin{array}{r}\\\end{array}\right)$$

DOI: 10.4324/9781003179030-8

Here the objective is nonlinear while the constraints are linear. Most of the problems to be discussed in this chapter are nonlinear in the objective only.

One of the reasons as to why nonlinear programming is of interest to geographers and planners is that many real-world problems, when expressed mathematically turn out to possess nonlinearities. Some examples are presented in the material which follows.

A further reason for the relevance of nonlinear programming relates to the fact that a linear programming model of the form (4.1)-(4.3) implies the existence of certain conditions which do not always hold. Reconsider the linear programming problem objective (4.1). Its form is such that each c_j remains constant no matter what values the X_j's take ; yet, in practice, this is not always the case. In the case of (say) profit maximisation as in (4.21), economies of scale can cause the per unit profit achieved, c_j, to increase as X_j increases; again, in the case of (say) cost minisation as in (4.28), economies of scale can cause the per unit cost to be paid, c_j, to decrease as X_j increases. We show in the next section how the explicit incorporation of economies of scale of these types in the objective (4.1) cause it to become nonlinear. Reconsider a linear programming constraint set e.g. (4.2). Here the a_{ij}'s remain constant no matter what values the X_j's take. Again, in practice, economies of scale may cause the a_{ij} values to alter as the X_j's increase or decrease which, if considered explicitly in a mathematical sense, will introduce nonlinearities into the constraints. Another situation which is not catered for by the general linear programming model is where interdependencies exist among the variables as in the objective:

$$\text{Maximise :} \quad X_1/X_2 + X_2/X_3 \qquad \qquad \text{----(8.5)}$$

which is nonlinear in X_1, X_2, X_3

8.1.2 Some Nonlinear Objectives

Consider once again the objective:

$$\text{Maximise : Profit} = \sum_{j=1}^{n} c_j X_j \qquad \qquad \text{----(8.6)}$$

where c_j =The profit achieved per unit of product j sold and suppose now, following the preceding section, that c_j increases with X_j. Specifically if c_j increases according to the linear relationship:

$$c_j = (d_j + e_j X_j) \qquad \qquad \text{----(8.7)}$$

where d_j and e_j are known constants, the objective (8.6) becomes:

$$\text{Maximise} : \quad \sum_{j=1}^{n} (d_j + e_j X_j)\ X_j \qquad \text{----}(8.8)$$

which is nonlinear in X_j (and in fact, due to the linear
nature of (8.7) is a quadratic)).

As mentioned previously, many entities which present
themselves as natural inputs to mathematical programming
models are by their very nature nonlinear. One such entity
is distance which recall (Section 7.8) is usually expressed
via a statement of the form (7.22) which is nonlinear.

Another objective of interest in certain situations and
which turns out to be nonlinear is the minimisation of
variance. Consider the following problem summarised by Scott
(1971a). n subregions with populations p_j, $j=1, \ldots, n$ are to
be aggregated into m (<n) electoral districts whose populations are to be as equal as possible. This objective can be
expressed as choosing the populations of the m electoral
districts, P_i, $i=1, \ldots, m$ such that the variance of the P_i
values is minimised i.e. such that:

$$\frac{1}{m} \sum_{i=1}^{m} (P_i - \bar{p})^2 \qquad \text{----}(8.9)$$

is minimised where:

$$\bar{p} = \frac{1}{m} \sum_{j=1}^{n} p_j \qquad \text{----}(8.10)$$

(8.9) may be expressed more manageably as finding λ_{ij} (= 1 if
subregion i is assigned to district j; = 0 otherwise) to
minimise:

$$Z = \frac{1}{m} \sum_{i=1}^{m} \left(\sum_{j=1}^{n} p_j\ \lambda_{ij} - \bar{p} \right)^2 \qquad \text{----}(8.11)$$

which is nonlinear in the zero-one variable λ_{ij}. In addition
to requiring that each subregion is assigned to exactly one
electoral district, a further set of constraints requiring
that each electoral district be composed of a set of contiguous
subregions would be necessary.

A nonlinear objective which has formed the basis for a
number of recent mathematical programming studies concerns
the maximisation of what is known as entropy. The idea of
maximising entropy is equivalent to that of finding the most
likely outcome to a particular set of events. To illustrate,
and following Gould (1972), consider tossing two coins.
Denoting 'Heads' by H and 'Tails' by T there are four possible
outcomes:

H, H ; H, T ; T, H ; T, T

Assuming that the precise coin which shows a head or tail is immaterial, it can be said that the most likely outcome from the foregoing experiment is H,T. Mathematically, if n coins are tossed, the number of ways in which one can finish up with N_1 heads and N_2 tails $(N_1 + N_2 = n)$ is given by:

$$f(N_1, N_2) = \frac{n\,!}{N_1\,!\;\;N_2\,!}$$

Checking for n = 2 we have:

$$f(2,0) = \frac{2!}{2!\;\;0!} = 1$$

$$f(1,1) = \frac{2!}{1!\;\;1!} = 2$$

$$f(0,2) = \frac{2!}{0!\;\;2!} = 1$$

which confirms the preceding results. If now for same number of coins n we are asked to find the values of N_1 and N_2 associated with the most likely outcome, this can be expressed mathematically as finding N_1 and N_2 which:

$$\text{Maximise} : f(N_1, N_2) = \frac{n!}{N_1!\;\;N_2!} \qquad \text{----(8.12)}$$

$$\text{s.t.} \qquad N_1 + N_2 = n \qquad \text{----(8.13)}$$

More generally, for a process involving n descrete entities each of which can adopt one of k possible outcomes, the objective of finding the most likely outcome can be expressed as finding N_1, N_2, ...; N_k to:

$$\text{Maximise} : f(N_1, N_2, \ldots, N_k) = \frac{n!}{\prod\limits_{i=1}^{k} N_i\,!} \qquad \text{----(8.14)}$$

$$\text{s.t.} \qquad \sum_{i=1}^{k} N_i = n \qquad \text{----(8.15)}$$

Objectives of the form (8.12) and (8.14) which seek to find the most likely outcome are said to maximise the entropy of the system being modelled. They are nonlinear in terms of the decision variables N_1, ..., N_k. Two examples of entropy maximising models are presented in Section 8.5.

8.2 SOME POTENTIAL DIFFICULTIES IN SOLVING NONLINEAR AS OPPOSED TO LINEAR PROGRAMMING PROBLEMS

Before investigating specific methods for solving nonlinear
programming problems, it is worth remarking that in general,
these problems are more difficult to solve than linear problems.
In order to appreciate some of the reasons for this, consider
a problem involving two decision variables, X_1 and X_2, with a
nonlinear objective, three linear constraints and the usual
non-negativity conditions. Recalling Section 4.3, the solution space will be similar to OA_1 SUC_2 in Figure 4.1. The
lines relating to given values of the objective i.e. the
equivalent of P_1 P_1', P_2 P_2' in Figure 4.1(c) will now be nonlinear. Their precise pattern will depend on the mathematical
form of the objective. Four geometrical possibilities are
indicated in Figure 8.1 (a)-(d). In Figure 8.1(a), the nature

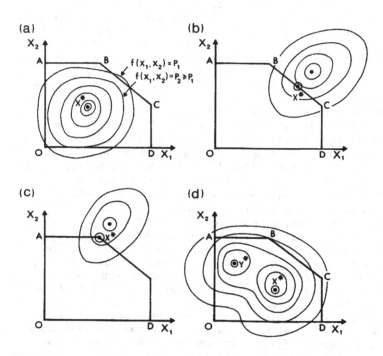

Figure 8.1 Some Hypothetical Nonlinear Programming Problems

of $f(X)=f(X_1,X_2)$ is such as to achieve a single maximum at a point X* within the solution space; in the case of Figures 8.1(b) and 8.1(c), the maximum occurs on a constraint bounding the solution space and at an outer point of the solution space respectively; finally, in the case of Figure 8.1(d), the mathematical form of f(X) is such as to possess two maxima within the solution space : a *local optimum*[+] at Y* and a *global optimum*[+] at X*. Recall (Section 4.3) the important finding in the case of linear programming that while the solution space comprises an infinite number of points, the optimal solution will almost certainly lie at one of the outer points and therefore that these alone need to be checked explicitly in the solution process. The foregoing examples demonstrate that the same generalisation cannot be made in the case of a nonlinear problem. The optimal solution can generally lie anywhere within the solution space which suggests that more complicated solution methods will be required.

A key factor controlling the location of the optimal solution to a particular nonlinear programming problem is, quite obviously, the mathematical nature of the nonlinearities involved. Suppose that when solving a particular problem, an optimal value (i.e. the equivalent of X* or Y* in Figure 8.1 (a)-(d)) has been found; now , if it is known that the mathematical form of f(X) is such that it possesses a single global optimum only (i.e. no local optima), then the point which has been identified must comprise that optimum and the solution process may cease.

In order to understand further how the mathematical nature of the underlying nonlinearities in a problem can aid in identifying a global optimum, consider the maximisation of a nonlinear objective comprising one variable, $f(X_1)$. Now, suppose that it is known that $f(X_1)$ is known to be such as to rise to a single peak and then fall off as X_1 increases (Figure 8.2(a)). $f(X_1)$ is actually said to be *concave*[+]. Now, suppose that the single constraint condition $a_1 \leq X_1 \leq a_2$ is imposed. The optimal solution lies at X_1*. Now, instead, suppose that the single constraint condition $a_2 \leq X_1 \leq a_3$ is imposed. The optimal solution now lies at a_2 i.e. at one of the constraint boundaries. Suppose now that $f(X_1)$ is known to be such as to fall to a single trough and then rise again as X_1 increases (Figure 8.2(b)). $f(X_1)$ is actually said to be *convex*[+]. Now, if a single constraint condition of the form $a_1 \leq X_1 \leq a_2$ is imposed, the point where $f(X_1)$ is maximised must lie at either a_1 or a_2 but not between them due to the shape of $f(X_1)$. To summarise the foregoing, we have shown that determining the point where $f(X_1)$ is maximised

---

[+]Terms so designated where they first appear in the text are defined in Appendix A.2.

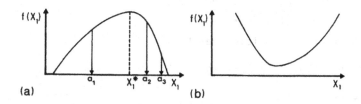

(a)   (b)

Figure 8.2 Two Hypothetical Nonlinear Objectives Involving
One Variable

subject to a condition of the form $a_1 \leq X_1 \leq a_2$ is more
straightforward when it is known in advance that $f(X_1)$ is
convex because, in that case, the optimal solution must lie
at a_1 or a_2. In general, for more complicated problems and
solution methods, we shall often find it necessary to impose
conditions relating to the convexity or concavity of the
nonlinearities in a problem in order to simplify the search
for the optimal solution.

8.3   UNCONSTRAINED OPTIMISATION

8.3.1   Quadratic Objective

The most straightforward type of nonlinear programming
problem comprises the optimisation of a nonlinear objective
in the absence of constraints i.e.

$$\text{Optimise} : f(X) = f(X_1, \ldots, X_n) \qquad \text{----(8.16)}$$

Such problems are said to involve *unconstrained optimisation*.
The most straightforward case of unconstrained optimisation
is where $f(X)$ is a *quadratic function*[+] of one variable, X_1,
i.e. of the form:

$$f(X_1) = aX_1{}^2 + bX_1 + c \qquad \text{----(8.17)}$$

where a, b and c are known constants. In this case, as discussed in Appendix A.2, the single optimal value of X_1 can be
determined by differentiation.

One investigation which involved finding the optimal
value of an objective of the form (8.17) is that carried out
by the Port of New York Authority to determine the maximum
traffic flow possible through the Lincoln Tunnel which
connects the northern New Jersey suburbs to mid-Manhattan.

255

Nonlinear Programming

This summary is based on Catanese (1972). Letting:

S = Speed of Vehicles (Miles per Hour)

D = Density of Vehicles (per mile)

F = Flow of traffic (Vehicles per Hour)

it is required that F be maximised. Now:

$$F = S.D. \qquad\qquad\qquad ----(8.18)$$

and S is obviously inversely related to D. Specifically, studies of the flow of traffic through the tunnel revealed that:

$$S = 42.1 - 0.324 \, D \; ; \; 0 \leq D \leq 130 \qquad ----(8.19)$$

Thus, substituting (8.19) in (8.18) :

$$F = (42.1 - 0.324 \, D) \, D$$

$$= (42.1 \, D - 0.324 D^2)$$

Using calculus, the value of D which optimises F, D*, is given by:

$$\frac{dF}{dD} \overset{\text{SET}}{=} 42.1 - 0.648 \, D = 0$$

i.e. D* = 64.9

which we note, lies within the range for which (8.19) holds. A negative second derivative demonstrates that this is a maximum. Substituting in (8.19) and (8.18) respectively yields:

$$S* = 21.0$$

and F* = 1363

i.e. the maximum flow of vehicles that the tunnel can handle is 1363 vehicles per hour which will travel at a speed of 21.0 miles per hour.

After a quadratic function in one variable, the next most complicated type of function to be called upon to optimise is a quadratic in more than one variable. Here, following the material presented in Appendix A.2, the *partial derivative*[+] of the function with respect to each decision variable is found and set to zero. The resulting set of linear equations is then solved for the decision variables to yield a solution whose nature (maximum, minimum etc) can then be checked. An interesting study which involves optimising a quadratic function in many variables is that described by Pearl (1974) who for an urban area seeks to determine the population and employment positions which should be placed in each of n zones in order to maximise the total desirability rating of the zones whilst approaching given employment and population targets as closely as possible. Certain aspects of the formulation of Pearl's model relate to goal programming which is discussed in Chapter Ten.

8.3.2 Non Quadratic Objectives

One of the advantages of a quadratic objective in one or more variables is that differentiation yields one or more linear equations which can be generally solved to give the required global optimum. In the case of more complex objectives, the first order derivative expressions will not be linear. There may be more than one solution to these expressions and these solutions might be hard or even impossible to determine. (For a further discussion, see Appendix A.2.)

By way of example, reconsider the objective underlying the one facility location-allocation problem (7.22):

$$\text{Minimise} : Z = \sum_{i=1}^{m} P_i \ \{(X_i - X*) + (Y_i - Y*)^2\}^{\frac{1}{2}} \quad \text{---}(8.20)$$

Now, in order to find the optimal values of X* and Y* respectively, we differentiate (8.20) with respect to these variables which yields:

$$\frac{\delta Z}{\delta X*} = \sum_{i=1}^{m} \tfrac{1}{2}. \ P_i \ \{(X_i - X*)^2 + (Y_i - Y*)^2 \}^{-\frac{1}{2}}.2(X_i - X*)(-1)$$

$$\text{----}(8.21)$$

$$\frac{\delta Z}{\delta Y*} = \sum_{i=1}^{m} \tfrac{1}{2}. \ P_i \ \{(X_i - X*)^2 + (Y_i - Y*)^2 \}^{-\frac{1}{2}}.2(Y_i - Y*)(-1)$$

$$\text{----}(8.22)$$

which, when set to zero, cannot be solved simultaneously for (X*,Y*) due to their complexity. It is because of this complexity that resource must be made to the heuristic methods summarised in Chapter Seven. The same type of difficulty arises in the case of many other nonlinear objectives.

8.3.3 Optimising an Imprecisely Defined Nonlinear Objective Whose General Form Is Known : The Method of Golden Sections

Up to this, it has been assumed that the objective to be optimised is exactly defined in terms of a mathematical expression and the discussion has focussed on methods for finding the optimal values of the decision variables. In certain research situations, the precise form of an objective under consideration i.e. in terms of a mathematical expression is not known. Instead, knowledge exists concerning its general form e.g. that it rises to a single peak and then declines and, on the basis of this information alone, it is required that the optimum be found.

In order to demonstrate the way in which this type of situation can arise and a method appropriate to dealing with it, we consider the study of Batty (1971) who focusses attention on the following model which aims to provide an estimate of the flow of consumer expenditure between zones. Specifically, it is hypothesised that if:

S_{ij} = Flow of consumer expenditure from residences in zone i to shops in zone j for all sales (to be predicted)

e_i = Expenditure per capita in zone i

p_i = Population of zone i

w_j = Shopping floorspace provided in zone j (being a measure of the relative attractiveness of zone j for shopping)

d_{ij} = Distance apart of zones i and j

then:

$$S_{ij} = \frac{(e_i \, p_i) \, w_j^{\mu} \cdot d_{ij}^{-\lambda}}{\sum\limits_{j=1}^{n} (w_j^{\mu} \, d_{ij}^{-\lambda})} \qquad \text{----(8.23)}$$

where $\sum\limits_{j=1}^{n} S_{ij} = e_i \, p_i$ for $i = 1, \ldots, n$ ----(8.24)

$$\sum\limits_{i=1}^{n} \sum\limits_{j=1}^{n} S_{ij} = \sum\limits_{j=1}^{n} S_j = \sum\limits_{i=1}^{n} e_i \, p_i \qquad \text{----(8.25)}$$

and where λ and μ are unknown parameters. For the initial part of his analysis, Batty assumed $\lambda = 0$ which reduces (8.23) to:

$$S_{ij} = \frac{(e_i \, p_i) \cdot w_j^{\mu}}{\sum\limits_{j=1}^{n} w_j^{\mu}} \qquad \text{----(8.26)}$$

For the purposes of his study, Batty had for 30 zones in Kristiansand, Sweden data for e_i, p_i, w_j, d_{ij} and S_{ij}. Thus, assuming a value for μ, estimates for S_{ij} could be

258

obtained from (8.26) and compared with the actual values.
Batty performed this comparison by calculating the coefficient
of determination, R^2, ($0<R^2\leq 1$ and $R^2= 1$ implies a perfect
match) for the estimated versus the actual values of S_{ij}. He
wished to find the value of the parameter μ in (8.26) which
produced S_{ij} values as close as possible to the actual values
i.e. which maximised R^2. All that was known in advance was
that the best value of μ lay between 0.00 and 5.00. Looking
at this situation in terms of a graph (Figure 8.3), it is

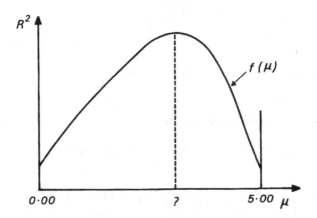

Figure 8.3 Hypothetical Plot for R^2 Against μ For Consumer
Expenditure Flow Model

known that R^2 rises to a peak between $\mu = 0.00$ and $\mu= 5.00$;
what is required is the value of μ associated with this peak.
We are thus seeking the optimum associated with an imprecisely
defined nonlinear function whose general form is known. The
strategy generally used in this type of situation involves what
is known as *adaptive search*. The precise version of adaptive
search employed by Batty is that known as the *method of golden
sections* which is now described. A further application of the
method can be found in Baxter and Williams (1975).

Use of the method of golden sections hinges on the following. Suppose that it is known that an objective (R^2 in the
present case) reaches a maximum between two given limits A_1 and
A_2 (Figure 8.4). Suppose now that its value is determined at
some two intermediate points between A_1 and A_2, say A_3 and A_4
and suppose that its value at A_3 is found to exceed that at
A_4. What information does this reveal concerning the location
of the optimum? First, it could lie between A_3 and A_4 as

259

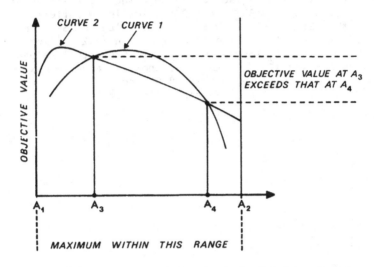

Figure 8.4 Logic Underlying Method of Golden Sections

indicated by curve 1 ; second, it could lie between A_1 and A_2 as indicated by curve 2. The one area in which it could not lie is between A_4 and A_2. Putting these facts together, it can be said that the optimal value of the objective definitely lies between A_1 and A_4 i.e. the intermediate point which is associated with the poorer value of the objective provides a new outer limit for the range within which the optimum must lie. The reader should satisfy himself that if the value of the objective at A_3 was less than that at A_4, the peak being sought would have to lie between A_3 and A_2 i.e. once again, the poorer value of the objective provides a new outer limit for the range within which the optimum must lie. Application of the method of golden sections involves applying the foregoing procedure iteratively thereby successively reducing the interval within which the optimum must lie. At each iteration, the intermediate points at which the objective is evaluated (the equivalent of A_3 and A_4 in Figure 8.4) are those at .382 and .618 times the distance from the current left hand to the current right hand boundary. In order to understand the advantage of this particular definition of the intermediate points, we consider the results obtained by Batty.

Recall that it is known that the value of μ in (8.26) which produces a set of S_{ij} values which maximise R^2 lies between 0.0000 and 5.0000. Thus, in order to initiate the search process, R^2 is calculated for:

Nonlinear Programming

$$\mu = 0.0000 + 0.382 \ (5.0000 - 0.0000) = 1.9098$$

$$\mu = 0.0000 + 0.618 \ (5.0000 - 0.0000) = 3.0902.$$

The corresponding values of R^2 for these values of μ turn out to be .9642 for $\mu = 1.9098$ and .8782 for $\mu = 3.0902$ which shows that the value of μ which maximises R^2 must lie between 0.0000 and 3.0902. The revised points for which R^2 must be calculated are thus:

$$\mu = 0.0000 + 0.382 \ (3.0902 - 0.0000) = 1.1804$$

$$\mu = 0.0000 + 0.618 \ (3.0902 - 0.0000) = 1.9098$$

Notice that one of these boundary values ($\mu = 1.9098$) is the same as in the previous iteration. Thus, only one further calculation of R^2 is required. In fact, in the method of golden sections, this will always be the case after the first iteration which explains the choice of the indices 0.382 and 0.618.

The results emerging from Batty's study are summarised in Figure 8.5. As is emphasied by the graph, the method of golden sections does not identify the optimal solution explicitly; rather it successively reduces the interval within which this solution lies. Thus the reduction process must continue until an acceptable level of accuracy has been achieved.

Recall that the initial expression of the consumer expenditure model to be tested by Batty (8.23) involved two unknown parameters: μ and λ. If it can be assumed that a graph of R^2 against μ and λ (i.e. a three dimensional equivalent of Figure 8.3) rises to a single peak, Batty suggests that the values of μ and λ associated with this peak may be found by first holding (say) λ constant and optimising μ by the method of golden sections, then by keeping μ at its optimal value and optimising λ , then of keeping λ at its current optimum and optimising μ and so on until constancy in both μ and λ is achieved. The reader must be warned, however, that many iterations may be required to reach the required optimum and that in some instances, it will not emerge at all. An advanced text e.g. Cooper and Steinberg (1970) should be consulted for details.

8.4 OPTIMISING A NONLINEAR OBJECTIVE WITH LINEAR EQUALITY CONSTRAINTS : THE METHOD OF LAGRANGE MULTIPLIERS

We now consider optimisation problems of the form:

$$\text{Optimise} : f(X_1, \ldots, X_n) \qquad\qquad ----(8.27)$$

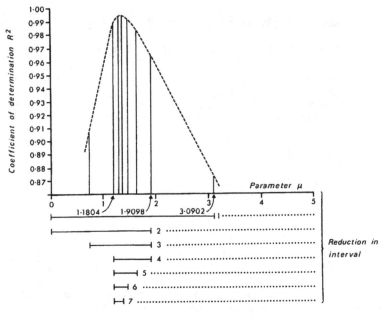

Figure 8.5 Search by Golden Section : Graphical Summary of Results

From: BATTY, M., (1971), Exploratory Calibration of a Retail Location Model Using Search by Golden Section, *Environment and Planning*, 3, 411-32, Figure 3.

Redrawn by permission.

$$\text{s.t.} \quad g_i(X_1, \ldots, X_n) = 0 \; ; \; i = 1, \ldots, m \quad \text{----(8.28)}$$

where $f(X_1, \ldots, X_n)$ is a nonlinear objective similar to those considered in the previous section while $g_i(X_1, \ldots, X_n)$ $i = 1, \ldots, m$ represent a set of m linear constraints which must hold at the optimal solution. Note that the usual condition that $X_j \geq 0$; $j = 1, \ldots, n$ is not imposed explicitly. The introduction of constraints obviously imposes complications in terms of solution method. In the case of unconstrained optimisation (Section 8.3), one is merely seeking the peak(s) or trough(s) in the objective i.e. the point(s) where the partial derivatives equal zero; with the imposition of constraints, the global optimal solution may no longer lie at a *stationary point*[+] but at a point located on one or more of the constraints (e.g. as in Figure 8.1(b), (c)).

The most usual approach for solving a problem of the type (8.27), (8.28) is by using what are known as Lagrange multipliers. The overall strategy is to convert the

262

constrained problem (8.27), (8.28) to one involving unconstrained optimisation and then to use the calculus methods outlined in the previous section. In order to illustrate, consider the following problem adapted from Taha (1976):

$$\text{Minimise} : X_1^2 + X_2^2 + X_3^2 \qquad \text{----}(8.29)$$

$$\text{s.t.} \quad \left.\begin{array}{l} X_1 + X_2 + 3X_3 = 2) \\ ) \\ 5X_1 + 2X_2 + X_3 = 5) \end{array}\right\} \qquad \text{----}(8.30)$$

Converting the constraints (8.30) to the form of (8.28) we have:

$$\text{Minimise} : X_1^2 + X_2^2 + X_3^2 \qquad \left.\begin{array}{l}) \\ ) \end{array}\right.$$

$$\text{s.t.} \quad \left.\begin{array}{l} X_1 + X_2 + 3X_3 - 2 = 0) \\ ) \\ 5X_1 + 2X_2 + X_3 - 5 = 0) \end{array}\right\} \qquad \text{----}(8.31)$$

Consider now the mathematical objective formed by the original objective plus the left hand side of each constraint in (8.23) multiplied by a constant, λ_i, which is known as a *Lagrange multiplier*, i.e.:

$$\text{Optimise} : f(X_1, \ldots, X_n) + \sum_{i=1}^{m} \lambda_i \cdot g_i (X_1, \ldots, X_n)$$

$$\text{----}(8.32)$$

In the case of (8.31) which possesses two constraints, this yields:

$$\text{Minimise} : (X_1^2 + X_2^2 + X_3^2) + \lambda_1 (X_1 + X_2 + 3X_3 - 2)$$

$$+ \lambda_2 (5X_1 + 2X_2 + X_3 - 5)$$

$$\text{----}(8.33)$$

The objectives (8.32), (8.33) are known as *Lagrange functions*. We show later that to solve (8.33) for the unknowns X_1, X_2, X_3, λ_1, λ_2 is equivalent to solving (8.31) for X_1, X_2, X_3 and that in general, solving an unconstrained problem of the form (8.32) is equivalent to solving the constrained problem (8.27), (8.28) from which it has been derived. Returning to (8.33) and following the methods of the previous section, the optimal values for the unknowns X_1, X_2, X_3, λ_1, λ_2 can be found by determining the partial derivative with respect to each unknown in turn, setting the resulting expressions to zero and solving. Designating the Lagrange function (8.33) as $L = L(X_1, X_2, X_3, \lambda_1, \lambda_2)$, this gives:

$$\frac{\delta L}{\delta X_1} = \quad 2X_1 \qquad\qquad + \lambda_1 + 5\lambda_2 \quad \overset{\text{SET}}{= 0}$$

$$\frac{\delta L}{\delta X_2} = \qquad 2X_2 \qquad + \lambda_1 + 2\lambda_2 \quad \overset{\text{SET}}{= 0}$$

$$\frac{\delta L}{\delta X_3} = \qquad\qquad 2X_3 + 3\lambda_1 \quad \lambda_2 \quad \overset{\text{SET}}{= 0} \qquad \text{----(8.34)}$$

$$\frac{\delta L}{\delta \lambda_1} = -(X_1 + \quad X_2 + 3X_3 \qquad\qquad -2) \overset{\text{SET}}{= 0}$$

$$\frac{\delta L}{\delta \lambda_2} = -(5X_1 + 2X_2 + \quad X_3 \qquad\qquad -5) \overset{\text{SET}}{= 0}$$

which when solved as five linear equations with five unknowns yields the unique solution:

$$X_1 = 0.81 \; ; \; X_2 = 0.35 \; ; \; X_3 = 0.28 \; \lambda_1 = -0.0867 \; ; \; \lambda_2 = -0.3067$$

from which $X_o = 0.8570$. Following the methods of the previous section and Appendix A.2, we must now check that this solution does indeed represent a minimum. A description of how this task may be undertaken lies beyond the scope of this text and the reader is referred to a more advanced treatment e.g. Taha (1976) for details. It is worth noting that in many applied situations, the researcher will know in advance from his knowledge of the system being modelled whether a particular solution is a maximum or minimum which obviates the necessity for checking explicitly.

That the values for X_1, X_2, X_3 obtained by solving (8.33) are indeed the optimal values associated with (8.31) can be seen by noting that the derivatives of L with respect to λ_1 and λ_2 (the last two expressions in (8.34)) require that X_1, X_2, X_3 shall be such in the solution that the two original constraints (8.30) hold. Given that this is so, the solution is such that the last two terms in (8.33) are zero which means in effect that the objective which is optimised is (8.29). The foregoing logic can be extended to show that any problem of the form (8.27),(8.28) can be solved by forming the equivalent unconstrained problem (8.32).

A point of interest surrounding the method of Lagrange multipliers concerns the interpretation that may be placed on the values of the multipliers themselves i.e. the λ_i values in the final solution. Reconsider the expression (8.33) and, in particular, the term:

$$\lambda_1 (X_1 + X_2 + 3X_3 - 2) \qquad\qquad \text{----(8.35)}$$

As mentioned previously, because the first constraint in the original problem must hold, (8.35) reduces at optimality to $\lambda_1(0) = 0$. Suppose now, however, that the first constraint in

(8.30) is altered to:

$$X_1 + X_2 + 3X_3 = 3$$

and, in the same way as in Chapter Five, the question is asked as to what effect the increase of one in the right hand side of the constraint will have on X_o assuming that all other values in the optimal solution remain the same. The answer is given by substitution in (8.33) which yields:

$$X_o = 0.8570 + \lambda_1 \, (-1) + \lambda_2 \, (0)$$

$$= 0.9437$$

Thus, in the same sense as in Chapter Five, λ_1 is the sensitivity coefficient associated with the right hand side of the first constraint and in general, λ_i is the sensitivity coefficient associated with the right hand side of the i th constraint. However, a special word of caution concerning the interpretation of these coefficients is necessary. Because we are dealing with a nonlinear objective, the rate at which the value of that objective changes as one moves away   from the current optimal solution is itself changing all the time. The values of λ_i express the rates of change at the current optimal solution point and hold exactly at that point only. They should hold approximately in the vicinity of that point but will become less and less accurate as one moves away from it. Translated into practical terms, this means that if (8.29), (8.30) was in fact re-solved but with the right hand side of the first constraint in (8.30) increased by one, the revised optimal value of the objective would probably be in the region of 0.9437 but would be unlikely to exactly equal that value.
      A final point worth noting in the case of the foregoing numerical example (8.29), (8.30) is that the objective is quadratic which means that each of the conditions (8.34) is linear. More complex nonlinearities in the objective would lead to nonlinearities in the equivalent of (8.34) which (recall Section 8.3.3) would make the task of determining the required solution(s) difficult or even impossible.

8.5   TWO ENTROPY MAXIMISING MODELS

Recall the objective of maximising entropy (Section 8.1.2). We now discuss two models involving entropy maximisation subject to equality constraints which are solved using the method of Lagrange multipliers.

8.5.1 A Trip Distribution Model

Consider a region divided into n zones.

Let o_i = The number of (say) worktrips which commence in zone i per day i.e. at residences; $i = 1, \ldots, n$

d_j = The number of worktrips which have their destination in zone j per day i.e. at workplaces; $j = 1, \ldots, n$

f_{ij} = Some measure of the cost of travelling between zone i and zone j.

Given this information, it is required that the pattern of trips between the zones be predicted. Conventionally, within the context of transportation planning (for a summary, see for example Bruton (1975), Stopher and Meyburg (1975)), this task is undertaken using the *fully constrained gravity model* which hypothesises that for any two zones i and j:

$$T_{ij} = A_i \, B_j \, o_i \, d_j \, f_{ij} \qquad \qquad ----(8.36)$$

where : T_{ij} = The number of trips between zone i and zone j

and A_i, B_j are constants relating to zones i and j as producers and attracters of trips respectively.

Two forms of f_{ij} which are commonly employed in (8.36) are:

$$f_{ij} = e^{-\alpha c_{ij}} \qquad \qquad ----(8.37)$$

and $$f_{ij} = c_{ij}^{-\beta} \qquad \qquad ----(8.38)$$

where c_{ij} is the cost of a journey from zone i to zone j and where α and β are known constants.
It is assumed that either (8.37) or (8.38) has been used in each of the formulations which follows. Any set of values for T_{ij} for some set of zones must fulfill two conditions:

$$\sum_{i=1}^{n} T_{ij} = d_j \; ; \; j = 1, \ldots, n \qquad \qquad ----(8.39)$$

$$\sum_{j=1}^{n} T_{ij} = o_i \; ; \; i = 1, \ldots, n \qquad \qquad ----(8.40)$$

where it is assumed that:

$$\sum_{i=1}^{n} o_i = \sum_{j=1}^{n} d_j = \sum_{i=1}^{n} \sum_{j=1}^{n} t_{ij} = t \qquad \text{----(8.41)}$$

where t is the total number of trips.

Given for a set of zones (say for the present day) values for T_{ij}, o_i, d_j, f_{ij}, methods exist by which values for A_i and B_i can be deduced which cause (8.36) to yield T_{ij} values which fulfill (8.39) and (8.40) as closely as possible. Then (say for some future year), given A_i, B_j, o_i, d_j and f_{ij}, (8.36) can be used to predict values for T_{ij}.

Wilson (1970) (for a summary and further discussion see Gould (1970), Wilson and Senior (1974), Baxter (1976), Wilson *et al.* (1981)) views the formulation (8.36), (8.39)-(8.41) in a different light. Given for a set of zones o_i and d_j, Wilson considers the task of determining the most likely pattern of trips between zones. Recall (Section 8.1.2) that this is equivalent to seeking the T_{ij} values which maximise entropy. In this instance, there are t discrete entities (trips) and 2n possible outcomes (routes) for which a flow level (T_{ij}) is required. Recalling (8.14), the most likely outcome is given by the values of T_{ij} which:

$$\text{Maximise} : f(T_{ij} \text{ for all } i, j) = \frac{t\,!}{\displaystyle\prod_{i=1}^{n} \prod_{j=1}^{n} t_{ij}!} \qquad \text{----(8.42)}$$

Wilson imposes the equality constraints (8.39), (8.40) together with the condition that the total amount of money spent on trip making equal a given total, c i.e.

$$\sum_{i=1}^{n} \sum_{j=1}^{n} c_{ij} T_{ij} = c \qquad \text{----(8.43)}$$

where c_{ij} is as in (8.37), (8.38).

The formulation (8.42), (8.39), (8.40), (8.43) comprises a nonlinear objective subject to linear equality constraints which can therefore be tackled *via* the methods introduced in the previous section. Rewriting the model in the form (8.28) yields:

$$\text{Maximise} : \frac{t\,!}{\displaystyle\prod_{i=1}^{n} \prod_{j=1}^{n} T_{ij}!}$$

$$\text{s.t.} \quad o_i - \sum_{j=1}^{n} T_{ij} = 0 \quad i=1, \ldots, n \qquad \text{----(8.44)}$$

$$d_j \; - \; \sum_{i=1}^{n} \; T_{ij} = 0 \; ; \; j=1, \; \ldots, \; n \qquad \text{----}(8.45)$$

$$c \; - \; \sum_{i=1}^{n} \; \sum_{j=1}^{n} \; c_{ij} \; T_{ij} = 0 \qquad \text{----}(8.46)$$

Unfortunately, the objective is not a quadratic which suggests that solving the partial derivatives of the associated Lagrange function might prove difficult. Fortunately, it can be shown that the values of T_{ij} which maximise (8.42) are also those which maximise the natural logarithm of the same expression i.e. are those which:

$$\text{Maximise : } f_{TRANS} = \ln \frac{t \, !}{\displaystyle\prod_{i=1}^{n} \; \prod_{j=1}^{n} \; T_{ij}!} \qquad \text{----}(8.47)$$

Also, provided that the T_{ij} values are reasonably large:

$$\frac{\delta f_{TRANS}}{\delta T_{ij}} = \; - \; \ln \; T_{ij} \qquad \text{----}(8.48)$$

Now, forming the Lagrange function from the revised objective together with the constraints (8.44)-(8.46) gives:

$$
\begin{array}{cccc}
 & (1) & (2) & (3) \\
L = L(T_{ij}, & \lambda_i, & \lambda_j, & \lambda \;)
\end{array}
$$

$$= \ln\left(\frac{t!}{\displaystyle\prod_{i=1}^{n} \; \prod_{j=1}^{n} \; T_{ij} \, !}\right) + \sum_{i=1}^{n} \lambda_i \overset{(1)}{(o_i - T_{ij})}$$

$$+ \sum_{j=1}^{n} \lambda_j \overset{(2)}{(d_j - T_{ij})} + \lambda \overset{(3)}{(c} - \sum_{i=1}^{n} \; \sum_{j=1}^{n} \; c_{ij} \; T_{ij}) $$

$$\text{----}(8.49)$$

$$
\begin{array}{ccc}
(1) & (2) & (3)
\end{array}
$$

where λ_i $i=1, \ldots, n$ λ_j, $j=1, \ldots, n$ and λ are the Lagrange multipliers associated with the constraints (8.44), (8.45), (8.46) respectively and L is to be maximised. Differentiating L with respect to each of the T_{ij}'s and setting to zero yields the 2n conditions:

$$\frac{\delta L}{\delta T_{ij}} = \; - \; \ln \; T_{ij} - \lambda_i^{(1)} - \lambda_j^{(2)} - \lambda^{(3)} \; c_{ij} \overset{SET}{=} \; 0 \quad \text{----}(8.50)$$

while differentiation with respect to the Lagrange multipliers yields the (2n+1) equality constraints (8.44)-(8.46). Simultaneous solution of (8.50) with (8.44)-(8.46) which has to be achieved iteratively due to the underlying mathematics yields the required T_{ij} values which can be shown to be associated with a global maximum. The reader is referred to one of the references cited at the outset for the mathematical details.

A study which applies the foregoing methods in the context of real-world data is that described by Walsh (1980) who, given o_i and d_j for eight zones comprising County Limerick, Ireland and using distance as a proxy for cost, determines the T_{ij} values which maximise entropy. The T_{ij} values obtained accord closely with those actually occurring. Walsh presents evidence to show that in this instance at least, the entropy maximising approach for estimating tripmaking levels is superior to the gravity model discussed at the outset of this section. In a planning context, he suggests that the entropy maximising model has a potential role to play in predicting trip patterns for possible future residence and employment patterns and in assessing the impact on trip patterns of possible transport system changes e.g. road improvements which would reduce certain c_{ij} values.

Before leaving the foregoing entropy maximisation formulation, it is interesting to note that it can be shown to be related to both the fully constrained gravity model (8.36), (8.39), (8.40) and to the transportation problem (3.4)-(3.7). Indeed, it forms an interesting link between these two formulations. First, it can be shown that if in the entropy maximising model A_i and B_j are defined by:

$$A_i = e^{-\lambda_i^{(1)}} / o_i \qquad \text{----(8.51)}$$

$$B_j = e^{-\lambda_j^{(2)}} / d_j \qquad \text{----(8.52)}$$

the doubly constrained gravity model results. Bearing in mind (Section 8.4) that $\lambda_i^{(1)}$ and $\lambda_j^{(2)}$ comprise, in effect, the sensitivity coefficients associated with the right hand sides of (8.44) and (8.45) respectively, the definitions (8.51), (8.52) have led to more meaningful interpretations for A_i and B_j in (8.36).

The relationship between the foregoing entropy maximising formulation and the transportation problem is set out rigorously by Evans (1973). An intuitive explanation only is offered here. Recall (Section 8.4) that in effect, $\lambda^{(3)}$ comprises a sensitivity coefficient for the right hand side of the constraint (8.46). Specifically it gives an estimate of the change in (8.42) if the right hand side of (8.46) becomes unity. A large value for $\lambda^{(3)}$ would suggest that the foregoing hypothesised change from zero to unity in the right hand side of (8.46) would cause a large change in (8.42) and *vice versa*. Consider now what altering (8.46) to:

$$c - \sum_{i=1}^{n} \sum_{j=1}^{n} c_{ij} T_{ij} = 1 \qquad \text{----(8.53)}$$

means in reality. In (8.46), the first and second terms on the left hand side must be equal but in (8.53), the second term, i.e. the cost of the optimal transport pattern must be one money unit less. Thus $\lambda^{(3)}$ estimates the effect of requiring in the optimal solution to (8.49) that the cost of the resultant transport pattern be one money unit less. A high value for $\lambda^{(3)}$ thus suggests that a reduction of one money unit in the amount spent on transport will have a relatively great effect on the optimal solution or, more loosely, that the amount of money available to be spent is an important determinant of the precise nature of this solution.

Recall now (Section 3.3.3) the use by Wheeler (1967, 1970) of the transportation problem (3.4)-(3.7) to determine the pattern of work trips from residences to workplaces which minimises total distance travelled. Using the notation of the present section, Wheeler's objective is:

$$\text{Minimise :} \quad \sum_{i=1}^{n} \sum_{j=1}^{n} f_{ij} T_{ij} \qquad \text{----(8.54)}$$

while the relevant constraints are (8.44), (8.45) and the non-negativity conditions. Evans (1973) proves that the solution to the transportation problem will be the same as for the foregoing entropy maximising formulation in the case where $\lambda^{(3)} \to \infty$. Recalling the foregoing interpretation of $\lambda^{(3)}$, $\lambda^{(3)} \to \infty$ is equivalent to assuming that the amount of money spent on travel and its reduction is of infinite importance which is precisely the implication of the objective (8.54) where f_{ij} and c_{ij} are related *via* (8.37) or (8.38).

Before leaving the foregoing trip distribution model it is worth noting an application of it within the context of the location-allocation problem (Section 7.8). Recall that in the latter problem, individuals are assigned to i.e. are assumed to use the facility nearest to them. Hodgson (1978) recasts the location-allocation problem under the assumption that the pattern of travel between a set of users (origins) and central facilities (destinations) will be as given by the foregoing trip distribution model. The reader should consult the original publication for details.

8.5.2 The Herbert-Stevens Residential Landuse Model Revisited

Recall (Section 4.2.1) the residential landuse model due to Herbert and Stevens (1960). Senior and Wilson (1974) (for a summary see Haggett *et al.* (1977)) recast this model and various developments of it within an entropy maximising framework. Employing the notation of (4.10)-(4.13), recall (4.10) that the objective was to find the values of X_{jk}^i, $i = 1,\ldots,\ell$; $j = 1,\ldots,m$; $k = 1, \ldots,n$ which maximise total rent paying ability. Now, reinterpreting the objective as finding the most likely values for the X_{jk}^i's i.e. of maximising entropy, the revised objective following (8.42) is:

$$\text{Maximise } f(X_{jk}^i \text{ for all } i,j,k) = \frac{(\sum_{i=1}^{\ell} \sum_{j=1}^{m} \sum_{k=1}^{n} X_{jk}^i)\,!}{\prod_{i=1}^{\ell} \prod_{j=1}^{m} \prod_{k=1}^{n} X_{jk}^i\,!}$$

$$----(8.55)$$

Maximisation of (8.55) is equivalent to maximisation of:

$$- \text{Log } \prod_{i=1}^{\ell} \prod_{j=1}^{m} \prod_{k=1}^{n} X_{jk}^i\,! \qquad ----(8.56)$$

which is in fact the objective Senior and Wilson employ. The first two constraints in their model are (4.11) and (4.12) expressed as equalities i.e.:

$$\sum_{i=1}^{\ell} \sum_{k=1}^{n} X_{jk}^i = n_j \; ; \; j=1, \ldots, m \qquad ----(8.57)$$

$$\sum_{j=1}^{m} \sum_{k=1}^{n} s_k^i \, X_{jk}^i = a_i; \; i=1, \ldots, \ell \qquad ----(8.58)$$

Finally, and in the same manner as (8.43) was appended in the entropy maximising trip distribution model, it is required that the rent paying ability in the solution equal some fixed value r i.e.

$$\sum_{i=1}^{\ell} \sum_{j=1}^{m} \sum_{k=1}^{n} (b_{jk} - c_{jk}^i) \, X_{jk}^i = r \qquad ----(8.59)$$

(8.56)-(8.59) comprises a programming problem which can easily be written in the form (8.27) (8.28) and solved by introducing Lagrange multipliers $\lambda_j^{(1)}$, $\lambda_i^{(2)}$ and $\lambda^{(3)}$

relating to (8.57), (8.58) and (8.59) respectively. The reader is referred to the works cited at the outset for details. A particularly interesting finding by Senior and Wilson is that when $\lambda^{(3)} \to \infty$, the solution to (8.56)-(8.59) tends to that for (4.10)-(4.13). Thus, the linear programming formulation (4.10)-(4.13) can be looked upon as a special case of the more general entropy maximising formulation just as (recall Section 8.5.1) the transportation problem can be viewed as a special case of the entropy maximising trip distribution model.

8.6 OPTIMISING A NONLINEAR OBJECTIVE WITH LINEAR INEQUALITY CONSTRAINTS

8.6.1. Kuhn-Tucker Conditions

In this section, the methods discussed in Section 8.4 are developed to deal with a problem of the form:

$$\text{Optimise}: f(X_1, \ldots, X_n) \quad\quad\quad\text{----(8.60)}$$

$$\text{s.t. } g_i(X_1, \ldots, X_n) \leq \text{ or } \geq 0; \ i=1, \ldots, m \text{ ----(8.61)}$$

where $f(X_1, \ldots, X_n)$ is a nonlinear objective and $g(X_1,\ldots,X_n)$ are linear inequality constraints. Some of these constraints may be of the form $X_i - 0$. The overall strategy employed to solve a problem of this type is to write out equations stating certain mathematical conditions which must hold at optimality and which, together, completely specify the optimal solution. These equations are then solved for that solution. The conditions represented by the equations are known as the *Kuhn-Tucker conditions*. They are derived as follows.

Consider the constraints (8.61). As in the case of the simplex method (Chapter 4), these can be converted to equalities by adding (in the case of a less than or equals constraint) or subtracting (in the case of a greater than or equals constraint) a slack variable. On this occasion, the quantity added to or subtracted from the i th constraint is designated S_i^2. Thus, (8.61) becomes:

$$g_i(X_1, \ldots, X_n) \pm S_i^2 = 0 \ ; \ i=1, \ldots, m \quad\quad \text{----(8.62)}$$

Proceeding now as in the previous section to form the Lagrange function associated with (8.60) and (8.62):

$$L = L(X_1, \ldots, X_n; S_1, \ldots, S_m; \lambda_1, \ldots, \lambda_m)$$

$$= f(X_1, \ldots, X_n) + \sum_{i=1}^{m} \lambda_i \{ g_i(X_1, \ldots, X_n) \pm S_i^2 \} \text{--(8.63)}$$

First, differentiating L with respect to X_j, the condition:

272

$$\frac{\delta L}{\delta X_j} = \frac{\delta f(X_1, \ldots, X_n)}{\delta X_j} + \sum_{i=1}^{m} \lambda_i \frac{\delta g_i(X_1, \ldots, X_n)}{\delta X_j} \overset{SET}{=} 0$$

$$j = 1, \ldots, n \text{----}(8.64)$$

must hold. Second, differentiating L with respect to S_i, $i = 1, \ldots, m$ yields the condition:

$$\frac{\delta L}{\delta S_i} = \pm 2\lambda_i S_i \overset{SET}{=} 0; \quad i = 1, \ldots, m \qquad \text{----}(8.65)$$

i.e. λ_i or S_i (or both) must equal zero

i.e. λ_i or S_i^2 (or both) must equal zero

i.e. λ_i or the slack variable associated with the i th constraint, however expressed (or both) must equal zero. Finally, as in the previous section, differentiating L with respect to λ_i, $i = 1, \ldots, m$ yields the constraint set (8.62).

To summarise, the foregoing analysis demonstrates that any solution to (8.60), (8.61) must fulfill the conditions (8.64), (8.65) and (8.62). Furthermore, it can be shown that solving these conditions will yield the required solution. Thus the usual approach is to write them out and then to solve them for the unknown variables. For an example, consider:

Maximise : $4X_1 + 6X_2 - 2X_1^2 - 2X_1 X_2 - 2X_2^2$)

s.t. $\quad X_1 + 2X_2 \qquad \qquad \leq 2$)----(8.66)

$\qquad X_1 \qquad \qquad \geq 0$)

$\qquad\qquad\qquad X_2 \qquad \geq 0$)

The condition (8.64) requires that:

$4 - 4X_1 - 2X_2 + \lambda_1 + \lambda_2 \qquad = 0$)

$6 - 2X_1 - 4X_2 + 2\lambda_1 \qquad + \lambda_3 = 0$) ----(8.67)

Designating T_i $(=S_i^2)$ as the slack variable associated with the i th constraint in exactly the same way as Chapter Three, the constraint conditions in (8.62) become:

$X_1 + 2X_2 + T_1 \qquad\qquad = 0$)

$X_1 \qquad\qquad -T_2 \qquad = 0$) ----(8.68)

$\qquad X_2 \qquad\qquad -T_3 = 0$)

while (8.65) requires that either λ_i or $T_i = 0$ for $i = 1,...,3$
solution   of (8.67) and (8.68) subject to (8.65) may be
conveniently achieved by re-expressing the equations as a
linear programming problem. Recalling the logic underlying
the "Big-M" method (Section 4.6.1), we form the problem:

$$\text{Maximise } R_o \qquad\qquad\qquad -MR_1 \; -MR_2$$

$$
\begin{aligned}
\text{s.t.} \quad & 4X_1 + 2X_2 - \lambda_1 - \lambda_2 && +R_1 && = 4) \\
& && && \quad) \\
& 2X_1 + 4X_2 - 2\lambda_1 \quad - \lambda_3 && +R_2 && = 6) \\
& && && \quad) \\
& X_1 + 2X_2 && +T_1 && = 2) \\
& && && \quad) \\
& X_1, \; X_2 \geq 0 && && \quad)
\end{aligned}
$$

$$\text{----}(8.69)$$

At optimality, provided that a feasible solution exists, R_1
and R_2 will equal zero which reduces the problem (8.69) to
that of solving (8.67), (8.68). The conditions X_1, $X_2 \geq 0$
account for the last two conditions in (8.68). The system
of equations (8.69) can be solved *via* the simplex method
commencing with R_1, R_2, T_1 as the basis. However, a modifi-
cation is needed. Recall, that (8.65) requires that in the
solution to (8.69):

$$
\begin{aligned}
& \lambda_1 \text{ and/or } T_1 = 0 \;) \\
& \qquad\qquad\qquad\quad) \\
& \lambda_2 \text{ and/or } T_2 = 0 \;) \qquad\qquad \text{----}(8.70) \\
& \qquad\qquad\qquad\quad) \\
& \lambda_3 \text{ and/or } T_3 = 0 \;)
\end{aligned}
$$

Neither T_2 nor T_3 appear explicitly in (8.69) as they refer
to conditions of the form $X_i > 0$. However, the form of these
conditions in (8.68) is such that $X_{i-1} = T_i$ for $i = 2,3$. Thus the
conditions (8.70) can be expressed as:

$$
\begin{aligned}
& \lambda_1 \text{ and/or } T_1 = 0 \;) \\
& \qquad\qquad\qquad\quad) \\
& \lambda_2 \text{ and/or } X_1 = 0 \;) \qquad\qquad \text{----}(8.71) \\
& \qquad\qquad\qquad\quad) \\
& \lambda_3 \text{ and/or } X_2 = 0 \;)
\end{aligned}
$$

In order to ensure that these conditions hold when (8.69) is
solved by the simplex method, we restrict the variables which
are allowed to enter the basis or any iteration. Specifically, if λ_i is in the basis at a particular point in the
simplex calculations, T_i or X_{i-1} as appropriate may not enter
on the next iteration unless the corresponding λ_i is the
variable which leaves; conversely, if T_i or X_{i-1} as appropriate

is in the basis, λ_i is not permitted to enter unless the corresponding value of T_i or X_i is the variable which leaves. These restrictions comprise what is known as a *restricted basis entry rule*. The full simplex tabulations for problem (8.69) are presented in Taha (1976). The optimal solution is:

$$X_1 = 0.33; \quad X_2 = 0.83; \quad X_o = 4.16$$
$$\lambda_1 = -1 ; \quad \lambda_2 = \lambda_3 = 0$$

Before leaving the theory underlying Kuhn-Tucker conditions, two further points should be noted. First, if the optimal values of λ_i, $i = 1, \ldots, m$ are such that $\lambda_i \leq 0$, the corresponding values of X_i refer to a maximum point. Furthermore, this is a global maximum if $f(X_1, \ldots, X_n)$ in (8.60) is concave and if the solution space formed by $g_i(X_1, \ldots, X_n)$ is *convex*. (All of these conditions can be shown *via* methods which lie outside the scope of this text to hold in the case of (8.66).) On the other hand, if the optimal values of λ_i, $i = 1, \ldots, m$ are such that $\lambda_i \geq 0$, the corresponding values of X_i refer to a minimum point. This is a global minimum if $f(X_1, \ldots, X_n)$ in (8.60) is convex and if the solution space formed by $g_i(X_1, \ldots, X_n)$ is convex. The second point to note in the context of Kuhn-Tucker conditions is that the foregoing calculations were made relatively straightforward by the fact that $f(X_1, \ldots, X_n)$ was a quadratic. This caused the conditions (8.64) to be linear thus enabling the complete problem to be cast as a linear programming formulation. Solution of the Kuhn-Tucker conditions associated with a non-quadratic objective would obviously pose additional difficulties.

8.6.2 Example

Two studies which involve optimising a quadratic objective subject to linear equality constraints are those of Louwes *et al.* (1963) and Rae (1970). The former deals with the optimal use of surplus milk production in the Netherlands while the latter considers the optimal production pattern for horticultural products. In both studies, the nonlinearities in the objective arise as a result of the type of interaction between fixed and decision variables as exemplified by (8.6) – (8.8).

Louwes *et al.* consider the amounts of four products which should be produced: consumption milk, butter, fat cheese and 40^+ cheese. Following Chapter Four and letting these amounts be $X_1, \ldots, X_4$ respectively and if $p_1, \ldots, p_4$ are known prices per thousand tons sold of the four products, the objective of maximising return is given by the linear expression:

Maximise: $P = p_1X_1 + p_2X_2 + p_3X_3 + p_4X_4$ ----(8.72)

Now, in reality, in the case of milk products, prices fetched depend on production levels. Specifically, in the case of the Netherlands at the time of the study under review, it was known that supply and price were linked _via_ the relationships:

$$X_1 = -1.5413p_1 + 2671$$

$$X_2 = -0.203p_2 + 135$$

$$X_3 = -0.0136p_3 + 0.0015p_4 + 103$$ ----(8.73)

$$X_4 = 0.0016p_3 - 0.0027p_4 + 19$$

Now, reinterpreting the problem as one of finding the prices (now designated by capitals as they have become the decision variables) and hence the production levels which maximise total returns and substituting the relations (8.73) in (8.72), the objective becomes:

$$\text{Maximise: } -1.5413P_1^2 - 0.0203P_2^2 - 0.0136P_3^2 - 0.0027P_4^2$$
$$+0.0031P_3P_4 + 2671P_1 + 135P_2 + 103P_3 + 19P_4$$

----(8.74)

Louwes _et al._ use the methods of the previous section to solve (8.74) subject initially to two linear inequality constraints and the usual non-negativity conditions.

8.7 SOME OTHER NONLINEAR PROGRAMMING SOLUTION APPROACHES

8.7.1 Geometric Programming

Geometric programming comprises special methods to deal with nonlinear programming problems where the objective and some or all of the constraint left hand sides (if any) are of the form:

$$\prod_{j=1}^{m} c_j \sum_{i=1}^{n} X_i^{a_{ij}}$$ ----(8.75)

where $c_i > 0$, a_{ij} is unrestricted and $X_i > 0$. To a large extent, geometric programming owes its development to Duffin _et al._ (1967). The overall solution strategy involves making a substitution which transforms the original programming problem to one involving the solution of a set of eq-

uations; once the equations are solved, the transformation
is applied in the opposite direction to determine the optimal
values for the original decision variables.

In order to demonstrate, consider the following unconstrained problem presented by Beightler and Phillips (1976):

$$\text{Minimise: } X_o = 60X_1^{-3} X_2^{-2} + 50X_1^3 X_2^{-2} + 20X_1^{-3} X_2^3$$

$$----(8.76)$$

Denoting the optimal values of the decision variables in
(8.76) as $X_i^*, i = 1, \ldots, n$ and the optimal value of the objective as X_o^*, we define a new set of variables Y_j,
$j = 1, \ldots, m$ where:

$$Y_j = \frac{c_j \prod_{i=1}^{n} (X_i)^{a_{ij}}}{X_o} \qquad ----(8.77)$$

It can be shown that the optimal values of Y_j, Y_j^*, $j=1,\cdots,m$
which when substituted in the relations (8.77) yield the
optimal values $X_i, i=1, \ldots, n$ are given by:

$$\text{Solve : } \sum_{j=1}^{m} a_{ij} Y_j = 0 ; i = 1, \ldots, n \qquad ----(8.78)$$

$$\sum_{j=1}^{m} Y_j = 1 \qquad ----(8.79)$$

Thus for (8.76), (8.78) and (8.79) give:

$$\text{Solve : } \left. \begin{array}{r} -3Y_1 + 3Y_2 - 3Y_3 = 0 \\ -2Y_1 - 2Y_2 + 3Y_3 = 0 \\ Y_1 + Y_2 + Y_3 = 1 \end{array} \right\} \qquad ----(8.80)$$

from which $Y_1^* = 0.4; \quad Y_2^* = 0.5 ; \quad Y_3^* = 0.1.$

In the context of geometric programming, the conditions
(8.78) and (8.79) are often referred to as the *orthogonality*
and *normality conditions* respectively. Together they are
known as the *dual constraints*. Given values for $Y_1^*,\ldots,Y_m^*$
and   the transformation (8.77), it can be shown that:

$$X_o^* = \prod_{j=1}^{m} \left(\frac{c_j}{Y_j^*} \right)^{Y_j^*} \qquad ----(8.81)$$

and that:

$$Y_j^*. \quad X_o^* = c_j \prod_{i=1}^{n} (X_i^*)^{a_{ij}} \; ; \; j = 1, \ldots, m \qquad \text{----(8.82)}$$

(8.81) can be solved for X_o^* while (8.82) yields m equations which can be solved for X_j^* , $j = 1, \ldots, m$.

An example of geometric programming applied in a planning context is the study of Dinkel *et al.* (1973) who consider the following problem: given a region of m districts the total population to be housed in the region, p, and an upper and lower bound on the population that may be placed in each of the districts, p_i^{MAX} and p_i^{MIN} respectively for i = 1, ..., m, determine the population which should be housed in each district in order to maximise total accessibility. The accessibility of district i from district j is defined as:

$$\{k_1 \exp \{-k_2 d_{ij} \} \} P_i \cdot P_j \qquad \text{----(8.83)}$$

where d_{ij} = Distance from district i to district j

P_i, P_j = Populations of districts i and j (decision vars.)

k_1, k_2 = Given constants

Thus the objective of maximising accessibility over all districts is given by:

$$\text{Maximise} : \sum_{i=1}^{m} \sum_{j=1}^{m} \{k_1 \exp \{-k_2 d_{ij}\}\} P_i \cdot P_j \qquad \text{----(8.84)}$$

Subject to the constraints:

$$\left. \begin{array}{l} \sum_{i=1}^{n} P_i = p \\[2mm] P_i \geq p_i^{MIN}; \; i = 1, \ldots, n \\[2mm] P_i \leq p_i^{MAX}; \; i = 1, \ldots, n \end{array} \right\} \qquad \text{----(8.85)}$$

The objective (8.84) is of the same form as (8.75). Thus, given values for the fixed variables, it could be solved using the foregoing methods but for the constraints (8.85) which impose additional complications but do not, in fact, alter the general solution strategy. The reader is referred to the original paper for the mathematical details.

Dinkel *et al.* demonstrate their model by applying it to a hypothetical region comprising seven urban centres whose distances apart by road are known (Figure 8.6). 100000 people are to be housed and the population limits for each centre are given. The results obtained by solving (8.84), (8.85) are:

$$P_1 = 7000 \; ; \; P_2 = 10500 \; ; \; P_3 = 43000 \; ; \; P_4 = 13500 \; ;$$

$$P_5 = 7000 \; ; \; P_6 = 12000 \; ; \; P_7 = 7000.$$

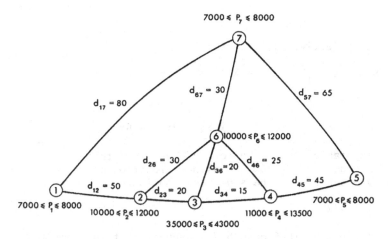

Figure 8.6 Input Data for Geometric Programming Model

From: DINKEL, J.J., KOCHENBERGER, G.A., and SEPPALA, Y., (1973), On the Solution of Regional Planning Models Via Geometric Programming, *Environment and Planning*, 5, 397-408, Figure 1.

Redrawn by permission.

As expected, the points in the centre of the network i.e. in accessible locations are assigned the maximum permissible population while those at the extremities i.e. in inaccessible locations are assigned the minimum allowable population.

8.7.2   Separable Programming

Separable programming comprises a means by which a nonlinear objective function and/or constraints can be approximated by a series of line segments. Mathematically, this transforms a nonlinear programming problem into a linear programming problem which yields approximately the same optimal solution. In order for the methods to be discussed to be applicable, the nonlinear expressions in the programming model concerned must be *separable* in terms of the decision variables by which

is meant it must be possible to write every nonlinear function, $f(X_1, \ldots, X_n)$, in the form:

$$\sum_{j=1}^{n} f_j (X_j) \qquad\qquad \text{----(8.86)}$$

Thus, the objective (8.29) i.e.

$$\text{Minimise } X_1^2 + X_2^2 + X_3^2$$

is separable whereas the objective (8.66) i.e.

$$\text{Maximise } 4X_1 - 2X_1^2 - 2X_1X_2 - 2X_2^2 + 6X_2$$

is not separable due to the form of the third term.

In order to see how a nonlinear function can be approximated by a series of line segments, consider the function:

$$f(X) = X^2 \qquad\qquad \text{----(8.87)}$$

which is depicted in Figure 8.7. Suppose that interest in

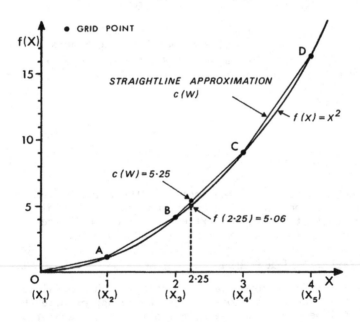

Figure 8.7 Approximation of a Nonlinear Function By Straightline Segments

this function lies in the interval $0 \leq X \leq 4$ and that a number of grid points which include the upper and lower bounds of the interval of interest — say, 0, 1, 2, 3, 4 are chosen. The function comprising the series of line segments joining $f(X)$ at the chosen grid points i.e. O A B C D in Figure 8.7 approximates the course of $f(X)$. Consider now the task of using this function which we shall call $c(W)$ in lieu of $f(X)$. For $X = 2.25$ (say), $f(X) = 5.06$. The corresponding value on $c(W)$ is 5.25. Thus in this instance and because $f(X)$ is concave, $c(W)$ overestimates its value. Nevertheless, the degree of overestimation is small.

Consider now the task of expressing $c(W)$ mathematically. It can be shown that $c(W)$ is given by the linear expression formed by summing the value of $f(X)$ at each of the grid points $i = 1, \ldots, 5$ multiplied by a new decision variable W_i i.e.

$$c(W) = f(X_1) . W_1 + f(X_2) . W_2 + f(X_3) W_3 + f(X_4) . W_4 + f(X_5) . W_5$$

$$= \quad 0 . W_1 + \quad 1 . W_2 + \quad 4 . W_3 + \quad 9 . W_4 + \quad .16 . W_5$$

$$----(8.88)$$

where:

$$\sum_{i=1}^{n} W_i = 1 \qquad ----(8.89)$$

and where either one W_i or, at most two adjacent W_i's i.e. W_i and W_{i+1} exceed zero with all the other W_i's equalling zero.

In order to see why (8.88) together with the foregoing conditions represents the line segments OABCD in Figure 8.7, we seek an interpretation for the W_i values. We shall interpret them as:

$$W_i = 1 - \lambda_i \qquad ----(8.90)$$

where λ_i is the proportion of the total distance from grid point i to grid point $(i+1)$ or $(i-1)$ as appropriate which must be covered in order to reach X, the point for which $f(X)$ is being approximated and where:

$$W_i = 0 \qquad ----(8.91)$$

if X does not lie between gridpoints i and $(i+1)$ or i and $(i-1)$.

In order to demonstrate, consider once again the task of using $c(W)$ to approximate $f(X)$ at $X = 2.25$. $X = 2.25$ lies between the third and fourth grid points. Thus from (8.91):

$$W_1 = W_2 = W_5 = 0 \qquad ----(8.92)$$

Nonlinear Programming

The value 2.25 lies at $\lambda_i = 0.25$ of the total distance from the third to the fourth grid point. Thus, from (8.90):

$$W_3 = (1 - 0.25) = 0.75 \ )$$
$$W_4 = (1 - 0.75) = 0.25 \ ) \qquad \text{----(8.93)}$$

Now, substituting in (8.88):

$$c(W) = 0 + 0 + (4)(0.75) + (9)(0.25) + 0 = 5.25$$

which confirms the result deduced from Figure 8.7.

In order to see how the foregoing methods for approximating nonlinear functions by line segments can be used to approximate nonlinear programming problems by linear programming problems, consider:

$$\text{Maximise: } (6X_1 - 3X_1^2) + X_2^2 \ )$$
$$X_1 + 2X_2 \leq 4 \ )$$
$$X_1, X_2 \geq 0 \qquad) \qquad \text{----(8.94)}$$

where it is known that at optimality: $0 \leq X_1 \leq 3$; $0 \leq X_2 \leq 2$. The objective is separable. Let the grids be:

$$X_1 : 0, 1, 2, 3$$

$$X_2 : 0, 0.5, 1.5, 2$$

The objective function thus becomes:

$$\text{Maximise: } 6 \ (0.U_1 + 1.U_2 + 2.U_3 + 3.U_4)$$
$$-3 \ (0.U_1 + 1.U_2 + 4.U_3 + 9.U_4)$$
$$+1 \ (0.V_1 + 0.25.V_2 + 2.25.V_3 + 4.V_4)$$

i.e. Maximise: $0.U_1 + 3.U_2 + 0.U_3 - 9.U_4 + 0.V_1 + 0.25V_2$
$$+ 2.25V_3 + 4.V_4 \quad \text{----(8.95)}$$

while the constraint gives:

$$0.U_1 + 1.U_2 + 2.U_3 + 3.U_4 + 0.V_1 + 1.V_2 + 3.V_3 + 4.V_4 \leq 4$$
$$\text{----(8.96)}$$

Maximisation of (8.95) subject to (8.96) and to the non-negativity conditions comprises a linear programming problem. In solving it, the condition (8.89) *et seq.* must be imposed on the U_i and V_j; in practice, if certain assumptions can

282

be made about the nature of the objective and constraints, this imposition poses few problems in terms of the solution method. In the case of (8.95), (8.96) the solution is:

$$U_1 = 0.0; \quad U_2 = 0.34; \quad U_3 = -0.66; \quad U_4 = 0.0$$
$$V_1 = 0.12; V_2 = 0.88; \quad V_3 = 0.0; \quad V_4 = 0.0$$

from which the solution to (8.94) is estimated to be:

$$X_1 = (1)(0.66) + (2)(0.34) = 1.34$$
$$X_2 = (0)(0.88) + (0.5)(0.12) = 0.06$$

The formulation (8.95), (8.96) highlights one of the potential disadvantages of separable programming: the number of decision variables increases rapidly both with the number of nonlinear components to be approximated and with the fineness of the grid. For this reason, the method is particularly appropriate where a single nonlinearity enters a linear problem and/or where the region within which the optimal solution lies is known in advance. One such instance of the former situation is that treated by Baritelle and Holland (1975) who develop the transhipment problem (3.13)-(3.16) to consider the transhipment nodes as processing points where the cost per unit of product processed is a nonlinear function of the amount of product involved. Baritelle and Holland also develop the transhipment problem to consider a number of time periods and products.

8.7.3 Direct Linearisation

The technique of *direct linearisation* involves using some type of mathematical transformation to change a nonlinear programming problem into a linear programming problem. The occasions upon which such transformations can be used are rare. Their exact nature depends on the mathematics of the original problem.

For an example of a situation in which direct linearisation might be of help, consider the *quadratic assignment problem* discussed by Koopmans and Beckmann (1957) which comprises a direct development of the assignment problem (3.1) - (3.4). n industrial plants are to be assigned to n given locations, one to each location. The plants must ship known amounts of product to each other. The per unit transport costs between each pair of locations is known. It is required that the n plants be assigned to the n locations such that the total transport costs associated with the required shipments are minimised. Mathematically, the problem may be expressed as follows:

Let c_{ij} = The per unit transport cost associated with the route from i to j

$f_{k\ell}$ = The flow which must occur from plant k to plant ℓ

X_{ik} = 1 if plant k is assigned to location i
      = 0 otherwise

$X_{j\ell}$ = 1 if plant ℓ is assigned to location j
      = 0 otherwise

Then the quadratic assignment problem is to find X_{ik}, $X_{j\ell}$ in order to:

$$\text{Minimise:} \quad \sum_{i=1}^{n} \sum_{j=1}^{n} \sum_{k=1}^{n} \sum_{\ell=1}^{n} c_{ij} f_{k\ell} X_{ik} X_{j\ell} \quad ----(8.97)$$

$$\sum_{i=1}^{n} X_{ik} = 1; \ k = 1, \ldots, n \ ----(8.98)$$

$$\sum_{k=1}^{n} X_{ik} = 1; \ i = 1, \ldots, n \ ----(8.99)$$

The objective (8.97) is nonlinear in terms of the decision variables X_{ik}, $X_{j\ell}$. However, it can be linearised by re-formulation in terms of decision variables of the form $X_{ikj\ell}$ where:

$X_{ikj\ell}$ = 1 if plant i is assigned to location k *and* plant j is assigned to location ℓ
      = 0 otherwise

The revised problem which is linear in the zero-one decision variables $X_{ikj\ell}$ could presumably be solved using the methods discussed in the previous chapter. Unfortunately, this is hampered by the fact that unless n is small, the re-formulation increases the number of decision variables by an exhorbitant amount.

It has been suggested that the quadratic assignment model might have a role to play in the context of landuse plan design where in effect, the overall objective is to assign landuses between which there will be known inter-actions to plots of land. The reader is referred to the interesting discussions in Gordon and MacReynolds (1974), Hopkins (1977) and Hopkins (1979) for details.

9

DYNAMIC PROGRAMMING

9.1 INTRODUCTION

The preceding chapters have described various mathematical
programming models together with methods appropriate to solving
them. Each particular programming type e.g. linear programming concerned a problem with a particular mathematical
structure e.g. (4.1)-(4.3). The methods devised to deal with
each programming type e.g. the simplex method reflected the
nature of this mathematical structure.

In contrast to what has gone before, dynamic programming
does not involve solving problems with a given mathematical
structure. Rather, the term refers to a general problem
solving approach which can be employed in many different contexts. The approach is to subdivide a large problem into a
number of smaller problems or *stages*. The smaller problems
are solved sequentially with the results obtained at each stage
entering the next stage calculations in an explicit manner.

Dynamic programming was developed in the early 1950's
by Richard Bellman who has written seminal texts on the subject
(Bellman (1957), Bellman and Dreyfus (1962)). Other descript-
ions are available in Hastings (1973), Jacobs (1967), Kaufmann
and Kruon (1967), Nemhauser (1966) and Taha (1971). Wagner
(1972) offers a particularly lucid treatment at an elementary
level. A review of dynamic programming applications in
subject areas of interest to geographers and planners is given
by MacKinnon (1970).

Dynamic programming offers two particular features
which cause it to be of interest to geographers and planners.
First, as was implied by the foregoing definition, it is
useful when dealing with large problems. Many real world programming problems are indeed of considerable magnitude. Second,
as indicated, the method involves solving a set of 'sub-
problems' sequentially. As will be seen, the output comprises
not only the optimal solution to the overall problem but also,
where appropriate, the order in which various decisions should
be taken in order to reach that solution. Very often,

DOI: 10.4324/9781003179030-9

especially in a planning sense, the optimal ordering of decisions on (say) a year by year basis is of as much interest as the final overall solution towards which one is striving. The overall approach of dynamic programming is now illustrated by means of an example.

9.2   THE SHORTEST ROUTE PROBLEM

Reconsider the shortest route problem discussed in Section 2.3.1 and illustrated in Figure 9.1. For convenience, the

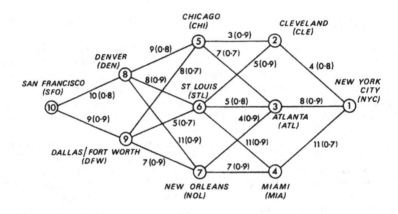

Figure 9.1 Shortest Route Problem

various nodes on the network (cities) have been numbered. The bracketed values associated with each route can be ignored for the present. We shall now solve the shortest route problem using dynamic programming.

Recall that dynamic programming proceeds by decomposing a problem into stages. In the case of the present example, any journey between New York and San Francisco will involve traversing four links. We shall view the process of determining in turn the four links which should be traversed in order to minimise total journey cost   as the four stages of the problem. Consider one particular stage e.g. that when the traveller is one link removed from New York. He will be in one of three locations or situations : Cleveland, Atlanta or Miami. The particular situations which can pertain at the outset of a particular stage of the solution process are referred to as the *state variable values* or *states* of the system for that stage. For the n th stage of the solution process, the associated state variable values are generally designated X_n.

Given the current stage of the problem being considered and its associated state variable values, one can also define the set of possible decisions that can be taken to enable one to proceed to the next stage. In the case of a traveller at Cleveland, Atlanta or Miami, the possible decisions are obviously to travel to Chicago, St. Louis or New Orleans. The possible decisions available at a particular stage of the solution process are referred to as the *decision variables* of the system for that stage. For the n th stage of the solution process, the associated decision variables are generally designated D_n.

We have now defined three important entities underlying the problem to be solved : the stages, the state variables associated with each stage and the decision variables associated with each stage. Any solution achieved *via* dynamic programming commences by defining these entities.

As is the case with many dynamic programming applications, the shortest route problem can be solved using one of two approaches : the *forwards method* or the *backwards method*. The former involves commencing at New York and examining in some systematic manner the state variables and decision variables associated with each stage until San Francisco is reached; the latter method involves commencing at San Francisco and tracing back in some systematic manner the least cost route stage by stage to New York. For reasons which lie beyond the scope of this text, the backwards method, although it might seem less logical in overall approach, often turns out to be mathematically less complex. Thus we shall use it here.

For the first stage of the solution process, we are thus considering the last step in the least cost route. There are two possible states : node eight or node nine or, more succinctly :

$$X_1 = \text{(Node) 8 or 9}$$

There is but one possible decision i.e. travel to node ten i.e. $D_1 = 10$. This information together with the costs associated with each possible state/decision combination can be summarised in tabular form as follows :

		DECISION VARIABLE (D_1)	D_1^*	$f_1(X_1)$
		10		
STATE VAR-IABLE (X_1)	8	10	10	10
	9	9	10	9

The columns labelled D_1^* and $f_1(X_1)$ may be ignored for the present.

Consider now the second stage of the solution process. The possible values associated with the state and decision variables are :

$$X_2 = 5 \text{ or } 6 \text{ or } 7$$

and $\quad D_2 = 8 \text{ or } 9$

which duly form the rows and columns respectively of the following table. Within the body of the table is recorded in each position the cost of taking the decision concerned *plus* the cost of proceeding onwards from the state to which that decision gives rise to node ten :

		DECISION VARIABLE (D_2)		D_2^*	$f_2(X_2)$
		8	9		
STATE VAR-IABLE (X_1)	5	9 + 10=19	8 + 9=17	9	17
	6	8 + 10=18	5 + 9=14	9	14
	7	11 + 10=21	7 + 9=16	9	16

Thus for $X_2 = 5$, $D_2 = 8$, the cost of proceeding from node five to node eight is nine units ; from the first stage table, the cost of proceeding onwards to node ten is a further ten units. Therefore the total cost value for $X_2 = 5$; $D_2 = 8$ is 19 units.

Suppose now that it is known that the least cost route does indeed pass through node five. To which node (eight or nine) should it proceed next ? Comparing the cost values associated with the two possible decisions, node nine should obviously be chosen as the total cost of proceeding there and onwards to node ten is less than that involved in proceeding *via* node eight. Thus, for the state $X_2 = 5$, the optimal decision is $D_2 = 9$ with an associated total cost for the rest of the journey of 17 ; these values are recorded as

288

D_2^* and f_2 (X_2) in the $X_2 = 5$ row of the table. Furthermore, the same values have been recorded for $X_2 = 6$ and $X_2 = 7$. Inspection of the first stage table reveals that, in effect, D_1^* and f_1 (X_1) yield the same information for that stage.

Consider now extending the solution process back one further stage. The relevant table is :

DECISION VARIABLE (D_3)

		5	6	7	D_3^*	f_3 (X_3)
STATE	2	3 + 17=20	5 + 14=19	-	6	19
VARIABLE	3	7 + 17=24	5 + 14=19	4 + 16=20	6	19
(X_3)	4	-	11 + 14=25	7 + 16=23	7	23

Thus, for example, should it be found that the least cost route passes through node three, it should pass next to node six ; the total minimum cost of proceeding from node three to node ten will be 19. Note that in the case of this table, no entries occur for $X_3 = 4$, $D_3 = 5$ and $X_3 = 2$, $D_3 = 7$ which reflects the fact that these stage/decision variable combinations are not permitted i.e. the relevant links do not occur in the network.

Consider now extending the solution back yet one further stage. The state variable X_4 takes one possible value and there are three associated possible decisions which yield :

DECISION VARIABLE (D_4)

	2	3	4	D_4^*	f_4 (X_4)
STATE VARIABLE (X_4) 1	4+19=23	8+19=27	11+23=34	2	23

Thus, commencing at New York, the optimal decision is to proceed to node two ; the total cost of the least cost journey is 23 which corresponds to the result obtained in Section 2.3.1. The complete least cost route can be obtained by noting the optimal decisions associated with the relevant states in the previous tables. From the stage three table the optimal decision for $X_3 = 2$ is to proceed to node 6 ; from the stage two table for $X_2 = 6$, $D_2^* = 9$; finally, from the stage one table for $X_1 = 9$, $D_1^* = 10$. The complete route is thus:

$$NYC \rightarrow CLE \rightarrow STL \rightarrow DFW \rightarrow SFO$$

which corresponds to the previously obtained result.

When compared with the solution approach used in Section 2.3.1, the foregoing method can be seen to possess two important advantages which pertain to dynamic programming in general. First, the amount of information to be retained through the solution process increases at a relatively modest rate from stage to stage ; furthermore, its final volume can be assessed in advance of commencing the solution process which is important when determining the extent to which a large problem will tax available computer capacity. Concerning information volume, it is to be noted that once the calculations for a particular stage have been carried out, the only values which need to be retained for each state variable value are the associated optimal decision, D_n^*, which might be required when tracing back through the tables at the end of the solution process to determine the complete optimal solution and the associated $f_n(X_n)$ value which might be required as input during the next stage of the calculations but which can be discarded once those calculations are complete. Note that in the case of the solution approach discussed in Section 2.3.1 no prior estimate can be made of the amount of information which will have to be stored: a least-cost tree network (e.g. Figure 2.6) is built up step by step until at some stage, unpredictable in advance and perhaps only after a very large number of links have been added, the destination node of interest and thus the optimal solution is reached.

A second advantage of the dynamic programming approach as exemplified by the foregoing example is that the tabular output from each stage of the calculations yields information which can be immensely helpful in analysing individual decisions. Consider the case of two individuals at New York choosing what they believe to be the least cost route to San Francisco and suppose that the routes they choose on the basis of their perceptions are:

$$NYC \rightarrow MIA \rightarrow NOL \rightarrow DFW \rightarrow SFO : Cost\ 34$$
$$NYC \rightarrow ATL \rightarrow NOL \rightarrow DFW \rightarrow SFO : Cost\ 28$$

At first sight, the second individual would appear to have made the more successful choice because he has chosen a route with a lower associated total cost. Yet in a sense, the first individual has acted in a more rational manner. From the fourth stage solution table, a mistake was obviously made when the decision was taken in New York to travel to Miami ; however, once there, and noting the stage three, two and one solution tables respectively, the first individual followed the best possible route. In the case of the second individual, a mistake was also made on the first stage of the journey by choosing to travel to Atlanta ; however, a second mistake was then made by travelling from there to New Orleans rather than to St. Louis as is suggested by the Stage Three solution table.

A particularly interesting study which involves an

application of dynamic programming to the shortest route
problem with an assessment of the number of mistakes made by
individuals is that of Scarlett (1971). For a section of
Montreal which was affected by severe snowstorms thereby
altering the travel times on links of the road network,
Scarlett compares for a sample of commuters their optimal
route and the number of mistakes made in the route actually
chosen. The number of journeys with none, one, two, ...
mistakes is then compared against a hypothesised poisson
distribution.

9.3   GENERALISATION

We now formalise the ideas presented in the previous section.
First, the objective of the shortest route problem involves
finding the route from the source node (NYC) to the sink
node (SFO) which minimises:

$$\sum_{i=1}^{N} R_i \qquad \qquad ----(9.1)$$

where R_i is the cost of traversing the link comprising the
i th stage of the journey and the summation is over some
series of links which form a continuous route from the source
to the sink. Consider some intermediate stage of the solution process, n. Associated with this stage are a number of
states, X_n, and a number of decisions, D_n. Each allowable
combination of state and decision variables has a cost associated with it. Denoting this cost as $R_n (X_n, D_n)$, we have
choosing two specific examples from the shortest route
problem:

$$R_2(X_2 = 5, D_2 = 9) = 8$$

and $$R_3(X_3 = 3, D_3 = 6) = 5$$

Now recall that for each stage n state variable/decision
variable combination we calculate a quantity equal to the
cost of making the decision concerned and of proceeding
optimally from the state in which that decision places us to
the final state. Denoting this quantity as $Q_n (X_n, D_n)$ and
the cost of proceeding optimally onwards from the state in
which the decision places us (which is obtainable from the
stage (n-1) table) as $f_{n-1}(X_{n-1})$, we have:

$$Q_n (X_n, D_n) = R_n (X_n, D_n) + f_{(n-1)} (X_{(n-1)}) \qquad ----(9.2)$$

Thus, for the example:

$$Q_2 \ (X_2 = 5, \ D_2 = 9) = R_2 \ (X_2 = 5, \ D_2 = 9) + f_1 \ (X_1 = 9)$$

$$= \qquad 8 \qquad + 9 \qquad = 17$$

Next, for each possible stage n state, recall that we determine over all possible decisions that associated with the minimum cost. Denoting this quantity ad $f_n \ (X_n)$, we have :

$$f_n(X_n) = \begin{array}{c} \text{Min over} \\ \text{all } D_n \end{array} \{ R_n \ (X_n, \ D_n) + f_{(n-1)} (X_{(n-1)}) \} \text{---} (9.3)$$

The expression (9.3) offers a formal statement of the recursive relationship by which the dynamic programming solution process proceeds. In effect it states that at a particular stage, n, in the solution process, the decision which should be taken is the one whose cost, when added to the costs accruing from proceeding optimally onward from the relevant stage (n-1) state is minimised. This statement is sometimes referred to as the *principle of optimality*.

Two further points concerning the statements (9.2), (9.3) are required to complete the general presentation. First, for a particular stage, n, and given a value for X_n and D_n, it must be clear as to which stage (n-1) state this gives rise . Thus it is formally required that $X_{(n-1)}$ is some explicit function of X_n and D_n i.e.

$$X_{(n-1)} = t_n \ (X_n, \ D_n) \qquad\qquad \text{----} (9.4)$$

In the case of the present example, the interrelationship between the stage n states, the decisions and the relevant stage (n-1) states is shown explicitly *via* the network (Figure 9.1). Thus if $X_n = 2$ and $D_n = 6$, then, automatically $X_{n-1} = 6$. Very often the interrelationship between the states and decisions is more subtle than this.

Second, the conditions (9.2), (9.3) must obviously be adjusted for the case where n = 1. Specifically, because there are no previous stage returns, the $f_{(n-1)} \ (X_{(n-1)})$ terms disappear to give :

$$Q_1 \ (X_1, \ D_1) = R_1 \ (X_1, \ D_1) \qquad\qquad \text{----} (9.5)$$

and $\quad f_1 \ (X_1, \ D_1) = \begin{array}{c} \text{Min. over} \\ \text{all} \quad D_1 \end{array} \{ R_1 \ (X_1, \ D_1 \} \} \quad \text{----} (9.6)$

The foregoing generalised presentation refers to a minimisation problem where the terms $R_n \ (X_n, \ D_n)$, $Q_n (X_n, \ D_n)$ and $f_n (X_n)$ relate to costs and the optimisations (9.3), (9.6) involve minimisation. In the case of maximisation, the terms $R_n \ (X_n, \ D_n)$, $Q_n (X_n, \ D_n)$ and $f_n \ (X_n)$ would relate to some type of returns and the optimisations (9.3), (9.6) would involve

Dynamic Programming

maximisation. Some examples of problems involving maximisation are given in the next section.

9.4   EXAMPLES

9.4.1   A Network Development Problem

Consider the following problem adapted from Funk and Tillman
(1968) and Scott (1971 a). On a network (Figure 9.2) to which

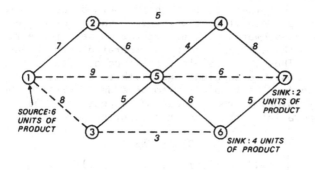

Figure 9.2 Network Development Problem

four links are to be added, one in each of the next four years,
six units of product originate at node one. Four of these
units are destined for node six and two for node seven. The
costs per unit flow of product for each link are known. The
product is always sent *via* the least cost i.e. 'shortest'
route. Thus, prior to construction of the additional links,
the product destined for node six will be routed *via* nodes
two and five at a total per unit cost of 19 units while that
for node seven will be routed *via* nodes two and four at a
total per unit cost of 20 units. The total transportation
cost associated with the initial network will thus be :

293

$$19 \times 4 + 20 \times 2 = 116$$

Likewise, after construction of the four new links, this cost will be 74. The problem to be solved *via* dynamic programming involves finding the order year by year in which the four additional links should be incorporated into the network in order to minimise the total transport costs over the four year transition period.

In order to proceed, we shall define the four yearly periods as the four stages of the problem. For each stage, the states will comprise the various combinations of links which could be already incorporated in the network whilst the decisions will comprise the links which could be added. Following the approach of Section 9.2, we shall solve the problem *via* the backwards method. At the outset of the final stage, three links will have been incorporated into the network already. Thus the possible stages appropriate to this stage are all possible combinations of three links ; the decision concerns the final link to be added. Listing the stages and decisions by row and column respectively and noting the operating cost of the resultant network yields:

	DECISIONS					
STATES	(1,3)	(1,5)	(3,6)	(5,7)	D_1^*	f_1^-
(1,3)(1,5)(3,6)	-	-	-	74	(5,7)	74
(1,3)(1,5)(5,7)	-	-	74	-	(3,6)	74
(1,3)(3,6)(5,7)	-	74	-	-	(1,5)	74
(1,5)(3,6)(5,7)	74	-	-	-	(1,3)	74

Note that for each state, there is but one possible decision i.e. one link that can be added. This yields the final network whose operating cost is 74.

Consider now the stage two calculations. The states now comprise all possible networks with two links added whilst the decisions involve the link to be added next. Following the logic of the previous section, we record for each feasible state/decision variable combination the cost of the resultant network *plus* the cost of taking the optimal decision concerning that network in the following year which can be extracted from the stage one table. This yields:

	DECISIONS					
STATES	$(1,3)$	$(1,5)$	$(3,6)$	$(5,7)$	D^*_2	f_2
$(1,3)(1,5)$	–	–	76+74	90+74	$(3,6)$	150
$(1,3)(3,6)$	–	76+74	–	76+74	$(1,5)$or $(5,7)$	150
$(1,3)(5,7)$	–	90+74	76+74	–	$(3,6)$	150
$(1,5)(3,6)$	76+74	–	–	90+74	$(1,3)$	150
$(1,5)(5,7)$	90+74	–	90+74	–	$(1,3)$ or $(3,6)$	164
$(3,6)(5,7)$	76+74	90+74	–	–	$(1,3)$	150

In the case of two of the states, there are two decisions which yield equally optimal solutions. Both are therefore recorded in the D^*_2 column.

The reader should check that the appropriate stage three and stage four solution tables are:

	DECISIONS					
STATES	$(1,3)$	$(1,5)$	$(3,6)$	$(5,7)$	D^*_3	f_3
$(1,3)$	–	100+150	76+150	114+150	$(3,6)$	226
$(1,5)$	100+150	–	100+150	100+164	$(1,3)$or$(3,6)$	250
$(3,6)$	76+150	100+150	–	114+150	$(1,3)$	226
$(5,7)$	114+150	90+164	114+150	–	$(1,5)$	254

and

	DECISIONS					
STATES	$(1,3)$	$(1,5)$	$(3,6)$	$(5,7)$	D^*_4	f_4
None	116+226	100+250	116+226	114+254	$(1,3)$or$(3,6)$	342

We now wish to read back through the tables to determine the optimal policy for link addition. First, from the stage four table, link $(1,3)$ or $(3,6)$ may be added initially. Assuming for the present that link $(1,3)$ is chosen i.e. the state of the system in the stage three calculations is $(1,3)$, $(3,6)$ should be added next. With the appropriate stage two state as $(1,3)(3,6)$, either $(1,5)$ or $(5,7)$ should be added next. If it is $(1,5)$, $(5,7)$ is added last to yield the overall policy:

$$(1,3) \rightarrow (3,6) \rightarrow (1,5) \rightarrow (5,7)$$

Choosing (5,7) in the third year yields the alternative policy:

$$(1,3) \rightarrow (3,6) \rightarrow (5,7) \rightarrow (1,5)$$

Finally, choosing (3,6) initially yields two further optimal policies:

$$(3,6) \rightarrow (1,3) \rightarrow (1,5) \rightarrow (5,7)$$

$$(3,6) \rightarrow (1,3) \rightarrow (5,7) \rightarrow (1,5)$$

A feature of this example which distinguishes it from that in Section 8.2 concerns the nature of the state variables: Here they represent all combinations of three, two, one and no links respectively drawn from a given set of four possibilities. Consider what would happen if the size of the problem in terms of the number of links to be added increased even modestly (say) to 20. The number of possible state variables would increase dramatically e.g. to 190 for stage two in the case of 20 links. A large real world problem would probably be of unmanageable size even with the aid of a modern computer. Within the context of dynamic programming, this problem of having to cope with very large numbers of state variables at the various stages is often referred to as the *curse of dimensionality*.

The foregoing example indicates one area within the general field of network/transportation modelling where dynamic programming can be used to advantage. Another area of application has been that of devising timetables for public transport services. Three contrasting models are those of Nemhauser (1969), Salzborn (1969) and Turnquist (1979).

9.4.2 The Stepwise Location-Allocation Problem

Recall (Section 7.8) the location-allocation problem which seeks to locate central facilities to serve persons in such a way that the total distance travelled to these facilities will be minimised. Scott (1971a) extends this problem to consider the order in which the central facilities should be located (built) in order to minimise the total distances travelled through the interim period. Specifically, assuming that one new facility can be provided per year, the solution process proceeds in the same manner as with the previous example. The states associated with each stage represent all combinations of facilities which could have been provided so far whilst the decisions concern the facility to be built next. Scott demonstrates for an example that the dynamic programming solution is superior to that where the policy followed is to build the most central facility first,

then the facility whose addition most reduces initial travel
times next and so on.

9.4.3 The Optimal Allocation Problem

Consider the following problem. An area has been divided into
three regions. For each region, a set of plans, one of which
will be implemented, has been identified. Each plan has
associated with it a cost and return (Table 9.1). Central

TABLE 9.1

OPTIMAL ALLOCATION PROBLEM : INPUT DATA

PLAN	REGION 1		REGION 2		REGION 3	
	COST	RETURN	COST	RETURN	COST	RETURN
1	0	0	0	0	0	0
2	1	5	2	4	1	3
3	2	6	3	6	-	-
4	-	-	4	8	-	-

government has decided to allocate up to six units of capital
between the regions. The plan which should be adopted in each
region in order to maximise total return whilst not over-spending the budget available is required.

Proceeding in the same general manner as before, we shall
consider each region to represent a stage. For each stage,
the state variables shall be the sum of money from the total
allocated to the region currently being considered together
with all previously considered regions. The decision variables
shall be the various plans which could be adopted for the
region currently being considered. Retaining the notion of
proceeding in backwards fashion (although the arbitrary
numbering of the regions precludes the necessity to do so in
this case), consider region three. The state variable values
give the amount out of the total budget which could be allocated to this region while the decision variable values denote
the plans which could be adopted. Entering the relevant
returns in the body of the table yields:

		DECISION VARIABLES (D_1)			
		1	2	D_1^*	$f_1(X_1)$
STATE	0	0	-	1	0
VARIABLES	1	0	3	2	3
	2	0	3	2	3
(X_1)	3	0	3	2	3
	4	0	3	2	3
	5	0	3	2	3
	6	0	3	2	3

Note that no value occurs for $X_1 = 0$, $D_1 = 2$ for, if no finance
is available, it is not possible to adopt plan two in region
three. Note too that because the problem involves maximisation, D_1^* refers to the decision associated with the maximum
possible return which is recorded as $f_1(X_1)$. The foregoing
table demonstrates that when considering region three on its
own, if no money is available, plan one should be adopted;
otherwise plan two should be adopted.

Consider now the stage two calculations. The state
variables now give the amount of money allocated to regions
three and two. The relevant solution table is:

		DECISION VARIABLES (D_2)					
		1	2	3	4	D_2^*	$f_2(X_2)$
	0	0+0	-	-	-	1	0
	1	0+3	-	-	-	1	3
STATE	2	0+3	4+0	-	-	2	4
	3	0+3	4+3	6+0	-	2	7
VARIABLES	4	0+3	4+3	6+3	8+0	3	9
	5	0+3	4+3	6+3	8+3	4	11
(X_2)	6	0+3	4+3	6+3	8+3	4	11

The values within the body of the table are arrived at as
follows. Consider $X_2 = 5$, $D_2 = 2$. This corresponds to a
situation where a total of five units of money are available
for investment in regions two and three and where plan two
is to be adopted in region two. The return from adopting
this plan is four money units. The cost is two money units
which leaves three money units over for investment in region

three. Consulting the stage one solution table yields the information that plan two should be adopted there for an additional return of three units yielding a total second stage return of seven units. Consider now the case $Y_2 = 3$, $D_2 = 4$. Here, the total amount of money allocated is not even suffic- ient to permit the adoption of plan four in region two; thus a blank appears in the relevant position in the solution table. We leave as an exercise for the reader the task of extending the foregoing calculations back by one further stage thereby yielding the strategies which should be followed if 0,1,2, ..., 6 money units were made available for investment between all three regions.

An important difference between this example and (say) that discussed in Section 9.2 concerns the nature of the interrelationship between a given stage n state and decision variable and the appropriate stage (n-1) state. Recall that in the case of the shortest route problem and for a given state (node) and decision, the appropriate stage (n-1) state (i.e. destination node) was automatically defined by the net- work. In this case, if X_n is the value of the stage n state· variable and the cost of the plan associated with the decision D_n is $c_n(D_n)$, then:

$$X_{(n-1)} = X_n - c_n(D_n) \qquad \text{----}(9.7)$$

where X_{n-1} is the amount of money available for stages (n-1), ..., 1. Thus (9.7) gives the actual form of the general relationship (9.4) in the case of this example. A further example set within this general context is offered by Miller (1979).

9.4.4. A Water Resources Problem

One of the earliest areas of application of dynamic programm- ing was in the general field of inventory modelling which involves determining for (say) a firm the amount of product which should be produced in each of a set of consecutive time periods and the amount which should be stored from one time period to another in order to minimise total production and storage costs while meeting a given demand pattern. An example of an inventory type model set within an agricultural context is described by Low and Brookhouse (1967).

A problem of interest to geographers and planners which closely resembles the inventory problem in terms of overall structure is that concerning the optimal use of water resources in a river. Specifically, we shall assume that water can be drawn from a river at various points along its course to serve the needs of the surrounding area (Figure 9.3).A varying amount of water (D_n) can be drawn off at each point and will fetch varying known amounts of money (returns) (R_n). As the

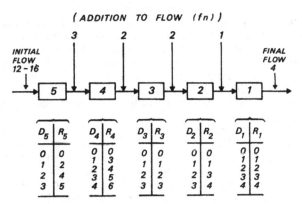

Figure 9.3   Water Resources Problem : Input Data

river proceeds downstream from one water withdrawal site to
the next, a certain known amount of water is added *via*
precipitation etc.   The amount of water which should be drawn
off at each point in order to maximise the total returns from
the sale of water whilst not overusing this resource are
required.   In the case of the current example, this latter
condition is interpreted as requiring that four units of
water emerge past the last withdrawal point.   It is assumed
also that the initial flow in the system i.e. before reaching
the first withdrawal point varies and at any one time equals
12, 13, 14, 15 or 16 units.   The way in which the withdrawals
policy should vary (if at all) as the initial flow varies is
required.

The foregoing problem may be solved relatively easily *via*
dynamic programming.   The stages are the water withdrawal
points.   The states associated with each stage are the possible
amounts of water entering that stage ; the decisions concern
the amounts of water to withdraw.   Following the logic underlying the previous examples, the problem is solved in backwards fashion i.e. considering the last withdrawal point first.
Thus the withdrawal points have been numbered in reverse order
in Figure 9.3.

Given that the final flow must equal four units, the

possible stage one states are $X_1 = 4, 5, 6, 7, 8$ respectively. The relevant dynamic programming solution table is:

DECISION VARIABLE (D_1)

		0	1	2	3	4	D_1^*	$f_1(X)$
	4	0	-	-	-	-	0	0
STATE	5	-	1	-	-	-	1	1
VAR.	6	-	-	2	-	-	2	2
(X_1)	7	-	-	-	3	-	3	3
	8	-	-	-	-	4	4	4

where the values in the body of the table give the return from making the relevant decision.

Consider now the stage two calculations. Given that the possible range of states for stage one is $X_1 = 4, \ldots, 8$ and that one unit is added to the flow downstream from withdrawal point two, the possible range of flow outwards from this point is $3, \ldots, 7$. Given the possible stage two decisions: $D_2 = 0, \ldots, 3$, the range of possible states for stage two is $X_2 = 3, \ldots, 10$. The relevant dynmaic programming solution table is then:

DECISION VARIABLE (D_2)

		0	1	2	3	D_2^*	$f_2^*(X)$
	3	0+0	-	-	-	0	0
	4	0+1	1+0	-	-	0,1	1
STATE	5	0+2	1+1	3+0	-	2	3
	6	0+3	1+2	3+1	4+0	2,3	4
VARIABLE	7	0+4	1+3	3+2	4+1	2,3	5
(X_2)	8	-	1+4	3+3	4+2	2,3	6
	9			3+4	4+3	2,3	7
	10	-	-	-	4+4	3	8

In order to understand how the values in the body of the table are arrived at, consider the case of $X_2 = 7$, $D_2 = 2$. Seven units of water enter the stage two withdrawal point. Two are withdrawn yielding a return of, three money units and leaving five units of water to exit downstream. The addition of one unit of water yields the appropriate stage one state of $X_1 = 6$; the optimal return associated with this decision, which can be read from the stage one table is two units. Thus the total stage two return is five units. In general, for the current problem the appropriate stage $(n-1)$ state is given by:

$$X_{(n-1)} = X_n - D_n + f_n \qquad \text{----}(9.8)$$

where f_n is the flow automatically added after leaving withdrawal point n. Thus (9.8) represents the precise form that (9.4) takes in the case of the example.

We leave the completion of the calculations as an exercise for the reader. The stage five table will comprise the states $X_5 = 12$, 13, 14, 15, 16. The optimal policy associated with each of these values will be obtainable *via* the D_i^* values in the preceding tables.

The foregoing example represents just one context within the general area of water resources research where dynamic programming has been used to advantage. Other straightforward yet contrasting examples are described by Hall and Buras (1961), Butcher *et al.* (1969), Morin and Esgobue (1971) and Glickman and Allison (1973) which should be consulted for details.

9.4.5. Decision Making Under Conditions of Uncertainty : Maximisation of Expected Value

Each of the foregoing examples has assumed that for each state and decision variable combination, a known return/cost $R_n(X_n, D_n)$ will accrue. In many real-world situations, this is not the case. Rather at any stage and for each state and decision, a number of possible outcomes can occur each with a given probability and return. Consider the case of a farmer deciding which of two crops should be grown next year. The yield and hence the return which would be received for each crop might depend on whether the growing conditions for it turn out to be good, medium or poor. Let us suppose that the probabilities of each of these events occurring for each crop are known (Table 9.2). Which crop should be grown ? We define as *the expected return from a particular decision* e.g. to grow crop A the sum of the actual returns possible each multiplied by its probability of occurrence. Thus, for crop A:

Expected Return $= (12)(0.3) + (6)(0.5) + (3)(0.2) = 7.2$

while for crop B:

Expected Return $= (9)(0.3) + (8)(0.6) + (4)(0.1) = 7.9$

TABLE 9.2

CROP GROWING DECISION PROBLEM

CONDITIONS	CROP A		CROP B	
	PROBABILITY	RETURN	PROBABILITY	RETURN
Good	0.3	12	0.3	9
Medium	0.5	6	0.6	8
Poor	0.2	3	0.1	4

In general terms :

$$E \{ R_n \} = \sum_{i=1}^{k} R_i \, P_i \qquad \text{----(9.9)}$$

where $E \{ R_n \}$ = Expected return from decision D_n

R_i, $i = 1, ..., k$ The possible actual returns associated with decision D_n

P_i = The probability of the return R_i accruing

Quite obviously, $E\{D_n\}$ is computed in such a way that the larger it turns out to be, the more attractive will be the corresponding decision to the individual seeking to maximise his return. When deciding between a number of possible decisions, that with the largest expected return should be chosen. Thus, in the case of the example, crop B represents the preferable alternative.

Within the context of dynamic programming and given for each stage and decision variable combination a set of possible outcomes each with an associated probability, the objective becomes one of maximising the total expected return over all stages i.e.

$$\text{Maximise} \quad \sum_{n=1}^{N} E \{ R_n \} \qquad \text{----(9.10)}$$

The values within the body of the stage n solution table, $Q_n(X_n, D_n)$ now give the expected return from taking the decision concerned plus the optimal expected return associated with the appropriate stage (n-1) state variable.

An excellent example of dynamic programming applied within this context is that of Burt and Allison (1963) who consider the production of wheat in the Great Plains region of the United States. Each stage of the solution process

corresponds to a single year. The state variable values give
the possible soil moisture level pertaining at the outset of
a year while the decisions are whether to plant wheat or
leave the land fallow. Burt and Allison show that the optimal
policy is to plant wheat unless soil moisture is at its
lowest level.

9.4.6 A Multiplicative Objective Function

Reconsider the shortest route problem discussed in Section 9.2
and suppose that associated with each route is a probability
value (bracketed values in Figure 9.1) which gives the chance
that a flight booked on that route will in fact operate on
schedule. Suppose that it is required that the most reliable
route from New York to San Francisco be found together with
the associated probability that all four flights involved
will operate on schedule.

In order to understand the appropriate mathematical form
of the objective, consider two consecutive links e.g. NYC→ATL
and ATL→CHI. If the probabilities associated with each of
these are 0.9 and 0.7 respectively, the probability of *both*
of them operating is given by the product of these values i.e.
0.63. Extending this to a complete route from NYC to SFO,
the objective is to find the set of routes which maximises:

$$\pi_{(I,j)} R_{ij} \qquad \text{----(9.11)}$$

where R_{ij} is the probability that a flight on route (ij) will
operate to schedule and where the multiplication is over some
set of links forming a continuous route.

For the dynamic programming formulation, the state and
decision variables are as in Section 9.2. The values within
the body of the stage n solution table now comprise the
product of the probability associated with the relevant stage
n decision and that associated with the optimal route from the
relevant stage $(n-1)$ state to the final destination i.e.

$$Q_n (X_n, D_n) = R_n (X_n, D_n) \cdot f_{(n-1)} (X_{(n-1)}) \qquad \text{----(9.12)}$$

In the case of the example, the relevant stage three solution
table is thus:

DECISION VARIABLES (D₃)

		5	6	7	D_3^*	$f_3(X_3)$
STATE	2	(0.9)(0.64)	(0.9)(0.72)		6	0.648
VARIABLES	3	(0.7)(0.64)	(0.8)(0.72)	(0.9)(0.81)	7	0.729
(X_3)	4	-	(0.9)(0.72)	(0.9)(0.81)	7	0.729

The reader should check that by extending the calculations by one further state, the optimal route turns out to be:

NYC → ATL → NOL → DFW → SFO

with an associated probability value of 0.6561.

9.5   SOME ADVANCED TOPICS

9.5.1 Continuous Variable Problems

In the dynamic programming problems considered up to this, it has been assumed that at each stage, the state and decision variables may take certain distinct values only e.g. $X_3 = 2$, 3, 4 ; $D_3 = 5$, 6, 7 in the previous table. In certain instances, this is not the case. Rather, the state and decision variables can vary over some continuous range.
  Consider the problem:

$$\text{MAXIMISE : } Y_1^2 + Y_2^2 + Y_3^2$$
$$\text{s.t.} \quad Y_1 + Y_2 + Y_3 \leq b \qquad \text{----(9.13)}$$

This is in fact a nonlinear programming problem which could be solved *via* the methods discussed in the previous chapter. It can also be solved using dynamic programming by viewing it as an optimal allocation problem of the type described in Section 9.4.3. Up to b units of money are available for investment in three regions. In the case of each region i, i=1, ..., 3, an investment of $y_i (\leq b)$ units of money yields a return of y_i^2. The formulation (9.13) expresses the problem of finding the appropriate level of investment for each region in order to maximise the total return.
  Proceeding in the same manner as before and taking as the state variable X_1 the amount of the budget allocated to region three and D_1 the amount actually spent on region three, both of these variables can vary continuously between 0 and b. The corresponding solution   table where x_1 and d_1 are some intermediate values of X_1 and D_1 is:

DECISION VARIABLES (D_1)

		0	...	d_1	...	b	d_1	$f_1(X_1)$
	0	0	...	-	...	-	0	0
STATE	:	:		:		:	:	:
VARIABLES	x_1	0	...	d_1^2 if $d_1 \leq x_1$		-	x_1	x_1^2
	:	:		:		:	:	:
X_1	b	0	...	d_1^2	...	b^2	b	b^2

Imagining a diagonal drawn from the upper left hand corner to lower right hand corner of the body of the table, all returns above this diagonal are blank as the corresponding decision variable value i.e. the amount of money to be invested exceeds that available as given by the state variable value. On or below the main diagonal, the stage one return is given by x_1^2. For any value of X_1, x_1,

$$f_1(X_1) = \max_{0 \leq d_1 \leq x_1} d_1^2 = x_1^2$$

Thus, at stage one, if $X_1 = x_1$ money units are available for investment in region three, the total return will be maximised if all of the money available is spent on the region.

Consider now the relevant stage two calculations. X_2, which can vary between zero and b gives the total allocation to regions two and three. D_2 which can also vary between zero and b gives the allocation to region two. The relevant solution table is:

DECISION VARIABLES (D_2)

		0	...	d_2	...	b	D_2^*	$f_2(X_2)$
STATE	0	0+0	...	-	...	-	0	0
VARIABLES	:	:		:		:	:	:
(X_2)	x_2	$0+x_2^2$	...$d_2^2+(x_2-d_2)^2$ if $d_2 \leq x_2$		-	$x_2/2$	$2(x_2/2)^2$
	:	:		:		:	:	:
	b	$0+b^2$	...$d_2^2+(b-d_2)^2$	...	b^2+0	b/2	$2(b/2)^2$

Once again, blank readings occur where $d_2 > x_2$. Consider now the case where $d_2 < x_2$. If d_2 units of money are assigned to region two, the return will be d_2^2. $(x_2 - d_2)$ units of money will remain for spending on region three. From the previous stage table, the optimal policy is to spend all of it there yielding a further return of $(x_2 - d_2)^2$. The total stage two return is thus given by:

$$Q_2 (X_2 = x_2, D_2 = d_2) = d_2^2 + (x_2 - d_2)^2 \qquad \text{----}(9.14)$$

The optimal value of d_2 given x_2 is that value which maximises the total return i.e.

$$f_2(X_2) = \max_{0 \le d_2 \le x_2} \{ d_2^2 + (x_2 - d_2)^2 \} \qquad \text{----}(9.15)$$

Differentiating the right hand side of (9.14) with respect to d_2 and setting to zero yields:

$$2d_2 + 2(x_2 - d_2)(-1) \overset{\text{SET}}{=} 0$$

i.e. $\qquad\qquad d_2 \qquad = x_2/2$

which demonstrates that if a sum of money x_2 is allocated to regions two and three and if the total return is to be maximised, one half of this sum should be allocated to region two and one half of it to region three. We leave as an exercise for the reader the task of extending the calculations back one further stage to show that if three regions are being considered, one-third of the total budget available should be allocated to each. Details of the full solution appear in Nemhauser (1966).

A particular feature to note concerning the foregoing problem is that the right hand side of the single constraint in (9.13) determines the range of permissible state variable values. The solution approach can be extended to cope with a number of constraints by introducing multidimensional state variables of the type discussed in Section 9.4.1 - one for each constraint right hand side. Thus dynamic programming can in fact be used to solve conventional linear and nonlinear programming problems. In practice, due to the inherent superiority of the solution methods discussed in the previous chapters, it is not often employed for these purposes.

9.5.2 More Complex Decision Making Processes

Up to this, it has been assumed that the situation being modelled can be represented by a set of sequential stages each involving a series of states and decisions. It is to be noted that dynamic programming can be extended for use in cases where at some intermediate stage, the decision making process splits into two separate branches, or where two separate decision making branches combine or where a loop occurs. The reader is referred to an advanced text e.g.

Nemhauser (1966) for details.

9.5.3 The Nature of the Objective Function

The expressions (9.1), (9.10), (9.11) and (9.13) each express the objective of a dynamic programming problem. In the most general sense, the objective is to optimise some function of the individual stage returns i.e.

$$\text{Optimise } g_i \ (R_1, \ \ldots, \ R_n) \qquad\qquad \text{----(9.16)}$$

where g_i might imply addition as in (9.1), multiplication as in (9.11) etc. It is to be noted that for any dynamic programming formulation, the function $g_i \ (R_1 \ \ldots, \ R_n)$ must fulfill two conditions. First, it must be separable in the sense defined in Section 8.5.2 for if it is not, it will not be possible to break the problem down into stages. Second, $g_i(R_1, \ldots, R_n)$ must be *monotonically nondecreasing* by which is meant the individual returns associated with each stage and decision variable combination at each stage must be greater than or equal to zero.

10

GOAL   PROGRAMMING
AND   RELATED   TOPICS

10.1   GOAL PROGRAMMING : INTRODUCTION

Virtually all of the mathematical programming models discussed in the previous chapters have involved optimising an
objective relating to single entity e.g. profit, total distance travelled subject to stated constraints. The reason as
to why these models are of such importance is that they do
indeed replicate the contexts within which many real world
decisions are made. Thus, as discussed in Section 1.2, they
play an important role both in the study of current patterns
and in the devising of future policies. Despite their
relevance however, there are some decision and policy making
situations which are not represented adequately by these
models. One such situation is where there are a number of
partly conflicting objectives involving contrasting entities
and where the overall desire is that all of these objectives
or *goals* be met to as large an extent as possible simultaneously. One method which seeks to treat this type of
situation is *goal programming*.
    In terms of the preceding material, goal programming
does not represent a new mathematical technique. Rather, it
represents a means by which certain of the previously discussed programming methods can be altered to cope with the
revised type of situation mentioned in the last paragraph.
As the examples will show, the method is very flexible in
terms of the precise formulation of the input model. We
restrict the discussion here to goal programming as applied
within the context of linear programming. A full discussion
of the technique is given in Lee (1972). Summaries appear in
Charnes and Cooper (1961), Johnsen (1968), Kornbluth (1973)
and in most of the examples discussed in Section 10.3.

DOI: 10.4324/9781003179030-10

10.2 GOAL PROGRAMMING : GENERAL FORMULATION

Reconsider the general linear programming formulation (4.1)-(4.3) i.e.

$$\text{Optimise} : \quad \sum_{j=1}^{n} c_j X_j \qquad \qquad \text{----(10.1)}$$

$$\text{s.t.} \quad \sum_{j=1}^{n} a_{ij} X_j \overset{\leq}{=} \text{ or } = \text{ or } \overset{\geq}{=} b_i; \; i = 1, \ldots, m$$

$$\text{----(10.2)}$$

$$X_j \overset{\geq}{=} 0 \; ; \; j = 1, \ldots, n \qquad \text{----(10.3)}$$

Up to this, the b_i values in the constraints (10.2) have been viewed as the available amounts of scarce resources in the case of 'less than or equals' constraints and as requirements to be equalled or exceeded in the case of 'greater than or equals' constraints. We shall now view these values as goals to be achieved as closely as possible. Specifically, a set of values is required for the X_j such that:

$$\sum_{j=1}^{n} a_{ij} X_j \rightarrow b_i; \; i = 1, \ldots, m \qquad \text{----(10.4)}$$

where '$\rightarrow$' is interpreted as meaning 'approaches as closely as possible to' or 'tends to'. In practice, for a given solution, the values of X_j will probably be such as to cause the left hand side of (10.4) to fall short of or exceed b_i at least for certain of the constraint expressions. We can thus rewrite (10.4) as:

$$\sum_{j=1}^{n} a_{ij} X_j + D_i^- - D_i^+ = b_i; \; i = 1, \ldots, m \qquad \text{----(10.5)}$$

Where D_i^- gives the amount by which the solution values of X_j cause the quantity $\sum_{j=1}^{n} a_{ij} X_j$ to fall short of b_i and D_i^+ gives the amount by which the solution values of X_j cause the quantity $\sum_{j=1}^{n} a_{ij} X_j$ to exceed b_i. Quite obviously, for a particular constraint expression and set of solution values $X_j, j = 1, \ldots, n$:

$$D_i^- \text{ and/or } D_i^+ = 0 \qquad \text{----(10.6)}$$

If the values of X_j are such as to cause an expression of the form (10.5) to hold exactly:

$$D_1^- = D_1^+ = 0 \qquad\qquad ----(10.7)$$

The larger the value of D_i^- or D_i^+, the greater the amount by which the goal expressed as b_i is underfulfilled or over-fulfilled.

The conditions (10.5) together with (10.3) and:

$$D_i^- \geq 0 \; ; \; D_i^+ \geq 0 \; ; \; i = 1, \ldots, m \qquad ----(10.8)$$

(which cause (10.6) to hold automatically) are those appropriate to a goal programming formulation derived from linear programming.

We now consider the formulation of an appropriate object-ive. Given that it is required that the goals (10.5) be met as closely as possible, it is required that the values D_i^+, D_i^- be as small as possible. Thus one appropriate objective is:

$$\text{Minimise :} \quad \sum_{i=1}^{m} (D_i^- + D_i^+) \qquad ----(10.9)$$

In many goal programming applications, it can be argued that the fulfillment of some goals is more important than others. In order to take account of this, the terms in (10.9) can be weighted to yield:

$$\text{Minimise :} \quad \sum_{i=1}^{m} w_i (D_i^- + D_i^+) \qquad ----(10.10)$$

where w_i represents the relative importance of satisfying the i th goal. Specifically, if it is considered of immense importance that the i th constraint be satisfied, w_i will be assigned a large value which, given the nature of the optim-isation and in a similar manner to the incorporation of big-M in a linear programming minimisation objective (Section 4.6.3) will cause D_i^-, D_i^+ to tend to zero.

The objective (10.10) presupposes that the weight to be given to the i th goal being underfulfilled ($D_i^- > 0$) and overfulfilled ($D_i^+ > 0$) is the same. If, the problem is such that this is not so, separate weights, w_i^- and w_i^+ respective-ly can be assigned to D_i^- and D_i^+ to yield the revised object-ive:

$$\text{Minimise :} \quad \sum_{i=1}^{m} w_i^- D_i^- + \sum_{i=1}^{m} w_i^+ D_i^+ \qquad ----(10.11)$$

Thus, for example, if the i th constraint is such that it is very important that the values of X_i be such that b_i is achieved (i.e. $D_i^- = 0$) but it is of little concern if b_i is exceeded, then w_i^- would be chosen to be a relatively large number while w_i^+ would be chosen to be relatively small.

In the case of certain goals, their nature is such as to disallow either underestimation or overestimation which will cause the term D_i^- or D_i^+ as appropriate to be dropped from (10.5) and the objective. Consider, for example, the task of subdividing an area of land between n uses. If X_j is the proportion of land allocated to the jth use, $j=1, \ldots, n$ and it is a goal that all of the land be allocated, then:

$$\sum_{j=1}^{n} X_j \to 1 \qquad\qquad ----(10.12)$$

Quite obviously, the summation in (10.12) cannot exceed one i.e. over-use of the land cannot occur. Thus, intrdocuing D_i^- only, (10.12) becomes:

$$\sum_{j=1}^{n} X_j + D_i^- = 1 \qquad\qquad ----(10.13)$$

and only D_i^- appears in the objective.

In order to indicate one further development of the basic goal programming model, we shall reconsider the objective (10.10); the development could be discussed equally well within the context of (10.11) or (10.12) and where certain of the terms D_i^-, D_i^+, $i=1, \ldots, m$ are deleted. Suppose that in (10.10), a set of weighting values $w_i = p_i$, $i = 1, \ldots, m$ are chosen such that:

$$p_i >>>> p_{(i+1)}; \quad i = 1, \ldots, (m-1) \qquad\qquad ----(10.14)$$

where the inequality '>>>>' means 'is very much greater than'. The revised objective is now:

$$\text{Minimise :} \quad \sum_{i=1}^{m} p_i \, (D_i^- + D_i^+) \qquad\qquad ----(10.15)$$

where the coefficient of the first term is very large, the coefficient of the next term is significantly smaller and so on. Provided the coefficients p_i are different enough from each other (for a summary of how this can be achieved see for example Field (1973) and, once more, following the logic underlying the big-M method (Section 4.6.3), the optimisation will proceed by satisfying the first goal (i.e. causing D_1^-, D_1^+ to tend to zero) to the greatest extent possible first and then, and only then, by satisfying the second goal to the greatest extent possible and so on. A goal programming problem where the weights satisfy the condition (10.14) i.e. with an objective of the form (10.15) is referred to as a *pre-emptive goal programming problem*; a problem with an objective of the form (10.10) comprises a *weighted goal programming problem*.

312

It should be noted that the pre-emptive and weighted formulation can be combined. Specifically, suppose that in a given goal programming problem comprising m goals, the first subgroup of a goals whose weights relative to each other are w_1, w_2, ..., w_a respectively are of top priority and must be satisfied insofar as is possible before all others, that the next subgroup of b goals of weights w_{a+1}, ..., w_{a+b} are of second priority and so on, then, assigning pre-emptive weights P_1, P_2, ... to the subgroups, the appropriate objective is:

$$\text{Minimise} : P_1 \, w_1 \, (D_1^- + D_1^+) + \ldots + P_1 \, w_a \, (D_a^- + D_a^+)$$

$$+ P_2 \, w_{(a+1)} \, (D_{(a+1)}^- + D_{(a+1)}^+) + \ldots$$

$$+ P_2 \, w_{(a+b)} \, (D_{(a+b)}^- + D_{(a+b)}^+) + \ldots \quad ----(10.16)$$

10.3 GOAL PROGRAMMING EXAMPLES

10.3.1 Recreational and Forest Landuse

McGrew (1975) presents the following problem which amply demonstrates the goal programming approach. An area which is subdivided into two planning regions contains seven state parks (Table 10.1). For each park, a proposal for an expansion in the number of campsites has been drawn up. Each proposal has an associated cost. It is required that the expansion plan chosen come as close as possible to meeting a number of goals. First, the total cost of the overall plan chosen must be as close to 5.0 million dollars as possible i.e.

$$1.0X_1 + 0.5X_2 + 1.5X_3 + 4.0X_4 + 2.0X_5 + 1.25X_6 + 0.75X_7$$

$$+ D_1^- - D_1^+ = 5.0 \quad ----(10.17)$$

where X_i = The proportion of the proposed development undertaken in state park i.

Next, for political reasons, it is required that if at all possible, at least one-third of the total budget available be spent in each region i.e.

$$1.0X_1 + 0.5X_2 + 1.5X_3 + D_2^- - D_2^+ = 1.67$$

and $$4.0X_4 + 2.0X_5 + 1.25X_6 + 0.75X_7 + D_3^- - D_3^+ = 1.67$$

$$----(10.18)$$

Next, due to local pressures against the full development of

TABLE 10.1 : RECREATIONAL LANDUSE PROBLEM

PLANNING REGION	STATE PARK	DATA INPUTS		MODEL RESULTS	
		PROPOSED EXPANSION (Campsites)	COST ($ mill.)	ACTUAL EXPANSION (Campsites)	COST ($ m.)
Northern	White Oak Lake	200	1.0	100	0.5
	Golden Hill	100	0.5	100	0.5
	Reedfoot	300	1.5	300	1.5
Southern	Trail Forks	800	4.0	0	0
	Drake Reservoir	400	2.0	100	0.5
	Fort Baker	250	1.25	250	1.25
	Lone Pine	150	0.75	150	0.75

From: MCGREW, J.C. Jr., (1975), Goal Programming and Complex Problem Solving in Geography, *Papers in Geography*, 12, Pennsylvania State University, University Park, Pennsylvania, Tables 1 and 4.

Reprinted by permission

Goal Programming and Related Topics

200 campsites at White Oak Lake, it is required that the expansion not exceed 100 campsites if possible i.e.

$$X_1 + D_4^- - D_4^+ = 0.5 \qquad\qquad ----(10.19)$$

Next, because verbal commitments have been made already to the media, it is required that the Lone Pine development be completed fully if at all possible i.e.

$$X_7 + D_5^- = 1.0 \qquad\qquad ----(10.20)$$

Following (10.13), note the absence of the term D_5^+ from (10.20) indicating the impossibility of 'over-completing' the project.

Each of the goals (10.17)-(10.20) is of equally top priority. Thus the relevant terms in the objective are:

$$P_1 D_1^+ + P_1 D_2^- + P_1 D_3^- + P_1 D_4^+ + P_1 D_5^- \qquad ----(10.21)$$

Because all of these top priority goals are of equal importance, individual weightings (i.e. the equivalent of the w_i in (10.16)) are set to unity. Note too that the incorporation of the relevant D_i^+ or D_i^- value in (10.21) reflects the nature of the underlying goal in terms of the undesirability of over achievement or under achievement respectively.

In addition to the foregoing top priority goals, two second priority goals are identified : to complete the Golden Hill and Reedfoot Developments i.e.

$$\left.\begin{array}{l} X_2 + D_6^- = 1.0) \\ \\ X_3 + D_7^- = 1.0) \end{array}\right\} \qquad ----(10.22)$$

The relevant importances of these within the second priority grouping is perceived as being 80 and 100 respectively. Thus, following (10.16) the relevant terms for incorporation within the objective are:

$$80 \, P_2 D_6^- + 100 \, P_2 D_7^- \qquad\qquad ----(10.23)$$

A third, fourth and fifth levels of priority relate to the completion of White Oak Lake and Fort Baker, to the completion of Trail Forks and Drake Reservoir and to the completion of Lone Pine respectively. A final (sixth level) of priority incorporates the goal of not underspending the budget. There are thus six additional expressions of the type (10.17)-(10.20), (10.22) within the model. The complete objective is:

$$\text{Minimise} : P_1 \ D_1^+ + P_1 \ D_2^- + P_1 \ D_3^- + P_1 \ D_4^+ + P_1 \ D_5^- + 80 P_2 D_6^-$$
$$+ \ 100 \ P_2 \ D_7^- + 80 \ P_3 \ D_8^- + 60 \ P_3 \ D_9^- + 40 \ P_4 D_{10}^-$$
$$+ \ 80 \ P_4 \ D_{11}^- + 20 \ P_5 \ D_{12}^- + P_6 \ D_1^- \text{----} (10.24)$$

Solving the complete problem using the methods discussed in Chapter Three (for a complete description of the use of the simplex method in a goal programming context see Lee (1972)) yielded the results given in Table 10.1. The first priority goals are met in their entirety : the various financial constraints are obeyed, White Oak Lake is 50 per cent completed and Lone Pine is completed in its entirety. The second priority goals are also met in their entirety : the Reedfoot and Golden Hill developments are completed. The third priority goals are partially met : Fort Baker is 100 per cent completed but White Oak Lake is only 50 per cent completed having been so constrained by a goal of higher (first) priority. The fourth priority goal is partially attained : Drake Reservoir is 25 per cent completed but no development is programmed for Trail Forks. The fifth and sixth priority goals are met in their entirety.

A number of other studies employ goal programming within the general context of forestry/recreational landuse planning. Field (1973) considers the case of an individual who has purchased 600 acres of woodland in West Central Maine, U.S.A. The forest will be harvested. In addition, the area contains a cabin which the individual will use for his summer vacation and for an autumn (fall) hunting trip. At other times, the cabin will be rented. The individual's management goals comprise achieving an annual income from the wood harvest and cabin rental of $2100 and ensuring that his own and his tenants' occupations of the cabin do not exceed the number of days available. Field reports on the results of various runs of the model each with a different set of priority weightings in the objective.

Schuler and Meadows (1975) and Schuler et al. (1977) consider landuse planning for approximately 10000 acres of the Mark Twain National Forest, Missouri, U.S.A. Some mix of eight landuses is to achieve a number of goals concerning the annual wood harvest, the amount of land available for grazing and the provision of recreational amenities. A further goal requires that a given annual budget not be over-spent. One particularly interesting aspect of this work is that the initial solution emerging is subjected to a sensitivity analysis in the sense discussed in Chapter Five Specifically, the extent to which various goals would be met as the available budget changes is investigated. Figure 10.1 illustrates the results emerging in the case of four of the goals. The goals of achieving a stated output of hardwood sawtimber and hardwood pulpwoods are

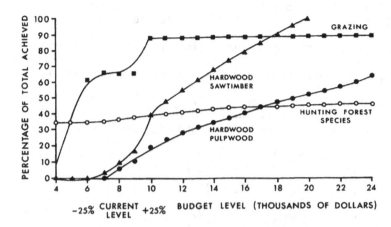

Figure 10.1 Goal Achievements at Various Budget Levels for a Sample Landuse Study

From: SCHULER, A.J., WEBSTER, H.H. and MEADOWS, J.C., (1977), Goal Programming in Forest Management, *Journal of Forestry*, 75, 320-4, Figure 3.

Redrawn by permission.

very sensitive to budget changes. In contrast, those concerning the provision of hunting forest species and, once the annual budget exceeds $10000 per annum, grazing land are relatively insensitive to such changes.

A further study within the same subject area is that discussed by Dane *et al.* (1977) who consider part of the Mount Hood Forest Park, Oregon, U.S.A. The reader is referred to the original paper for details.

10.3.2 Residential and Industrial Location

Courtney *et al.* (1972) consider the residential location decisions of a homogeneous group of individuals e.g. undergraduate students, migrant farm workers arriving in an area and seeking places to live. It is assumed that the area is divided into m sectors. The characteristics of each sector as perceived by the incoming group are summarised *via* a set of k scores each relating to one of k characteristics of the sector as it would exist if the complete group settled there. The k characteristics include such items as average land value and population density. As far as each characteristic is concerned, the group has a goal score which it would like to achieve for that characteristic. In a sense, this set of goal scores

317

represents the characteristics of the 'perfect' residential location sector as perceived by the incoming group.

In order to formalise the foregoing, let:

a_{ij} = The score for sector j in terms of characteristic i

g_i = The desired or goal score for characteristic i.

The complete set of scores, a_{ij}; i=1, ..., k ; j=1, ..., m can be envisaged as being arranged in the form of a (kXm) matrix A with the g_i scores arranged in a (kx1) matrix G:

$$A = \begin{pmatrix} a_{11} & \cdots & a_{im} \\ \vdots & & \vdots \\ a_{k1} & \cdots & a_{km} \end{pmatrix} \; ; \quad G = \begin{pmatrix} g_1 \\ \vdots \\ g_k \end{pmatrix}$$

Now, comparing each column of A with G in turn, if there was some sector j for which:

$$a_{ij} = g_i; \; i = 1, \ldots, k \qquad \qquad \text{----(10.24)}$$

i.e. for each characteristic, the actual rating of the sector equalled the goal level of the individuals comprising the incoming group, then, presumably, all of the individuals would settle in that sector. In reality, this is unlikely to arise. For any sector, certain of its characteristics will approach the required goal level but others will fall well below it or above it. In this case, the various residential location decisions made by the group will represent a compromise. Courtney *et al.* argue that the final result will be such that:

$$\left.\begin{array}{l} a_{11} X_1 + a_{12} X_2 + \cdots + a_{1m} X_m \to g_1 \\ a_{21} X_1 + a_{22} X_2 + \cdots + a_{2m} X_m \to g_2 \\ \vdots \\ a_{k1} X_1 + a_{k2} X_2 + \cdots + a_{km} X_m \to g_k \end{array}\right\} \qquad \text{----(10.25)}$$

where X_j, j=1, ..., m gives the proportion of individuals who choose to live in sector j and, as before, the symbol '$\to$' means 'approaches as closely as possible to'. The overall hypothesis is thus that the group will divide itself among the sectors in such a way as to cause the average score achieved in terms of each characteristic to approach the desired goal level as closely as possible. Using the methods of the previous section, the goal programming formulation which ensures that this occurs is given by:

Goal Programming and Related Topics

$$\text{Minimise}: \quad \sum_{i=1}^{k} (w_i^- D_i^- + w_i^+ D_i^+)$$

$$\text{s.t.} \quad \sum_{j=1}^{m} a_{ij} X_j + D_i^- - D_i^+ = g_i; \quad i=1, \ldots, k$$

$$----(10.26)$$

and where, obviously :

$$D_i^- . D_i^+ = 0; \quad i=1, \ldots, k$$

$$\sum_{j=1}^{m} X_j = 1$$

$$X_j \geq 0 ; \quad j=1, \ldots, m$$

$$w_i^-, w_i^- \geq 0 ; \quad i=1, \ldots, k$$

and where the various w_i^-, w_i^+ values are chosen by the
researcher. The foregoing formumation presupposes a single
homogeneous group of individuals. If, in fact, an incoming
group comprised a number of distinct subgroups each with its
own matrices A and G the model (10.26) could be solved for
each subgroup in turn. Courtney *et al.* test out their model
within the context of three subgroups of students (Freshman/
Sophomore-no car; Freshman/Sophomore-car; Juniors/Seniors-car)
seeking residential locations in the area surrounding the
University of Texas campus at Austin, Texas. The sectors
comprise seven areas each offering accommodations of contrasting characteristics e.g. dormitories, fraternity/sorority
houses, low cost private housing and suburban residential.
The values placed on the characteristics of these different
accommodation types vary by student group. Thus three
independent runs of the model are undertaken.

One of the disadvantages of ·Courtney *et al.*'s model in the
form (10.26) is that it takes no account of the supply of
residential locations available within each sector and thus
of the possible competition which might occur for a limited
number of locations within a particular sector. Furthermore,
in the case of an incoming group comprising a number of subgroups, no account is taken of the possible effect of one
subgroup's decisions e.g. female students on those of another
subgroup e.g. male students. Courtney *et al.* attempt to over-
come these deficiencies *via* a special linking programme. The
reader is referred to the original publication for details

A study which casts the problem of optimal landuse design
within a goal programming format is that of Werczberger
(1976) who considers a planning authority which intends to
develop an area at the outskirts of a metropolitan region.
The goals concern the nature of the residential development to
occur, the provision of a minimum amount of floorspace for
manufacturing and, finally, the desire first that the local

319

electricity generating station which is already *in situ*
operates in such a way as to keep the annual sulphur dioxide
concentration below a stated level and second that the cost of
electricity be kept below a stated level. A number of runs of
the model are undertaken with both various priority orderings
of the goals and various goal targets for manufacturing floorspace.

In an interesting application of goal programming, Barber
(1977b) uses the method to determine for a set of planning
districts comprising Metropolitan Toronto the increase in
basic employment necessary in each district in order to minimise the deviation from targetted population increases. The
interrelationship between a given increase in basic employment
in some planning district i and the resultant population
increase in each of the planning districts is controlled *via*
relationships developed for use in the Garin-Lowry model of
urban development (for a summary see Barber's paper). Basic
employment increases appropriate to three population growth
strategies are determined:

(1) A suburbanisation strategy comprising zero population
growth in the six inner city planning districts(1-6)
and a population increase of 5000 persons in each of
the other ten outer area zones (7-16)

(2) A lakeshore growth limitation strategy comprising
zero growth in all planning districts contiguous with
Lake Ontario (1, 2, 6, 7, 14, 15) and a population
increase of 5000 in each other district

(3) An Eastern Toronto growth strategy defined as zero
population growth in the six westernmost districts
(2, 3, 7, 8, 9, 10) and a population increase of 5000
persons in each of the other zones.

The results are summarised in Table 10.2. The growth target
goals were approached most closely in the case of the eastern
growth strategy where 31485 of the 50000 persons to be allocated to growth districts (62.9%) were actually so placed by the
model; the suburbanization strategy proved to be the most
difficult to achieve with only 18773 persons (37.5%) being
allocated to districts where growth was actually targetted to
take place.

A final example of goal programming used within a planning
context which deserves mention is that of Charnes *et al.*(1975)
who consider the development of the coastal area of Texas,
U.S.A. This application is particularly interesting in that it
incorporates two notions discussed previously in this text:
interregional linear programming (Section 4.2.2) and sequential
decision making (Chapter Nine). The reader is referred to the
original presentation for details.

320

TABLE 10.2

THREE EMPLOYMENT AND POPULATION ALLOCATION STRATEGIES FOR METROPOLITAN TORONTO

Zone	Suburbanization strategy			Lakeshore growth limitation strategy			Eastern growth strategy		
	Basic employment	Population[a]	Target	Basic employment	Population[a]	Target	Employment	Population[a]	Target
1		3841	0		3632	0	5089	5000	5000
2		7438	0		7257	0		6621	0
3		6720	0		7304	5000		6021	0
4		5629	0		5871	5000		5722	5000
5		1479	0		1495	5000		1591	5000
6		6525	0		6475	0		7513	5000
7	6153	2247	5000		1192	0		997	0
8		3773	5000		3772	5000		2887	0
9	1985	837	5000	9869	1485	5000		597	0
10		1327	5000		1934	5000		1096	0
11		2603	5000		2933	5000		2483	5000
12		211	5000		149	5000		251	5000
13		5000	5000	5056	5000	5000		5000	5000
14	6787	1981	5000		1249	0	9836	2571	5000
15		366	5000		349	0		906	5000
16		428	5000		349	5000		448	5000

[a]Totals may not add to 50,000 due to rounding.

From: BARBER, G.M., (1977), Urban Population Distribution Planning, Annals of the Association of American Geographers, 67, 239–45, Table 2. Reprinted by permission

10.3.3 Goal Programming in the Context of the Transportation Problem

Recall the transportation problem (3.4)-(3.7). A feature of this model is that the supply of product available at each origin (s_i) and the demand for it at each destination (d_j) are assumed to be fixed. Kwak and Schniederjans (1979) consider how goal programming might be used to improve on a particular optimal solution to a transportation problem when the demand requirement at each destination is altered to be stated in terms of an interval i.e.

$$d_j^{min} \le d_j \le d_j^{max} \qquad ----(10.27)$$

As a first priority goal in their model, Kwak and Schniederjans require that the total number of units of product transported in their final solution come as close as possible to the total supply available i.e.

$$\sum_{i=1}^{m} \sum_{j=1}^{n} X_{ij} + D_1^- - D_1^+ = \sum_{i=1}^{m} s_i \qquad ----(10.28)$$

where the notation is as in (3.4)-(3.7). Next, as a second priority, it is is required that the total number of units transported from each origin approach the total supply available there i.e.

$$\sum_{j=1}^{n} X_{ij} + D_{1+i}^- - D_{1+i}^+ = s_i; \; i = 1, \ldots, m \qquad ----(10.29)$$

Further goals require, for example that deliveries to relatively 'low cost' destinations i.e. destinations which receive their deliveries *via* relatively low cost routes in the initial optimal solution be increased, if possible; towards d_j^{max} whilst those to relatively 'high cost' destination be decreased, if possible, towards d_j^{min}. The reader is referred to the original presentation for details.

10.4   MULTICRITERIA ANALYSIS

The overall prupose of goal programming as set out in the previous sections is to devise the policy or plan which simultaneously comes as close as possible to achieving a series of appropriately weighted goals. Sometimes, the actual task facing the planner is different : he is required to choose from a set of possible plans, each with its own characteristics in terms of a number of contrasting criteria e.g. employment generated, pollution caused that plan which, overall, is

the most desirable. Traditionally, this task has been performed using *cost-benefit analysis* which involves quantifying
the various costs and benefits inherent in each plan in money
terms with a view to discerning which plan is most desirable.
A major drawback of cost-benefit analysis is that the conclusions drawn in a specific study obviously depend very much
on how the various cost and benefits associated with the
various features of the proposed plans are actually quantifi-
ed in money terms. Nijkamp (1975) and van Delft and Nijkamp
(1976, 1977a) discuss various alternative approaches (for a
further discussion within this general subject area, see
Cohon and Marks (1975)) and discuss one, *multicriteria
analysis*, in detail.

In order to provide an illustration, Nijkamp (1975) considers seven plans proposed for reclaiming land in a particular area in the Netherlands. Each plan has been evaluated
in terms of eight criteria. These criteria include the
effect of the plan on regional accessibility, the total cost
involved and the number of new jobs created. The complete
set of evaluations is presented as a 8X7 matrix, R. It is to
be noted that the units of measurement in each row of R i.e.
for each criterion vary; for example, the three criteria
cited previously were measured respectively on an ordinal
scale from '1' (very good) to '10' (very bad), in money
values and in thousands of man-years respectively. In order
to proceed with the multicriteria analysis, these values are
first normalised i.e. transformed to be of 'like' magnitude
via the expression:

$$r_{jk}' = r_{jk}/(\sum_{k=1}^{k_{tot}} r_{jk}^2)^{1/2} \qquad ----(10.30)$$

where r_{jk} = Score achieved by plan k in terms of criterion
j

r'_{jk} = Normalised score of plan k in terms of
criterion j.

and k_{tot} = The total number of plans (seven in this
instance)

Now, the relative importance each criterion j in terms of the
overall plan is decided upon and an appropriate score or
weight is assigned to it. This yields a 1Xj$_{tot}$ matrix of
weights, W, where j$_{tot}$ is the total number of criteria
involved. These are then transformed *via* (10.30) to yield a
revised matrix of normalised weights, W'.

Nijkamp now uses the matrices R' and W' to calculate two
further matrices from which the desirability or otherwise of
the various plans relative to each other can be determined
and the 'best' plan chosen. The first of these, a

k_{tot} x k_{tot} *concordance matrix*, C, gives for each plan pair
k and k' the extent to which plan k scores more highly than
plan k' in terms of the various criteria. Specifically, if:

w_j = Weight (normalised) associated with criterion j

$c_{kk'}$ = The concordance of plan k relative to plan k'

$$c_{kk'} = \Sigma \, w'_j \quad / \quad \sum_{j=1}^{j_{tot}} w'_j \qquad \text{----(10.31)}$$

where the summation in the numerator of (10.31) is over all
criteria for which plan k scores more highly than plan k'.
Quite obviously:

$c_{kk'} = 1 \Rightarrow$ Plan k scores more highly than plan k' for all
criteria

$c_{kk'} = 0 \Rightarrow$ Plan k scores lower than plan k' for all criteria.

In general, for k_{tot} possible plans, the desired plan is one
for which

$c_{kk'} \rightarrow 1$ for k'= 1, 2, ..., k_{tot} (k' $\neq$ k).

The second matrix determined by Nijkamp is a k_{tot} X k_{tot}
discordance matrix, D, which gives for each plan pair k
and k' the extent to which the maximum deviation between k
and k' in terms of some criterion approaches the maximum
between two plans in terms of some criterion in the complete
data set. In this case $d_{kk'} \rightarrow 0$ implies that plan k is to be
preferred over plan k'.

Given the matrices C and D, Nijkamp demonstrates how these
may be inspected logically to yield ultimately the most preferred plan. The main advantage cited for multicriteria
analysis is that it provides a means by which unlike criteria
can be employed simultaneously within the optimal plan choice
process. Quite obviously however, certain arbitrary decisions
must be taken within the process e.g. concerning the methods
for calculating the concordance and discordance indices, for
using the matrices C and D to identify the best plan and the
choice of suitable w_j values. These and other matters together
with further examples are discussed in some detail in van
Delft and Nijkamp (1976, 1977a) who suggest in particular
that the sensitivity of the solution i.e. the plan finally
chosen should be tested for changes in the w_j values.

Goal Programming and Related Topics

10.5   HIERARCHICAL OPTIMISATION

Recall (Section 4.7.1) the observation that in practice, the
true objective underlying a particular planning exercise can
seldom be defined precisely in terms of a single objective in
advance.   Recall too, that one approach for dealing with this
situation in the case of a particular problem is to solve it
for a number of objectives in order to see by how much and in
what ways the resultant optimal solutions vary.   One way in
which these solutions could be evaluated is via the methods
discussed in the previous section.   In cases where the
individual objectives can be ranked in order of importance,
van Delft and Nijkamp (1977b) suggest an alternative approach:
hierarchical optimisation.
  Consider the constraint set:

$$g_i \ (X_1, \ \ldots, \ X_n) = g_i \ (X) \leq \text{ or } = \text{ or } \geq b_i; \ i=1, \ \ldots, \ m \quad)$$
$$X_i \geq 0; \ i = 1, \ \ldots, \ m \qquad\qquad)$$

$$\text{----} (10.32)$$

where $g_i(X)$ may or may not be linear together with the ℓ
objectives:

Maximise : $f_1 \ (X_1, \ \ldots, \ X_n) = f_1 \ (X)$ ----(10.33)

Maximise : $f_2 \ (X)$ ----(10.34)

Maximise : $f_\ell \ (X)$ ----(10.35)

(The use of objectives involving maximisation causes no loss
of generality.)   Now, suppose that the objective (10.33) is of
greatest importance followed by (10.34) etc. van Delft and
Nijkamp suggest a solution process which begins by solving
(10.33), (10.32) to yield an optimal value for $f_1(X)$, say
$f_1^*(X)$.   Now, (10.34), (10.32) is solved together with an
additional constraint of the form:

$$f_1(X) \geq \beta_{12} \ f_1^*(X) \qquad\qquad \text{----}(10.36)$$

where $\beta_{12} \leq 1$.   Appending the condition (10.36) ensures that
in solving (10.34), (10.32), the optimal values of the decision variables are such as to still cause $f_1(X)$ to approach
its optimal value, $f_1^*(X)$ to at least a certain extent.   In
effect, β_{12} represents the partial tradeoff for (10.33) with
respect to (10.34).   Continuing in this manner, the next
problem to be solved is:

Maximise : $f_3(X)$

s.t. $\quad f_1(X) \geq \beta_{13} \, f_1{}^* (X)$

$\qquad f_2(X) \geq \beta_{23} \, f_2{}^* (X)$

and (10.32). Continuing in this manner ultimately yields a maximisation of (10.35) subject to (10.32) and $(\ell - 1)$ additional constraints which yields decision variable values which cause $f_1(X), \ldots, f_{(\ell-1)}(X)$ to be within acceptable limits of $f_1{}^*(X), \ldots, f^*_{(\ell-1)}(X)$.

van Delft and Nijkamp refer to the foregoing solution approach as *hierarchical optimisation*. Various versions of the method are discussed and difficulties arising especially concerning the feasibility of the successive intermediate solutions are considered. Other related approaches are cited. The reader is referred to the original publication for details.

APPENDIX

A.1 MATRIX ALGEBRA

A matrix is a rectangular array of numbers. The following are matrices:

$$A = \begin{pmatrix} 1 & 2 & 1 & 5 \\ 3 & 1 & 0 & 2 \end{pmatrix}$$

$$B = \begin{pmatrix} 1 & 3 \\ 2 & 7 \\ 5 & 0 \\ 1 & 1 \end{pmatrix}$$

$$C = \begin{pmatrix} 1 & 1 & 1 \\ 3 & 2 & 1 \\ 1 & 2 & 1 \end{pmatrix}$$

A matrix comprising r rows and c columns is called an (r x c) matrix. Thus A, B and C are (2 x 4), (4 x 2) and (3 x 3) matrices respectively. The element in the i th row and the j th column of a matrix, A, is usually designated a_{ij}. Thus in A above, $a_{24} = 2$.

Just as there are rules for adding, subtracting, multiplying and dividing real numbers, there are rules for performing the equivalent operations on matrices. In order to add two matrices, each element in a given position in the second is added to the element in the corresponding position in the first. Thus, for example,

$$\begin{pmatrix} 1 & 2 & 1 & 5 \\ 3 & 1 & 0 & 2 \end{pmatrix} + \begin{pmatrix} 1 & 8 & 2 & 7 \\ 3 & 0 & 4 & 2 \end{pmatrix} = \begin{pmatrix} 2 & 10 & 3 & 12 \\ 6 & 1 & 4 & 4 \end{pmatrix}$$

Only matrices of similar size can be added.

In order to subtract two matrices, each element in a given position in the second is subtracted from the corresponding element in the first. Only matrices of similar size can be subtracted.

In order to multiply two matrices, the number of rows in the second must equal the number of columns in the first. A number of calculations are performed focussing on each occasion on a particular row in the first matrix and, simultaneously, on a particular column in the second. Specifically, the first, second, third ... elements in the row of the first matrix upon which attention is being focussed (say i) are multiplied respectively by the first, second, third ... elements in the column of the second matrix upon which attention is being focussed (say j). The resultant products are summed and the result placed in position (i,j) of the resultant matrix. Specifically, for A and B above, consider the task of multiplying them to yield D i.e.

$$\begin{pmatrix} 1 & 2 & 1 & 5 \\ 3 & 1 & 0 & 2 \end{pmatrix} \begin{pmatrix} 1 & 3 \\ 2 & 7 \\ 5 & 0 \\ 1 & 1 \end{pmatrix} = D$$

This multiplication is possible because the number of columns in A equals the number of rows in B. Focussing attention initially on row one of A and column one of B, the relevant sum of products is:

$$d_{11} = (1)(1) + (2)(2) + (1)(5) + (5)(1) = 15$$

This product, d_{11}, is written in position (1,1) of the resultant matrix D. Matrix multiplication involves performing the calculations described above for all possible combinations of rows in the first matrix and columns in the second. In the case of AB, this yields additionally:

$$d_{12} = (1)(3) + (2)(7) + (1)(0) + (5)(1) = 22$$
$$d_{21} = (3)(1) + (1)(2) + (0)(5) + (2)(1) = 7$$
$$d_{22} = (3)(3) + (1)(7) + (0)(0) + (2)(1) = 18$$

Appendix

i.e. $D = \begin{pmatrix} 15 & 22 \\ 7 & 18 \end{pmatrix}$

Note that, in general, multiplication of an $(r_1 \times c_1)$ matrix by an $(r_2 \times c_2)$ matrix where $c_1 = r_2$ yields a matrix of dimension $(r_1 \times c_2)$.

It is not possible to divide two matrices. In the case of a square matrix, however, an equivalent operation is to find the inverse of the matrix. The *inverse of a matrix* A, generally written A^{-1}, is that matrix which when multiplied by A yields a matrix with values of one along the diagonal running from the top left hand corner to the bottom right hand corner of the matrix and zeros elsewhere. This latter matrix is called the *identity matrix*. In the case of C above, its inverse is:

$$C^{-1} = \begin{pmatrix} -4 & 3/2 & 1/2 \\ -1 & 0 & 1 \\ 2 & -1/2 & -1/2 \end{pmatrix}$$

because:

$$\begin{pmatrix} -4 & 3/2 & 1/2 \\ -1 & 0 & 1 \\ 2 & -1/2 & -1/2 \end{pmatrix} \begin{pmatrix} 1 & 1 & 1 \\ 3 & 2 & 1 \\ 1 & 2 & 1 \end{pmatrix} = \begin{pmatrix} 1 & 0 & 0 \\ 0 & 1 & 0 \\ 0 & 0 & 1 \end{pmatrix}$$

A discussion of how the inverse of a matrix can be calculated falls beyond the scope of this summary.

A.2 CALCULUS

We summarise here some basic ideas from Calculus which are required to aid a full understanding of the material in Chapter Eight. The reader is cautioned that the presentation represents no more than a summary of the main ideas and that some of the definitions given are not those which would be given in a rigorous mathematical treatment. The reader requiring further details should consult a basic text e.g. Wilson and Kirkby (1975).

A notion underlying much of Calculus is that of a *function* which can be defined loosely as a mathematical rule which states the value a quantity $f(X) = f(X_1, \ldots, X_n)$ takes for given values of $X_1, \ldots, X_n$. The following are examples of functions:

Appendix

$$f_1(X) = f(X_1) \qquad = -4 + 6X_1 - X_1^2 \qquad\qquad ----(A.1)$$

$$f_2(X) = f(X_1,X_2) \quad = X_1^2 + X_2^2 \qquad\qquad ----(A.2)$$

$$f_3(X) = f(X_1,X_2,X_3) = X_1^3 + 2X_2^3 - 3X_3^3 + 4X_1 X_2 - 4X_2 X_3 ---(A.3)$$

(The subscript i in $f_i(X)$ has been introduced to distinguish (A.1)-(A.3) in the discussion which follows.) The function $f_1(X)$ concerns one variable, X_1. For any given value of X_1, the expression (A.1) states the value which $f_1(X)$ will take e.g. for $X_1 = 6$:

$$f_1(X) = f(X_1) = -4 + 6 (6) - (36) = -4$$

The functions (A.2) and (A.3) concern two and three variables respectively. Once again, the values they would take for given values of X_1, X_2 and in the case of $f_3(X)$, X_3 can be duly determined. The function $f_3(X)$ is more complex than the other two, not only because it contains more variables and terms but also because these terms contain cubes in some X_i's. The functions $f_1(X)$ and $f_2(X)$ are said to be *quadratic functions* as the most complex terms they contain involve squares of the original variables; $f_3(X)$ is a *cubic function*. A *linear function* is one containing the original variables multiplied by constants only.

It is often convenient to represent a function graphically with f(X) plotted on the vertical axis. Figure A.1 shows such a representation for $f_1(X)$ and $f_2(X)$; from these graphs, the value taken by the function for given values of X_1 in the case of $f_1(X)$ and for given values of X_1 and X_2 in the case of $f_2(X)$, can be read off. A graphical representation such as that in Figure A.1 would not be possible for $f_3(X)$ as four axes would be required.

A point of interest concerning a function is the slope it possesses at given points on its surface. In the case of a function involving one variable e.g. (A.1) a general expression for its slope at some point can be found by determining what is known as its *derivative* or, more correctly, its *first derivative* with respect to that variable. Rules exist for finding the derivatives of functions of different mathematical forms and we assume that the reader is familiar with some of these. In the case of (A.1) and denoting the first derivative as $df(X_1)$, we have:
$$\overline{dX_1}$$

$$\frac{df(X_1)}{dX_1} = + 6 - 2X_1 \qquad\qquad ----(A.4)$$

Thus the slope of $f(X_1)$ at (say) $X_1 = 2$ is + 2. This latter

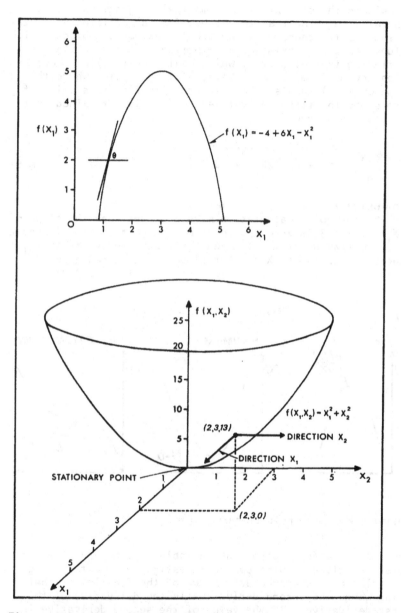

Figure A.1 Graphs of Functions

value is, in fact, the tangent of the angle θ as depicted in Figure A.1.

Within the context of mathematical programming, it is generally required that the values for (a) decision variables be found which cause a mathematically expressed objective i.e. a function to be maximised or minimised. Consider the task of finding the value of X_1 which maximises $f(X_1)$. By definition the maximum, if it exists, will be a point where the slope of $f(X_1)$ equals zero. In order to find this point of zero slope the first derivative of $f(X_1)$ is determined, set to zero and solved for X_1 i.e.

$$\frac{df(X_1)}{dX_1} = + 6 - 2X_1 \overset{SET}{=} 0 \qquad\qquad ----(A.5)$$

from which $X_1 = 3$.

The foregoing calculation merely proves that the slope of $f(X_1)$ at $X_1 = 3$ is zero and therefore that it is what is known as a *stationary point*. It does not however prove that $f(X_1)$ reaches a maximum at $X_1 = 3$ for slopes of zero can also indicate a minimum or an inflection point (Figure A.2). In

(a)   **(b)**   **(c)**

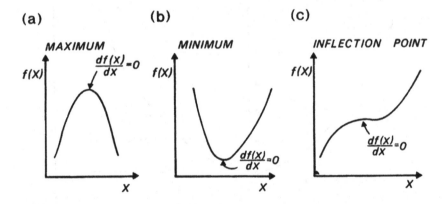

Figure A.2 Types of Stationary Point

the case of a function of one variable, the nature of a particular stationary point can be investigated by determining the value of the *second derivative* of the function at that point where the second derivative is the derivative of the first derivative. If the value of the second derivative is negative, the stationary point is a maximum; if the value of the second derivative is positive, the stationary point is a minimum; if the value of the second derivative is zero, further analysis is required to check whether the stationary point is a maximum, a minimum or an inflection point. The reader is referred to a specialised text for details. Returning to the example, and denoting the second derivative of $f(X_1)$ with respect to X_1 as:

$$\frac{d^2f(X_1)}{dX_1^2}, \text{ we have:}$$

$$\frac{d^2f(X_1)}{dX_1^2} = -2$$

which, because it is negative, proves that $f(X_1)$ reaches a maximum at $X_1 = 3$. The actual value attained at this maximum can be determined by substitution in the original expression (A.1) which yields:

$$f(X_1) = -4 + 18 - 9 = 5.$$

The foregoing methods for determining the maximum/minimum of a single variable function can be adapted relatively easily to deal with a function involving more than one variable. We define the *partial derivative of a function* with respect to some variable X_i which is written:

$$\frac{\delta f_{(X)}}{\delta X_i} = \frac{\delta f(X_1, \ldots, X_n)}{\delta X_i}$$

as the derivative of $f(X_1, \ldots, X_n)$ with respect to X_i treating all of the other variables as constants. Thus, in the case of (A.2) we have:

$$\frac{\delta f(X_1, X_2)}{\delta X_1} = 2X_1$$

$$\frac{\delta f(X_1, X_2)}{\delta X_2} = 2X_2$$

Geometrically, the partial derivatives give a general expression for the slope of the function concerned in the direction corresponding to the variable in the denominator of the partial derivative. Thus, in the case of $f(X_1, X_2)$, the slope of the surface illustrated in Figure A.1 at some point (X_1, X_2) is $2X_1$ in the direction X_1 and $2X_2$ in the direction X_2. Specifically, at the point $X_1 = 2$ and $X_2 = 3$, the slope of the surface in the directions X_1 and X_2 is +4 and +6 respectively. These values are in fact the tangents of the relevant angles.)

Continuing to apply the logic underlying the methods described for functions of one variable, we are generally interested within the context of mathematical programming in identifying (a) stationary point(s) which, in this case, will be points in which the slope of the function concerned is simultaneously zero in all directions. We thus seek values for X_1, X_2, ... which simultaneously cause $\dfrac{\delta f(X)}{\delta X_1}$, $\dfrac{\delta f(X)}{\delta X_2}$, ...

to equal zero. Specifically, in the case of the two variable function (A.2) we seek values for X_1 and X_2 such that:

$$\frac{\delta f(X_1, X_2)}{\delta X_1} \overset{\text{SET}}{=} 2X_1 = 0$$

$$\frac{\delta f(X_1, X_2)}{\delta X_2} \overset{\text{SET}}{=} 2X_2 = 0$$

which yields $X_1 = X_2 = 0$. That this is in fact a stationary point can be checked by inspection of Figure A.1. The mathematical method by which the nature of this point (maximum, minimum, inflection) can be investigated once more involves calculating second order derivatives. The precise details fall beyond the scope of this summary.

Before leaving the problem of determining the location and nature of stationary points, it is worth recalling that the functions (A.1) and (A.2) are quadratics. Geometrically, such functions possess a single stationary point. This is confirmed mathematically by the fact that the n partial derivatives of a quadratic function $f(X_1, \ldots, X_n)$ yield, when set to zero, n linear expressions in $X_1, \ldots, X_n$ which can be solved to yield the coordinates of a single point whose nature can then be checked. Consider now a more complex function e.g. a cubic function as in (A.3). Geometrically, such functions generally possess a number of stationary points. In the case of a function with a number of maxima, minima and inflection points (Figure A.3), the stationary points associated with the greatest and least values of $f(X)$ are known as the *global maximum* and *global minimum* respectively; the other stationary points are referred to as *local maxima*, *local minima* and inflection points as appropriate. Mathematically, the existence of a number of stationary points is confirmed by the fact that the relevant partial derivatives of a non-quadratic function when set to zero, are not linear and do not generally possess a single unique solution. Thus, taking (A.3) as an example:

Appendix

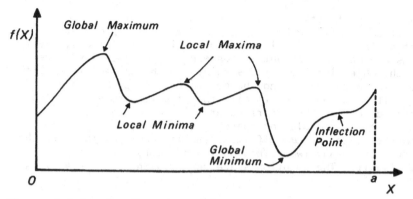

Figure A.3 Complex Function With Seven Stationary Points
NOTE: f(X) exists within the interval $0 \leq X \leq a$ only.

$$\frac{\delta f(X_1, X_2, X_3)}{\delta X_1} = 3X_1{}^2 + 4X_2 \overset{SET}{=} 0$$

$$\frac{\delta f(X_1, X_2, X_3)}{\delta X_2} = 6X_2{}^2 + 4X_1 - 4X_3 \overset{SET}{=} 0 \qquad ----(A.6)$$

$$\frac{\delta f(X_1, X_2, X_3)}{\delta X_3} = -9X_3 - 4X_3 \overset{SET}{=} 0$$

Because they contain quadratic terms, the equations (A.6) cannot be solved to yield a single unique set of values for X_1, X_2, X_3; rather there is more than one possible solution i.e. stationary points. Given the form of (A.6), these would be difficult to identify.

In dealing with nonlinear functions in the context of actual applications, the general shape of a nonlinear object-ive or constraint e.g. that it rises to a single maximum is often known in advance. This usually simplifies the mathe-matical calculations as it obviates the need to test the nature of (a) stationary point(s) explicitly. The shape of a function is usually expressed in the following terms. A function such as that depicted in Figure A.2 (a) is said to be *strictly concave* because if any two points on the function are chosen, the straight line joining those two points will always fall below the function. A *strictly convex* function (e.g. Figure A.2 (b)) is one where the straight line joining any two points on the function will always fall above the function.

If the function is such that for (a) certain choice(s) of
point pairs, the straight line joining these points actually
touches the function at some intermediate point(s), the
function is said to be *concave* or *convex* as appropriate. Very
often, in specific nonlinear programming formulations, assumptions are made at the outset concerning the concavity/convexity
of the objective and/or constraints which can facilitate both
locating and identifying the nature of the optimal solution.

It is to be noted finally that the term convex is also
applied to describe a particular solution space shape.
Specifically, a solution space is said to be *convex* or to
comprise a *convex hull* if its shape is such that the straight
line joining any two points on its boundary does not pass
outside it. The solution space depicted in Figure A.4(a) is

(a)   (b)

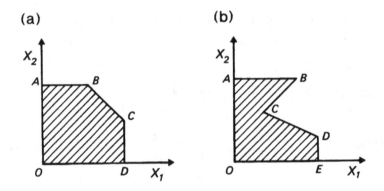

Figure A.4 Two Hypothetical Solution Spaces

convex whereas that in Figure A.4(b) is not.

REFERENCES

*ABLER, R., ADAMS, J.S. and GOULD, P., (1971), *Spatial Organisation : The Geographer's View of the World*, Prentice Hall, Englewood Cliffs.

ANDERSON, M.G., (1971), A Computer Based Model for Nuclear Power Station Site Selection, *Area*, 3, 35-41.

BACON, R.W., (1971), An Approach to the Theory of Consumer Shopping Behaviour, *Urban Studies*, 8, 55-64.

BAMMI, D. and BAMMI, D., (1975), Land Use Planning : An Optimizing Model, *Omega*, 3, 583-94.

BARBER, G.M., (1975), A Mathematical Programming Approach to a Network Development Problem, *Economic Geography*, 51, 128-41.

BARBER, G.M., (1977a), Sequencing Highway Network Improvements: A Case Study of South Sulawesi, *Economic Geography*, 53, 55-69.

BARBER, G.M., (1977b), Urban Population Distribution Planning, *Annals of the Association of American Geographers*, 67, 239-45.

BARITELLE, J.L. and HOLLAND, D.W., (1975), Optimum Plant Size and Location : A Case for Separable Programming, *Agricultural Economics Research*, 27, 73-84.

BARR, B. and SMILLIE, K., (1972), Some Spatial Interpretations of Alternative Optimal and Suboptimal Solutions to the Transportation Problem, *Canadian Geographer*, 16, 356-64.

* - General reference ; not cited in text.

337

References

BATTY, M., (1971), Exploratory Calibration of a Retail Location Model Using Search By Golden Section, *Environment and Planning*, 3, 411-32.

BAXTER, R.S., (1976), *Computer and Statistical Techniques for Planners*, Methuen London.

BAXTER, R. and WILLIAMS, I., (1975), An Automatically Calibrated Urban Model, *Environment and Planning A*, 7, 3-20.

BEAUMONT, J.R., (1979), Some Issues in the Application of Mathematical Programming in Human Geography, *Working Paper*, 256, School of Geography, University of Leeds.

BEIGHTLER, C.S. and PHILLIPS, D.J. (Ed.), (1976), *Applied Geometric Programming*, Wiley, New York.

BELLMAN, R.E., (1957), *Dynamic Programming*, Princeton, New Jersey.

*BELLMAN, R.E., COOKE, K.L. and LOCKETT, J.A., (1970), *Algorithms Graphs and Computers*, Academic Press, New York.

BELLMAN, R.E. and DREYFUS, S.E., (1962), *Applied Dynamic Programming*, Princeton University Press, Princeton, New Jersey.

BEN-SHAHAR, H., MAZOR, A. and PINES, D., (1969), Town Planning and Welfare Maximisation : A Methodological Approach, *Regional Studies*, 3, 105-13.

BOYCE, D.E., FARHI, A. and WEISCHEDEL, R., (1973), Optimal Network Problem : A Branch and Bound Algorithm, *Environment and Planning*, 5, 519-33.

BOYE, Y., (1965), Routing Methods : Principles for Handling Multiple Travelling Salesman Problems, *Lund Studies in Geography, Series C*, 5, Gleerup, Lund.

BRUTON, M.J., (1975), *Introduction to Urban Transportation Planning*, Hutchinson, London.

BURT, O.R. and ALLISON, J.R., (1963), Farm Management Decisions With Dynamic Programming, *Journal of Farm Economics*, 45, 121-36.

BUTCHER, W.S., HAIMES, Y.Y. and HALL, W.A., (1969), Dynamic Programming for the Optimal Sequencing of Water Supply Projects, *Water Resources Research*, 5, 1196-1204.

* - General reference ; not cited in text.

References

CASETTI, E., (1966), Optimal Location of Steel Mills Serving the Quebec and Southern Ontario Steel Market, *Canadian Geographer*, *10*, 27-39.

CASTRO LOPO, N., DE, (1967), An Analysis of Internal Migration in Bihar, North India, *Geografisk Tijdschrift*, *66*, 1-23.

CATANESE, A.J., (1972), *Scientific Methods of Urban Analysis*, Leonard Hill Books, Aylesbury, England.

CHADWICK, G., (1971), *A Systems View of Planning*, Pergamon Press, Oxford, Chapter 10.

CHARNES, A. and COOPER, W.W, (1961), *Management Models and Industrial Applications of Linear Programming*, Wiley, New York.

CHARNES, A., HAYNES, K.E., HAZLETON, J.E. and RYAN, M.J., (1975), A Hierarchical Goal-Programming Approach to Environmental Land Use Management, *Geographical Analysis*, *7*, 121-30.

CHEUNG, H.K. and AUGER, J.A., (1976), Linear Programming and Land Use Allocation : Suboptimal Solutions and Policy, *Socio-Economic Planning Sciences*, *10*, 43-5.

CHURCH, R.L. and MEADOWS, M.E., (1977), Results of a New Approach to Solving the p-Median Problem With Maximum Distance Constraints, *Geographical Analysis*, *9*, 364-78.

CHURCH, R. and REVELLE, C., (1974), The Maximal Covering Location Problem, *Papers of the Regional Science Association*, *32*, 101-18.

COHON, J.L. and MARKS, D.H., (1975), A Review and Evaluation of Multiobjective Programming Techniques, *Water Resources Research*, *11*, 208-20.

CONNOLLY, J., (1974), Linear Programming And The Optimal Capacity of Range Under Common Use, *Journal of Agricultural Science-Cambridge*, *83*, 259-65.

*CONVERSE, A.O., (1970), *Optimization*, Holt, Rinehart and Winston, New York.

COOPER, L. (1968), An Extension of the Generalised Weber Problem, *Journal of Regional Science*, *8*, 181-97.

---

* - General reference ; not cited in text.

References

COOPER, L. and STEINBERG, D., (1970) *Introduction To Methods of Optimisation*, Saunders, Philadelphia.

*COOPER, L. and STEINBERG, D., (1974), *Methods and Applications of Linear Programming*, Saunders, Philadelphia.

COURTNEY, J.F. Jr., KLASTORIN, T.D. and RUEFLI, T.W., (1972), A Goal Programming Approach To Urban-Suburban Location Preferences, *Management Science*, *18*, B258-68.

COX, K.R., (1965), The Application of Linear Programming to Geographic Problems, *Tijdschrift Voor Economische en Sociale Geografie*, *56*, 228-36.

DAELLENBACH, H.G. and BELL, E.J., (1970), *User's Guide To Linear Programming*, Prentice Hall, Englewood Cliffs.

DANE, C.W., MEADOR, N.C. and WHITE, J.B., (1977), Goal Programming in Land-Use Planning, *Journal of Forestry*, *75*, 325-9.

*DANTZIG, G.B., (1963), *Linear Programming and Extensions*, Princeton University Press, Princeton.

DAY, J.C., (1973), A Linear Programming Approach to Floodplain Land Use Planning in Urban Areas, *American Journal of Agricultural Economics*, *55*, 165-74.

DE CASTRO, S. and LAURITZ, J., (1967), Some Steps Towards An Optimal Foodstuffs Consumption, Production and Importation Programme for Trinidad and Tobago, *Social and Economic Studies*, *16*, 349-64.

DELFT, A. VAN and NIJKAMP, P., (1976), A Multi-objective Decision Model for Regional Development, Environmental Quality Control and Industrial Land Use, *Papers of the Regional Science Association*, *36*, 35-57.

DELFT, A. VAN and NIJKAMP, P., (1977a), Multi-criteria Analysis and Regional Decision Making, *Studies in Applied Regional Science*, *8*, Martinus Nijhoff, Leiden.

DELFT, A. VAN and NIJKAMP, P., (1977b), The Use of Hierarchical Optimization Criteria in Regional Planning, *Journal of Regional Science*, *17*, 195-205.

DICKEY, J.W. and AZOLA, M.P., (1972), An Adaptive Programming Technique For Sequencing Highway Improvements to Affect Land Use Growth, *Regional Studies*, *6*, 331-42.

---

* - General reference ; not cited in text

References

DINKEL, J.J., KOCHENBERGER, G.A. and SEPPALA, Y., (1973), On The Solution of Regional Planning Models Via Geometric Programming, *Environment and Planning*, 5, 397-408.

DOKMECI, V.F., (1973), An Optimization Model for a Hierarchical Spatial System, *Journal of Regional Science*, 13, 439-51.

*DORFMAN, R., SAMUELSON, P.A. and SOLOW, R.M., (1958), *Linear Programming and Economic Analysis*, McGraw-Hill, New York.

DUFFIN, R.J., PETERSON, E.L. and ZENER, C., (1967), *Geometric Programming*, Wiley, New York.

EVANS, A.W., (1972), A Linear Programming Solution to the Shopping Problem Posed By R.W. Bacon, *Urban Studies*, 9, 221-2.

EVANS, S.P., (1973), A Relationship Between the Gravity Model for Trip Distribution and the Transportation Problem of Linear Programming, *Transportation Research*, 7, 39-61.

FIELD, D.B., (1973), Goal Programming for Forest Management, *Forestry Science*, 19, 125-35.

FULKERSON, D.R., (1961), An Out-of-Kilter Method for Minimal Cost Flow Problems, *Journal of the Society for the Industrial Application of Mathematics*, 9, 18-27.

FUNK, M.L. and TILLMAN, F.A., (1968), A Dynamic Programming Approach to Optimal Construction Staging, *American Society of Civil Engineers Journal of the Highway Division*, 94, 255-65.

*GARFINKEL, R.S. and NEMHAUSER, G.L., (1972), *Integer Programming*, Wiley, New York.

*GARRISON, W.L., (1959), Spatial Structure of the Economy : II, *Annals Association American Geographers*, 49, 471-82.

*GARRISON, W.L., (1960), Spatial Structure of the Economy : III, *Annals Association American Geographers*, 50, 357-73.

GARRISON, W.L. and MARBLE, D.F., (1958), Analysis of Highway Networks : a Linear Programming Formulation, *Proceedings of the Highway Research Board*, 37, 1-17.

*GASS, S.I., (1969), *Linear Programming : Methods and Applications*, McGraw-Hill, New York.

---

* - General reference ; not cited in text

References

GAUTHIER, H.L., (1968), Least Cost Flows in a Capacitated Network : A Brazilian Example in : HORTON, F. (Ed.), Geographic Studies of Transportation and Network Analysis, *Northwestern University Studies in Geography*, 16, 102-27.

GILBERT, E.N., and POLLAK, H.O., (1968), Steiner Minimal Trees, *SIAM Journal on Applied Mathematics*, 16, 1-29.

GLICKMAN, T.S. and ALLISON, S.V., (1973), Investment Planning for Irrigation Development Projects, *Socio-Economic Planning Sciences*, 7, 113-22.

GOODCHILD, M.F., (1978), Spatial Choice in Location-Allocation Problems : The Role of Endogenous Attraction, *Geographical Analysis*, 10, 65-72.

GOODCHILD, M.F. and MASSAM, B.H., (1969), Some Least-Cost Models of Spatial Administrative Systmes in Southern Ontario, *Geografiska Annaler*, 52B, 86-94.

GORDON, P. and MAC REYNOLDS, W.K., (1974), Optimal Urban Forms, *Journal of Regional Science*, 14, 217-31.

GOULD, P.R., (1972), Pedagogic Review, *Annals of the Association of American Geographers*, 62, 689-700.

GOULD, P.R. and LEINBACH, T.R., (1966), An Approach to the Geographic Assignment of Hospital Services, *Tijdschrift voor Economische en Sociale Geografie*, 57, 203-6.

GOULD, P. and SPARKS, J.P., (1969), The Geographical Context of Human Diets in Southern Guatemala, *Geographical Review*, 59, 58-82.

GRANHOLM, A. and OHLSSON, O., (1975), A Note on Distribution Analysis in a Linear Programming Model, *Regional Science and Urban Economics*, 5, 483-91.

*GREENBERG, H., (1971), *Integer Programming*, Academic Press, New York.

GREENBERG, M.R., (1978), *Applied Linear Programming for the Socioeconomic and Environmental Sciences*, Academic Press, New York.

GRIFFITHS, T.W. and CONNIFFE, D., (1974/5), Aspects of Compound Animal Feed Formulation in the Republic of Ireland, 1972-3, *Irish Journal of Agricultural Economics and Rural Sociology*, 5, 131-44.

---

* - General reference ; not cited in text

References

GULDMANN, J-M. and SHEFER, D., (1977), Optimal Plant Location And Air Quality Management Under Indivisibilities and Economies of Scale, *Socio-Economic Planning Sciences, 11,* 77-93.

*HADLEY, G., (1962), *Linear Programming,* Addison-Wesley, Reading, Mass.

HAGGETT, P., CLIFF, A.D. and FREY, A., (1977), *Locational Analysis in Human Geography,* Arnold, Chapter 15.

HALL, W.A. and BURAS, N., (1961), The Dynamic Programming Approach to Water Resources Development, *Journal of Geophysical Research, 66,* 517-20.

HARVEY, M.E., HOCKING, R.T. and BROWN, J.R., (1974a), The Chromatic Travelling Salesman Problem and its Application to Planning and Structuring Geographic Space, *Geographical Analysis, 6,* 33-52.

HARVEY, M.E., HUNG, M-S. and BROWN, J.R., (1974b), The Application of a p-Median Algorithm to the Identification of Nodal Hierarchies and Growth Centres, *Economic Geography, 50,* 187-202.

HASHIM, S.R. and MATHUR, P.N., (1975), Interregional Programming Models For Economic Development in CRIPPS, E.L. (Ed.), *Regional Science - New Concepts and Old Problems,* London Papers in Regional Science, Pion, London, 109-25.

HASTINGS, N.A.J. (1973), *Dynamic Programming With Management Applications,* Butterworths, London.

HAY, A., (1977), *Linear Programming : Elementary Geographical Applications of the Transportation Problem,* Concepts and Techniques in Modern Geography Monograph No. 11, Geo Abstracts, Norwich.

HEADY, E.O. and EGBERT, A.C., (1962), Programming Models of Interdependence Among Agricultural Sectors and Spatial Allocation of Crop Production, *Journal of Regional Science, 4,* 1-20.

HENDERSON, J.M., (1958), *The Efficiency of the Coal Industry : an Application of Linear Programming,* Harvard University Press, Cambridge, Mass.

---

* - General reference ; not cited in text

References

HENDERSON, J.M., (1968), The Utilization of Agricultural
Land : An Empirical Inquiry in : SMITH, R.H.T., TAAFFE,
E.J. and KING, L.J. (Eds.), *Readings in Economic Geography*,
Rand McNally, Chicago, 281-6.

HERBERT, J.D. and STEVENS, B.H., (1960), A Model For The
Distribution of Residential Activity in Urban Areas,
Journal of Regional Science, 2, 21-36.

HEROUX, R.L. and WALLACE, W.A., (1975), New Community Development With The Aid of Linear Programming, in : SALKIN, H.
and SAHA, J. (Eds.), *Studies in Linear Programming*, North
Holland, Amsterdam, 309-22.

HODGART, R.L., (1978), Optimizing Access to Public Services :
a Review of Problems, Models and Methods of Locating
Central Facilities, *Progress in Human Geography*, 2, 17-48.

HODGSON, M.J., (1978), Toward a More Realistic Allocation in
Location-Allocation Problems : An Interaction Approach,
Environment and Planning A, 10, 1273-85.

HOLMES, J., WILLIAMS, F.B. and BROWN, L.A., (1973), Facility
Location Under A Maximum Travel Restriction : An Example
Using Day Care Facilities, *Geographical Analysis*, 4, 258-66.

HOPKINS, L.D., (1977), Land-Use Plan Design - Quadratic Assignment and Central Facility Models, *Environment and Plan-
Planning A*, 9, 625-42.

HOPKINS, L.D., (1979), Quadratic Versus Linear Models For
Land-Use Plan Design, *Environment and Planning A*, 11, 291-8.

HORNER, A., (1980), Population Distribution and the Location
of Airports in Ireland, *Proceedings of the Royal Irish
Academy*, 80C, 159-85.

HORNER, A. and TAYLOR, A-M., (1979), Grasping the Nettle -
Locational Strategies for Irish Hospitals, *Administration*,
27, 348-70.

HORTON, F.E. and WITTICK, R.I., (1969), A Spatial Model for
Examining the Journey to Work in a Planning Context,
Professional Geographer, 21, 223-6.

ISARD, W., (1958), Interregional Linear Programming : An
Elementary Presentation and a General Model, *Journal of
Regional Science*, 1, 1-59.

References

*ISARD, W., (1960), *Methods of Regional Analysis : an Introduction to Regional Science*, Massachusetts Institute of Technology Press, Cambridge, Mass.

ITTIG, P.T., (1978), An Optimization Model for Planning Community Health Services, *Socio-Economic Planning Sciences*, 12, 221-8.

JACOBS, O.L.R., (1967), *An Introduction to Dynamic Programming*, Chapman and Hall, London.

JENKINS, P.M. and ROBSON, A., (1974), An Application of Linear Programming Methodology For Regional Strategy Making, *Regional Studies*, 8, 267-79.

JOHNSEN, E., (1968), *Studies in Multiobjective Decision Models*, Studentlitteratur, Lund.

KAUFMANN, A. and KRUON, R., (1967), *Dynamic Programming - Sequential Scientific Management*, Academic Press, New York.

KEARNEY, B., (1971), Linear Programming and Pig Feed Formulation, *Irish Journal of Agricultural Economics and Rural Sociology*, 3, 145-55.

KHUMAWALA, B.M., (1973), An Efficient Algorithm for the p-Median Problem With Maximum Distance Constraints, *Geographical Analysis*, 5, 309-21.

KHUMAWALA, B.M., (1975), Algorithm for the p-Median Problem With Maximum Distance Constraints : Extension and Reply, *Geographical Analysis*, 7, 91-5.

*KILLEN, J.E., (1979), *Linear Programming : The Simplex Method With Geographical Applications*, Concepts and Techniques in Modern Geography Monograph Series Number 24, Geo Abstracts, Norwich.

KING, L.J., (1972), Models of Urban Land-Use Development in: SWEET, D.C. (Ed.), *Models of Urban Structure*, Lexington Books, Lexington, 3-26.

KING, L., CASETTI, E., ODLAND, J., and SEMPLE, K., (1971), Optimal Transportation Patterns of Coal in the Great Lakes Region, *Economic Geography*, 47, 401-13.

*KOLMAN, B. and BECK, R.E., (1980), *Elementary Linear Programming With Applications*, Academic Press, New York.

---

* - General reference ; not cited in text

References

KOOPMANS, T.C. and BECKMANN, M., (1957), Assignment Problems and the Location of Economic Activities, *Econometrica, 25,* 53-76.

KORNBLUTH, J., (1973), A Survey of Goal Programming, *Omega, 1,* 193-205.

KUENNE, R.E. and SOLAND, R.M., (1972), Exact and Approximate Solutions To The Multisource Weber Problem, *Mathematical Programming, 3,* 193-209.

KUHN, H.W. and KUENNE, R.E., (1962), An Efficient Algorithm for the Numerical Solution of the Generalised Weber Problem in Spatial Economics, *Journal of Regional Science, 4,* 21-33.

*KWAK, N.K., (1973), *Mathematical Programming With Business Applications,* McGraw-Hill, New York.

KWAK, N.K. and SCHNIEDERJANS, M.J., (1979), A Goal Programming Model for Improved Transportation Problem Solutions, *Omega, 7,* 367-70.

LAIDLAW, C.D., (1972), *Linear Programming for Urban Development Plan Evaluation,* Praeger Publishers, New York.

LAND, A.H., (1957), An Application of Linear Programming to the Transport of Coking Coal, *Journal of the Royal Statistical Society Series A, 120,* 308-19.

LEE, S.M., (1972), *Goal Programming for Decision Analysis,* Auberach, Philadelphia.

*LEINBACH, T.R., (1976), Networks and Flows, *Progress in Geography, 8,* 180-207.

LEONARDI, G., (1981a), A Unifying Framework for Public Facility Location Problems - part 1 : A Critical Overview and Some Unsolved Problems, *Environment and Planning A, 13,* 1001-28.

LEONARDI, G., (1981b), A Unifying Framework for Public Facility Location Problems - Part 2 : Some New Models and Extensions, *Environment and Planning A, 13,* 1085-1108.

LOUWES, S.L., BOOT, J.C.G. and WAGE, S., (1963), A Quadratic Programming Approach to the Problem of the Optimal Use of Milk in the Netherlands, *Journal of Farm Economics, 45,* 309-17.

---

* - General reference ; not cited in text

346

References

LOW, E.M. and BROOKHOUSE, J.K., (1967), Dynamic Programming
and The Selection of Replacement Policies in Commercial Egg
Production, *Journal of Agricultural Economics*, *18*, 339-50.

MCGREW, J.C. Jr., (1975), Goal Programming and Complex
Problem-Solving in Geography, *Papers in Geography*, *12*,
Pennsylvania State University, University Park, Pennsylvan-
ia.

MACKINNON, R.D., (1970), Dynamic Programming and Geographical
Systems, *Economic Geography*, *46(2) Supplement*, 350-66.

MACKINNON, R.D. and BARBER, G.M., (1977), Optimisation Models
of Transportation Network Improvement, *Progress in Human
Geography*, *1*, 387-412.

MACKINNON, R.D. and HODGSON, M.J., (1970), Optimal Transportation Networks : a Case Study of Highway Systems, *Environment and Planning*, *2*, 267-84.

*MACMILLAN, C., (1975), *Mathematical Programming*, Wiley, New
York.

MANDELL, P.I. and TWEETEN, L.G., (1971), The Location of
Cotton Production in the United States Under Competitive
Conditions : A Study of Crop Location and Comparative
Advantage, *Geographical Analysis*, *3*, 334-53.

MASSAM, B.H., (1972), *The Spatial Structure of Administrative
Systems*, Commission on College Geography Resource Paper No.
12, Association of American Geographers, Washington D.C.

MAXFIELD, D.W., (1969), An Interpretation of the Primal and
Dual Solutions of Linear Programming, *Professional Geographer*, *21*, 255-63.

MAXFIELD, D.W., (1972), Spatial Planning of School Districts,
Annals of The Association of American Geographers, *62*, 582-90

MEIER, R.C., (1968), Programming of Recreational Land
Acquisition, *Socio-Economic Planning Sciences*, *2*, 15-24.

MILLER, R.E., (1963), Alternative Optima, Degeneracy and
Imputed Values in Linear Programs, *Journal of Regional
Science*, *5*, 21-39.

MILLER, R.E., (1979), *Dynamic Optimization and Economic
Applications*, McGraw-Hill, New York.

---

* - General reference ; not cited in text

References

MINIEKA, E., (1978), *Optimization Algorithms for Networks and Graphs*, Marcel Dekker, New York.

MORIN, T.L. and ESGOBUE, A.M.O., (1971), Some Efficient Dynamic Programming Algorithms for the Optimal Sequencing and Scheduling of Water Supply Projects, *Water Resources Research*, 7, 479-84.

MORRILL, R.L., (1973), Ideal and Reality in Reapportionment, *Annals of the Association of American Geographers*, 63, 463-77.

*MORRILL, R.L. and SYMONS, J., (1977), Efficiency and Equity Aspects of Optimum Location, *Geographical Analysis*, 9, 215-25.

NARULA, S.C. and OGBU, U.I., (1979), An Hierarchical Location-Allocation Problem, *Omega*, 7, 137-43.

NEMHAUSER, G.L., (1966), *Introduction to Dynamic Programming*, Wiley, New York.

NEMHAUSER, G.L., (1969), Scheduling Local and Express Service, *Transportation Science*, 3, 164-75.

NIJKAMP, P., (1975), A Multicriteria Analysis for Project Evaluation : Economic-Ecological Evaluation of a Land Reclamation Project, *Papers of the Regional Science Association*, 35, 87-111.

OCHS, J., (1969), An Application of Linear Programming to Urban Spatial Organisation, *Journal of Regional Science*, 9, 451-7.

OSAYIMWESE, I., (1974), An Application of Linear Programming to the Evacuation of Groundnuts in Nigeria, *Journal of Transport Economics and Policy*, 8, 58-69.

OSLEEB, J.P. and SHESKIN, I.M., (1977), Natural Gas : A Geographical Perspective, *Geographical Review*, 67, 71-85.

OSTRESH, L.M., (1975), An Efficient Algorithm for Solving the Two Center Location-Allocation Problem, *Journal of Regional Science*, 15, 209-16.

OSTRESH, L.M., (1977), The Multifacility Location Problem : Applications and Descent Theorems, *Journal of Regional Science*, 17, 409-19.

---

* - General Reference ; not cited in text

References

OSTRESH, L.M., (1978), The Stepwise Location-Allocation Problem : Exact Solutions in Continuous and Discrete Spaces, *Geographical Analysis, 10,* 174-85.

O'SULLIVAN, P., (1972), Linear Programming as a Forecasting Device For Interregional Freight Flows in Great Britain, *Regional and Urban Economics, 1,* 383-96.

O'SULLIVAN, P., (1975), Modelling The Distribution of Interregional Freight Traffic In Great Britain, in : SALKIN, H. and SAHA. J. (Eds.), *Studies in Linear Programming,* North Holland, Amsterdam, 293-307.

*O'SULLIVAN, P., HOLTZCLAW, G.D., and BARBER, G., (1979), *Transport Network Planning,* Croom Helm, London.

*PANNE, C. VAN DE., (1971), *Linear Programming and Related Techniques,* North Holland, Amsterdam.

PEARL, L., (1974), A Land Use Design Model, *Urban Studies, 11,* 315-21.

*PLANE. D.R. and MCMILLAN, C., (1971), *Discrete Optimization: Integer Programming and Network Analysis For Management Decisions,* Prentice Hall, Englewood Cliffs, New Jersey.

PUTERBAUGH, H.L., KEHRBERG, E.W. and DUNBAR, J.O., (1957), Analyzing The Solution Tableau of a Simplex Linear Programming Problem in Farm Organization, *Journal of Farm Economics, 39,* 478-89.

QUANDT, R.E., (1960), Models of Transportation and Optimal Network Construction, *Journal of Regional Science, 2,* 27-45.

RAE, A.N., (1970), Profit Maximisation and Imperfect Competition - An Application of Quadratic Programming to Horticulture, *Journal of Agricultural Economics, 45,* 309-17.

REIF, B., (1973), *Models in Urban and Regional Planning,* Leonard Hill Books, Aylesbury, Chapters 10, 14.

REVELLE, C.S. and SWAIN, R.W., (1970), Central Facilities Location, *Geographical Analysis, 2,* 30-42.

REVELLE, C., TOREGAS, C., and FALKSON, L., (1976), Applications of The Location Set Covering Problem, *Geographical Analysis, 8,* 65-76.

---

* - General Reference ; not cited in text.

References

RIDLEY, T.M., (1968), An Investment Policy to Reduce The Travel Time in a Transportation Network, *Transportation Research*, 2, 409-24.

RIDLEY, T.M., (1969), Reducing the Travel Time in a Transport Network, in SCOTT, A.J. (Ed.), *Studies in Regional Science*, London Papers in Regional Science, Pion, London, 73-87.

RIMMER, P.J., (1968), The Transportation Method of Linear Programming With a New Zealand Example, *New Zealand Geographer*, 24, 90-9.

ROBERTSON, I.M.L., (1974a), Scottish Population Distribution: Implications for Locational Decisions, *Transactions of the Institute of British Geographers*, 63, 111-24.

ROBERTSON, I.M.L., (1974b), Road Networks and the Location of Facilities, *Environment and Planning A*, 6, 199-206.

ROBERTSON, I.M.L., (1976), Accessibility to Services in the Argyll District of Strathclyde : a Locational Model, *Regional Studies*, 10, 89-95.

ROBERTSON, I.M.L., (1978), Planning the Location of Recreation Centres in an Urban Area : A Case Study of Glasgow, *Regional Studies*, 12, 419-27.

ROJESKI, P. and REVELLE, C., (1970), Central Facilities Location Under An Investment Constraint, *Geographical Analysis*, 2, 343-60.

SALKIN, H.M., (1975), *Integer Programming*, Addison-Wesley, Reading, Mass.

SALKIN, H.M. and BALINSKY, W.L., (1973), Integer Programming Models and Codes in the Urban Environment, *Socio-Economic Planning Sciences*, 7, 739-53.

SALZBORN, F.J.M., (1969), Timetables for a Suburban Rail Transit System, *Transportation Science*, 3, 297-316.

SCARLETT, M.J., (1971), Dynamic Programming and the Solution of a Problem in Urban Transportation, *Canadian Geographer*, 15, 1-12.

SCHLAGER, K.J., (1965), A Land-Use Plan Design Model, *Journal of the American Institute of Planners*, 31, 103-11.

---

* - General Reference ; not cited in text

References

SCHULER, A.T. and MEADOWS, J.C., (1975), Planning Resource Use On National Forests to Achieve Multiple Objectives, *Journal of Environmental Management*, 3, 351-66.

SCHULER, A.T, WEBSTER, H.H. and MEADOWS, J.C., (1977), Goal Programming in Forest Management, *Journal of Forestry*, 75, 320-4.

SCOTT, A.J., (1969a), The Optimal Network Problem : Some Computational Procedures, *Transportation Research*, 3, 201-10.

SCOTT, A.J., (1969b), Combinatorial Programming and the Planning of Urban and Regional Systems, *Environment and Planning*, 1, 125-42.

SCOTT, A.J., (1969c), On the Optimal Partitioning of Spatially Distributed Point Sets, in SCOTT, A.J. (Ed.), *Studies in Regional Science*, London Papers in Regional Science, Pion, London, 57-72.

SCOTT, A.J., (1970), Location-Allocation Systems : A Review, *Geographical Analysis*, 2, 95-119.

SCOTT, A.J., (1971a), *Combinatorial Programming, Spatial Analysis and Planning*, Methuen, London.

*SCOTT, A.J., (1971b), *An Introduction to Spatial Allocation Analysis*, Commission on College Geography Resource Paper Number 9, Association of American Geographers, Washington D.C.

SENIOR, M.L. and WILSON, A.G., (1974), Explorations and Syntheses of Linear Programming and Spatial Interaction Models of Residential Location, *Geographical Analysis*, 6, 209-38.

SHAW, J.R., (1970), The Location of Maincrop Potato Production in Britain - An Application of Linear Programming, *Journal of Agricultural Economics*, 21, 267-81.

SMITH, K.V., PHILLIPS, C.T. and LEWIS, R.J., (1972), Network Evaluation of Complex Transportation Systems, *Transportation Research*, 6, 103-11.

SOLTANI-MOHAMMADI, G.R., (1972), Problems of Choosing Irrigation Techniques in a Developing Country, *Water Resources Research*, 8, 1-6.

---

* - General Reference ; not cited in text

References

STEENBRINK, P.A., (1974), *Optimization of Transport Networks*, Wiley, New York.

STEVENS, B.H., (1958), An Interregional Linear Programming Model, *Journal of Regional Science*, 1, 60-98.

STEVENS, B.H., (1961), Linear Programming and Location Rent, *Journal of Regional Science*, 3, 15-26.

STOPHER, P.R. and MEYBURG, A.H., (1975), *Urban Transportation Modeling and Planning*, Lexington Books, Lexington.

SWART, W.W., GEARING, C., VAR, T. and CANN, G., (1975), Investment Planning for the Tourism Sector of a Developing Country With the aid of Linear Programming in : SALKIN, H.M. and SAHA, J. (Eds.), *Studies In Linear Programming*, North Holland, Amsterdam, 227-49.

TAAFFE, E.J. and GAUTHIER, H.L., (1973), *Geography of Transportation*, Prentice Hall, Englewood Cliffs.

TAHA, H.A., (1976), *Operations Research : An Introduction*, Macmillan, New York, Second Edition.

TAYLOR, P.J., (1977), *Quantiative Methods in Geography*, Houghton Mifflin, Atlanta, 312-3.

*THIERAUF, R.J. and KLEKAMP, R.C., (1975), *Decision Making Through Operations Research*, Wiley, New York.

*THOMPSON, W.W., (1967), *Operations Research Techniques*, Merrill, Columbus.

TOREGAS, C. and REVELLE, C., (1972), Optimal Location Under Time and Distance Constraints, *Papers of the Regional Science Association*, 28, 133-43.

TOREGAS, C. and REVELLE, C., (1973), Binary Logic Solutions to a Class of Location Problem, *Geographical Analysis*, 5, 144-55.

TORNQVIST, G., NORDBECK, S., RYSTEDT, B. and GOULD, P., (1971), Multiple Location Analysis, *Lund Studies in Geography, Series C, 12*, Gleerup, Lund.

TRIFON, R. and LINVAT, A., (1973), The Spatial Allocation of Schools Over Time in Cities, *Regional and Urban Economics*, 2, 387-400.

---

* - General Reference ; not cited in text

References

TURNQUIST, M.A., (1979), Zone Scheduling of Urban Bus Routes, *American Society of Civil Engineers Transportation Engineering Journal*, 105, 1-13.

*VAJDA, S., (1974), *Theory of Linear and Non-Linear Programming*, Longman, London.

WAGNER, H.M., (1969), *Principles of Operations Research With Applications to Managerial Decisions*, Prentice Hall, Englewood Cliffs, New Jersey.

WALSH, J., (1980), An Entropy Maximising Analysis of Journey to Work Patterns in County Limerick, *Irish Geography*, 13, 33-53.

WARE, G.O., and DICKERT, P.M., (1976), A Management Planning Model for the Delivery of Family Planning Services, *Socio-Economic Planning Sciences*, 10, 155-8.

WERCZBERGER, E., (1976), A Goal Programming Model For Industrial Location Involving Environmental Considerations, *Environment and Planning A*, 8, 173-88.

WERNER, C., (1968), The Role of Topology and Geometry in Optimal Network Design, *Regional Science Association Papers*, 21, 173-89.

WERNER, C., (1969), Networks of Minimum Length, *Canadian Geographer*, 13, 47-69.

WHEELER, J.O., (1966), Occupational Status and Work-Trips : A Minimum Distance Approach, *Social Forces*, 45, 508-15.

WHEELER, J.O., (1970), Transport Inputs and Residential Rent Theory : An Empirical Analysis, *Geographical Analysis*, 2, 43-54.

WHITE, J.A. and CASE, K.E., (1974), On Covering Problems and the Central Facilities. Location Problem, *Geographical Analysis*, 6, 281-93.

WILSON, A.G., (1970), *Entropy in Urban And Regional Modelling*, Pion, London.

WILSON, A.G., COELHO, J.D., MACGILL, S.M. and WILLIAMS, H.C.W.L., (1981), *Optimization in Locational and Transport Analysis*, Wiley, Chichester.

---

* - General Reference ; not cited in text

References

WILSON, A.G. and KIRKBY, M.J., (1975), *Mathematics for Geographers and Planners*, Clarendon Press, Oxford.

WILSON, A.G. and SENIOR, M.L., (1974), Some Relationships Between Entropy Maximising Models, Mathematical Programming Models and Their Duals, *Journal of Regional Science*, 14, 207-15

YEATES, M.H., (1963), Hinterland Delimitation : A Distance Minimising Approach, *Professional Geographer*, 16, 7-10.

YOUNG, W., (1972), Planning - a Linear Programming Model, *Greater London Intelligence Quarterly*, 19, 5-13.

YOUNG, W., (1974), The Language of Linear Programming, *Greater London Intelligence Quarterly*, 29, 19-28.

*ZIONTS, S., (1974), *Linear and Integer Programming*, Prentice Hall, Englewood Cliffs, New Jersey.

---

* - General Reference ; not cited in text

AUTHOR INDEX

SUBJECT INDEX

optimal network problem
11-14, 216-7
optimisation model 1
orthogonality conditions 277
out-of-kilter algorithm
30-2, 41, 65, 67

p-median problem
and the transportation
problem with setup
costs 229
definition 227
examples 228-9, 231-2
general formulation 227-9
with a maximum distance
constraint 230
with an investment cons-
traint 230
parametric linear programming
172
partial cover problem 225-7
partial derivative 257, 263,
264, 268, 273, 333
partial enumeration algorithm
211
partial tours method 220-2
pivotting (of equations) 102
plan evaluation 322-4
point of minimum aggregate
travel 233
positive parts 198
pre-emptive goal programming
312
principle of optimality 292
programming 1

quadratic assignment problem
283-4
quadratic function 255-7,
265, 275-6, 330

recreational landuse 122-4
156, 313-7
reducible link 26
regional development 82-7,
174-5, 179-85, 278-9
restricted basis entry rule
275

school districts 38-9

second derivative 256, 332
second shortest route 22-4
secondary constraints 172
sensitivity analysis
addition of a new var-
iable 167-9
addition of a constraint
169-72
and Lagrange multipliers
264-5, 269-72
change in constraint
coefficient 165-7
change in objective
coefficients 157-64
change in right hand side
coefficients 148-57
definition 6, 143
types 144
separable programming 279-83
separability 279, 308
shadow costs 47, 160
shadow prices See dual variable values
shopping 195-6, 258-61
shortest route problem
17-22, 286-91, 304-5
simplex method 78, 106-19
simplex multipliers 145,
147, 150-7, 178, see also
dual variable values
simplex tableau 106
simultaneous equations (solution of) 98-100
sink 18
slack variable 96
source 18
state variable 287
stationary point 262, 332
Steiner minimal spanning
tree 14-17
Steiner point 15-17, 233
stepping stone 45
strictly concave function
335
strictly convex function
335

technological coefficients
167
temporary degeneracy 136